# iOS® 8

## FOR PROGRAMMERS:
## AN APP-DRIVEN APPROACH
## WITH SWIFT™
### VOLUME 1, THIRD EDITION
### DEITEL® DEVELOPER SERIES

Many of the designations used by manufacturers and sellers to distinguish their products are claimed as trademarks. Where those designations appear in this book, and the publisher was aware of a trademark claim, the designations have been printed with initial capital letters or in all capitals.

The authors and publisher have taken care in the preparation of this book, but make no expressed or implied warranty of any kind and assume no responsibility for errors or omissions. No liability is assumed for incidental or consequential damages in connection with or arising out of the use of the information or programs contained herein.

For information about buying this title in bulk quantities, or for special sales opportunities (which may include electronic versions; custom cover designs; and content particular to your business, training goals, marketing focus, or branding interests), please contact our corporate sales department at corpsales@pearsoned.com or (800) 382-3419.

For government sales inquiries, please contact governmentsales@pearsoned.com.

For questions about sales outside the U.S., please contact international@pearsoned.com.

Visit us on the web: informit.com/ph

*Library of Congress Cataloging-in-Publication Data*

On file

ISBN-13: 978-0-13396526-1
ISBN-10: 0-13-396526-0

Text printed in the United States at Edwards Brothers Malloy in Ann Arbor, Michigan.
First printing, December 2014

# iOS® 8

## FOR PROGRAMMERS:
## AN APP-DRIVEN APPROACH
## WITH SWIFT™
### VOLUME 1, THIRD EDITION
#### DEITEL® DEVELOPER SERIES

Paul Deitel, Harvey Deitel and Abbey Deitel
*Deitel & Associates, Inc.*

PRENTICE
HALL

Upper Saddle River, NJ • Boston • Indianapolis • San Francisco
New York • Toronto • Montreal • London • Munich • Paris • Madrid
Capetown • Sydney • Tokyo • Singapore • Mexico City

# Deitel® Series Page

## Deitel® Developer Series

Android for Programmers: An App-Driven
   Approach, 2/E, Volume 1
C for Programmers with an Introduction to C11
C++11 for Programmers
C# 2012 for Programmers
iOS® 8 for Programmers: An App-Driven Approach
   with Swift™
Java™ for Programmers, 3/E
JavaScript for Programmers

## How To Program Series

Android How to Program, 2/E
C++ How to Program, 9/E
C How to Program, 7/E
Java™ How to Program, Early Objects Version, 10/E
Java™ How to Program, Late Objects Version, 10/E
Internet & World Wide Web How to Program, 5/E
Visual C++® 2008 How to Program, 2/E
Visual Basic® 2012 How to Program, 6/E
Visual C#® 2012 How to Program, 5/E

## Simply Series

Simply C++: An App-Driven Tutorial Approach
Simply Java™ Programming: An App-Driven
   Tutorial Approach
*(continued in next column)*

*(continued from previous column)*
Simply C#: An App-Driven Tutorial Approach
Simply Visual Basic® 2010: An App-Driven
   Approach, 4/E

## CourseSmart Web Books

www.deitel.com/books/CourseSmart/

C++ How to Program, 8/E and 9/E
Simply C++: An App-Driven Tutorial Approach
Java™ How to Program, 9/E and 10/E
Simply Visual Basic® 2010: An App-Driven
   Approach, 4/E
Visual Basic® 2012 How to Program, 6/E
Visual Basic® 2010 How to Program, 5/E
Visual C#® 2012 How to Program, 5/E
Visual C#® 2010 How to Program, 4/E

## LiveLessons Video Learning Products

www.deitel.com/books/LiveLessons/

Android App Development Fundamentals, 2/e
C++ Fundamentals
Java™ Fundamentals, 2/e
C# 2012 Fundamentals
C# 2010 Fundamentals
iOS® 6 App Development Fundamentals
JavaScript Fundamentals
Swift Fundamentals

To receive updates on Deitel publications, Resource Centers, training courses, partner offers and more, please join the Deitel communities on

- Facebook®—facebook.com/DeitelFan
- Twitter®—@deitel
- Google+™—google.com/+DeitelFan
- YouTube™—youtube.com/DeitelTV
- LinkedIn®—linkedin.com/company/deitel-&-associates

and register for the free *Deitel® Buzz Online* e-mail newsletter at:

   www.deitel.com/newsletter/subscribe.html

To communicate with the authors, send e-mail to:

   deitel@deitel.com

For information on *Dive-Into® Series* on-site seminars offered by Deitel & Associates, Inc. worldwide, write to us at deitel@deitel.com or visit:

   www.deitel.com/training/

For continuing updates on Pearson/Deitel publications visit:

   www.deitel.com
   www.pearsonhighered.com/deitel/

Visit the Deitel Resource Centers that will help you master programming languages, software development, Android and iOS app development, and Internet- and web-related topics:

   www.deitel.com/ResourceCenters.html

*In Memory of Amar G. Bose, MIT Professor and Founder and Chairman of the Bose Corporation:*

*It was a privilege being your student—and members of the next generation of Deitels, who heard our dad say how your classes inspired him to do his best work.*

*You taught us that if we go after the really hard problems, then great things can happen.*

*Harvey Deitel*
*Paul and Abbey Deitel*

## Trademarks

DEITEL, the double-thumbs-up bug and DIVE-INTO are registered trademarks of Deitel & Associates, Inc.

Apple, iOS, iPhone, iPad, iPod touch, Xcode, Swift, Objective-C, Cocoa and Cocoa Touch are trademarks or registered trademarks of Apple, Inc.

Java is a registered trademark of Oracle and/or its affiliates. Other names may be trademarks of their respective owners.

Google, Android, Google Play, Google Maps, Google Wallet, Nexus, YouTube, AdSense and AdMob are trademarks of Google, Inc.

Microsoft and/or its respective suppliers make no representations about the suitability of the information contained in the documents and related graphics published as part of the services for any purpose. All such documents and related graphics are provided "as is" without warranty of any kind. Microsoft and/or its respective suppliers hereby disclaim all warranties and conditions with regard to this information, including all warranties and conditions of merchantability, whether express, implied or statutory, fitness for a particular purpose, title and non-infringement. In no event shall Microsoft and/or its respective suppliers be liable for any special, indirect or consequential damages or any damages whatsoever resulting from loss of use, data or profits, whether in an action of contract, negligence or other tortious action, arising out of or in connection with the use or performance of information available from the services.

The documents and related graphics contained herein could include technical inaccuracies or typographical errors. Changes are periodically added to the information herein. Microsoft and/or its respective suppliers may make improvements and/or changes in the product(s) and/or the program(s) described herein at any time. Partial screen shots may be viewed in full within the software version specified.

Microsoft® and Windows® are registered trademarks of the Microsoft Corporation in the U.S.A. and other countries. Screen shots and icons reprinted with permission from the Microsoft Corporation. This book is not sponsored or endorsed by or affiliated with the Microsoft Corporation.


Throughout this book, trademarks are used. Rather than put a trademark symbol in every occurrence of a trademarked name, we state that we are using the names in an editorial fashion only and to the benefit of the trademark owner, with no intention of infringement of the trademark.

# Contents

# 2    Welcome App                                        43

*Dive-Into® Xcode: Introducing Visual User Interface Design with Cocoa
Touch, Interface Builder, Storyboarding and Auto Layout, Universal
Apps, Accessibility, Internationalization*

# 3    Tip Calculator **App**                                                75

*Introducing Swift, Text Fields, Sliders, Outlets, Actions, View Controllers, Event Handling, NSDecimalNumber, NSNumberFormatter and Automatic Reference Counting*

## 5    Flag Quiz **App**                                              **158**

*UISegmentedControls, UISwitches, Outlet Collections, View Animations, UINavigationController, Segues, NSBundle, Scheduling Tasks with Grand Central Dispatch*

# 6  Cannon **Game App**    **198**

*Xcode Game Template, SpriteKit, Animation, Graphics, Sound, Physics,
Collision Detection, Scene Transitions, Listening for Touches*

# 7    Doodlz App                                                    242

*Multi-Touch Event Handling, Graphics, **UIBezierPath**s, Drawing
with a Custom **UIView** Subclass, **UIToolbar**, **UIBarButtonItem**,
Accelerometer Sensor and Motion Event Handling*

# 8    Address Book App                                            273

*Core Data Framework, Master-Detail Template with Core Data*
*Support, Xcode Data Model Editor, UITableView with Static Cells,*
*Programmatically Scrolling UITableViews*

# Preface

Welcome to the world of iOS® 8 app development with Apple's new and rapidly evolving Swift™ programming language, the Cocoa Touch® frameworks and the Xcode® 6 development tools.

*iOS® 8 for Programmers: An App-Driven Approach with Swift™, Volume 1, 3/e* presents leading-edge mobile computing technologies for professional software developers. At the heart of the book is our *app-driven approach*—we present concepts in the context of *seven completely coded and fully tested iOS 8 apps* rather than using code snippets. We've always favored teaching by example—in an app-development world, the best examples are real, working apps.

Chapters 2–8 each present one app. We begin each of these chapters with an introduction to the app, an app test-drive showing one or more sample executions and a technologies overview. Then we proceed with a detailed source code walkthrough. We don't try to be exhaustive—our goal is to get you developing apps quickly with the Xcode 6 integrated development environment, the Swift programming language and the Cocoa Touch frameworks. All of the source code is available at

```
http://www.deitel.com/books/iOS8FP1
```

We recommend that you keep the code open in the IDE as you read the book. You should study the apps sequentially because each introduces technologies that are used in subsequent apps.

This book is Volume 1 of what will become a multi-volume set. Volume 1 presents seven fully coded apps of increasingly rich functionality. The apps cover a range of topics from simple visual programming (without code), to simple programming with Swift, to more involved programming.

## Explosive Growth of the iPhone and iPad Is Creating Opportunity for Developers

iPhone and iPad device sales have been growing exponentially, creating significant opportunities for iOS app developers. The first-generation iPhone, released in June 2007, sold 6.1 million units in its initial five quarters of availability.[1] The iPhone 5s and the iPhone 5c, released simultaneously in September 2013, sold over nine million combined in the first three days of availability.[2] The most recent iPhone 6 and iPhone 6 Plus, announced in September 2014, pre-sold four million combined in just one day—double the number of

---

1. http://www.apple.com/pr/library/2009/07/21results.html.
2. https://www.apple.com/pr/library/2013/09/23First-Weekend-iPhone-Sales-Top-Nine-Million-Sets-New-Record.html.

iPhone 5 pre-sales in its first day of pre-order availability.[3] Apple sold 10 million iPhone 6 and iPhone 6 Plus units combined in their first weekend of availability.[4]

Sales of the iPad are equally impressive. The first generation iPad, launched in April 2010, sold 3 million units in its first 80 days of availability[5] and over 40 million worldwide by September 2011.[6] The iPad mini with Retina display (the second-generation iPad mini) and the iPad Air (the fifth-generation iPad) were released in November 2013. In just the first quarter of 2014, Apple sold a record 26 million iPads.[7]

There are over 1.3 million apps in the App Store[8] and over 75 billion iOS apps have been downloaded.[9] The potential for iOS app developers is enormous.

## SafariBooksOnline e-Book and LiveLessons Videos

If you have a subscription to Safari Books Online (www.safaribooksonline.com), check out the e-book and LiveLessons video versions of *iOS® 8 for Programmers: An App-Driven Approach with Swift*. Safari is a subscription service popular with large companies, colleges, libraries and individuals who would like access to video training and electronic versions of print publications.

## Copyright Notice and Code License

*All of the code and iOS apps in the book are copyrighted by Deitel & Associates, Inc. The sample iOS apps are licensed under a Creative Commons Attribution 3.0 Unported License (http://creativecommons.org/licenses/by/3.0),* **with the exception that they may not be reused in any way in educational tutorials and textbooks, whether free or for a fee and whether in print or digital format.** *Additionally, the authors and publisher make no warranty of any kind, expressed or implied, with regard to these programs or to the documentation contained in this book. The authors and publisher shall not be liable in any event for incidental or consequential damages in connection with, or arising out of, the furnishing, performance, or use of these programs. You're welcome to use the apps in the book as shells for your own apps, building on their existing functionality. If you have any questions, contact us at* deitel@deitel.com.

## Intended Audience

This book is part of the *Deitel Developer Series* intended for experienced programmers who know object-oriented programming in a C-based programming language such as Objective-C, Java, C# or C++. Objective-C experience is helpful, but not specifically required. If you have not worked in any of these languages, you should still be able to learn a good amount of iOS 8 app development and object-oriented programming in Swift and Cocoa

---

3.  http://techcrunch.com/2014/09/15/apple-sells-4m-iphone-6-and-6-plus-pre-orders-in-opening-24-hours/.
4.  http://www.apple.com/pr/library/2014/09/22First-Weekend-iPhone-Sales-Top-10-Million-Set-New-Record.html.
5.  http://www.ipadinsider.com/tag/ipad-sales-figures/.
6.  http://www.statista.com/statistics/180656/sales-of-tablets-and-ipads-in-the-us-until-2012/.
7.  http://www.theverge.com/2014/1/27/5350106/apple-q1-2014-earnings.
8.  http://mashable.com/2014/09/09/apple-1-3-million-apps-app-store/.
9.  http://techcrunch.com/2014/06/02/itunes-app-store-now-has-1-2-million-apps-has-seen-75-billion-downloads-to-date/.

Touch by reading the code and our code walkthroughs, running the apps and observing the results. We review the basics of object-oriented programming in Chapter 1. We also assume that you're comfortable with OS X, as you'll need to work on a Mac to develop iOS apps. The book does not include exercises.

This book is *not* a Swift tutorial, but it presents a significant amount of Swift in the context of iOS 8 app development. If you're interested in learning Swift, check out our publications:

- *Swift for Programmers* print book (www.deitel.com/books/swiftfp). This book is also available as an e-book on SafariBooksOnline.com, Informit.com, Amazon® Kindle® and a growing number of other electronic platforms.

- *Swift Fundamentals: Parts I, II and III* LiveLessons videos (www.deitel.com/books/LiveLessons), available on SafariBooksOnline.com, Informit.com, Udemy.com and soon on other popular e-learning platforms.

## Academic Bundle iOS® 8 for Programmers and Swift™ for Programmers

The *Academic Bundle iOS® 8 for Programmers and Swift™ for Programmers* is designed for professionals, students and instructors interested in learning or teaching iOS 8® app development with a broader and deeper treatment of Swift. You can conveniently order the Academic Bundle with one ISBN: 0-13-408775-5. The Academic Bundle includes:

- *Swift™ for Programmers* (print book)

- *iOS® 8 for Programmers: An App-Driven Approach with Swift™, Volume 1, 3/e* (print book)

- Access Code Card for Academic Package to accompany *Swift™ for Programmers*

- Access Code Card for Academic Package to accompany *iOS® 8 for Programmers: An App-Driven Approach with Swift™, Volume 1, 3/e*

The two Access Code Cards for the Academic Packages (when used together) give you access to the companion websites, which include self-review questions (with answers), short-answer questions, programming exercises, programming projects and selected videos chosen to get you up to speed quickly with Xcode 6, visual programming and basic Swift-based, iOS 8 programming.

### Ordering the Books and Supplements Separately

The print books and Access Code Cards may be purchased separately using the following ISBNs:

- *Swift™ for Programmers* (print book): ISBN 0-13-402136-3

- Standalone access code card for Academic Package to accompany *Swift™ for Programmers*: ISBN 0-13-405818-6

- *iOS® 8 for Programmers: An App-Driven Approach with Swift™* (print book): ISBN 0-13-396526-0

- Standalone access code card for Academic Package to accompany *iOS® 8 for Programmers: An App Driven Approach with Swift™, Volume 1, 3/e*: ISBN 0-13-405825-9

*Instructor Supplements*

Instructor supplements are available online at Pearson's Instructor Resource Center IRC). The supplements include:

- Solutions Manual with selected solutions to the short-answer exercises.

- Test Item File of multiple-choice examination questions (with answers).

- PowerPoint® slides with the book's source code and tables.

**Please do not write to us requesting access to the Pearson Instructor's Resource Center. Certified instructors who adopt the book for their courses can obtain password access from their regular Pearson sales representatives (`www.pearson.com/replocator`). Solutions are *not* provided for "project" exercises.**

## Key Features of *iOS*® *8 for Programmers: An App-Driven Approach with Swift™, Volume 1, 3/e*

Here are some of this book's key features:

*App-Driven Approach.* Chapters 2–8 each present one completely coded app—we discuss what the app does, show screen shots of the app in action, test-drive it and overview the technologies and architecture we'll use to build it. Then we build the app's GUI and re-source files, present the complete code and do a detailed code walkthrough. We discuss the Swift programming concepts and demonstrate the functionality of the Cocoa Touch APIs used in the app.

*Swift Programming Language.* Swift was arguably the most significant announcement at Apple's Worldwide Developers Conference in 2014. Although apps can still be programmed in Objective-C, Swift is Apple's language of the future for app development and systems programming.

We've programmed all the book's apps in Swift—previous editions were programmed in Objective-C. Swift is a contemporary language with simpler syntax than Objective-C. It enables a clean, concise coding style and has a strong focus on error prevention. Our own experience with Swift has been that we can develop apps faster and with significantly less code than when we program in Objective-C.

At the time of this writing, Apple had not as yet published coding guidelines for Swift—we'll conform to them when they appear. We use a mix of Apple's Objective-C coding guidelines and Deitel coding guidelines for this edition.

*Cocoa Touch Frameworks.* Cocoa Touch is the groups of reusable components (known as frameworks) for building iOS apps. Throughout this edition, we use many of the Cocoa Touch features and frameworks, even though they're programmed mostly in Objective-C. Apple has made this easy with a technique called "bridging." We simply call Cocoa Touch methods and receive the returns *transparently*—it feels as if Cocoa Touch is written in Swift.

*iOS SDK 8.* Between Volumes 1 and 2 of *iOS*® *8 for Programmers: An App-Driven Approach with Swift™, Volume 1, 3/e*, we cover a broad range of the features included in iOS Software Development Kit (SDK) 8.

*Xcode 6.* Apple's Xcode integrated development environment (IDE) and its associated tools for Mac OS X, combined with the iOS 8 Software Development Kit (SDK), provide all the software you need to develop and test iOS 8 apps.

*Instruments.* The Instruments tool, which is packaged with the SDK, is used to inspect apps while they're running to check for memory leaks, monitor processor (CPU) usage and network activity, and review the objects allocated in memory.

*iOS Human Interface Guidelines.* We encourage you to read Apple's *iOS Human Interface Guidelines* (HIG) and follow them as you design and develop your apps. The HIG discusses human interface principles, app design strategies, user experience guidelines, iOS technology usage guidelines and more. We gradually introduce HIG issues as we encounter them in the apps we develop. Section 9.3 overviews the HIG, discusses features and functionality required to get your app accepted on the App Store and lists reasons why Apple rejects apps.

*Multimedia.* The apps use iOS 8 multimedia capabilities, including graphics, images, animation and audio. We'll present video capabilities in Volume 2.

*iOS App Design Patterns.* This book adheres to Apple's app coding standards, including design patterns, such as Model-View-Controller (MVC), Delegation, Target-Action and Observer.

## Features

*Syntax Coloring.* For readability, we syntax color the code, similar to Xcode's use of syntax coloring. Our syntax-coloring conventions are as follows:

```
comments appear like this
keywords appear like this
constants and literal values appear like this
all other code appears in black
```

*Code Highlighting.* We highlight the key code segments in each app that exercise the new technologies the app features.

*Using Fonts for Emphasis.* We place key terms and the index's page reference for each term's defining occurrence in **bold blue** text for easier reference. We emphasize on-screen components in the **bold Helvetica** font (e.g., the **File** menu) and emphasize Swift program text in the Lucida font (for example, var x = 5).

*Source Code.* All of the source-code examples are available for download from:

```
http://www.deitel.com/books/iOS8FP1/
```

*Documentation.* All of the manuals that you'll need to develop iOS 8 apps are available free at http://developer.apple.com/ios.

*Chapter Objectives.* Each chapter begins with a list of objectives.

*Figures.* Abundant tables, source-code listings and iOS screen shots are included.

*Index.* We include an extensive index, which is especially useful when you use the book as a reference. Defining occurrences of key terms are highlighted with a **bold** page number.

## iOS® 8 for Programmers: An App-Driven Approach with Swift™, Volume 2

Volume 2 of this series will contain additional app-development chapters. **For the status of Volume 2 and for continuing book updates, visit**

http://www.deitel.com/books/iOS8fp2

## iOS® 8 Fundamentals LiveLessons Video Training Products

Our *iOS 8 Fundamentals* LiveLessons videos show you what you need to know to start building robust, powerful iOS apps with the iOS Software Development Kit (SDK) 8, the Swift programming language, Xcode and Cocoa Touch. It will include 10+ hours of expert training synchronized with *iOS® 8 for Programmers: An App-Driven Approach with Swift™, Volume 1, 3/e*. For additional information about Deitel LiveLessons video products, visit

www.deitel.com/livelessons

or contact us at deitel@deitel.com. You can also access our LiveLessons videos if you have a subscription to Safari Books Online (www.safaribooksonline.com). You can get a free 10-day subscription to SafariBooksOnline at

http://www.safaribooksonline.com/register

## Acknowledgments

We'd like to thank Barbara Deitel for long hours spent researching iOS 8 and its many related technologies.

### Pearson Education Team

We're fortunate to have worked on this project with the dedicated publishing professionals at Prentice Hall/Pearson. We appreciate the extraordinary efforts and 19-year mentorship of our friend and professional colleague Mark L. Taub, Editor-in-Chief of Pearson Technology Group. Kim Boedigheimer recruited distinguished members of the iOS community to review the manuscript and she managed the review process. We selected the cover art and Chuti Prasertsith designed the cover. John Fuller managed the book's publication.

### Reviewers

We wish to acknowledge the efforts of our current and recent editions reviewers. They scrutinized the text and the programs and provided countless suggestions for improving the presentation.

*iOS 8 edition reviewers:* Scott Bossak (Lead iOS Developer, Thrillist Media Group), Charles E. Brown (Independent Contractor affiliated with Apple and Adobe), Matt Galloway (iOS Developer and author of *Effective Objective-C 2.0*), Michael Haberman (Software Engineer, Instructor at University of Illinois), Rob McGovern (Indie Developer) and Rik Watson (Technical Team Lead, HP Enterprise Services).

*Earlier iOS editions reviewers:* Cory Bohon (Indie Developer at CocoaApp.com and Writer at Mac|Life), Scott Gustafson (Owner/Developer, Garlic Software LLC), Firoze Lafeer (Master Developer, Capital One Labs), Dan Lingman (Partner, www.nogotogames.com), Marcantonio Magnarapa (Chief Mobile Officer, www.bemyeye.com), Nik Saers (iOS Developer, SAERS), Zach Saul (Founder, Retronyms) and Rik Watson (then a Senior Software Engineer, Lockheed Martin).

### Keeping in Touch with the Authors

As you read the book, we'd appreciate your comments, criticisms, corrections and suggestions for improvement. Please address all correspondence to:

```
deitel@deitel.com
```

We'll respond promptly. For updates on this book, visit

```
http://www.deitel.com/books/iOS8FP1
```

subscribe to the *Deitel® Buzz Online* newsletter at

```
http://www.deitel.com/newsletter/subscribe.html
```

and join the Deitel social networking communities on

- Facebook® (http://www.deitel.com/deitelfan)
- Twitter® (@deitel)
- LinkedIn® (http://linkedin.com/company/deitel-&-associates)
- Google+™ (http://google.com/+DeitelFan)
- YouTube® (http://youtube.com/DeitelTV)

Well, there you have it! We hope you enjoy working with *iOS® 8 for Programmers: An App-Driven Approach with Swift, Volume 1, 3/e* as much as we enjoyed writing it!

*Paul, Harvey and Abbey Deitel*

## About the Authors

**Paul Deitel**, CEO and Chief Technical Officer of Deitel & Associates, Inc., is a graduate of MIT, where he studied Information Technology. He holds the Java Certified Programmer and Java Certified Developer designations, and is an Oracle Java Champion. Paul was also named as a Microsoft® Most Valuable Professional (MVP) for C# in 2012–2014. Through Deitel & Associates, Inc., he has delivered hundreds of programming courses worldwide to clients, including Cisco, IBM, Siemens, Sun Microsystems, Dell, Fidelity, NASA at the Kennedy Space Center, the National Severe Storm Laboratory, White Sands Missile Range, Rogue Wave Software, Boeing, SunGard, Nortel Networks, Puma, iRobot, Invensys and many more. He and his co-author, Dr. Harvey Deitel, are the world's best-selling programming-language textbook/professional book/video authors.

**Dr. Harvey Deitel**, Chairman and Chief Strategy Officer of Deitel & Associates, Inc., has over 50 years of experience in the computer field. Dr. Deitel earned B.S. and M.S. degrees in Electrical Engineering from MIT and a Ph.D. in Mathematics from Boston University. He has extensive college teaching experience, including earning tenure and serving as the Chairman of the Computer Science Department at Boston College before founding Deitel & Associates, Inc., in 1991 with his son, Paul. The Deitels' publications have earned international recognition, with translations published in Japanese, German,

Russian, Spanish, French, Polish, Italian, Simplified Chinese, Traditional Chinese, Korean, Portuguese, Greek, Urdu and Turkish. Dr. Deitel has delivered hundreds of programming courses to corporate, academic, government and military clients.

**Abbey Deitel**, President of Deitel & Associates, Inc., is a graduate of Carnegie Mellon University's Tepper School of Management where she received a B.S. in Industrial Management. Abbey has been managing the business operations of Deitel & Associates, Inc. for 17 years. She has contributed to numerous Deitel & Associates publications including *Swift™ for Programmers* and, together with Paul and Harvey, is the co-author of *iOS® 8 for Programmers: An App-Driven Approach with Swift™, Volume 1, 3/e, Android for Programmers: An App-Driven Approach, 2/e, Internet & World Wide Web How to Program, 5/e, Visual Basic 2012 How to Program, 6/e* and *Simply Visual Basic 2010, 5/e*.

## About Deitel® & Associates, Inc.

Deitel & Associates, Inc., founded by Paul Deitel and Harvey Deitel, is an internationally recognized authoring and corporate training organization, specializing in mobile app development, computer programming languages, object technology and Internet and web software technology. The company's training clients include many of the world's largest companies, government agencies, branches of the military, and academic institutions. The company offers instructor-led training courses delivered at client sites worldwide on major programming languages and platforms, including Swift™, Objective-C and iOS® app development, Java™, Android app development, C++, C, Visual C#®, Visual Basic®, Python®, object technology, Internet and web programming and a growing list of additional programming and software development courses.

Through its 40-year publishing partnership with Pearson/Prentice Hall, Deitel & Associates, Inc., publishes leading-edge programming textbooks and professional books in print and a wide range of e-book formats, and *LiveLessons* video courses. Deitel & Associates, Inc. and the authors can be reached at:

```
deitel@deitel.com
```

To learn more about Deitel's *Dive-Into® Series* Corporate Training curriculum, visit:

```
http://www.deitel.com/training
```

To request a proposal for worldwide on-site, instructor-led training at your organization, send an e-mail to `deitel@deitel.com`.

Individuals wishing to purchase Deitel books and *LiveLessons* video training can do so through `www.deitel.com`. Bulk orders by corporations, the government, the military and academic institutions should be placed directly with Pearson. For more information, visit

```
http://www.informit.com/store/sales.aspx
```

# Before You Begin

This section contains information you should review before using this book. Updates will be posted at:

```
http://www.deitel.com/books/iOS8FP1
```

## Font and Naming Conventions

We use fonts to distinguish between on-screen components (such as menu names and menu items) and Swift code. Our convention is to emphasize on-screen components in a sans-serif bold **Helvetica** font (for example, **File** menu) and to emphasize Swift code and commands in a sans-serif Lucida font (for example, import UIKit). When building user interfaces (UIs) using Xcode's Interface Builder, we also use the bold **Helvetica** font to refer to property names for UI components (such as a **Label**'s **Text** property).

## Conventions for Referencing Menu Items in a Menu

We use the > character to indicate selecting a menu item from a menu. The notation **File > Open...** indicates that you should select the **Open...** menu item from the **File** menu.

## Software Used in this Book

To execute our apps and write your own iOS 8 apps, you must install Xcode 6. You can install the currently released Xcode version for free from the Mac App Store. When you open Xcode for the first time, it will download and install additional features required for development. For the latest information about Xcode, visit

```
https://developer.apple.com/xcode
```

### *A Note Regarding the Xcode 6 Toolbar Icons*

We developed this book's examples with Xcode 6 on OS X Yosemite. If you're running OS X Mavericks, some Xcode toolbar icons we show in the text may differ on your screen.

## Becoming a Registered Apple Developer

Registered developers have access to the online iOS documentation and other resources. Apple also now makes Xcode pre-release versions (such as the next point release or major version) available to all registered Apple developers. To register, visit:

```
https://developer.apple.com/register
```

To download the next pre-release Xcode version, visit:

```
https://developer.apple.com/xcode/downloads
```

Once you download the DMG (disk image) file, double click it to launch the installer, then follow the on-screen instructions.

## Fee-Based Developer Programs

### iOS Developer Program
The fee-based iOS Developer Program allows you to load your iOS apps onto iOS devices for testing and to submit your apps to the App Store. If you intend to distribute iOS apps, you'll need to join the fee-based program. You can sign up at

```
https://developer.apple.com/programs
```

### iOS Developer Enterprise Program
Organizations may register for the iOS Developer Enterprise Program at

```
https://developer.apple.com/programs/ios/enterprise
```

which enables developers to deploy proprietary iOS apps to employees within their organization.

### iOS Developer University Program
Colleges and universities interested in offering iOS app-development courses can apply to the iOS Developer University Program at

```
https://developer.apple.com/programs/ios/university
```

Qualifying schools receive free access to all the developer tools and resources. Students can share their apps with each other and test them on iOS devices.

## Adding Your Paid iOS Developer Program Account to Xcode

Xcode can interact with your paid iOS Developer Program account on your behalf so that you can install apps onto your iOS devices for testing. If you have a paid iOS Developer Program account, you can add it to Xcode. To do so:

1. Select **Xcode > Preferences…**.
2. In the **Accounts** tab, click the **+** button in the lower left corner and select **Add Apple ID…**.
3. Enter your Apple ID and password, then click **Add**.

## Obtaining the Code Examples

The final versions of the apps you'll build in this book are available for download as a ZIP file from

```
http://www.deitel.com/books/iOS8FP1
```

under the heading **Download Code Examples and Other Premium Content**. When you click the link to the ZIP file, it will be placed by default in your user account's Downloads folder. We assume that the examples are located in the iOS8Examples folder in your user account's Documents folder. You can use Finder to move the ZIP file there, then double click the file to extract its contents.

## Xcode Projects

For each app, we provide a project that you can open in Xcode by double clicking its project file, which has the .xcodeproj extension. You'll use these projects to test-drive the apps before building them.

## Configuring Xcode to Display Line Numbers

Many programmers find it helpful to display line numbers in the code editor. To do so:

1. Open Xcode and select **Preferences...** from the **Xcode** menu.
2. Select the **Text Editing** tab, then ensure that the **Editing** subtab is selected.
3. Check the **Line Numbers** checkbox.

## Configuring Xcode's Code Indentation Options

Xcode uses four space indents by default. To configure your own indentation preferences:

1. Open Xcode and select **Preferences...** from the **Xcode** menu.
2. Select the **Text Editing** tab, then ensure that the **Indentation** subtab is selected.
3. Specify your indentation preferences.

You're now ready to begin working with *iOS® 8 for Programmers: An App-Driven Approach with Swift™, Volume 1, 3/e.* We hope you enjoy the book! If you have any questions, please email us at deitel@deitel.com.

# Introduction to iOS 8 App Development and Swift

| Carrier 🔋 | 3:36 PM | |
|---|---|---|
| Bill Amount | | |
| $56.32 | | |
| Custom Tip Percentage: 25% | | |
| | 15% | 25% |
| Tip | $8.45 | $14.08 |
| Total | $64.77 | $70.40 |

| 1 | 2 ABC | 3 DEF |
|---|---|---|
| 4 GHI | 5 JKL | 6 MNO |
| 7 PQRS | 8 TUV | 9 WXYZ |
| | 0 | ⌫ |

## Objectives

In this chapter we discuss:

- iPhone and iPad gestures, sensors and accessibility features.
- History and features of the iOS operating system.
- iPhone 6, iPhone 6 Plus and Apple Watch.
- Key software for iOS app development, including the Xcode® 6 integrated development environment, the iOS simulator, the Swift programming language and the Cocoa Touch® frameworks.
- Review of object-oriented programming concepts.
- Test-driving an app in the iOS simulator.
- Characteristics of great iOS apps.
- iOS security.
- Key Apple publications for iOS developers.

## 1.1 Introduction

Welcome to iOS 8 app development! We hope that using *iOS 8 for Programmers: An App-Driven Approach with Swift, Volume 1* will be an informative, challenging, entertaining and rewarding experience for you.

This book is geared toward experienced programmers who have worked in a C-based object-oriented language such as Objective-C®, C++, Java™ or C#. If you don't specifically know Apple's Swift programming language and the Cocoa Touch® frameworks, you should be able to absorb a good amount of them by running the book's iPhone and iPad apps and studying the feature presentations and detailed code walkthroughs.

### App-Driven Approach

We use an **app-driven approach**—new features are discussed in the context of complete working iPhone or iPad apps, with one app each in Chapters 2–8. Some of our apps are built as **universal apps** so they can run on iPhone, iPad and iPod touch devices. For each app, we start by describing it, then have you test-drive it. Next, we briefly overview the key

Xcode® integrated development environment, Swift and Cocoa Touch technologies we use to implement the app. We walk through designing each app's user interface (UI) *visually*. Then we provide the complete source-code listing with *line numbers, syntax coloring* and *code highlighting* to emphasize the key portions of the code. We also show one or more screen shots of the running app. Then we do a detailed code walkthrough, emphasizing the new programming concepts introduced in the app. You can download the source code for all of the book's apps from `http://www.deitel.com/books/iOS8FP1`. See the Preface for the code license details.

## 1.2 iPhone and iPad Sales Data

iPhone and iPad device sales have been growing exponentially, creating enormous opportunities for iOS app developers.

- *First-generation iPhone*: The first-generation iPhone was released in June 2007 and was an instant blockbuster success. Sales have grown significantly with each new version. According to Apple, 6.1 million first-generation iPhones were sold in the initial five quarters of availability.[1]

- *iPhone 3G*: The second-generation iPhone 3G included GPS and was released in July 2008; it sold 6.9 million units in the first quarter alone.

- *iPhone 3GS*: The third-generation iPhone 3GS included a compass; it was launched in June 2009 and sold 5.2 million in its first month of availability.

- *iPhone 4*: The iPhone 4, launched in June 2010, sold over three million units in its first three weeks.

- *iPhone 4S*: The iPhone 4S, released in October 2011, sold over four million in its first three days.[2] Apple sold 35.1 million iPhones during the first three months of 2012, helping the company to nearly double its profits from the previous quarter.[3]

- *iPhone 5*: The iPhone 5, released in September 2012, sold over five million in its first three days.[4]

- *iPhone 5s* and *iPhone 5c*: The iPhone 5s and the iPhone 5c, released simultaneously in September 2013, sold over nine million combined in the first three days of availability.[5] In mid-January 2014, China Mobile—the world's largest mobile carrier —began selling the iPhone for the first time in mainland China. Analysts predict sales of over 20 million iPhones by China Mobile in 2014.[6]

---

1. `http://www.apple.com/pr/library/2009/07/21results.html`.
2. `http://www.apple.com/pr/library/2011/10/17iPhone-4S-First-Weekend-Sales-Top-Four-Million.html`.
3. `http://money.cnn.com/2012/04/25/technology/apple-supplier-stocks/index.htm`.
4. `http://www.apple.com/pr/library/2012/09/24iPhone-5-First-Weekend-Sales-Top-Five-Million.html`.
5. `https://www.apple.com/pr/library/2013/09/23First-Weekend-iPhone-Sales-Top-Nine-Million-Sets-New-Record.html`.
6. `http://www.forbes.com/sites/connieguglielmo/2013/12/23/apple-inks-important-china-mobile-deal-could-sell-17-million-iphones-in-first-year/`.

- *iPhone 6*: The iPhone 6 and iPhone 6 Plus, released in September 2014, pre-sold four million combined in just one day—double the number of iPhone 5 pre-sales in its first day of pre-order availability.[7] Apple sold 10 million units in the first weekend that the iPhone 6 was available.[8]

Sales of the iPad are equally impressive. Gartner predicts that global tablet sales will rise from 207 million in 2013 to 321 million in 2015.[9] Here are some sales statistics by iPad model:

- *First-generation iPad*: The iPad, launched in April 2010, sold three million units in its first 80 days of availability[10] and a total of over 40 million worldwide by September 2011.[11]

- *iPad 2*: The thinner, lighter and faster iPad 2 was launched in March 2011 and sold one million units in just the first weekend of availability. By the end of 2011, the iPad accounted for 58% of worldwide tablet market share.[12]

- *The New iPad*: The third-generation iPad went on sale in March 2012; three million of these devices were sold in just three days.[13] Overall iPad sales in the first quarter of 2012 reached 11.8 million units—a 151% increase over same quarter the previous year.

- *First-generation iPad Mini* and the *fourth-generation iPad*: The WiFi-only versions of the first-generation iPad Mini—which featured a 7.9-inch display—and the fourth-generation iPad were released in November 2012. They sold a combined three million units in the first weekend of availability.[14]

- *Second-generation iPad Mini* (also referred to as the *iPad mini with Retina® display*) and the *iPad Air* (the fifth-generation iPad) were released in November 2013. In just the first quarter of 2014, Apple sold a record 26 million iPads.[15]

## 1.3 Gestures

Apple's Multi-Touch screen allows you to control the device with **gestures** involving one touch or multiple simultaneous touches (Fig. 1.1). You'll learn how to recognize and respond to gestures in your code.

---

7.  http://techcrunch.com/2014/09/15/apple-sells-4m-iphone-6-and-6-plus-pre-orders-in-opening-24-hours/.
8.  http://www.apple.com/pr/library/2014/09/22First-Weekend-iPhone-Sales-Top-10-Million-Set-New-Record.html.
9.  http://www.gartner.com/newsroom/id/2791017.
10. http://www.apple.com/pr/library/2010/06/22Apple-Sells-Three-Million-iPads-in-80-Days.html.
11. http://www.statista.com/statistics/180656/sales-of-tablets-and-ipads-in-the-us-until-2012/.
12. http://finance.yahoo.com/news/why-google-android-tablet-market-185500797.html.
13. http://www.apple.com/pr/library/2012/03/19New-iPad-Tops-Three-Million.html.
14. https://www.apple.com/pr/library/2012/11/05Apple-Sells-Three-Million-iPads-in-Three-Days.html.
15. http://www.theverge.com/2014/1/27/5350106/apple-q1-2014-earnings.

| Gesture | Action | Used to |
|---|---|---|
| Tap | Tap the screen once. | Open an app, click a button. |
| Double Tap | Tap the screen twice. | Select text to cut, copy and paste. |
| Touch and Hold (also called a Long Press) | Touch the screen and hold your finger in position. | Move the cursor in e-mail and SMS messages, move app icons, and so on. This can also be used to select text to cut, copy and paste. |
| Drag | Touch and drag your finger across the screen. | Move a slider left and right or up and down, move around to different areas on a map or web page. |
| Swipe | Touch the screen, then move your finger in the swipe direction and release. | Flip item-by-item through a series, such as photos or music album covers. A swipe automatically stops at the next item. |
| Flick | Touch and quickly flick your finger across the screen in the direction you'd like to move. | Scroll through a **Table View** (e.g., Contacts) or a **Picker View** (e.g., dates and times in the Calendar). Unlike a swipe, a flick does not have a specific stop point. If you overshoot or undershoot your target, you can then drag to get to the desired stop point. |
| Pinch | Using two fingers, touch and pinch your fingers together, or spread them apart. | Zoom out and in on the screen (for example, enlarging text and pictures). |
| Shake | Shake the device. | Undo or redo an action (e.g., undo or redo typing). |

**Fig. 1.1** | iPhone and iPad gestures.

## 1.4 Sensors

The iPhone and iPad include several sensors.

- The **accelerometer** allows the device to respond to up/down, left/right and forward/backward acceleration. For example, you can rotate the device from *portrait* to *landscape* (vertical to horizontal) to change the orientation of pictures, e-mails, web pages and more. You can also use the accelerometer to control games by shaking or tilting the device. You can shake the device to "shuffle" randomly to a different song in your music library, or turn the device sideways to display a **landscape keyboard** for easier typing (Fig. 1.2). We use the accelerometer in Chapter 7's **Doodlz** app, where we allow the user to shake the device to erase the current drawing.

- The **three-axis gyro** (a gyroscope; introduced with the iPhone 4) works with the accelerometer, making the device more responsive and sensitive to motion by allowing apps to detect the device's rotation around the *x*-, *y*- and *z*-axes (left/right, up/down and forward/backward, respectively). The gyroscope helps the **Camera** app stabilize images for better pictures and video, helps improve game controllers and more.[16] We use the gyroscope in Chapter 7.

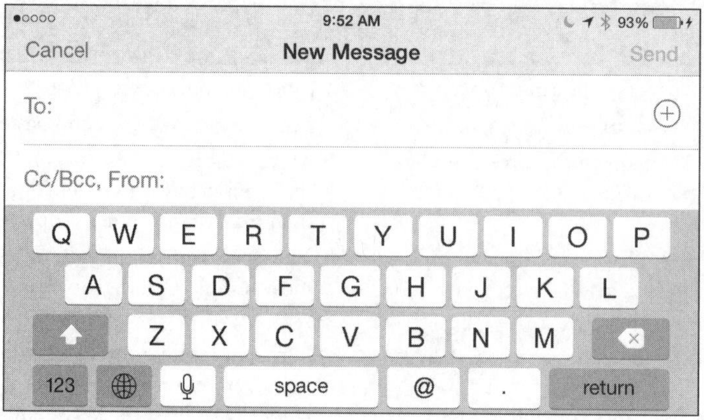

**Fig. 1.2** | Landscape keyboard.

- The digital **compass** (included on iPhone 3GS and higher and on the iPad) allows you to orient maps to point in the direction the device is facing.

- The **ambient light sensor** determines the amount of light around the device and adjusts the screen's brightness to preserve the battery.

- The iPhone **proximity sensor** determines whether the device is near your face (e.g., when you're on a phone call). The screen turns off when the iPhone is held close to your face and turns back on when the device is moved away from your face. This sensor is not included on the iPad or iPod touch.

- The iPad **magnetic sensor** determines whether an iPad smart cover—which is attached to the device magnetically and covers the screen—is open or closed, and turns the screen on or off, respectively.

- The **GPS sensor** supplies global-positioning satellite data for location-based and mapping apps.

- The **Touch ID sensor**, which was introduced with the iPhone 5s, is a fingerprint authentication feature built into the *Home* button. You can use your fingerprint to unlock the device and to make purchases from the App Store. As of iOS 8, app developers can use Touch ID for in-app security.

- The **NFC sensor**, new in the iPhone 6 and iPhone 6 Plus, currently is used only for the Apple Pay service—Apple's new payment technology for mobile and online payments. Apple Pay and NFC are introduced in Fig. 1.3.

## 1.5 Accessibility

iOS includes several **accessibility** features to help vision-, hearing- and physically impaired users. **VoiceOver** is a gesture-based screen-reader program available in numerous languages. It lets vision-impaired users interact with objects on the screen and understand their context. For example, users can touch the screen to hear a description of the item they

16. www.zdnet.com/blog/apple/inside-the-iphone-4s-vibrational-gyroscope/7410.

touch, then drag their finger to hear descriptions of the surrounding content. VoiceOver is also used with the keyboard to speak each character touched, or each complete word. Starting with iOS 7, VoiceOver is integrated with **Maps**. The voice-recognition capabilities allow you to use voice commands to access features on the phone, such as making phone calls and playing music. Vision-impaired users can also pair their device with a Bluetooth-enabled refreshable braille display.

Users with low vision can change their device display to **Large Text** for readability, **White on Black** for higher contrast, or use **Zoom** to magnify the screen 100–500% (including the home screen, all apps, etc.). To magnify the screen, double tap with three fingers and drag your fingers up to zoom in or down to zoom out. To set **Zoom, White on Black** and other accessibility features on the device, go to **Settings > General > Accessibility.**

For hearing-impaired users, iOS has closed-captioning capabilities, MMS texting, visible and vibrating alerts, **FaceTime** video calling and more. For physically impaired users, **AssistiveTouch** enables entry of multi-touch gestures with one finger or a stylus (sold separately). Also, Siri®—the iOS personal digital assistant—enables voice entry of numerous commands.

To help users with autism, attention deficit and sensory disorders, **Guided Access** allows you to restrict the device to one app, disable touch input on specific areas or all of the screen, control the user's access to the **Settings** app, turn off motion sensors and more. To set up restrictions, go to **Settings > General > Accessibility > Guided Access.**

Check out the overview of accessibility features at

```
http://www.apple.com/accessibility/
```

To view the *Accessibility Programming Guide for iOS*, visit

```
https://developer.apple.com/library/ios/documentation/UserExperi-
   ence/Conceptual/iPhoneAccessibility/Introduction/Introduc-
   tion.html
```

## 1.6  iPhone 6 and iPhone 6 Plus

The iPhone 6 and the larger iPhone 6 Plus were announced by Apple in September, 2014. Figure 1.3 discusses a few of the key new iPhone 6 features.

| Feature | Description |
|---------|-------------|
| A8 64-bit chip | This new chip provides 25% faster processing power and 50% faster graphics performance than its predecessor. |
| Retina HD display | The new Retina HD display is brighter and more color-accurate than in previous models. The ion-strengthened glass is harder to scratch or break. The iPhone 6 has a 4.7", 1334 x 750-pixel display. The iPhone 6 Plus has a 5.5", 1920 x 1080-pixel high definition (HD) display—it plays games in higher resolution than many game consoles. |
| Memory | Both iPhones are available in three memory sizes—16GB, 64GB and the new 128GB. |

**Fig. 1.3** | Key new iPhone 6 and iPhone 6 Plus features. (Part 1 of 2.)

| Feature | Description |
|---|---|
| Barometer | The barometer sensor determines your elevation based on air pressure. You can use it for health and fitness apps to more accurately track how far a user has run, the number of stairs the user has climbed and more. |
| Camera | iPhones are now used to take more pictures than any other camera (`http://www.apple.com/iphone-6/`). The iPhone 6 and iPhone 6 Plus feature a new 8-megapixel iSight camera. The camera's sensor includes focus pixels—previously available in only professional cameras—that enable faster and improved autofocus. You can record 1080p high-definition video at 60 frames per second and 720p slow-motion videos at 240 frames per second. The improved auto-image stabilization helps eliminate motion blur. For additional information about the new cameras, see `http://www.apple.com/iphone-6/cameras/`. |
| Near-Field Communications | **Near-field communication (NFC)**—new in the iPhone 6 and iPhone 6 Plus—is a short-range wireless connectivity standard that enables communication between two devices within a few centimeters. Currently, NFC can be used only with Apple Pay for mobile payments and is not available for developers to use in their apps. |
| Apple Pay | Apple's new wireless payment technology, **Apple Pay**, uses NFC and TouchID authentication to make secure one-touch payments at participating retailers. You can link the credit card that's associated with your iTunes account or submit other credit cards for authentication. The cards are added to your **Passbook** app. The actual card numbers are not stored and other Apple Pay data is encrypted on a dedicated secure storage chip so it's not vulnerable if your phone is lost or stolen. When you pay at an approved retailer, simply select the card you want to use from the **Passbook** app, touch the *Home* button to authenticate and simultaneously hold the iPhone up to an NFC device at the retailer's point-of-sale terminal. A one-time-use credit card number is used for the transaction, so the retailer never sees your sensitive information including name, credit-card number and security code. This is particularly important given recent security breaches at large retailers. Apple Pay can also be used for online payments, eliminating the need to share your credit card numbers, etc. through websites. For more information, visit `https://www.apple.com/iphone-6/apple-pay/`. |

**Fig. 1.3** | Key new iPhone 6 and iPhone 6 Plus features. (Part 2 of 2.)

## 1.7 iOS Operating System History and Features

In this section we provide a brief history and feature summary of the various versions of the iOS mobile operating system. Though originally designed for the iPhone, iOS also runs on the iPod touch, iPad and Apple TV, and Apple Watch. It's a proprietary operating system tightly controlled by Apple and available only on Apple's devices. Google's Android operating system is open source and available for use on third-party devices. iOS does use various open-source libraries—for information on this, visit:

```
http://opensource.apple.com
```

### 1.7.1 iPhone Operating System

The iPhone operating system (later renamed iPhone OS, then iOS) was released in June 2007 along with the first-generation iPhone. The operating system included the **iPod** (built-in media player), **Messages** (for SMS text messaging; originally called **Text**), Calendar, **Camera**, **Photos**, **Maps** and a few other built-in apps.

### 1.7.2 iPhone OS 2: Introducing Third-Party Apps and the App Store

iPhone OS 2 and the iPhone 3G—released in 2008—introduced third-party apps. With the iPhone SDK, developers could create apps for the iPhone and iPod touch. Using the built-in frameworks, developers could build apps that access some of the core functionality of the phone, such as Contacts. The App Store was launched as a marketplace where users could download free and for-sale apps.

### 1.7.3 iPhone OS 3

iPhone OS 3.0 was released in 2009 and introduced many new features, including
- the ability to cut, copy and paste text within and between apps
- landscape keyboard
- recording audio voice memos using the built-in microphone
- multimedia messaging to send photos and videos via the **Messages** app
- Spotlight search for locating e-mail, contacts, calendars, notes and music
- iTunes access directly from an iPhone
- broader language support—30 spoken languages
- peer-to-peer Bluetooth connectivity for transferring data between phones

### 1.7.4 iOS 4

iOS 4 and the iPhone 4 were released in 2010. One notable new feature for users was *multitasking*, which allowed some types of apps to run in the background (such as apps that play music). iOS 4 also added several developer frameworks for integrating some of the core functionality of the device into your apps. For example, the Event Kit framework is used to access events in the **Calendar** app and the Core Motion framework replaced and enhanced earlier iOS capabilities for reading a device's motion data from sensors such as the accelerometer, gyroscope and magnetometer, which we discuss in Section 1.4. iOS 4 also added Grand Central Dispatch (GCD), which provided a new *asynchronous programming* model that was more efficient than the traditional multithreading model provided in earlier iOS versions. Figure 1.4 lists some key iOS 4 features.

| Feature | Description |
|---|---|
| Multitasking | For certain app types (e.g., GPS and Audio), you can run multiple apps simultaneously and switch between them without losing data. |

**Fig. 1.4** | Key iOS 4 features (https://developer.apple.com/library/ios/releasenotes/General/WhatsNewIniOS/Articles/iPhoneOS4.html). (Part 1 of 2.)

| Feature | Description |
|---|---|
| **FaceTime** | Takes advantage of the front- and rear-facing cameras, allowing you to make video calls on the phone. Select a contact from **Contacts** and tap the **FaceTime** button, or if you're already on a call, tap the **FaceTime** button to switch to a video call. An invitation to join the video call appears on your contact's device screen. If the invitation is accepted, the video call starts immediately. |
| iAd | The mobile advertising platform allows you to monetize your apps with in-app banner advertising. Many in-app ads when clicked will open the advertiser's website in a web browser, taking the user out of your app. iAd opens the ads—full-screen video and interactive ad content—within your app; when done viewing the content, users can close an ad and continue using the app. Apple handles all ad sales and delivers them to the users' devices. Developers who implement iAd in their apps receive 70% of iAd revenue. At the time of this writing, iAd was available in France, Germany, Italy, Japan, Spain, the United States and the U.K. We say more about iAd in Chapter 9. |
| Apple Push Notification | Allows apps to receive notifications, even when they aren't running. The service can be used, for example, to notify the user when a new version of your app is available for download or to send news and messages to users. |
| High Dynamic Range (HDR) Photos | Allows you to capture the best exposure for your photos. To create an HDR photo, three photos are taken in rapid succession at varying exposures—low, normal and high. The three photos are then merged using an algorithm that maps the tones across the three images into a single image with optimized tones throughout. The final HDR photo and the original photos are saved. |
| Game Center | The Game Center APIs allow you to create social, multiplayer games. Users can play against friends or find other opponents worldwide, track their scores and compare scores with those of other players. |
| iTunes TV Show Rentals | Rent commercial-free TV shows for $0.99 per episode. |
| Folders | Organize apps into folders by dragging and dropping one app icon on top of another. |
| Improved e-mail | Receive e-mails from multiple accounts in a single inbox, organize messages by threads, check spelling, search your messages and more. |
| **iBooks** | Download e-books from the **iBooks** store to read on an iPhone, iPad or iPod touch. |
| Create playlists | Create customized music playlists directly on the device. |
| Spell Checking | New spell-checking functionality works in **Mail**, **Notes**, **Messages** and more. |
| Wireless Keyboard Support | Pair your device with a wireless Bluetooth keyboard. |

**Fig. 1.4** | Key iOS 4 features (`https://developer.apple.com/library/ios/releasenotes/General/WhatsNewIniOS/Articles/iPhoneOS4.html`). (Part 2 of 2.)

## 1.7.5 iOS 5

iOS 5 featured several enhancements, including more than a thousand new APIs and tools (Fig. 1.5). For a detailed list, see

```
https://developer.apple.com/library/ios/releasenotes/General/
iOS50APIDiff/
```

| Feature | Description |
| --- | --- |
| iCloud | iCloud allows users to store data such as music, photos and videos, documents and e-mail virtually ("in the cloud") and then pushes the data to all of their iOS devices. **iCloud Storage APIs** allow you to create apps that write and store users' data in the cloud. That data can then be accessed and modified by users from any of their iOS or Mac devices without transferring files or syncing devices. |
| Game Center | As of iOS 5, you can post pictures to your **Game Center** profile and track your overall scores. You can play against people you know or find recommended opponents based on the games you play. |
| Notification Center | Places text, e-mail, voice mail, friend requests, stock prices, weather and other notifications in one place. To access the Notification Center on a device, swipe downward from the top of the screen. |
| Reminders | Create to-do lists that automatically sync with the **Calendar** and **Mail** apps and with your iCloud account. Location-based alerts remind you to complete an item on the list when you enter or leave a specified location. |
| Newsstand App | Places users' newspaper and magazine apps in one folder. When new subscriptions are released, they're automatically loaded into the **Newsstand** app. The **Newsstand Kit** and **Store Kit** frameworks allow you to create apps that *push* (i.e., automatically send) magazine and newspaper content to the app users' devices. |
| Camera | Quickly access the **Camera** app from the **Lock** screen and press the volume-up button to take a photo. You can use Photo Stream to automatically download photos to your other iOS devices through your iCloud account. |
| Twitter integration | Users can tweet directly from Camera, Photos, YouTube, Safari or Maps, and store friends' Twitter usernames in **Contacts**. The **iOS Twitter account API** allows you to integrate Twitter into your apps. |
| Safari browser | Improved performance plus new features such as tabbed browsing on the iPad and a **Reading List** that allows you to save web pages to read later on any of your iOS devices connected to iCloud. |
| PC Free | Wirelessly activate and update iOS devices via Wi-Fi without connecting directly to a computer. |
| AirPrint | Print wirelessly from apps on an iOS device to printers that support **Air-Print**. |

**Fig. 1.5** | iOS 5 features (`https://developer.apple.com/library/ios/releasenotes/General/WhatsNewIniOS/Articles/iOS5.html`). (Part 1 of 2.)

| Feature | Description |
|---------|-------------|
| Accessibility | Features include an LED flash and custom vibration settings that allow users to see or feel incoming calls, support for Bluetooth-enabled braille displays, audible alerts, speak selection to read highlighted text and more. |
| Mail | New formatting capabilities include italic, bold, underlined and indented text. You can also flag messages, add and delete folders, search within the body of a message and more. The free e-mail account for iCloud users syncs across iOS devices. |
| Siri | First available on the iPhone 4S, the Siri personal assistant allows you to use your voice to perform numerous tasks on the device. You can tell Siri to make a phone call, dictate and send SMS and e-mail messages, schedule events and appointments on your calendar, perform a web search, find a location on a map, check the weather and more. |

**Fig. 1.5** | iOS 5 features (`https://developer.apple.com/library/ios/ releasenotes/General/WhatsNewIniOS/Articles/iOS5.html`). (Part 2 of 2.)

## 1.7.6 iOS 6

iOS 6, announced at the Apple World Wide Developer Conference (WWDC) in 2012, included approximately 200 new features. Figure 1.6 summarizes some of the key updates and enhancements for developers.

| Feature | Description |
|---------|-------------|
| Game Center and the Game Kit framework | Some of the new and updated features include:<br>• *Challenges*, which allow users to invite their friends to beat an achievement (when a player meets a goal) or a score.<br>• Simultaneous submission of multiple achievements.<br>• Achievement, leaderboard and friend request UIs are now included in a tab in the Game Center UI.<br>• Increased control over *local-player authentication*.<br>• *Player timeout support*. You create a list of players; when a player takes a timeout, the next player in the list is asked to take a turn.<br>• Improved support for *matchmaking*, allowing you to match players to other players programmatically. Players can then send and receive match invitations.<br>• Support for *players' display names*.<br>• Determining which player has the *best connection* to Game Center. |

**Fig. 1.6** | Key iOS 6 features for developers (`https://developer.apple.com/library/ ios/releasenotes/General/WhatsNewIniOS/Articles/iOS6.html`). (Part 1 of 2.)

| Feature | Description |
| --- | --- |
| Social framework | Replaces the Twitter framework from iOS 5. The Social framework allows you to build apps that access the user's social media accounts—including Facebook, Twitter and Sina Weibo (China's most popular social media site)—to post status updates and images. Used in Chapter 4's **Twitter® Searches** app. |
| **Maps** | Enhancements to the **Maps** app and Map Kit framework including launching the **Maps** app from within your app to display directions or points of interest, registering apps that provide directions as routing apps to allow other apps—including **Maps**—to use the directions, and new interfaces allowing apps that do not offer routing information to query **Maps** for directions and points of interest. |
| Pass Kit | Passes are a digital replacement for tickets (e.g., concert tickets, airline boarding passes), membership cards, coupons, etc.—items that are normally printed and used or redeemed physically (not online). Passes include information for the user (e.g., event details, coupon description, etc.) and, if necessary, a bar code or other data to redeem the pass. Users manage their passes in the **Passbook** app. Your web service creates the pass and delivers it to the user either through your app, e-mail or Safari. |
| In-App Purchase | *Store content available for in-app purchase on Apple's servers* rather than hosting it yourself. Also, users can purchase iTunes content (e.g., other apps, music and books) from within your app. |
| iAd | *New larger banner sizes* designed for display in *iPad* apps. |
| **Reminders** | Apps can create and access reminders that appear in the **Reminders** app. These can be set for a time or triggered by entering or existing a location. |
| Collection views | Customize the layout of your data, include animated content, easily create and manage cells and views, and insert/move/delete items in batches. |
| Auto Layout | Set guidelines for laying out user-interface elements. |
| State Preservation | Apps can save and restore the user interface to the state it was in when the user last used the app. |

**Fig. 1.6** | Key iOS 6 features for developers (`https://developer.apple.com/library/ios/releasenotes/General/WhatsNewIniOS/Articles/iOS6.html`). (Part 2 of 2.)

iOS 6 included several updates and new features for users. Figure 1.7 lists some of the key user features.

| Feature | Description |
| --- | --- |
| Facebook integration | Facebook integration allows users to perform tasks such as posting updates via **Notification Center**, viewing friend details in **Contacts** and events in **Calendar**, and posting photos from within **Photos** or **Camera**, game scores from **Game Center** and location from **Maps**. |

**Fig. 1.7** | Key iOS 6 features. (Part 1 of 3.)

| Feature | Description |
|---|---|
| Siri | Siri added features, including:<br>• Sports scores, batting averages, player stats and team standings.<br>• Results from Rotten Tomatoes (movie information), Yelp! (business listings and reviews) and OpenTable (restaurant reservations).<br>• Launching apps.<br>• Posting status updates on Facebook and tweets on Twitter.<br>• Reading turn-by-turn directions.<br>• Car integration via the *Eyes Free* feature, enabling drivers to ask Siri for directions, change the radio station and more. Vehicle manufacturers planning support for this include Audi, BMW, General Motors, Mercedes-Benz and Toyota. |
| FaceTime | **FaceTime** is now available over cellular and can be used to make video calls among iPhone, iPad and Mac devices. **iMessage** works similarly. |
| Passbook | Stores the user's tickets, boarding passes, coupons and loyalty cards in one place. **Passbook**'s time- and location-based services display passes as they're needed; the barcodes can be scanned directly from iOS devices. For example, coupons, loyalty cards and gift certificates are displayed when the user visits the related business, and boarding passes are displayed when the user arrives at the airport. |
| Maps | New **Maps** features include:<br>• Turn-by-turn navigation, real-time traffic updates and an estimated time of arrival (ETA).<br>• Siri can access **Maps**, help users find a location and speak the directions.<br>• Users can rotate and tilt the iOS device to change the map view.<br>• Flyover provides a high-definition aerial view of metropolitan areas.<br>• Local search of business listings. |
| Photo sharing | Users can send pictures from the **Photos** app to friends who are using iCloud. The shared pictures appear in their friends' **Photos** app on iOS devices or in the iPhoto app on their Mac. Friends can also view the shared pictures on the web and Apple TV. Users and their friends can add comments to the photos. |

**Fig. 1.7** | Key iOS 6 features. (Part 2 of 3.)

| Feature | Description |
|---------|-------------|
| **Phone** | The **Do Not Disturb** setting allows users to block all calls or allow only certain callers to get through. Users can quickly respond to incoming calls with text messages and set reminders to call back. |

**Fig. 1.7** | Key iOS 6 features. (Part 3 of 3.)

## 1.7.7 iOS 7

iOS 7 was released in September, 2013. It has a redesigned user interface and many new features for developers that make it easier to create games, such as a new animation system, improved multitasking and more (Fig. 1.8).

| Feature | Description |
|---------|-------------|
| Sprite Kit framework | A hardware-accelerated animation system that allows you to create games more easily. Includes a physics simulation engine, graphics and animation support and sound playback. |
| Game Controller framework | Enables your apps to use game controllers—hardware devices connected to the iPhone or iPad physically or via Bluetooth. |
| Game Center | iOS 7 added a few improvements to Game Center including an increased number of leaderboards per app, exchanges (which let players in a multiplayer game take actions even when it's not their turn) and conditions for meeting challenges. |
| Maps | Enhancements include 3D map and overlay support, the ability to request directions from Apple and more. |
| AirDrop | Allows users to share documents, photos, and more with other devices nearby. |
| Inter-App Audio | Share audio between multiple apps on the same device. |
| Multipeer Connectivity framework | Connect with nearby devices using Bluetooth, a local-area Wi-Fi network or peer-to-peer Wi-Fi. |
| Media Accessibility framework | Manage closed-captioned content in your app's media files. |
| Enhanced Store Kit framework | You can now verify in-app purchases on the user's device. |
| Enhanced Message UI framework | Allows users to send files with messages. |

**Fig. 1.8** | Some key iOS 7 features (`https://developer.apple.com/library/ios/releasenotes/General/WhatsNewIniOS/Articles/iOS7.html`). (Part 1 of 2.)

| Feature | Description |
| --- | --- |
| CarPlay | Added in iOS 7.1 and available on select 2014 cars, CarPlay enables you to make phone calls, get driving directions, listen to and dictate text messages and play music from your iPhone in your car. Just plug in your iPhone to access the features through the car's built-in controls (e.g., touch screens or buttons) or using Siri voice controls. |

**Fig. 1.8** | Some key iOS 7 features (`https://developer.apple.com/library/ios/releasenotes/General/WhatsNewIniOS/Articles/iOS7.html`). (Part 2 of 2.)

## 1.8 iOS 8

iOS 8 was announced at Apple's WWDC in June 2014 and was released in September, 2014. It's supported on the iPhone 4s and higher. It includes several new APIs including a few that make it easier to create 3D games, sophisticated UIs, a new animation system, improved multitasking and more (Fig. 1.9). New *continuity* features enable users to start a task on one iOS device and finish it on another. Users can even make or answer phone calls and send or receive text messages through their iPhones via an iPad or Mac (running OS X 10.10 or higher) that's connected to the same WiFi network as the iPhone. In the future, devices other than iPhones, iPod touches, iPads and Apple Watches—such as the Apple TV—may be able to run iOS apps. To help developers prepare for this, Xcode now enables you to design adaptive UIs that can adjust based on a device's screen size and orientation. Also, the iOS 8 Simulator includes resizable iPhone and iPad "devices," enabling you to test your adaptive designs at different sizes. For additional information about what's new in iOS 8, visit

```
https://developer.apple.com/library/ios/releasenotes/General/
    WhatsNewIniOS/Articles/iOS8.html
```

| Feature | Description |
| --- | --- |
| App extensions | Enable you to make custom functionality and content from your app available to other apps. For example, sharing content between apps, editing photos and videos, viewing or modifying content within another app (e.g., adding **Calendar** entries), performing tasks in the **Notification Center**'s **Today** view, storing documents and sharing them with other apps, and creating custom keyboards that can be used system-wide. |
| Document Picker | Enables users to share, read and edit documents across multiple apps. |

**Fig. 1.9** | Some key iOS 8 features (`https://developer.apple.com/library/ios/releasenotes/General/WhatsNewIniOS/Articles/iOS8.html`. (Part 1 of 2.)

| Feature | Description |
|---------|-------------|
| Cloud Kit | Share data between your app and iCloud, even if the app user does not have an iCloud account. The data is stored in a repository associated with your app. You can use the Cloud Kit dashboard to monitor and manage the user data. |
| Handoff | Create apps that allow users to start an activity on one iOS device, then continue the activity on another (the devices must use the same Apple ID). For example, a user could start playing a game using your app on an iPad, then continue playing on an iPhone or Mac. For more information about continuity features, see `https://www.apple.com/ios/ios8/continuity/`. |
| Health Kit Framework | Create apps that keep track of user's health information and share it with other connected devices, such as fitness trackers, blood pressure monitors and more. The user maintains control over what information is shared with your app. Everything is stored securely in a central location, enabling the user to access all of their health information in the new **Health** app. |
| Home Kit Framework | Create apps that control or communicate with the user's connected home devices (e.g., security systems, thermostats, appliances, lighting, heating, cooling, etc.). |
| Photos framework | Includes new APIs for retrieving, displaying and editing photos and videos, video playback, working with iCloud Shared Albums and more. |
| PhotosUI framework | Helps you create extensions to the **Photos** app. |
| Touch ID Authentication (Local Authentication framework) | Improve security of your app by authenticating app users with Touch ID fingerprint authentication, rather than with a username and password. |
| SceneKit | Makes it easier for you to create 3D games and user interfaces. Includes a 3D physics engine that allows you to detect collisions, simulate gravity and more. |
| SpriteKit | Includes new features for creating advanced game effects, including pixel-perfect collision detection (collision detection based on an object's actual shape, rather than a rectangular bounding box), SceneKit integration, new animations, new physics effects, and more. |
| Unified storyboards | Create one storyboard for universal apps, rather separate ones for iPhones and iPads. This enables you to design a single user interface, then add customizations for specific screen sizes and orientations. |

**Fig. 1.9** | Some key iOS 8 features (`https://developer.apple.com/library/ios/releasenotes/General/WhatsNewIniOS/Articles/iOS8.html`. (Part 2 of 2.)

## 1.9 Apple Watch

In September, 2014, Apple announced the **Apple Watch**—to be released in early 2015. The Apple Watch uses Bluetooth to pair with your iPhone 5 or higher running iOS 8. The watch provides time accuracy within 50 milliseconds, and a new way for users to communicate directly from their wrists, track health and fitness, view maps, receive notifications, make payments using the new Apple Pay, check the weather and more. Tim Cook, Apple's CEO, has called the Apple Watch, "The most personal device Apple has ever created."

The Apple Watch features a flexible Retina display that senses both touch and force, so the device is able to recognize the difference between a tap and a press. You can swipe the **Home** screen to pan through your apps and tap to launch them. The **Digital Crown**—the dial on the right side of the watch—can be rotated forward or backward to zoom in and out, navigate and scroll through items on the screen. You can press the Digital Crown to return to the **Home** screen and to access Siri. By swiping upwards from the bottom of the screen, you can access your customized **Glances**, such as the weather, music, stock prices and more.

The **Taptic Engine** lightly vibrates the watch when a notification is received (e.g., an e-mail or text message). Simply lifting your wrist displays the notification on the screen. The **Maps** app shows you where you are and you can swipe or zoom in and out to see more of the area. When you use the app for directions, the Taptic Engine sends light taps to your wrist to let you know when to turn left or right. It uses different sensations for each direction so you don't have to look at the map to know which way to turn.

**Digital Touch**—the button below the Digital Crown on the right side of the watch—displays your **Contacts**. You can initiate a phone call, send text messages or create a live communication such as sending taps or your heartbeat to a friend.

**WatchKit** enables you to extend your iOS 8 iPhone apps to Apple Watch. For example, you can send notifications to the watch, use the watch to collect the user's health information (e.g., pulse, distance run so far) and more. Figure 1.10 provides a few examples of apps that have been designed for the Apple Watch.

| Example | Description |
| --- | --- |
| America Airlines | Get your boarding passes. |
| W Hotels (part of Starwood) | Check into the hotel and open your hotel room door by simply waving your Apple Watch in front of the lock on the door. |
| BMW | See the charge level in your electric car and find where you parked. |
| MLB | Check Major League Baseball scores. |
| Honeywell thermostats | Check and change your home thermostats remotely. |
| Fitness app | Monitor all of your fitness and activity throughout day. |
| Workout app | Set specific workout goals (e.g., running, cycling, etc.) and track your progress. |
| Apple TV | Control your Apple TV device. |

**Fig. 1.10** | Examples of apps designed for the Apple Watch.

# 1.10 App Store

At the time of this writing, there were over 1.3 million apps in the App Store[17] and over 75 billion iOS apps have been downloaded.[18] The potential for iOS app developers is enormous.. Figure 1.11 lists some popular apps by category. Visit the App Store to check out Apple's featured apps. This might give you ideas for the types of apps you'd like to create. Some apps are free and some are fee based. Developers set the prices for their apps sold through the App Store and receive 70 percent of the revenue. Many app developers offer free versions of their apps so users can try them. Then, if they like them, they can purchase more feature-rich versions or virtual goods. We discuss the so-called "lite" strategy and the freemium business model in more detail in Section 9.5.

| Category | Sample apps |
|---|---|
| Books | iBooks®, Kindle, Audio Books from Audible, Goodreads, NOOK |
| Business | TurboScan, Adobe Reader, Job Search, HotSchedules, SayHi Translate |
| Catalogs | Emoji, Pokedex Pro Elite, My Movies for iPhone Pro, cPRO |
| Education | Duolingo, Quizlet, Stack the States™, iTunes U, Fit Brains Trainer |
| Entertainment | iTube Pro, Netflix, Disney Movies Anywhere, Podcasts, WeFollow |
| Finance | My Weekly Budget, MileBug, Bank of America, PayPal™, Mint |
| Food & Drink | Starbucks, GrubHub, OpenTable, Craft Check, Clean and Green Eating |
| Games | Angry Birds, Cooking Academy, Fruit Ninja, Jaws™, Skee-Ball |
| Health & Fitness | Sleep Cycle, Fitbit, Lose It!, Weight Watchers Mobile, Fitness Buddy |
| Kids | Tiny Firefighters, Endless Reader, PlayKids, Toca Pet Doctor |
| Lifestyle | Lockster, Tinder, eBay, Amazon, CARFAX, Cupid Dating |
| Medical | Baby Connect, Doctor on Demand, SnoreLab, Epocrates, Pregnancy+ |
| Music | Spotify, Shazam, Pandora Radio, Slacker Radio, Beats Music, Rdio |
| Navigation | Google Maps, Waze, MapQuest®, Trailhead, MotionX™ GPS Drive |
| News | CNN, NYTimes, USA Today, WSJ, Flipboard, The Blaze, Yahoo!® |
| Newsstand | Time Magazine, Forbes Magazine, Women's Health Mag |
| Photo & Video | Instagram, Camera+, Snapchat, YouTube, iMovie, PicPlayPost |
| Productivity | Gmail, Dropbox, Evernote, Keynote, Pages, Zippy, Lookup+ |
| Reference | Google® Translate, Dictionary.com, Ancestry, WolframAlpha |
| Social Networking | Facebook®, Pinterest, Twitter, Skype™, LinkedIn®, WhatsApp Messenger |
| Sports | ESPN® ScoreCenter, NFL Live Football, Bike Repair, MLB.com At Bat |
| Travel | Uber, TripIt, Google Earth, Yelp®, Gas Buddy, Kayak, Hotels.com |
| Utilities | Globo, Scan, Chrome, Text Free with Pinger, Hushed, RedLaser |
| Weather | The Weather Channel®, WeatherBug®, Smoggy Air Quality |

**Fig. 1.11** | Popular iPhone and iPad apps in the App Store.

17. http://mashable.com/2014/09/09/apple-1-3-million-apps-app-store/.
18. http://techcrunch.com/2014/06/02/itunes-app-store-now-has-1-2-million-apps-has-seen-75-billion-downloads-to-date/.

## 1.11 Objective-C

The C programming language was developed in the early 1970s by Dennis Ritchie at Bell Laboratories. It initially became widely known as the UNIX operating system's development language. The **Objective-C** programming language, created by Brad Cox and Tom Love at StepStone in the early 1980s, added object-oriented programming capabilities to C. In 1988, NeXT licensed Objective-C from StepStone and developed an Objective-C compiler and libraries which were used to build the NeXTSTEP operating system's user interface. NeXT also developed **Interface Builder** for creating graphical user interfaces with drag-and-drop. Apple acquired NeXT in 1997, then Objective-C became enormously popular due to its use in developing iPhone and iPad apps.

## 1.12 Swift: Apple's Programming Language of the Future

The Swift programming language was arguably the most significant announcement at Apple's WWDC in 2014. Swift had been under development by Apple's Developer Tools team since 2010. Very few people—including Apple insiders—were aware of the project.[19] Although apps can still be developed in Objective-C, Apple says that Swift is its applications programming and systems programming language of the future. All of the apps in this book are coded in Swift.

### 1.12.1 Key Features

Swift is a contemporary language with simpler syntax than Objective-C. Figure 1.12 lists some of Swift's key features that are not in Objective-C.

| Swift feature | Description |
| --- | --- |
| Type inference | Though Swift is a strongly typed language, in many cases you do not need to specify a variable's or constant's type—Swift can *infer* the type based on the variable's or constant's initializer value. |
| switch statement enhancements | Unlike switch statements in other C-based languages, Swift's switch statement can test values of any type. Also, its cases are much more flexible than those in other languages—you can have cases for individual values, sets of values and ranges of values. You can also specify boolean criteria that must be true for a match to occur. |
| Closures | Swift supports functional-programming techniques via closures (anonymous functions that some languages call *lambdas*). Closures can be manipulated as data—they can be assigned to variables, passed to functions as arguments and returned from functions. Several of the Swift Standard Library's global functions receive closures as arguments—for example, there's a version of the sort function that receives a closure for comparing two objects to determine their sort order. |

**Fig. 1.12** | Some key Swift features that are not in Objective-C. (Part 1 of 3.)

---

19. http://nondot.org/sabre/.

| Swift feature | Description |
|---|---|
| Tuples | Swift provides *tuples*—collections of values that can be of the same or different types. The language provides syntax for *composing* (creating) and *decomposing* (extracting values from) a tuple. |
| Optionals | *Optionals* enable you to define variables and constants that might not have a value. The language provides mechanisms for determining whether an optional has a value and, if so, obtaining that value. Optionals work for any Swift type, whereas the corresponding concept in Objective-C—a pointer that points to an object or is `nil`—works only for reference types. |
| Dictionary type | Swift's `Dictionary` type provides built-in support for manipulating data in *key–value pairs*. |
| Array, String and Dictionary value types | Swift types `Array`, `String` and `Dictionary` are *value* types (not reference types as you might expect) that are implemented as `struct`s. Objects of value types are *copied* when you assign them to variables or constants, pass them to functions or return them from functions. The Swift compiler optimizes value-type copy operations, performing them only when necessary. |
| Array bounds checking | A *runtime* error occurs if you access an element outside an `Array`'s bounds. |
| Class-like struct and enum value types | Swift's `struct` and `enum` types have many class-like features, making them more robust than their Objective-C counterparts. Objects of `struct` and `enum` types are *value* types. |
| Functions with multiple return values (via tuples) | Functions can return multiple values of possibly different types as tuples. |
| Generics | Rather than writing separate code to perform identical tasks on different types (e.g., summing an `Array` of integers vs. summing an `Array` of floating-point values), *generics* enable you to write the code once and use placeholders to represent the type(s) of data to manipulate. The compiler substitutes actual types for the placeholders. In a generic function call, the compiler determines the actual types based on the arguments specified in the code that calls the function. For a generic type, the compiler uses the actual type you specify when declaring an object of that generic type. Swift's `Array` and `Dictionary` types are generic types, and many of its global functions are generic functions. When you use generic functions and types, compile-time type checking is performed to ensure that you use the functions and types correctly. For example, creating an `Array` of integers, then attempting to place a `String` into that `Array` is a compilation error. |
| Operator overloading | You can define functions that overload existing operators to work with new types, and you can also define *entirely new operators*—which you cannot do in C# or C++, for example. |
| Overflow checking in integer calculations | *By default*, all integer calculations check for *arithmetic overflow* and result in a runtime error if overflow occurs. |

**Fig. 1.12** | Some key Swift features that are not in Objective-C. (Part 2 of 3.)

| Swift feature | Description |
|---|---|
| String interpolation | String interpolation enables you to build Strings by *inserting* variable, constant and expression values into *placeholders* directly in String literals. |
| Nested types | You can define types *nested* in other type definitions—this is commonly used to define enums or utility classes and structs that are *hidden* in the scope of another type. |
| Nested functions | You can nest function definitions in other function definitions—such a nested function is callable in the scope of its enclosing function and can be returned from that function for use in other scopes. |

**Fig. 1.12** | Some key Swift features that are not in Objective-C. (Part 3 of 3.)

## 1.12.2 Performance

Swift was designed for better performance than Objective-C on today's multi-core systems. At Apple's WWDC 2014 main keynote address, Apple observed that Swift code was about 1.5 times faster than Objective-C code. Although Array, String and Dictionary are *value* types whose variables are normally *copied* when passed or assigned, the Swift compiler optimizes value-type copy operations by performing them only when necessary.

## 1.12.3 Error Prevention

Swift eliminates many common programming errors, making your code more robust and secure (Fig. 1.13). Many of these—such as not returning a value from the assignment operator—could not have been added to Objective-C, because doing so would have broken backward compatibility with legacy code.

### Some Swift features that eliminate common programming errors

- Curly braces ({}) are required around *every* control statement's body. For all control statements this helps ensure that you do not accidentally forget the braces around multi-statement bodies.
- Unlike Objective-C, C and C++, Swift does not include pointers.
- The assignment operator (=) does not return a value. A compilation error occurs if = is used in a condition rather than the equal-to operator (==), thus preventing the common error of typing a single = when you intend to use the equal-to operator (==).
- Semicolons are optional unless you need to separate multiple statements on the same line.
- Parentheses around conditions in control statements are optional, making the code a bit easier to read.
- Variables and constants *must* be initialized before they're used—either in their definitions or via initializer methods in type definitions.

**Fig. 1.13** | Some Swift features that eliminate common programming errors. (Part 1 of 2.)

Some Swift features that eliminate common programming errors

- Integer calculations are *checked for overflow by default*—a runtime error occurs if a calculation results in overflow.
- Swift *does not allow implicit conversions* between numeric types.
- Array indices (subscripts) are *bounds checked* at execution time—a runtime error occurs if you access an element outside an `Array`'s bounds.
- Automatic memory management *eliminates most memory leaks*—it's still possible to maintain references to objects that are no longer used and thus prevent their memory from being reclaimed by the runtime. Swift also has *weak references* for cases in which circular references between objects would prevent those objects' memory from being reclaimed.

**Fig. 1.13** | Some Swift features that eliminate common programming errors. (Part 2 of 2.)

## 1.12.4 Swift Standard Library

The **Swift Standard Library** contains Swift's built-in types (`String`, `Array`, `Dictionary` and the various integer and floating-point numeric types), protocols (`Equatable`, `Comparable` and `Printable`) and global functions (e.g., for printing and sorting). We discuss these as we use them throughout the book. For more details on these types, protocols and global functions, see Apple's *Swift Standard Library Reference* document at:

```
https://developer.apple.com/library/ios/documentation/General/Ref-
    erence/SwiftStandardLibraryReference
```

## 1.12.5 Swift Apps and the Cocoa® and Cocoa Touch® Frameworks

Swift, like Objective-C, can use OS X's **Cocoa frameworks** and iOS's **Cocoa Touch frameworks**. These powerful libraries of prebuilt components help you create apps that meet Apple's requirements for the look-and-feel of iOS and OS X apps. The frameworks are written mainly in Objective-C (some are written in C); Apple has indicated that new frameworks will be developed in Swift. See Section 1.14 for more details on these frameworks.

## 1.12.6 Swift and Objective-C Interoperability

You can combine Swift and Objective-C in the same app, so you can use Swift to code portions of existing apps without rewriting all your Objective-C code. Most of the Cocoa Touch APIs are still written in Objective-C, so Swift programmers typically create apps that interact with existing Objective-C code, as we'll do in this book's examples.

  In fact, you'll often pass Swift objects into methods of classes written in Objective-C, such as those in Cocoa Touch. Swift's numeric types and its `String`, `Array` and `Dictionary` types can all be used in contexts where their Objective-C equivalents are expected. Similarly, the Objective-C equivalents (`NSString`, `NSMutableString`, `NSArray`, `NSMutableArray`, `NSDictionary` and `NSMutableDictionary`), when returned to your Swift code, are automatically treated as their Swift counterparts. This mechanism—known as **bridging**—is transparent to you.

Apple's book *Using Swift with Cocoa and Objective-C*, available at:

```
https://developer.apple.com/library/ios/documentation/Swift/Concep-
    tual/BuildingCocoaApps
```

and in the iBooks store discusses:

- Setting up a Swift app project that can use the Cocoa or Cocoa Touch frameworks.
- Swift and Objective-C interoperability—e.g., interacting with the Objective-C APIs, creating Swift classes for use from Objective-C code and more.
- Projects that contain both Swift and Objective-C files.
- Tips for migrating your legacy Objective-C code to Swift.

### 1.12.7 Other Apple Swift Resources

In addition to the documents mentioned in Sections 1.12.4– and 1.12.6, Apple provides other resources to help you learn Swift:

- Apple's Swift Blog is located at:

```
https://developer.apple.com/swift/blog/
```

- The sample code for Apple's WWDC 2014 Swift demos is located at:

```
https://developer.apple.com/wwdc/resources/sample-code/
```

- Apple's book *The Swift Programming Language* introduces Swift and contains a brief tour of the language, the language guide (covering Swift's key features in more depth) and the language reference (presenting Swift's grammar and the details of each language feature). This is available in the iBooks store and at:

```
https://developer.apple.com/library/ios/documentation/Swift/
    Conceptual/Swift_Programming_Language/
```

- The WWDC 2014 videos are available at:

```
https://developer.apple.com/videos/wwdc/2014/
```

## 1.13  Can I Use Swift Exclusively?

This book is intended for the following audiences:

- Objective-C programmers who are developing new iOS apps in Swift.
- Objective-C programmers who are enhancing existing iOS apps with Swift.
- Java, C++ and C# programmers who are new to iOS development and who want to build their apps using Swift.

One of your biggest questions is probably, "Can I program my iOS apps purely in Swift?" Let's consider the issues by audience.

### 1.13.1 Objective-C Programmers Who Are Developing New iOS Apps in Swift

Apple encourages Objective-C programmers to use Swift for new app development. You can create entire apps in Swift, though you'll still use Cocoa Touch frameworks, which are largely written in Objective-C.

### 1.13.2 Objective-C Programmers Who Are Enhancing Existing iOS Apps with Swift

Apple also encourages Objective-C programmers to use Swift to enhance *existing* apps with Swift. Even if you write your enhancements using only Swift, they'll still interact extensively with your existing apps' Objective-C code and the Cocoa Touch frameworks. Rather than converting your existing apps to Swift, you can preserve the investments you've made in them by reusing your debugged, tested and performance-tuned Objective-C code. Be sure to read Apple's document *Using Swift with Cocoa and Objective-C* (discussed in Section 1.12.6) for details on Swift and Objective-C interoperability issues.

### 1.13.3 Java, C++ and C# Programmers Who Are New to iOS App Development

Apple also encourages Java, C++ and C# programmers who don't know Objective-C to use Swift for new iOS app development. Apple believes that for these programmers Swift lowers the barriers to entry to iOS app development. Its similarities to these other popular programming languages make it more familiar and easier to learn than Objective-C. You'll still need to use Cocoa Touch frameworks written in Objective-C, but Apple provides Swift interfaces for these existing frameworks.

### 1.13.4 Rapid Evolution Expected

Because Swift is so new, it has been evolving rapidly and is likely to continue doing so. Apple has stated that Swift will be *binary compatible* with future Swift versions and with Objective-C. However, future Swift versions might not be *source-code compatible* with older versions. Apple plans to provide code converters to help you update your existing Swift source code with new language features.

### 1.13.5 Mixing Swift and Objective-C Code

We believe most existing iOS app developers will mix Swift and Objective-C, rather than converting all of their legacy code to Swift. In this book, we write all of our application code in Swift, using existing Cocoa Touch frameworks as necessary.

## 1.14  Cocoa Touch® iOS Frameworks

The Cocoa frameworks evolved from projects at NeXT. OpenStep was developed as an object-oriented programming API for building an operating system. After Apple acquired NeXT, OpenStep evolved into Rhapsody, and many of the base libraries became the Yellow Box API. Rhapsody and Yellow Box eventually evolved into the Mac's OS X operating system and Cocoa, respectively. Cocoa Touch is the version of Cocoa for iOS devices—these are resource constrained (compared to desktop computers, mobile devices typically have smaller memory, slower processor speeds and limited battery power) and offer different functionality than desktop computers. Three key frameworks for OS X and iOS development are Foundation, AppKit and UIKit, each introduced below.

*Foundation Framework*
The **Foundation** framework—in both Cocoa and Cocoa Touch—includes class `NSObject` for defining object behavior. Foundation also has classes for basic types, storing data, work-

ing with text and strings, filesystem access, calculating differences in dates and times, inter-app notifications and much more.

### AppKit Framework

Cocoa's **AppKit** framework is for developing the UIs of OS X apps. AppKit provides controls (such as windows, menus, buttons, panels, text fields, dialogs), event-handling capabilities, gesture support and more. It also supports content sharing between services (e.g., e-mail), iCloud integration, printing, accessibility (for users with disabilities), push notifications, graphics and more.

### UIKit Framework

Cocoa Touch's **UIKit** framework is similar to AppKit, but optimized for developing iOS app UIs for mobile devices. UIKit includes multi-touch interface controls that are appropriate for mobile apps, event handling for motion-based events, event handling for sensors (e.g., proximity, motion, accelerometer, ambient light, gyroscope) and more.

### Other Cocoa Touch Frameworks

The Cocoa Touch frameworks allow you to conveniently access iOS features and incorporate them into your apps. The frameworks help you create apps which adhere to iOS's unique look and feel. Figures 1.14–1.17 list the frameworks and provide brief descriptions of each. To learn more about these frameworks, see the Frameworks section of the *iOS Developer Library* at

```
http://developer.apple.com/library/ios/navigation/index.html#sec-
    tion=Frameworks
```

| Framework | Description |
| --- | --- |
| AddressBookUI | Display contact information from the user's Address Book. |
| EventKitUI | Edit, create and display calendar events from within your apps. |
| GameKit | Voice, Bluetooth networking and other capabilities that can be used in games or other apps. |
| MapKit | Add maps and satellite images to location-based apps. Annotate maps, identify areas on a map using overlays and more. |
| MessageUI | Create e-mail messages from within an app. Create and send SMS messages from within an app. |
| NotificationCenter | Display information from your app in Notification Center and allow users to perform brief tasks for your app (such as responding to a message). |
| PhotosUI | Incorporate iOS photo and video editing features into your own apps. |
| Twitter | Add tweeting capabilities to any app. |
| UIKit | Classes for creating and managing a user interface, including event handling, drawing, windows, views and multi-touch interface controls. Introduced in Chapter 2's **Welcome** app and used throughout the book. |
| iAd | In-app advertising framework used to place full-screen or banner advertisements within an app for monetization. |

**Fig. 1.14** | Cocoa Touch layer frameworks for building graphical, event-driven apps.

| Framework | Description |
|---|---|
| AVFoundation | Interface for audio recording and playback (similar to the Audio Toolbox). Includes media asset management and editing, video capture and playback, track management, metadata management for media, stereophonic panning, sound synchronization and an Objective-C interface for determining the format, sample rate and number of channels for sound files. Also includes classes for playing a sequence of media objects, reading samples from media files and writing samples to a data file. Used in Chapter 6's **Cannon** game app. |
| AssetsLibrary | Framework for accessing the user's media library including photos and videos uploaded onto the device or stored in the user's **Photos** app. Also allows your app to save new photos and videos to the user's photo albums. |
| AudioToolbox | Interface for audio recording and playback of streamed audio and alerts. |
| AudioUnit | Interface for using the iPhone OS audio-processing plug-ins. |
| CoreAudio | Framework for declaring data types and constants used by other Core Audio interfaces. |
| CoreGraphics | API for drawing, rendering images, color management, gradients, coordinate-space transformations and handling PDF documents. Used in Chapter 6's **Cannon** game app. |
| CoreMidi | Enables apps to interact with MIDI (Musical Instrument Digital Interface) devices like synthesizers. |
| CoreText | APIs for text layout and handling fonts. |
| CoreVideo | C-based APIs for video playback, editing and processing. |
| GLKit | Provides capabilities that simplify creating OpenGL ES apps (e.g., games). |
| GameController | Enables apps to support game play via external game controllers connected to an iOS device. |
| ImageIO | Support for reading and writing various image formats. |
| MediaAccessibility | Capabilities for accessing closed captioning preferences so that you can use them when presenting closed captions for your app's media content. |
| MediaPlayer | Finds and plays audio and video files within an app. |
| Metal | Gives your apps access to the device's graphics processor for hardware-accelerated 3D graphics and offloading compute-intensive tasks from the device's CPU. |
| OpenAL | An open-source library for three-dimensional sound. |
| OpenGLES | A subset of OpenGL for 2D and 3D graphics in mobile apps. |
| QuartzCore | Used to create animations and effects that are then hardware rendered for performance. |
| SceneKit | For adding 3D models to an app's user interface. Commonly used in games. |
| SpriteKit | For 2D sprite-based games. Provides animation, physics simulation, collision detection and event-handling support. Used in Chapter 6's **Cannon** game app. |

**Fig. 1.15** | Media layer frameworks for adding audio, video, graphics and animation to your apps.

| Framework | Description |
| --- | --- |
| Accounts | Enables apps to access user account information in the Accounts database, rather than storing user credentials. Users can grant access to your apps to use their accounts so that they do not have to enter usernames and passwords. |
| AdSupport | Enables an app to serve ads and determine whether the user has limited ad tracking. |
| AddressBook | Framework for accessing the user's Address Book contacts. |
| CFNetwork | Framework using network protocols in apps to perform tasks including working with HTTP and authenticating HTTP and HTTPS servers, working with FTP servers, creating encrypted connections and more. |
| CloudKit | Used to manage data transfer between apps and iCloud. |
| CoreData | Framework for performing tasks related to object life-cycle and object graph management. Used in Chapter 8's **Address Book** app. |
| CoreFoundation | Library of programming interfaces that allow frameworks and libraries to share code and data. Introduced in Chapter 4's **Twitter® Searches** app and used throughout the book. |
| CoreLocation | For determining the location and orientation of an iPhone, then configuring and scheduling the delivery of location-based events. |
| CoreMedia | For creating, playing and managing audio and video. |
| CoreMotion | For receiving and handling accelerometer and other motion events. |
| CoreTelephony | Used to get information about the user's mobile service provider. |
| EventKit | Allows your apps to access data in the user's **Calendar** app and to add and edit events in the **Calendar** app. |
| HealthKit | For recording and tracking health and fitness data. |
| HomeKit | For controlling devices that support Apple's Home Automation Protocol. |
| JavaScriptCore | For executing JavaScript in an app. |
| MobileCoreServices | Includes standard types and constants. |
| MultipeerConnectivity | Enables apps to discover and communicate with services provided by nearby iOS devices. Communication occurs via WiFi networks, peer-to-peer WiFi connections directly between devices or via Bluetooth personal area networks. |
| NewsstandKit | Enables apps to download and process Newsstand content (e.g., magazine and newspaper subscriptions). |
| PassKit | For creating, distributing, updating and interacting with passes that are managed by the Passbook app. For the iPhone 6 and iPhone 6 Plus, PassKit is now also used to manage credit cards for Apple Pay. |
| PushKit | Enables apps to register for and receive data pushed from remote servers. |
| QuickLook | Displays previews of files even if they're in formats not directly supported by your app (e.g., Microsoft Office documents). |
| Social | Enables apps to integrate with social networking services to perform tasks such as posting messages and photos on your users' behalf. |

**Fig. 1.16** | Core Services layer frameworks. (Part 1 of 2.)

| Framework | Description |
|---|---|
| StoreKit | In-app purchase support for processing transactions. |
| SystemConfiguration | Determines network availability and state on an iPhone. |
| UIAutomation | Used to integrate automated user interface testing. |
| WebKit | Enables apps to render web content directly rather than opening the Safari browser. |

**Fig. 1.16** |   Core Services layer frameworks. (Part 2 of 2.)

| Framework | Description |
|---|---|
| Accelerate | For complex math and image processing. Includes functions for vector and matrix math, digital signal processing, large number handling and more. |
| CoreBluetooth | For communicating with Bluetooth low energy (Bluetooth LE) devices, such as heart rate monitors, fitness devices, proximity sensors, etc. |
| ExternalAccessory | Allows the iPhone to interact with third-party authorized accessories connected via Bluetooth or the dock connector. |
| LocalAuthentication | Enables apps to authenticate users with passphrases or TouchID (e.g., to authenticate a purchase). |
| Security | Framework for securing data used in an app. |
| System | BSD operating system and POSIX API functions. |

**Fig. 1.17** |   Core OS layer frameworks for accessing the iOS kernel.

### Web Services

**Web services** are software components stored on one computer that can be accessed by an app (or other software component) on another computer over the Internet. With web services, you can create **mashups,** which enable you to rapidly develop apps by combining complementary web services, often from multiple organizations and possibly with other forms of information feeds. 100 Destinations (http://www.100destinations.co.uk), for example, combines the photos and tweets from Twitter with the mapping capabilities of Google Maps to allow you to explore countries around the world through the photos of others.

Programmableweb (http://www.programmableweb.com/) provides a directory of over 11,150 APIs and 7,300 mashups, plus how-to guides and sample code for creating your own mashups. Figure 1.18 lists some popular web services. According to Programmableweb, the three most widely used APIs for mashups are Google Maps, Twitter and YouTube. Google provides many web services, which you can study at:

```
http://code.google.com/apis/gdata/docs/directory.html
```

We use Twitter web services in Chapter 4. Figure 1.19 lists a some popular web mashups.

| Web services source | How it's used |
|---|---|
| Google Maps | Mapping services |
| Twitter | Microblogging |
| YouTube | Video search |
| Facebook | Social networking |
| Instagram | Photo sharing |
| Foursquare | Mobile check-in |
| LinkedIn | Social networking for business |
| Groupon | Social commerce |
| Netflix | Movie rentals |
| eBay | Internet auctions |
| Wikipedia | Collaborative encyclopedia |
| PayPal | Payments |
| Last.fm | Internet radio |
| Amazon eCommerce | Shopping for books and lots of other products |
| Salesforce.com | Customer Relationship Management (CRM) |
| Skype | Internet telephony |
| Microsoft Bing | Search |
| Flickr | Photo sharing |
| Zillow | Real-estate pricing |
| Yahoo Search | Search |
| WeatherBug | Weather |

**Fig. 1.18** | Some popular web services (`http://www.programmableweb.com/apis/directory/1?sort=mashups`).

| URL | Description |
|---|---|
| `http://twikle.com/` | Twikle uses social networking web services to aggregate popular news stories being shared online. |
| `http://trendsmap.com/` | TrendsMap uses Twitter and Google Maps. It allows you to track tweets by location and view them on a map in real time. |
| `http://www.dutranslation.com/` | The Double Translation mashup uses Bing and Google translation services to translate text to and from over 50 languages. You can then compare the results between the two. |
| `http://musicupdated.com/` | Music Updated uses Last.fm and YouTube web services. Use it to track your favorite music artists for album releases, concert information and more. |

**Fig. 1.19** | A few popular web mashups.

# 1.15 Xcode 6® Integrated Development Environment

To program in Swift you'll need the **Xcode 6** integrated development environment (IDE), which includes support for the Swift, Objective-C, C++ and C languages. Xcode's editor provides syntax coloring, auto-indenting, auto-complete and more. It's available free through the Mac App Store—see the Before You Begin section of the book for details. Figure 1.20 lists several key new Xcode 6 features,[20] plus some other important features from recent releases.[21] We'll frequently refer to Xcode 6 simply as Xcode.

| Feature | Description |
|---|---|
| *Key New Features in Xcode 6* | |
| Playgrounds | A **Playground** is an Xcode window in which you can enter Swift code that executes as you type it, allowing you to fix errors immediately and see your code's results (text outputs, graphics, animations and more). You no longer have to build and run the code to debug it, saving you time as you develop your apps. Playgrounds also provide interesting features such as timelines that enable you to see how an algorithm executes over time—for example, using a slider you can view the results of each iteration of a loop or each frame of an animation. |
| Read-Eval-Print-Loop (REPL) | **Read-Eval-Print-Loop (REPL)** is a debugging tool for interacting with a running app. Like a playground, you can also use it to write statements that execute immediately, but REPL does not have a playground's capabilities for writing large amounts of code or rendering complex results (e.g., graphics and animations), though you can use it to run Swift files. REPL can be used directly in Xcode 6 or in OS X's Terminal app. |
| Interface Builder, Storyboarding and Auto Layout adaptive design | Xcode's Interface Builder enables you to create your apps' UIs using drag-and-drop UI design techniques. Typically, you create UIs in **Storyboards** that graphically map the paths a user can take through your app, including each screen and the transitions between screens. By default, new iOS storyboards use Interface Builder's **Auto Layout** capabilities, which enable you to create responsive UIs that adjust based on device orientation changes, screen size and the user's locale. Prior to Xcode 6, you'd provide multiple storyboards to support various device sizes (e.g., iPhone and iPad) and orientations (portrait and landscape). Xcode 6 adds Auto Layout **adaptive design**, which enables you to use one storyboard to design your app's UI for all supported device sizes and orientations. |
| iOS 8 Simulator | The iOS 8 Simulator enables you to test your iOS 8 apps on your Mac. It provides support for various iPhone and iPad devices. It also includes new resizable iPhone and iPad "devices" that enable you to test your Auto Layout adaptive designs by resizing the simulator window. |

**Fig. 1.20** | Key features in Xcode 6 and other recent releases. (Part 1 of 2.)

20. https://developer.apple.com/library/ios/documentation/DeveloperTools/Conceptual/WhatsNewXcode/Articles/xcode_6_0.html.
21. http://developer.apple.com/library/mac/documentation/DeveloperTools/Conceptual/WhatsNewXcode/00-Introduction/Introduction.html.

| Feature | Description |
| --- | --- |
| Live rendering in Interface Builder | As you design your UI (including custom UI components) and write code that manipulates it, Interface Builder renders the resulting UI so you can see what it will look like when the app runs. |
| View debugger | The view debugger allows you to find and fix user interface problems. When you use the view debugger to pause an app, the view debugger displays the app's user interface in a 3D rendering so that you can quickly see where an error has occurred. You can then go to the corresponding code to fix the problem. |
| Game design features | Xcode now has support for 2D and 3D game design as well as a particle editor that can be used to create complex animations (e.g., fire, smoke, moving water and fireworks). |
| *Other Xcode Features* | |
| LLVM compiler | LLVM (Low Level Virtual Machine; llvm.org)—primarily developed by Chris Lattner, creator of Swift—is a fast, open-source compiler for Swift, Objective-C and several other languages that's fully integrated into Xcode. |
| Fix-it | Fix-it feature flags code errors and suggests corrections as you type—you don't need to build the app first. Playgrounds also use this feature. |
| LLDB Debugger | Includes a fast, efficient multicore debugging engine. |
| Assistant editor | When you work in Xcode's editor with two panes, the Assistant editor anticipates other files that you might need to look at. For example, if you're working on a UI in Interface Builder, the Assistant editor displays the corresponding code file, or if a new Swift class you're defining inherits from a superclass, the Assistant editor displays the superclass. |
| Location Simulation | You can now select from a list of locations in the simulator to run location-based apps that use the Core Location framework, which enables an app to determine a device's location and heading (i.e., the direction in which the device is moving). |
| Version editor | If you use source-code control (such as GIT), Xcode's Version editor can show you multiple versions of your source code side by side so you can easily compare them, view a log of past events and more. |
| Instruments | The Instruments tool helps you test your app, monitor memory allocation, track graphics performance with OpenGL ES, track the interaction of system processes, locate and remove performance bottlenecks, and more. |
| XCTest | **XCTest** is a unit-testing tool. Unit tests help ensure that software components in an app function as expected. You can use XCTest to automate testing of your app's features, view the test results, determine whether any problems occurred and fix those problems. For more on unit testing, visit http://bit.ly/TestingWithXcode. |

**Fig. 1.20** | Key features in Xcode 6 and other recent releases. (Part 2 of 2.)

### *The iOS Simulator*

The iOS simulator allows you to test iOS apps on your Mac, so you don't have to buy an iOS device—however, if you intend to distribute your apps, testing them on actual devics is essential. Not all device capabilities are available in the simulator. For example, the camera—which is commonly used in iOS apps—does not work in the simulator. You can reproduce on the simulator many of the single-touch and multi-touch gestures using your Mac's keyboard and mouse (Fig. 1.21).

| Gesture | Simulator action |
| --- | --- |
| Tap | Click the mouse once. |
| Double Tap | Double click the mouse. |
| Touch and Hold | Click and hold the mouse. |
| Drag | Click, hold and drag the mouse. |
| Swipe | Click and hold the mouse, move the pointer in the swipe direction and release the mouse. |
| Flick | Click and hold the mouse, move the pointer in the flick direction and quickly release the mouse. |
| Pinch | Press and hold the *Option* key. Two circles that simulate the two touches will appear. Move the circles to the start position, click and hold the mouse and drag the circles to the end position. |
| Two-Finger Drag | Position the pointer where the two-finger drag will occur. Press and hold the *Option* key and move the circles to the start position. Press and hold the *Shift* key and move the circles to the center position, then release the *Shift* key. Press and hold the *Shift* key and the mouse to move the circles in the direction of the two-finger drag, then release both. |
| Rotate | Position the pointer where the rotation will occur. Press and hold the *Option* key and move the circles to the start position. Continue holding the *Option* key and press and hold the *Shift* key. Move the circles to the center position of the rotation and release the *Shift* key. Press and hold the mouse, rotate the circles to the end position, and release the *Option* key. |

**Fig. 1.21** | Gestures on the iOS simulator (`http://bit.ly/iOSSimulatorUserGuide`).

Although the iOS simulator can simulate orientation changes (to portrait or landscape mode) and the *shake gesture*, there's no built-in way to simulate accelerometer readings and readings from various other sensors. You can, however, install your app on an iPhone or iPad to test these features—you'll learn about requirements for installing your app on a device in Section 2.6.2. Only members of Apple's iOS Developer Program can install apps on a device for testing. (See the Before You Begin section of this book for more information.)

## 1.16 Object Oriented-Programming Review

Today, as demands for new and more powerful software are soaring, building software quickly, correctly and economically remains an elusive goal. *Objects*, or more precisely, the *classes* objects come from, are essentially *reusable* software components. There are date objects, time objects, audio objects, video objects, automobile objects, people objects, etc. Almost any *noun* can be reasonably represented as a software object in terms of *attributes* (e.g., name, color and size) and *behaviors* (e.g., calculating, moving and communicating). Software-development groups can use a modular, object-oriented design-and-implementation approach to be much more productive than with earlier popular techniques like "structured programming"—object-oriented programs are often easier to understand, correct and modify.

### 1.16.1 Automobile as an Object

Suppose you want to *drive a car and make it go faster by pressing its accelerator pedal*. What must happen before you can do this? Well, before you can drive a car, someone has to *design* it. A car typically begins as engineering drawings, similar to the *blueprints* that describe the design of a house. These drawings include the design for an accelerator pedal. The pedal *hides* from the driver the complex mechanisms that actually make the car go faster, just as the brake pedal "hides" the mechanisms that slow the car, and the steering wheel "hides" the mechanisms that turn the car. This enables people with little or no knowledge of how engines, braking and steering mechanisms work to drive a car easily.

Just as you cannot cook meals in the kitchen of a blueprint, you cannot drive a car's engineering drawings. Before you can drive a car, it must be *built* from the engineering drawings that describe it. A completed car has an *actual* accelerator pedal to make it go faster, but even that's not enough—the car won't accelerate on its own (hopefully!), so the driver must *press* the pedal to accelerate the car.

### 1.16.2 Methods and Classes

Let's use our car example to introduce some key object-oriented programming concepts. Performing a task in a program requires a **method**. The method houses the program statements that actually perform its tasks. The method hides these statements from its user, just as the accelerator pedal of a car hides from the driver the mechanisms of making the car go faster. In Swift, we create a program unit called a **class** to house the set of methods that perform the class's tasks. For example, a class that represents a bank account might contain one method to *deposit* money to an account, another to *withdraw* money from an account and a third to *inquire* what the account's current balance is. A class is similar in concept to a car's engineering drawings, which house the design of an accelerator pedal, steering wheel, and so on.

### 1.16.3 Instantiation

Just as someone has to *build a car* from its engineering drawings before you can actually drive a car, you must *build an object* of a class before a program can perform the tasks that the class's methods define. The process of doing this is called *instantiation*. An object is then referred to as an **instance** of its class.

### 1.16.4 Reuse

Just as a car's engineering drawings can be *reused* many times to build many cars, you can *reuse* a class many times to build many objects. Reuse of existing classes when building new classes and programs saves time and effort. Reuse also helps you build more reliable and effective systems, because existing classes and components often have undergone extensive *testing, debugging* and *performance* tuning. Just as the notion of *interchangeable parts* was crucial to the Industrial Revolution, reusable classes are crucial to the software revolution that has been spurred by object technology.

### 1.16.5 Messages and Method Calls

When you drive a car, pressing its gas pedal sends a *message* to the car to perform a task—that is, to go faster. Similarly, you *send messages to an object*. Each message is implemented as a **method call** that tells a method of the object to perform its task. For example, a program might call a bank-account object's *deposit* method to increase the account's balance.

### 1.16.6 Attributes and Properties

A car, besides having capabilities to accomplish tasks, also has *attributes*, such as its color, its number of doors, the amount of gas in its tank, its current speed and its record of total miles driven (i.e., its odometer reading). Like its capabilities, the car's attributes are represented as part of its design in its engineering diagrams (which, for example, include an odometer and a fuel gauge). As you drive an actual car, these attributes are carried along with the car. Every car maintains its *own* attributes. For example, each car knows how much gas is in its own gas tank, but *not* how much is in the tanks of *other* cars.

An object, similarly, has attributes that it carries along as it's used in a program. These attributes are specified as part of the object's class. For example, a bank-account object has a *balance attribute* that represents the amount of money in the account. Each bank-account object knows the balance in the account it represents, but *not* the balances of the *other* accounts in the bank. Attributes are specified by the class's **properties**.

### 1.16.7 Encapsulation and Information Hiding

Classes (and their objects) **encapsulate**, i.e., encase, their properties and methods. A class's (and its object's) properties and methods are intimately related. Objects may communicate with one another, but they're normally not allowed to know how other objects are implemented—implementation details are *hidden* within the objects themselves. This **information hiding**, as we'll see, is crucial to good software engineering.

### 1.16.8 Inheritance

A new class of objects can be created conveniently by **inheritance**—the new class (called the **subclass**) starts with the characteristics of an existing class (called the **superclass**), possibly customizing them and adding unique characteristics of its own. In our car analogy, an object of class "convertible" certainly *is an* object of the more *general* class "automobile," but more *specifically*, the roof can be raised or lowered.

### 1.16.9 Protocols

Swift also supports a concept known as a **protocol** which describes a set of methods that can be called on an object—this is similar to the concept of an "interface" in other programming languages. By default, protocol methods *must* be implemented by any class that says it *conforms to* (implements) the protocol. Protocols that are intended for use in both Swift and Objective-C code may also contain optional methods—in such cases, a class can implement a *subset* of the protocol's methods. By default, you must implement all methods in Swift protocols.

Classes may conform to any number of protocols, just as a car implements separate interfaces for basic driving functions, controlling the radio, controlling the heating and air conditioning systems, and the like. Just as car manufacturers implement capabilities *differently*, classes may conform to a protocol's methods *differently*. For example a software system may include a "backup" protocol that offers the methods *save* and *restore*. Classes may implement those methods differently, depending on the types of things being backed up, such as programs, text, audios, videos, etc., and the types of devices where these items will be stored.

### 1.16.10 Design Patterns

**Design patterns**[22] are proven, reusable architectures that programmers use to solve recurring problems in object-oriented software development. In iOS app development, design patterns establish a common design vocabulary among iOS app developers. By adhering to well-known iOS design patterns, you'll be able to shorten your app-design phase and take advantage of the powerful capabilities that the iOS APIs provide.

The notion of design patterns originated in the field of architecture. Architects use a set of established architectural design elements, such as arches and columns, when designing buildings. Designing with arches and columns is a proven strategy for constructing sound buildings—these elements may be viewed as architectural design patterns.

The most common design pattern you'll use in iOS app development is the **Model-View-Controller** (MVC) pattern, which separates app data (contained in the **model**) from graphical presentation components (the **view**) and processing logic (the **controller**).

Consider an address book app. When the user adds a new contact's information through the app's UI, the app's controller updates the model—that is, it stores the contact in a database or file. When the model changes, it notifies the controller which, in turn, updates the view—in this case, to display the updated contact list. As you build iOS apps, you'll use an extensive set of common Cocoa Touch design patterns. We'll present various design patterns as they're encountered in the design and implementation of the book's apps. For an overview of the most common design patterns used in iOS and OS X development, visit:

```
http://bit.ly/iOSDesignPatterns
```

## 1.17  Test-Driving the Tip Calculator App in the iPhone and iPad Simulators

In this section, you'll run and interact with your first iOS app using both the iPhone and iPad simulators. The Tip Calculator (Fig. 1.22(a))—which you'll build in Chapter 3—calculates and displays possible tips and bill totals for a restaurant bill amount. As you enter each digit of the bill amount by touching the *numeric keypad*, the app calculates and displays the

---

22. Some books you'll want to consult on design patterns are the seminal "gang of four" book, *Design Patterns: Elements of Reusable Object-Oriented Software*, by Gamma, Helm, Johnson and Vlissides, ©1994, Addison-Wesley, and *Cocoa Design Patterns*, by Buck and Yacktman, ©2010, Addison-Wesley.

tip amount and total bill amount for a 15% tip and a custom tip percentage (Fig. 1.22(b)). You specify the custom tip percentage by moving a **Slider**'s *thumb*—this updates the custom tip percentage **Labels** and displays the custom tip and bill total in the right-hand column of yellow **Labels** below the **Slider** (Fig. 1.22(b)). We chose 18% as the default custom percentage, because many restaurants in the U.S. add this tip percentage for parties of six people or more.

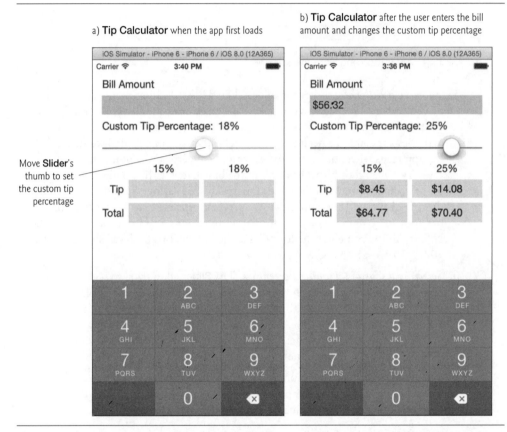

a) **Tip Calculator** when the app first loads

b) **Tip Calculator** after the user enters the bill amount and changes the custom tip percentage

Move **Slider**'s thumb to set the custom tip percentage

**Fig. 1.22** | **Tip Calculator** when the app first loads, then after the user enters the bill amount and changes the custom tip percentage.

### *Test-Driving the Completed Application Using the iPhone Simulator*
The following steps show you how to test-drive the app:

1.  *Checking your setup.* Confirm that you've set up your computer properly by reading the Before You Begin section located after the Preface.

2.  *Locating the app folder.* Open a **Finder** window and navigate to the Documents/ Examples folder or the folder where you saved the chapter's examples.

3.  *Opening the TipCalculator project.* Open the TipCalculator folder, then double click the file name TipCalculator.xcodeproj to open the project in Xcode.

4. *Launching the Tip Calculator app.* In Xcode, click the **Scheme** selector to the right of the **Run** and **Stop** buttons in the upper-left corner of the Xcode IDE (Fig. 1.23), then select the **iPhone 6** simulator. Next, click the **Run button** (or type ⌘ + *R*) to run the app in the simulator.

**Fig. 1.23** | Run button and **Scheme** selector.

5. *Entering a Bill Total.* Enter the bill total 56.32 by touching numbers on the displayed numeric keypad. If you make a mistake, press the delete button (⌧) in the bottom-right corner of the keypad to erase the last digit you entered. The keypad does *not* contain a decimal point. Each time you touch a digit or delete one, the app reads what you've entered so far and converts it to a number, divides the value by 100 and displays the result in the blue **Label** with two digits to the right of the decimal point, and calculates and updates the various tip and total amounts that are displayed. This app uses iOS's *locale-specific currency formatting* capabilities to display monetary values formatted for the user's current locale. For the U.S. locale, as you enter the four digits, the bill total is displayed successively as $0.05, $0.56, $5.63 and $56.32, respectively.

6. *Selecting a Custom Tipping Percentage.* The **Slider** allows you to select a custom percentage, and the **Labels** in the right column below the **Slider** display the corresponding tip and the total bill. Drag the **Slider**'s thumb to the right until the custom percentage reads **25%**. As you drag the thumb, the **Slider**'s value continuously changes. The app updates the custom tip percentage, amount and total accordingly for each **Slider** value until you release the thumb (Fig. 1.22(b)).

7. *Closing the app.* Close your running app by clicking the *Home* button on the simulator, or by clicking the **Stop** button in Xcode or by selecting **iOS Simulator > Quit iOS Simulator** from the menu bar.

### *Test-Driving the Completed Application Using the iPad Simulator*

To test-drive the app using the iPad simulator, click the **Scheme** selector, then select the **iPad Air** simulator. Next, click the **Run** button to run the app in the simulator.

### *Test-Drives for the Book's Apps*

To get a broad sense of the capabilities that you'll learn in this book, check out the test-drives of the book's apps in Chapters 2 and higher.

## 1.18 What Makes a Great App?

With over a million apps in the App Store, how do you create an iOS app that people will find, download, use and recommend to others? Consider what makes an app fun, useful, interesting, appealing and enduring. A clever app name, an attractive icon and an engaging description might lure people to your app on the App Store. Figure 1.24 lists some key characteristics of great apps.

**Characteristics of great apps**

*Great Games*
- Entertaining and fun.
- Challenging.
- Progressive levels of difficulty.
- Show your scores and use leaderboards to record high scores.
- Provide audio and visual feedback.
- Offer single-player, multiplayer and networked versions.
- Have high-quality animations.
- Innovate with augmented reality technology—enhancing a real-world environment with virtual components; this is particularly popular with video-based apps.

*Useful Utilities*
- Provide useful functionality and accurate information.
- Increase personal and business productivity.
- Make tasks more convenient (e.g., maintaining a to-do list, managing expenses).
- Make the user better informed.
- Provide topical information (e.g., stock prices, news, severe storm warnings, traffic updates).
- Use location-based services to provide local services (e.g., coupons for local businesses, best gas prices, food delivery).

*General Characteristics*
- Up-to-date with the latest iOS features.
- Access users' personal information only if necessary for the app's function.
- Do not require the user to sign in using a social media account such as Facebook or Twitter.
- Work properly.
- Bugs are fixed promptly.
- Follow Apple's *iOS Human Interface Guidelines* (http://bit.ly/iOSMobileHIG).
- Support the standard iOS gestures in the standard way.
- Launch quickly.
- Are responsive.
- Don't require too much memory, bandwidth or battery power.
- Use high-quality icons that will appear in the App Store and on the user's device.
- Are novel and creative.
- Enduring—something users will use regularly.
- Use quality graphics, images, animations, audio and video.
- Work well, given that the device displays only a single screen at a time.
- Are intuitive and easy to use (don't require extensive help documentation).

**Fig. 1.24** | Characteristics of great apps. (Part 1 of 2.)

| Characteristics of great apps |
|---|
| • Are accessible to people with disabilities (see the *Accessibility Programming Guide for iOS*). |
| • Give users reasons and a means to tell others about your app (e.g., you can give users the option to post their game scores to Facebook or Twitter). |
| • Provide additional content for content-driven apps (e.g., game levels, articles, puzzles). |
| • Localized for each country in which the app is offered (e.g., translate the app's text and audio files, use different graphics based on the locale, etc.). |
| • Take advantage of the device's built-in capabilities. |
| • Use Apple's universal app technology to run optimally across the variety of iOS devices. We'll develop several universal apps in this book. |

**Fig. 1.24** | Characteristics of great apps. (Part 2 of 2.)

# 1.19 iOS Security

As an iOS app developer, it's your responsibility to keep your user's personal data secure, not only within your app but also when transmitting it over the Internet and storing it on servers. Your apps should request and store only necessary information. For example, if your app does not provide location-based services, it should not request or store the user's location. Figure 1.25 provides a brief walk through the iOS security considerations discussed in the iOS Developer Library's *Security Overview*.

| Topic | Description |
|---|---|
| Risk Assessment and Threat Modeling | Topics include assessing and evaluating risk, determining potential threats and mitigating those threats. |
| Code Security | Discusses fixing security holes in your code, code signing for authentication, app sandboxing to ensure your app is performing only its intended tasks (and terminating the app if it's behaving suspiciously and thus suspected of having been exploited), and the principle of least privilege (i.e., dividing your app into multiple parts and granting each *only* the privileges required to perform its specific task). |
| Authentication and Authorization | Discusses *authentication* (i.e., verifying the user's or network's identity) and *authorization* (i.e., granting a user or a server permission to perform a restricted task). |
| Cryptographic Services | Discusses secure communications and storage using cryptography to encrypt and decrypt data so that it cannot be read by an unintended party, techniques for verifying that the data has not been altered, secure storage of data and more. |

**Fig. 1.25** | iOS *Security Overview* topics (`http://bit.ly/iOSSecurityOverview`).

To learn more about developing secure iOS apps, see the detailed *iOS Security* guide at

`http://images.apple.com/ipad/business/docs/iOS_Security_Feb14.pdf`

### Find My iPhone and Remote Wipe

iPhone and iPad devices include the **Find My iPhone** app. The app helps you find your device if it's lost or stolen. You must first set up iCloud on the device by going to **Settings**. If you misplace your device, log in to Apple's **iCloud** from any computer at www.icloud.com/find. You can view a map with the device's approximate location, have the device play a sound to help you locate it, or display a message to help the person who finds your device return it to you. If you're unable to find your device, the **Remote Wipe** feature restores it to the factory settings (removing all personal data), thus protecting the privacy of your information. As of iOS 7, your Apple ID and password are required before turning off Find My iPhone, removing all personal data using Remote Wipe and reactivating the device.

## 1.20 iOS Publications and Forums

Figure 1.26 lists some of the key documentation from the Apple iOS Developer site. Most of these are available free at developer.apple.com. As you dive into iOS app development, you may have questions about the tools, design issues, security and more. There are several iOS developer forums where you can get the latest announcements or ask questions (Fig. 1.27).

| Title | |
| --- | --- |
| iOS App Programming Guide | What's New in Xcode |
| iOS Human Interface Guidelines | Xcode Overview |
| Getting Started | Cocoa Core Competencies |
| Programming with Objective-C | Coding Guidelines for Cocoa |
| Objective-C Runtime Programming Guide | SDK Compatibility Guide |
| Accessibility Programming Guide for iOS | Sample Code |
| Game Center Programming Guide | What's New in iOS 8 |
| Social Framework Reference | Swift Standard Library Reference |
| The Swift Programming Language | |

**Fig. 1.26** | Key online documentation (most at developer.apple.com) for iOS developers.

| URL | Description |
| --- | --- |
| https://devforums.apple.com/community/ios | Login to your developer account to access Apple's iOS Developer Forums where you can post questions and find answers from iOS developers and Apple engineers. |
| http://stackoverflow.com/questions/tagged/ios | Search through the iOS questions or post your own on StackOverflow. |
| http://iphonedevsdk.com/ | Find several forums related to iPhone development, tutorials, sample code and more. |

**Fig. 1.27** | iOS forums. (Part 1 of 2.)

| URL | Description |
| --- | --- |
| `http://www.raywenderlich.com/`<br>    `forums/viewforum.php?f=18` | Includes an active general iOS development forum, plus tips, tricks and tutorials. |
| `http://iosdeveloperforums.com/` | Discussions include iOS development, Xcode tips and tricks, game development and tutorials. |
| `http://forums.macrumors.com/`<br>    `forumdisplay.php?f=135` | Includes an iPhone and iPad programming forum. |

**Fig. 1.27** | iOS forums. (Part 2 of 2.)

# 1.21 Wrap-Up

This chapter introduced the world of iOS. We discussed features of the iOS operating system and provided links to some popular free and fee-based apps on the App Store. You learned the various single-touch and multi-touch gestures, and how to perform each on iOS devices and the simulator. We walked through the various device sensors and their functionality. You learned about the accessibility features built into iOS devices. We introduced the Swift programming language, and listed the Cocoa Touch iOS frameworks that enable you to quickly develop iOS apps. You'll use many of these frameworks in this book and in *iOS 8 for Programmers: An App-Driven Approach, Volume 2*. We also introduced some key features of the Xcode toolset. We provided a quick refresher on basic object-technology concepts, including classes, objects, methods, properties and more. You test-drove the **Tip Calculator** app. We then discussed what makes a great app and introduced the iOS *Security Overview* document. Finally, we provided links to some of the key online documentation and to the newsgroups and forums you can use to connect with the developer community and get your questions answered. In the next chapter, you'll build your first iOS app using visual programming techniques and no coding. The app will display text and two images. You'll also learn about iOS accessibility and internationalization.

# Welcome App

Dive-Into® Xcode: Introducing Visual User Interface Design with Cocoa Touch, Interface Builder, Storyboarding and Auto Layout, Universal Apps, Accessibility, Internationalization

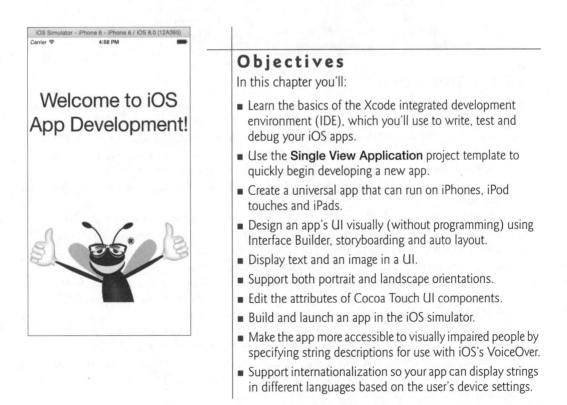

## Objectives

In this chapter you'll:

- Learn the basics of the Xcode integrated development environment (IDE), which you'll use to write, test and debug your iOS apps.
- Use the **Single View Application** project template to quickly begin developing a new app.
- Create a universal app that can run on iPhones, iPod touches and iPads.
- Design an app's UI visually (without programming) using Interface Builder, storyboarding and auto layout.
- Display text and an image in a UI.
- Support both portrait and landscape orientations.
- Edit the attributes of Cocoa Touch UI components.
- Build and launch an app in the iOS simulator.
- Make the app more accessible to visually impaired people by specifying string descriptions for use with iOS's VoiceOver.
- Support internationalization so your app can display strings in different languages based on the user's device settings.

## 2.1 Introduction

In this chapter, you'll build the **Welcome** app that displays a welcome message and an image of the Deitel bug corporate icon—and you'll do this *without writing any code*. You'll use the Xcode IDE—Apple's suite of development tools for creating and testing Mac OS X and iOS applications—to create a **universal app** that runs on iPhones, iPod touches and iPads. You'll see in later chapters that you can also create apps that run only on an iPhone/iPod touch or an iPad. From this point forward, we'll refer to iPhone/iPod touch simply as iPhone.

You'll create a simple iOS app (Fig. 2.1) using Xcode's Interface Builder, which allows you to create UIs using *drag-and-drop* techniques and *no* Swift programming. You'll execute your app in the iOS simulator for both iPhones and iPads. If you're a paid iOS Developer Program member, you'll also run the app on an iOS device.

Next we'll show how to make the app more accessible for people with impaired vision by providing accessibility strings that describe the image to the user. As you'll see, iOS's VoiceOver accessibility feature can speak the accessibility strings to the user.

Finally, we'll demonstrate how to localize your app so that it can display strings in different spoken languages based on the user's device settings. For demonstration purposes, we'll show one localization in which the app's strings (including the accessibility strings) are translated into Spanish, then incorporated into the app. You'll then run the app in Spanish on the iOS Simulator.

Fig. 2.1 | Welcome app running in the iPhone simulator.

## 2.2 Technologies Overview

This section introduces the technologies you'll learn in this chapter.

### 2.2.1 Xcode and Interface Builder

This chapter introduces the *Xcode IDE*. You'll use it to create a new project (Section 2.3). You'll use Xcode's integrated **Interface Builder** to build a simple user interface (UI) consisting of text and an image (Section 2.5). Interface Builder enables you to visually lay out your UI. You can use it to drag and drop Labels, Image Views, Buttons, Text Fields, Sliders and other UI components onto an app's UI. You'll use Interface Builder's **storyboarding** capability (Section 2.5) to design the app's UI—in later apps you'll also use storyboards to specify how the app will *transition between screens*.

### 2.2.2 Labels and Image Views

This app's text is displayed in a **Label** (an object of class `UILabel` from the Cocoa Touch's UIKit framework) and its picture is displayed in an **Image View** (an object of class `UIImageView`). Using Interface Builder, you'll drag and drop a Label and an Image View onto the UI (Section 2.5). Each will occupy half the screen, and iOS's **auto layout** capabilities will maintain this size relationship when the user rotates the device. You'll see how to edit UI component attributes (e.g., the Text attribute of a Label and the Image attribute of an Image View) to customize them for your app.

### 2.2.3 Asset Catalogs and Image Sets

When your app is installed on a device, its icon and name appear with all other installed apps in the iOS home screen. You'll specify the icon for your app as part of the app's settings (Section 2.5.2). Your app's icon appears in different sizes and resolutions based on the device and context in which it's displayed. For example, the icons on an iPad are larger than those on an iPhone, and the icons on a retina display device have twice the width and height of the icons on nonretina devices. As you'll see, iOS supports asset catalogs, which manage image resources that require different resolutions for different devices. An asset catalog contains image sets from which iOS automatically chooses the appropriate image based on the device running the app and the context in which the icon is used—such as in the iOS **Settings** app, in **Spotlight** search or as the app's icon on the home screen. You can also create your own image sets to manage your app's other image resources. If you do not provide icons for each size and resolution, iOS will scale the images that you do provide, using the image that's closest in size to what it needs.

### 2.2.4 Running the App

After building the app, you'll run it in the iOS simulator, which can be used to test iPhone and iPad apps. You'll also learn how to run the app on an iOS device (Section 2.6.2).

### 2.2.5 Accessibility

iOS contains many *accessibility* features to help people with various disabilities use their devices. For example, people with visual disabilities can use iOS's **VoiceOver** to allow a device to speak screen text (such as the text on a **Label** or **Button**) or text that you provide to help them understand the purpose and contents of a UI component. The user can touch the screen to hear VoiceOver speak what's on the screen near the touch. Section 2.7 shows how to enable these features and how to configure your app's UI components for accessibility.

### 2.2.6 Internationalization

iOS devices are used worldwide. To reach the largest possible audience with your apps, you should consider customizing them for various *locales* and spoken languages—this is known as **internationalization**. Section 2.8 shows how to provide Spanish text for the **Welcome** app's **Label** and for the **Image View**'s accessibility string, then shows how to test the app in a simulator configured for Spanish.

## 2.3 Creating a Universal App Project with Xcode

The book's examples were developed using the most current versions of Xcode (6) and the iOS SDK (8) at the time of this writing. *We assume that you're familiar with Mac OS X and that you've already set up Xcode, as discussed in the book's Before You Begin section.* This section overviews Xcode and shows you how to create a new universal app project. We'll introduce additional Xcode features throughout the book. To learn more about Xcode, visit:

```
https://developer.apple.com/xcode/
```

### 2.3.1 Launching Xcode

To launch Xcode, open a Finder window, select **Applications**, locate the Xcode icon ( 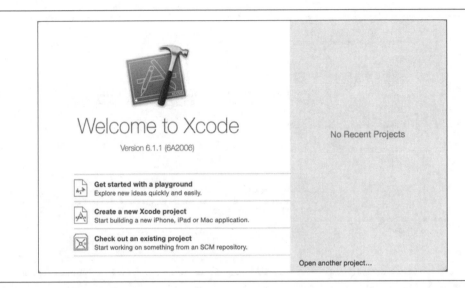 )
and double click it. If this is your first time running Xcode, the **Welcome to Xcode** win-
dow will appear (Fig. 2.2).

**Fig. 2.2**  |  **Welcome to Xcode** window.

The left side of the dialog contains links for:

- Getting started with a playground.

- Creating a new project.

- Checking out existing projects. This option allows you to connect to *source-code management (SCM) repositories*, which are often used to manage the interactions among many developers on a single project.

The right side of the dialog shows the list of recently opened projects and playgrounds;
you can also open these via the **File** menu. This list will be empty until you create your first
projects or playgrounds.

Close the **Welcome to Xcode** window for now—you can access it any time by selecting
**Window > Welcome to Xcode**. We use the > character to indicate selecting a menu item
from a menu. For example, the notation **File > Open...** indicates that you should select the
**Open...** menu item from the **File** menu.

### 2.3.2 Projects and App Templates

A **project** is a group of related files, such as the Swift code files and any media files (e.g.,
images, video, audio) that compose an app. To begin working on an app, select either
**File > New > Project...** to create a new project or **File > Open...** to open an *existing* project.
Selecting **File > New > Project...** displays a sheet containing the templates that you can use
as your new project's foundation (Fig. 2.3). A sheet is a type of dialog that slides down

from the top of a window. **Templates** save you time by providing preconfigured starting points for commonly used app designs. The dialog's left side shows the template categories for both iOS and OS X development. For the iOS apps you'll build in this book, you'll use the templates listed in the **iOS** category's **Application** subcategory. Figure 2.4 briefly describes each of the iOS app templates shown in Fig. 2.3.

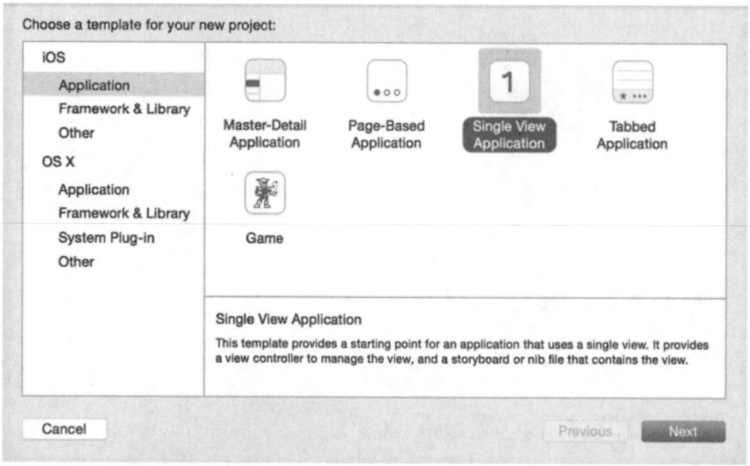

**Fig. 2.3** | Choosing a project template.

| Template | Template description |
|---|---|
| **Master-Detail Application** | Creates an app with a UI that displays a *master list* of items from which a user can choose one item to see its *details* (similar to the built-in **Mail** and **Contacts** apps). For iPad apps, this template also includes a *split view* that can display the master list and the details of one item at the same time. |
| **Page-Based Application** | Creates an app in which content is *displayed page by page* (similar to the built-in **iBooks** app). |
| **Single View Application** | Creates an app in which everything is *displayed on one screen*—as this chapter's **Welcome** app does. |
| **Tabbed Application** | Creates an *app with a tab bar* (similar to the built-in **Clock** app). The user touches a tab to change screens. |
| **Game** | Creates an app with features that support game development with one of iOS's gaming APIs—SceneKit, SpriteKit, OpenGL ES or Metal. |

**Fig. 2.4** | Xcode iOS app templates.

## 2.3.3 Creating and Configuring a Project

For this chapter, we'll use the **Single View Application** template. Select that app template in the dialog of Fig. 2.3, then click **Next** to display the **Choose options for your new project** sheet (Fig. 2.5). Specify the following options for the app (or use your own values), then click **Next**:

- **Product Name:** `Welcome`—This specifies *both* your project's name *and* app's name.

- **Organization Name:** `Deitel and Associates, Inc.`—The developer's company or institution name.

- **Company Identifier:** `com.deitel`—Typically, this is a *company's domain name in reverse*. It's combined with the app's name to form a *bundle identifier* that uniquely identifies the app in various app settings and in the App Store. Our domain name is `deitel.com`, so we used `com.deitel` as the company identifier. *If you're creating apps for learning purposes, some of Apple's tutorials suggest using the company identifier* `edu.self`.

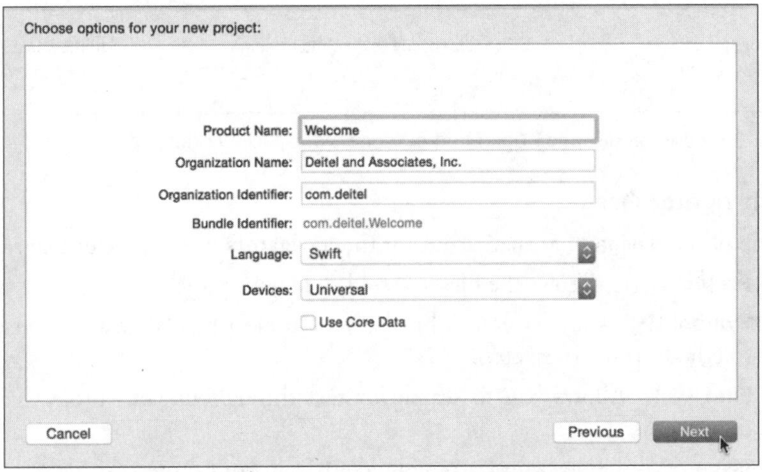

Choose options for your new project:

|  |  |
|---|---|
| Product Name: | Welcome |
| Organization Name: | Deitel and Associates, Inc. |
| Organization Identifier: | com.deitel |
| Bundle Identifier: | com.deitel.Welcome |
| Language: | Swift |
| Devices: | Universal |
|  | ☐ Use Core Data |

Cancel          Previous     Next

**Fig. 2.5** | Configuring the **Welcome** app.

- **Devices**—Specifies the device types on which your app can run. Select **Universal** to indicate that the app can run on iPhones and iPads. You can also create apps that run only on iPhones or only on iPads.

After clicking **Next**, specify where you'd like to save your project. You can also choose to use *Git* for source-code management. Git is a source-code control system often used to manage projects to which multiple developers contribute, but you can also use it yourself to manage and track the revisions you make to your app. Click **Create** to display the new project's window.

## 2.4 Xcode Workspace Window

A new project's window (Fig. 2.6) is known as a **workspace window**, which is divided into four main areas below the toolbar: the **Navigator** area, **Editor** area, **Utilities** area and the **Debug** area (which is not initially displayed—we'll explain how to display it shortly).

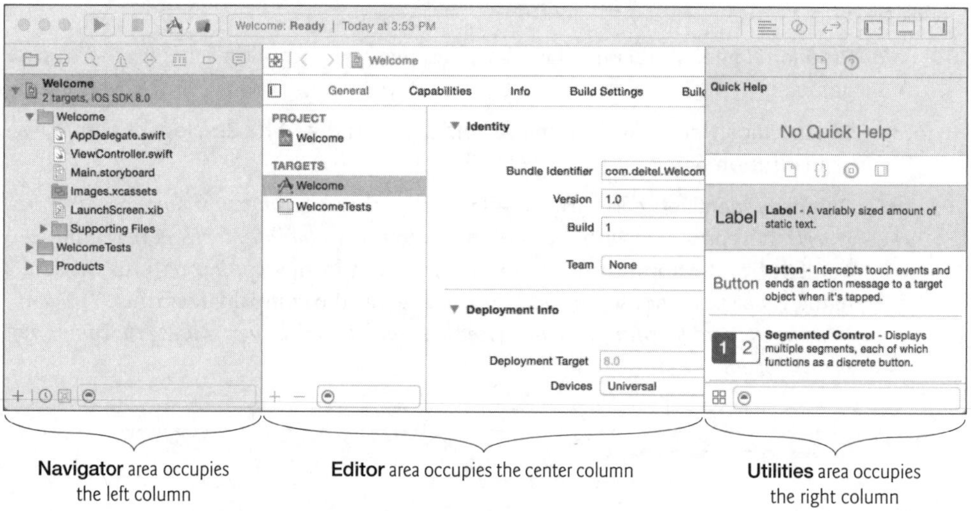

Navigator area occupies the left column

Editor area occupies the center column

Utilities area occupies the right column

**Fig. 2.6** | `Welcome.xcodeproj` open in the Xcode workspace window.

### 2.4.1 Navigator Area

At the top of the **Navigator** area are icons for the **navigators** that can be displayed there:

- **Project** (▭)—Shows the files and folders in your project.
- **Symbol** (▤)—Allows you to browse your project by classes and their contents (methods, properties, etc.).
- **Find** (Q)—Allows you to search for text throughout your project's files and frameworks.
- **Issue** (⚠)—Shows you warnings and errors in your project by file or by type.
- **Test** (⊖)—Enables you to manage your unit tests (for more about unit testing with Xcode, visit `http://bit.ly/TestingWithXcode`).
- **Debug** (▤)—During debugging, allows you to examine your app's threads and method-call stacks.
- **Breakpoint** (▷)—Enables you to manage your debugging breakpoints by file.
- **Report** (◁)—Allows you to browse log files created each time you build and run your app.

You choose which navigator to display by clicking the corresponding button above the **Navigator** area of the window.

### 2.4.2 Editor Area

To the right of the **Navigator** area is the **Editor** area for editing source code and designing UIs. This area is *always* displayed in your workspace window. When you select a file in the project navigator, its contents are displayed in the **Editor** area. There are three editors:

- The **Standard** editor (☰) shows the selected file's contents.

- The **Assistant** editor ( ⊘ ) shows the selected file's contents on the left and related file contents on the right—for example, if you're editing a class that extends another class, the **Assistant** editor will also show the superclass.

- The **Version** editor ( ↩→ ) allows you to compare different versions of the same file (e.g., old and new versions).

### 2.4.3 Utilities Area and Inspectors

At the right side of the workspace window is the **Utilities** area, which displays **inspectors** that allow you to view and edit information about items displayed in the **Editor** area. The set of inspectors you can choose from depends on what you're doing in Xcode. By default, the top half of the **Utilities** area shows either the **File** inspector ( 🗋 ) or the **Quick Help** inspector ( ⑦ ). The **File inspector** shows information about the currently selected file in the project. The **Quick Help** inspector provides context-sensitive help—documentation that's based on the currently selected item in a UI or the cursor position in the source code. For example, clicking on a method name shows a description of the method, its parameters and its return value.

### 2.4.4 Debug Area

When displayed, the **Debug** area appears at the bottom of the editor area and provides controls for stepping through code, inspecting variable contents and more. We discuss how to hide and show the **Navigator** area, **Utilities** area and **Debug** area momentarily.

### 2.4.5 Xcode Toolbar

The Xcode toolbar contains options for executing your app (Fig. 2.7(a)), a display area (Fig. 2.7(b)) that shows the progress of tasks executing in Xcode (e.g., project build status) and buttons (Fig. 2.7(c)) for hiding and showing areas in the workspace window. Figure 2.8 overviews the toolbar.

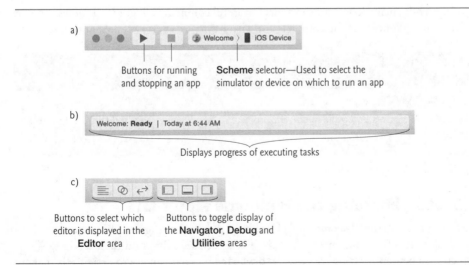

**Fig. 2.7** | Xcode 6 toolbar.

| Control | Description |
|---------|-------------|
| Run | Clicking the **Run** button builds then runs the project on the currently selected simulator or device as specified in the **Scheme** selector (Fig. 2.7(a)). Clicking and holding on this button displays **Run**, **Test**, **Profile** and **Analyze** options. The **Test** option allows you to run unit tests on your app. The **Pro-file** option collects information about your running code to help you locate performance issues, memory leaks and more. The **Analyze** option checks your source code for potential logic errors. |
| Stop | Terminates the running app. |
| Scheme | Specifies the simulator or device on which the app will run when the **Run** button is clicked. |
| **Editor** buttons | Click one of these buttons (Fig. 2.7(c)) to specify which editor is displayed in the **Editor** area. |
| **View** buttons | Click these toggle buttons (Fig. 2.7(c)) to specify whether the **Navigator**, **Debug** and **Utilities** areas of the workspace window are displayed. |

**Fig. 2.8** | Xcode 6 toolbar elements.

### 2.4.6 Project Navigator

The **Project** navigator (left side of Fig. 2.6) provides access to all of a project's components. It consists of a series of groups (folders) and files. The most used group is the **project structure group**, which Xcode names the same as the project. This group contains your project's source files, media files and supporting files. The **Products** group contains the .app files for your project. The .app files execute when you test your apps and are also used to distribute your apps via the iOS app store.

### 2.4.7 Keyboard Shortcuts

Xcode provides many keyboard shortcuts for useful commands. Figure 2.9 shows some of the most useful ones. For the complete list, visit http://bit.ly/XcodeShortcuts.

| Shortcut | Function | Shortcut | Function |
|----------|----------|----------|----------|
| *shift* + ⌘ + *N* | Create new project. | ⌘ + *B* | Build project. |
| ⌘ + *N* | Create new file in current project. | ⌘ + *R* | Build and run project. |
| ⌘ + *S* | Save current file. | *shift* + ⌘ + *K* | Clean project. |

**Fig. 2.9** | Common Xcode keyboard shortcuts.

## 2.5 Storyboarding the Welcome App's UI

Next, you'll create the **Welcome** app's UI. Recall that you configured the project as a *universal app* that runs on iPhones and iPads. The screen sizes differ on these devices. When you create a new app, Xcode creates a .storyboard file that you use to design UIs that are appropriate for the user-interface idiom of each type of device. The **Welcome** app you'll build here simply displays text and an image. In Chapter 3, you'll build your first app that contains Swift code. At that point we'll introduce other features of Interface Builder and storyboards that enable you to interact with your UIs programmatically.

## 2.5.1 Configuring the App for Portrait and Landscape Orientations

As you know, users can hold their devices in *portrait* (long edge vertical) or *landscape* (long edge horizontal) orientation. Many apps support *both* orientations by rearranging their UIs, depending on the current device orientation. You'll support *both* orientations in this app, which is the default.

To view the orientation settings, select the **Welcome** project in the **Project** navigator. This displays the project's settings in the **Editor** area (Fig. 2.10). In the **Deployment Info** section under **Device Orientation**, ensure that **Portrait**, **Landscape Left** and **Landscape Right** are selected as shown in Fig. 2.10—these are the default settings for supported orientations. Notice that **Upside Down** is *not* selected. If the phone is upside down when the user receives a call, it's more difficult to answer the phone. For this reason, Apple recommends that you *do not* support the **Upside Down** orientation in iPhone apps. With the exception of the **Upside Down** orientation for iPhones, Apple recommends supporting all possible device orientations.

**Fig. 2.10** | **Welcome** project's **Deployment Info** settings.

## 2.5.2 Providing an App Icon

When your app is installed on a device, its icon and name appear with all other installed apps in the iOS home screen. In this step, you'll add an app icon to the project. Due to the variety of iPhones and iPads on which iOS 8 can execute, you'll provide icons of various sizes to support the different screen sizes and resolutions. If you do not provide an icon for a particular size or if the icon you provide is not the correct size, Xcode will provide warnings.

### Asset Catalog

Scroll down to the **App Icons and Launch Images** section in the settings, then click the ⊕ icon to the right of **App Icons Source** (or click the project's Images.xcassets group) to display the **asset catalog** (Fig. 2.11), which manages image resources that require different resolutions for different devices. iOS automatically chooses the appropriate image from an image set based on the device running the app and the context in which the icon is used—that is, in the iOS **Settings** app, in **Spotlight** search or as the app's icon on the home screen.

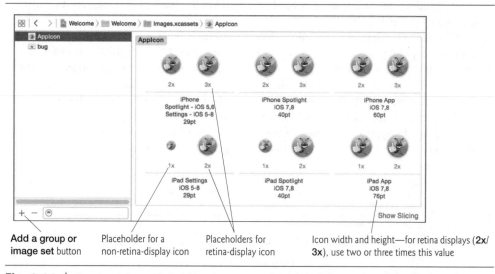

**Fig. 2.11** | Asset catalog with **AppIcon** image set selected and the app icons specified.

### Icon Placeholders

By default, the **AppIcon** image set is selected and empty placeholders are displayed for the various iPhone and iPad app icons. Each is labeled **1x**, **2x** or **3x**. These represent non-retina-display (**1x**) and retina-display (**2x** or **3x**) devices with difference pixel densities. The measurements are in points. For **1x** icons the relationship is one point = one pixel, for **2x** it's one point = two pixels and for **3x** (the iPhone 6 Plus) it's one point = three pixels.

### Icon Sizes

Below the **1x**, **2x** or **3x** the asset catalog provides additional information about the purpose of a given icon. For example, **iPhone Spotlight, iOS 7, 8, 40pt** indicates an icon that would appear in the Spotlight search results on iPhones running iOS 7 or iOS 8. Such an icon must be 40 points (**40pt**) wide and tall. For a placeholder that's labeled **1x**, you provide an icon of the specified size. If that icon is labeled **2x** or **3x**, you provide an image that's two or three times the specified size—80 or 120 points wide and tall, respectively.

### Adding the Icons to the Asset Catalog

Open a Finder window and locate the images folder provided with the book's examples, then drag the various DeitelOrange icons onto each the asset catalog's placeholders so that the image set appears as shown in Fig. 2.11. Each image file we provided is square (e.g., 29-by-29, 40-by-40, etc.). Place the images as follows:

- For each placeholder labeled **1x** use the image that's named with the listed resolution—for example, use `DeitelOrange_29x29.png` for a placeholder that indicates **29pt** and use `DeitelOrange_76x76.png` for a placeholder that indicates **76pt**.

- For each placeholder labeled **2x** or **3x** use the image that's named with *two* or *three* times the required resolution—for example, use `DeitelOrange_80x80.png` and `DeitelOrange_120x120.png`, respectively, for a placeholder that indicates **40pt**.

When you save your app, these images are all placed into the `Images.xcassets` group in the project's `Welcome` group.

*Launch Screen*

To improve the user's experience in an app that take several seconds to load, you can also specify a launch screen that your app displays while it's loading, so the user does not see a blank screen. In prior iOS versions, the launch screen was an image. As of iOS 8, it can be a resizable UI that adjusts to fit the device on which the app is running. Xcode adds the file `launchscreen.xib` to each new project you create. This file displays your app's name in the center of the screen. Though we do not do so in this app, you can select this file, then use Interface Builder to customize it.

## 2.5.3 Creating an Image Set for the App's Image

As with app icons, you'll typically provide multiple versions of each image your app displays to accommodate various device sizes and pixel densities. Placing such images into the asset catalog as image sets allows iOS to choose the correct image for you based on the device resolution. To add a new image set, you can drag an image from a Finder window onto the list of image sets at the left of the asset catalog—Xcode names the image set as the image name without its filename extension and uses that image for devices with **1x** resolution. You can then provide additional images for devices with **2x** and **3x** resolution.

Open a Finder window and locate the `images` folder provided with the book's examples, then from the subfolder `Welcome` drag the `bug.png` icon onto the asset catalog's list of image sets to create the **bug** image set. The new image set appears as shown in Fig. 2.12.

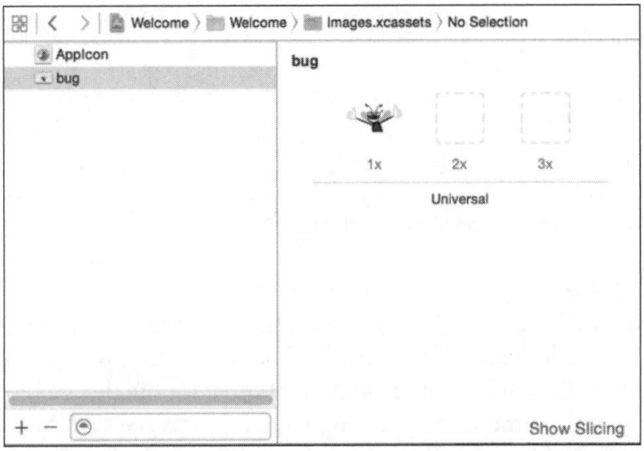

**Fig. 2.12** |  Asset catalog with **bug** image set selected.

We provided one image for all iOS devices. Images do not always scale well, so it's generally better to provide customized images. In Chapter 9, we discuss submitting apps to the App Store and list companies that offer free and fee-based icon and image design services.

### 2.5.4 Overview of the Storyboard and the Xcode Utilities Area

You design an app's UI in its storyboard. In the **Project** navigator, select the file Main.storyboard in the **Project** navigator to open the storyboard in the **Editor** area (Fig. 2.13). In a storyboard, each *screen* of information is represented as a **scene**—designated by a white rectangular area. For this app, we'll focus on manipulating UI components in the scene. In Chapter 3, we'll begin discussing other Interface Builder features that help you implement your app's logic for responding to user interactions.

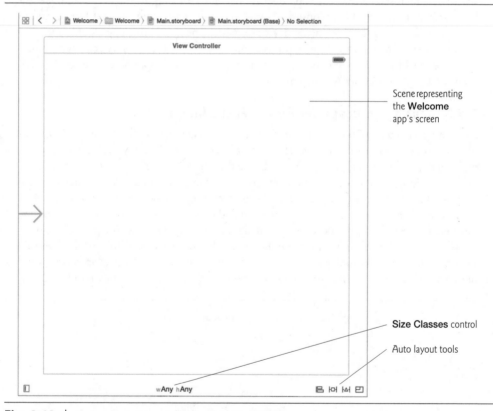

**Fig. 2.13** | Main.storyboard displayed in the **Editor** area.

*Size Classes and Auto Layout Tools*
iOS apps can currently execute on iPhones and iPads, and there will be other devices in the future, such as the Apple Watch. On current iOS devices, users can view your apps in either portrait or landscape orientation. At the bottom of Interface Builder are tools for specifying the scene's size classes and the auto layout properties for the scene's UI. **Size classes** help you design scenes for these different screen sizes and orientations. By default, the scene is configured for **Any** width and **Any** height, meaning that the scene is designed for any iOS device

and any device orientation. The **Any/Any** scene is 600-by-600 pixels. Later in the book, you'll learn how to use size classes to customize scenes so that they display differently based on the device size and orientation. The auto layout tools enable you to specify how UI components adjust their sizes and positions based on a device's size and orientation.

### Library Window

Once the storyboard is displayed, the bottom part of the **Utilities** area shows the **Library** window (Fig. 2.14), which contains four library tabs:

- **File Template** (⬜)—Common file types for quickly adding files to a project.

- **Code Snippet** ({})—Code snippets for quickly inserting and customizing commonly used code, such as control statements, exception handling and more. You can also create your own code snippets.

- **Object** (◉)—Standard Cocoa Touch UI components for designing iOS apps. A key component of Cocoa Touch is the **UIKit framework**, which contains the UI components we use throughout this book. You can also learn more at

```
http://bit.ly/CocoaTouch
```

- **Media** (🖼)—The project's media resources (images, audios and videos).

You drag and drop UI components from the **Object** library tab to add them to your scene.

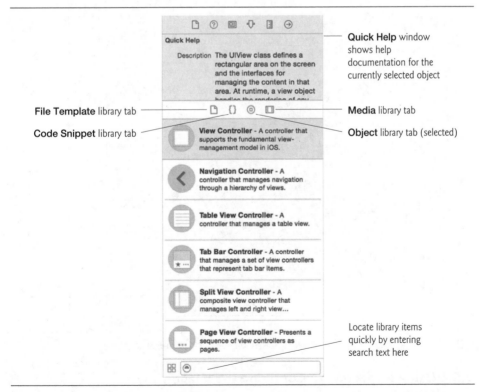

**Fig. 2.14**   |   **Utilities** area showing **Quick Help** and the **Library** window with the **Object** library selected.

### 2.5.5 Adding an Image View to the UI

You'll now begin customizing the app's UI. First, you'll add the **Image View** that will display the bug.png image. In Cocoa Touch, images are usually displayed by an object of class UIImageView.

1. In the **Library** window, ensure that the **Object** library tab (⊚) is selected, then locate **Image View** by scrolling or by typing Image View into the search field at the bottom of the window (Fig. 2.14).

2. Drag and drop an **Image View** from the **Library** onto the scene as shown in Fig. 2.15. By default, Interface Builder sizes the **Image View** to fill the scene.

Notice the dashed blue guide lines that appear as you drag the **Image View** around the scene. The guide lines suggest component spacing and alignments that help you conform to Apple's *Human Interface Guidelines (HIG)*, which include conventions for *spacing between components, component positioning* and *alignment, gestures used to interact with apps* and much more. You can learn more about the *HIG* at:

> http://bit.ly/iOSMobileHIG

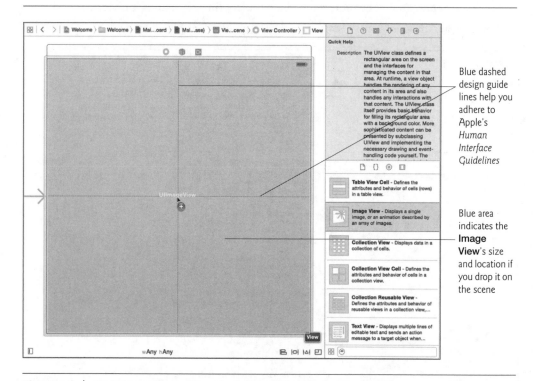

**Fig. 2.15** | Dragging an **Image View** from the **Object** library onto the scene.

### 2.5.6 Using Inspectors to Configure the Image View

Now you'll customize the **Image View** to display bug.png. When you're designing a UI, the top of the **Utilities** area will have additional tabs for the following inspectors:

- **Identity** inspector (▤)—Used to specify an object's class and accessibility information and to provide a name for the object that appears in the list of objects to the left of the scene design area.
- **Attributes** inspector (⇩)—Used to customize the selected object's attributes, such as the image to display in an **Image View**.
- **Size** inspector (▥)—Used to configure an object's size and position.
- **Connections** inspector (⊖)—Use to create connections between code and UI components (e.g., to respond to user interactions with particular components).

In the scene, click the **Image View** you just added to select it, then perform the following steps:

1. Select the **Attributes** inspector tab (⇩) in the **Utilities** area (Fig. 2.16).

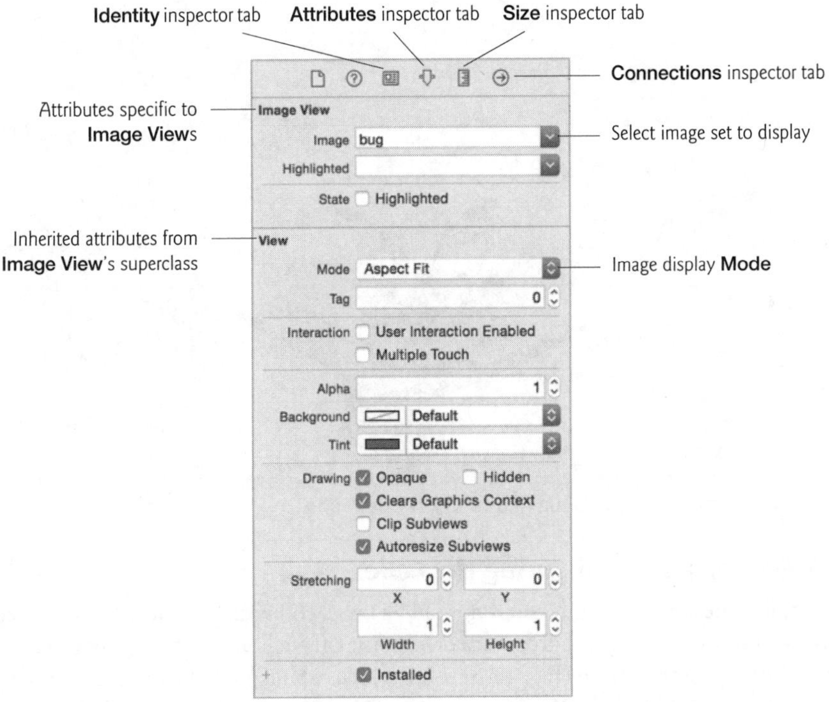

**Identity** inspector tab
**Attributes** inspector tab
**Size** inspector tab
**Connections** inspector tab
Attributes specific to **Image Views**
Select image set to display
Inherited attributes from **Image View**'s superclass
Image display **Mode**
Image View
Image
bug
Highlighted
State
Highlighted
View
Mode
Aspect Fit
Tag
0
Interaction
User Interaction Enabled
Multiple Touch
Alpha
1
Background
Default
Tint
Default
Drawing
Opaque
Hidden
Clears Graphics Context
Clip Subviews
Autoresize Subviews
Stretching
0
0
X
Y
1
1
Width
Height
Installed


**Fig. 2.16** | **Image View** attributes in the **Attributes** inspector tab of the **Utilities** area.

2. In the **Image View** section, click the drop-down arrow to the right of the **Image** field and select the `bug` image set that you added to the asset catalog in Section 2.5.3 as the image to display. By default, the image stretches to fill the **Image View**.
3. In the **Mode** field, select `Aspect Fit` to force your image to fit in the **Image View** and maintain its aspect ratio—its original width-to-height ratio.
4. Select the **Size** inspector (▥) in the **Utilities** area.

**5.** Change the **Height** attribute to 300 so the **Image View** occupies half the scene.

**6.** Change the **Y** attribute to 300 (half the scene's height), so that the **Image View**'s upper-left corner is positioned halfway down the scene. You could also drag the **Image View** to the bottom half of the scene.

The **Image View** should now appear as shown in Fig. 2.17. Interface Builder can also create the **Image View** for you and configure it to display the proper image—simply drag the image from the **Media** library onto the scene, then configure the **Image View**'s attributes. If you do this, you'll also need to resize the **Image View** by using the *sizing handles* that are displayed when the image is selected (also shown in Fig. 2.17).

Sizing handles

**Fig. 2.17** | **Image View** configured to display bug.png.

### 2.5.7 Adding and Configuring the Label

To complete the scene's design, you'll now add a **Label** containing the text "Welcome to iOS App Development!". Drag and drop a **Label** from the **Object** library into the upper-left corner of the scene above the image (Fig. 2.18). Notice that a blue guide line appears to help you position the **Label**. Next, use the **Size** inspector (▤) to change the **Label**'s **Width** attribute to 600 and **Height** attribute to 300 so that the **Label** occupies the scene's top half (Fig. 2.19).

Blue design guide lines for positioning the **Label** in the scene's top-left corner

**Fig. 2.18** | Adding a **Label** to the scene.

**Fig. 2.19** | Resizing the **Label**.

With the **Label** selected, modify the following attributes in the **Attributes** inspector:

- **Text** attribute—replace "Label" with "Welcome to iOS App Development!". You can also set the text by double clicking the **Label**.

- **Alignment** attribute—select the middle option for *centered* alignment.

- **Lines** attribute—enter 2 for two lines of text.

- **Font** attribute—hold the up arrow to the right of this attribute until the font size is 55. This is the default maximum font size we'd like to use.

- **Autoshrink** attribute—select **Minimum Font Scale**. If the text is too large to fit in the **Label** based on the device size or orientation, iOS by default scales the text by up to half the specified font size, as indicated by the value 0.5 below **Minimum Font Scale**.

The **Label** should now appear as shown in Fig. 2.20.

**Fig. 2.20** | **Welcome** app scene before setting auto layout constraints.

### 2.5.8 Using Auto Layout to Support Different Screen Sizes and Orientations

Though the design appears to be complete, if you were to run the app now using the iOS simulator, you'd see various problems (if you'd like to run it now, see Section 2.6):

- The **Label** and **Image View** will not resize based on the device and orientation.

- On an iPhone in portrait orientation the **Label** and **Image View** will be too wide for the screen, and in landscape orientation the screen will not be tall enough to display both components.

- On an iPad, the **Label** and **Image View** will be too small to fill the screen and will be positioned at the screen's left edge.

You use *auto layout constraints* to specify how UI components are positioned relative to other components and how components should resize and reposition based on the device and device orientation. You'll use auto layout constraints in this app to ensure that the **Label** and **Image View**:

- Fill the screen horizontally regardless of the screen orientation.

- Fill the screen vertically and scale appropriately regardless of the screen orientation.

- Resize based on the device running the app and the current device orientation.

When the user rotates the device, auto layout will use these constraints as it repositions and resizes the **Label** and **Image View** based on the new orientation. To configure this app's auto layout constraints:

1. In the bottom-left corner of the storyboard, click the **Show Document Outline (▢)** button to display the document outline window (Fig. 2.21), which appears to the left of the design area. The **document outline window** shows you all of the UI components that make up your scene(s) and other features that you'll learn about in later chapters.

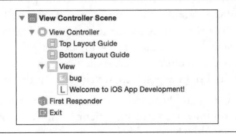

**Fig. 2.21** | Document outline window.

2. In the document outline, hold the *control* key, drag from the **Label** node (**Welcome to iOS App Development!**) to the **Top Layout Guide** node, which represents the top of the scene, then release the mouse to complete the drag—we'll refer to this operation as "*control* drag" going forward. From the popup menu that appears, select **Vertical Spacing** (Fig. 2.22)—this attaches the **Label**'s top edge to the top edge of the scene so the **Label** *always* appears at the top. Because the **Label** is already positioned at the top, this creates an auto layout constraint requiring 0 points of space between the **Label**'s top edge and the **Top Layout Guide**.

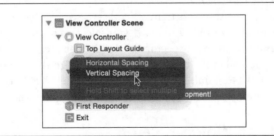

**Fig. 2.22** | Document outline.

3. *Control* drag from the **Image View (bug)** node to the **Bottom Layout Guide** node. From the popup menu, select **Vertical Spacing**—this attaches the **Image View**'s bottom edge to the bottom edge of the scene so the **Image View** *always* appears at the bottom. Because the **Image View** is already positioned at the bottom, this cre-

ates an auto layout constraint requiring 0 points of space between the **Image View**'s bottom edge and the **Bottom Layout Guide**.

4. In a **Single View Application**, the scene has a root **View** that contains the scene's other UI components—in this case the **Label** and **Image View** (nested below the **View** node in the document outline). In this app, the **Label** and **Image View** should each have the **View**'s width, which changes depending on the device and orientation. To accomplish this, you'll attach these components to the **View**'s leading and trailing edges. In left-to-right languages, the leading edge is at the left and the **trailing edge** is at the right. In right-to-left languages, this is reversed. This is an iOS *internationalization* feature that enables iOS to adapt your UIs based on the user's spoken language.

Next, *control* drag from the **Label** node to the **View** node, and select **Leading Space to Container Margin**, then *control* drag from the **Label** node to the **View** node and select **Trailing Space to Container Margin**. The **Label** is already the same width as the **View** (based on the settings in Section 2.5.7), so this creates auto layout constraints that require the **Label**'s left and right edges to be 0 points from the **Vi ew**'s left and right edges, respectively. Repeat this step for the **Image View**.

5. We'd like the **Label** and **Image View** to each occupy half the screen's height and to scale based on the screen size and orientation. To accomplish this, we'll indicate that they should have equal heights and that there should be a fixed amount of space between them vertically. *Control* drag from the **Label** to the **Image View** and select **Equal Heights**. Next, *control* drag from the **Label** to the **Image View** and select **Vertical Spacing**. Because there is no space between the components based on the prior design steps, this creates an auto layout constraint that requires the **Label**'s bottom edge to be 0 points from the **Image View**'s top edge.

The constraints set in *Step 5* above—combined with the **Label**'s vertical spacing constraint to the **Top Layout Guide** and the **Image Views**'s vertical spacing constraint to the **Bottom Layout Guide**—ensure that these components each occupy 50% of the screen's height and scale based on the device and orientation.

## Optional: Viewing the Constraints

You can view the complete list of constraints Xcode created by expanding the **Constraints** node in the document outline's **View** node. If you select a constraint, you can view and manipulate its attributes with the inspectors in the **Utilities** area. Also, if you select a UI component, you can view all of the constraints applied to it in the **Size** inspector, and you can click each constraint's **Edit** link to modify the constraint. We'll discuss constraints in more detail and show other ways to create constraints throughout the book.

# 2.6 Running the Welcome App

In this section, we discuss running the app on the iOS simulator and on an iOS device. To test on a device, you must be a member of the fee-based iOS Developer Program—see the Before You Begin section of this book for more information.

## 2.6.1 Testing on the iOS Simulator

You'll now execute the app using the iOS simulator.

1. Click the **Scheme** selector (Fig. 2.7(a)) on the Xcode toolbar to display the list of iOS simulators and devices on which you can test the app (Fig. 2.23). As you can see, there are various simulators that you can use including resizable simulators in which you can specify different widths and heights so you can see how your app's UI dynamically adjusts.

**Fig. 2.23** | List of iOS simulators and devices in the Scheme selector.

2. Select **iPhone 6** to indicate that you'd like to test the app on a simulator configured based on the size and features of an iPhone 6 device.

3. Click the **Run** (▶) button on the Xcode toolbar, select **Run** from the **Product** menu or type ⌘ + *R*. This builds the project, installs the **Welcome** app in the **iPhone 6** simulator and runs the app. Initially, the app is displayed in portrait orientation (Fig. 2.24(a)). Depending on your computer's screen size, the simulator

a) App running in portrait orientation

b) App running in landscape orientation

**Fig. 2.24** | **Welcome** app running on the iPhone simulator in portrait and landscape modes.

window might be too tall to show the entire app. In this case, use the simulator's **Window > Scale** menu to scale the simulator window to a smaller size.

4. To change the device orientation, select **Hardware > Rotate Left** or **Hardware > Rotate Right**. Figure 2.24(b) shows the app running in landscape orientation. While your app is running, the **Stop** (■) button in Xcode is enabled. Clicking **Stop** terminates the app, but leaves the simulator running. You can click the app's icon on the simulator's home screen to re-run the app in the Simulator.

5. To run the app on the iPad simulator, choose **iPad Air** from the **Scheme** selector, then run the app. Figure 2.25 shows the app executing in the iPad simulator.

a) Running on the iPad simulator in portrait orientation

b) Running on the iPad simulator in landscape orientation

**Fig. 2.25** │ **Welcome** app running on the iPad simulator in portrait and landscape modes.

### 2.6.2 Testing on a Device (for Paid Apple iOS Developer Program Members Only)

To test your app on an iOS device, you must first set up your paid developer account in Xcode.

1. Select **Xcode > Preferences…**.
2. Click the **Accounts** tab.
3. Click the **+** button and select **Add Apple ID…**.
4. Enter your Apple ID and password, then click **Add**.

Next, connect the iOS device to your computer. Once connected, the device will show up in Xcode's **Scheme** selector. Choose your device, then run the app. If the device has not yet been added to your developer account, Xcode will assume you want to use the device for testing and will handle the details of adding the device to your developer account for you. Then Xcode will build the app, install it onto your device and run it. Try rotating the device to see how the app adjusts to portrait and landscape orientations.

## 2.7 Making Your App Accessible

iOS contains various *accessibility* features to help people with various disabilities use their devices. For people with visual and physical disabilities, iOS's VoiceOver can speak the screen text (such as the text on a **Label** or **Button**) or text that you provide to help the user understand the purpose of a UI component. When VoiceOver is enabled and the user touches an accessible UI component, VoiceOver speaks the accessibility text associated with the component. All UIKit framework components support accessibility and many have it enabled by default. For example, when the user touches a **Label**, VoiceOver speaks the **Label**'s text. VoiceOver can be enabled in the **Settings** app under **General > Accessibility**. From there, you can also set the **Accessibility Shortcut** to **VoiceOver** so that you can triple click the device's *Home* button to toggle VoiceOver on and off. VoiceOver is *not* currently supported in the iOS simulator, so you must run this app on a device to hear VoiceOver speak the text. However, in the simulator you can use the **Accessibility Inspector** to view the text that VoiceOver will speak, as you'll see in Section 2.7.2.

### 2.7.1 Enabling Accessibility for the Image View

The Xcode **Identity** (▣) inspector's **Accessibility** section enables you to provide descriptive text that VoiceOver can speak when the user selects a given component. In the **Welcome** app, we don't need more descriptive text for the **Label**, because VoiceOver will read the **Label**'s content. Accessibility is *not* enabled by default for **Image Views**, so we'll show how to enable it and provide descriptive text for the **Image View** in the storyboard. Perform the following steps:

1. In Xcode, select `Main.storyboard` in the **Project** navigator.
2. Select the **Image View** in the scene.
3. Click the **Identity** inspector's icon (▣) in the **Utilities** area, then scroll to the **Accessibility** section (Fig. 2.26). The **Image** and **User Interaction Enabled** checkboxes are selected by default, but are used only if accessibility is enabled.

**Fig. 2.26** | **Accessibility** section of the **Identity** inspector.

4. Select the **Enabled** checkbox to enable accessibility for the **Image View**.

5. The **Label** provides a brief description of the UI component. In the **Label** field, enter "Deitel logo".

6. If a more detailed description is required to help the user understand the UI component's purpose, you can enter a string in the **Hint** field. Enter "Deitel double-thumbs-up bug logo" there now.

7. Save the storyboard.

Run this app on a device with VoiceOver enabled, then touch the **Label** or the **Image View** to hear VoiceOver speak the corresponding text.

Some apps dynamically generate UI components in response to user interactions. For such UI components, you can programmatically set the accessibility text using properties from the UIAccessibility protocol.

### 2.7.2 Confirming Accessibility Text with the Simulator's Accessibility Inspector a

If you're not a paid member of the iOS Developer Program, you can use the simulator's **Accessibility Inspector** to ensure that your accessibility text is set correctly. To do so:

1. With the app running in a simulator, select **Hardware > Home** from the simulator's menus to return to the simulator's home screen. If there are multiple pages of apps, you can "swipe" left or right by dragging the mouse in the appropriate direction.

2. Locate and open the **Settings** app, then navigate to **General > Accessibility**.

3. Enable the **Accessibility Inspector**. This opens an **Accessibility Inspector** window that hovers over what's currently displayed on the simulator's screen (Fig. 2.27(a)).

4. Next, select **Hardware > Home** to return to the home screen. You'll notice that you cannot swipe left or right with the mouse. To allow normal navigation in the simulator, click the **x** button in the upper-left corner of the **Accessibility Inspector** to minimize it. Then locate and run the **Welcome** app, and click the **x** button again to expand the **Accessibility Inspector**.

a) Accessibility Inspector enabled          b) **Label** selected          b) **Image View** selected

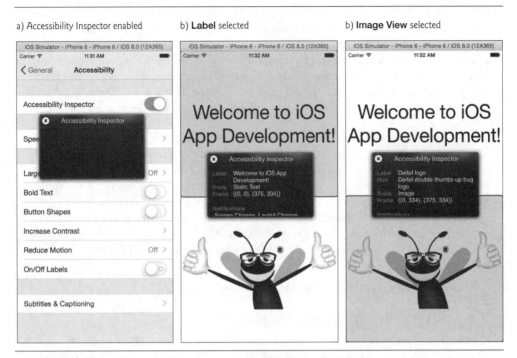

**Fig. 2.27** | iOS simulator with the **Accessibility Inspector** displayed.

5. Click the **Label** to view its accessibility text. The simulator highlights the entire **Label** and displays its accessibility information (Fig. 2.27(b))—the text in the **Accessibility Inspector**'s **Label** line is what VoiceOver will speak on a device.

6. Click the **Image View** to view its accessibility text. The simulator highlights the **Image View** and displays its accessibility information, including both the **Label** and the **Hint** that you added earlier in this section (Fig. 2.27(c))—VoiceOver will first speak the text in the **Accessibility Inspector**'s **Label** line, followed by the **Hint** text (if any).

# 2.8 Internationalizing Your App

To reach the largest possible audience with your apps, consider customizing them for various locales and spoken languages. Preparing your app to do this is known as **internationalization**, and creating the resources for each locale (such as text in different languages) is know as **localization**.

Using auto layout to design your UI is a key part of internationalization—when used correctly, auto layout enables iOS to present your UI in a manner appropriate for each locale. For example, a UI arranged left-to-right for some languages (e.g., English, French, Spanish, etc.) would typically be arranged right-to-left for others (e.g., Arabic, Hebrew, etc.).

Another important aspect of internationalization is preparing your string resources so that iOS can replace them with appropriate translated strings for the user's locale. Xcode now supports XLIFF (XML Localization Interchange File Format) files for managing localized string resources. XLIFF is a standard XML representation for localizable data. As you'll see, Xcode can export an XLIFF file containing all of your app's localizable text. You provide this file to a translator and then import the translated XLIFF file. When your app executes on devices with different locale settings, iOS automatically chooses the correct string resources for that locale. You can learn more about XLIFF at

```
http://en.wikipedia.org/wiki/XLIFF
```

By default, each app you create uses base internationalization—the string resources in your app are separated from your storyboard and used as a template for providing localized strings for other languages. The language you use during development (in our case, English) is known as your app's base language. If you don't provide strings in the appropriate language for a given locale, iOS uses the *base language* strings by default.

In this section, we'll demonstrate how to provide Spanish strings for the **Welcome** app's **Label** and for its **Image View**'s accessibility strings. Then, we'll demonstrate how to test the app for a Spanish locale. See Apple's *Internationalization and Localization Guide* for more information:

```
http://bit.ly/iOSInternationalization
```

## 2.8.1 Locking Your UI During Translation

Localization is best performed once you've completed your app's UI or when it's nearly complete. Each UI component has a unique ID that's used as part of the internationalization and localization process—if these IDs change (e.g., when you add/remove UI components), then Xcode will not be able to apply the localized string resources properly and some of your UI components might not have localized string resources.

If you're still developing your app and want to have your string resources translated in parallel, you can *lock* your UI components for an entire storyboard or individually so they cannot be modified accidentally. There are four locking options:

- **Nothing**—You can modify all of a UI component's properties.

- **All Properties**—You can't modify any of a UI component's properties.

- **Localizable Properties**—You can't modify a UI component's localizable properties (e.g., the text of a **Label** or the accessibility **Label** and **Hint** for a given UI component). You'd use this option to continue working on your UI while you wait for translated resources that you can import into your app project.

- **Non-localizable Properties**—You can modify only a UI component's localizable properties. You'd use this option when importing translated resources to ensure that you don't modify non-localizable properties accidentally.

If you wish to lock storyboard components:

1. Select the storyboard in the **Project** navigator.

2. Select **Editor > Localization Locking**, then select one of the locking options.

If you wish to lock a specific UI component:

1. Select the UI component in your storyboard.

2. In the **Identity** inspector's **Document** category, change the value of the **Lock** attribute. (For your reference, the UI component's unique ID is also shown in the **Identity** inspector's **Document** category.)

## 2.8.2 Exporting Your UI's String Resources

You'll now create an XLIFF file containing the app's string resources. You'll provide a copy of this file—renamed to indicate the locale it represents—to the person responsible for translating the strings. Perform the following steps:

1. Select your app in the Xcode **Project** navigator.

2. Select **Editor > Export for Localization…**, specify where to save the XLIFF file (outside your project's folders) and click **Save**. By default, Xcode creates a folder with your app's name and places the file en.xliff in that folder.

The filename depends on your app's base language—for our apps this is English, so the language ID en is used. You can see the complete list of language and locale IDs at:

```
http://bit.ly/iOSLanguageLocaleIDs
```

Xcode extracts the localizable strings from all the files in your project (not just the ones in the storyboard) and places them in the XLIFF file. For this demonstration, we'll discuss only the strings in the storyboard. Figure 2.28 shows the portion of the generated XLIFF file that corresponds to Main.storyboard (reformatted for readability). Lines 8–12 represent the **Label**'s string, lines 13–17 represent the **Image View**'s accessibility **Hint** string and lines 18–22 represent the **Image View**'s accessibility **Label** string. The unique IDs that Xcode assigned to the **Label** and **Image View** are highlighted—these must not be modified in the translated XLIFF file; otherwise, Xcode will not know what the corresponding strings apply to. The original source strings are specified in lines 9, 14 and 19.

```
1   <file original="Welcome/Base.lproj/Main.storyboard" source-language="en"
2      datatype="plaintext">
3      <header>
4         <tool tool-id="com.apple.dt.xcode" tool-name="Xcode"
5            tool-version="6.0" build-num="6A280e"/>
6      </header>
7      <body>
8         <trans-unit id="GCg-Ah-7Id.text">
9            <source>Welcome to iOS App Development!</source>
10           <note>Class = "IBUILabel"; text = "Welcome to iOS App
11              Development!"; ObjectID = "GCg-Ah-7Id";</note>
12        </trans-unit>
13        <trans-unit id="waJ-nz-oow.accessibilityHint">
14           <source>Deitel double-thumbs-up bug logo</source>
15           <note>Class = "IBUIImageView"; accessibilityHint = "Deitel
16              double-thumbs-up bug logo"; ObjectID = "waJ-nz-oow";</note>
17        </trans-unit>
```

**Fig. 2.28** | Portion of the XLIFF file that corresponds to Main.storyboard. (Part 1 of 2.)

```
18        <trans-unit id="waJ-nz-oow.accessibilityLabel">
19           <source>Deitel logo</source>
20           <note>Class = "IBUIImageView"; accessibilityLabel =
21              "Deitel logo"; ObjectID = "waJ-nz-oow";</note>
22        </trans-unit>
23     </body>
24  </file>
```

**Fig. 2.28** | Portion of the XLIFF file that corresponds to `Main.storyboard`. (Part 2 of 2.)

### 2.8.3 Translating the String Resources

Next, you'll make a copy of the `en.xliff` and add the Spanish language strings:

1. In Finder, locate the `en.xliff` file you created in Section 2.8.2, make a copy of it and rename it `es.xliff` (es is the language ID for Spanish).

2. Double click the `es.xliff` file to open it in Xcode.

3. In the XML, locate line 1 from Fig. 2.28 and modify it to include the XLIFF's `target-language` attribute. This tells Xcode which locale's strings the file represents. The line should now appear as follows.

```
<file original="Welcome/Base.lproj/Main.storyboard"
   source-language="en" target-language="es" datatype="plaintext">
```

4. Locate line 9 from Fig. 2.28, insert a blank line after it and enter the translated string resource:

```
<target>¡Bienvenido al Desarrollo de App iOS!</target>
```

5. Locate line 14 from Fig. 2.28, insert a blank line after it and enter the translated string resource:

```
<target>El logo de Deitel que tiene el insecto con dedos pulgares
   hacia arriba</target>
```

6. Finally, locate line 19 from Fig. 2.28, insert a blank line after it and enter the translated string resource:

```
<target>Logo de Deitel</target>
```

7. Save and close the file.

### 2.8.4 Importing the Translated String Resources

Next, you'll import the XLIFF file containing the app's Spanish string resources.

1. Select your app in the Xcode **Project** navigator.

2. Select **Editor > Import Localizations...**, locate the `es.xliff` file and click **Open**.

3. Xcode displays a sheet in which you can compare the source strings and the translated strings. In this case, it also shows several warnings, because we did not provide translated strings for various string resources (such as the app's product name that appears with the app icon on a device's home screen). Click **Import** to import the Spanish strings into the project.

Xcode extracts the storyboard's translated Spanish strings from the XLIFF file and places them into a file named `Main.strings`. This file is nested in the `Main.storyboard` node in the **Project** navigator.

### 2.8.5 Testing the App in Spanish

To test the app in Spanish, you must change the language settings in the iOS simulator (or your device). To do so, open the simulator by selecting **Xcode > Open Developer Tool > iOS Simulator**, then perform the following steps:

1. If the home screen is not displayed, select **Hardware > Home** from the iOS simulator menu or press the *home* button on your device.

2. Locate and select the **Settings** app.

3. Select **General** then **Language & Region**.

4. Select **iPhone Language**, then select **Español** from the list of languages and press **Done**, then confirm that you'd like to change the language.

The simulator or device will change its language setting to Spanish and return to the home screen. Use Xcode to run the **Welcome** app again. Figure 2.29 shows the app running in Spanish. VoiceOver supports many spoken languages. If you run the app on a device with VoiceOver enabled, VoiceOver will speak the Spanish versions of the accessibility strings. You can also confirm your Spanish accessibility strings using the simulator's **Accessibility Inspector**, as we showed in Section 2.7.2.

**Fig. 2.29** | **Welcome** app running in Spanish in the iOS simulator.

*Returning the Simulator (or Your Device) to Its Original Language Settings*
To return the simulator or your device back to its original language, you can perform the same steps you used in Section 2.8.5, but select **English** (or your own language). You can also return the simulator to its *default* settings. With the simulator running, select **iOS Simulator > Reset Content and Settings....** This displays a dialog asking you to confirm the operation. If you press **Reset**, any apps you've installed on that specific simulator for testing will be removed and all of its settings will return to their original values.

## 2.9 Wrap-Up

In this chapter, you used Xcode to create a universal app that can run on iPhones and iPads. You used Xcode's **Single View Application** template as the foundation for your new app and learned how to configure a new project. We discussed Xcode's workspace window, its toolbar and the various items that can be displayed in its **Navigator, Editor, Utilities** and **Debug** areas. We discussed an app's supported user-interface orientations, which can consist of portrait, upside down, landscape left and landscape right orientations.

You used Xcode's Interface Builder to drag an **Image View** (an object of the Cocoa Touch class UIImageView) and a **Label** (an object of class UILabel) from the Xcode **Object** library onto a storyboard scene.

We showed how to add an app's icon images to your project's Images.xcassets file and how to create a new image set containing an image that could be displayed in an **Image View**. You used inspectors in the Xcode **Utilities** area to edit UI component attributes, such as the **Text** attribute of the **Label** and the **Image** attribute of the **Image View**, to customize them for your app. You also used auto layout capabilities to support various iOS devices, to ensure that the **Image View** and **Label** had the same width and height and to maintain that size relationship when the user rotates a given device.

You executed the app using the iOS simulator for the iPhone and for the iPad, and you learned how to simulate device orientation changes with the iOS Simulator's **Hardware** menu. We also showed how to run an app on an iOS device if you're a member of Apple's paid iOS Developer Program. You learned how to make the app more accessible and how to internationalize the **Welcome** app so that it could display a different welcome message based on the language settings of the user's device.

In the next chapter, we introduce Swift programming. iOS development is a combination of UI design and Swift coding. You use Interface Builder to develop UIs visually—avoiding tedious UI programming—and Swift programming to specify the behavior of your apps.

You'll develop the **Tip Calculator** app, which calculates a range of tip possibilities when given a restaurant bill amount. You'll once again build a **Single View Application** and design its UI using Interface Builder and a storyboard, as you did in this chapter. You'll also add Swift code to specify how the app should respond to user interactions and display the tip calculation results.

# Tip Calculator App

Introducing Swift, Text Fields, Sliders, Outlets, Actions, View Controllers, Event Handling, NSDecimalNumber, NSNumberFormatter and Automatic Reference Counting

iOS Simulator - iPhone 6 - iPhone 6 / iOS 8.0 (12A365)
Carrier 🛜    3:36 PM

Bill Amount

$56.32

Custom Tip Percentage: 25%

|       | 15%      | 25%      |
|-------|----------|----------|
| Tip   | $8.45    | $14.08   |
| Total | $64.77   | $70.40   |

## Objectives

In this chapter you'll:

- Learn basic Swift syntax, keywords and operators.

- Use object-oriented Swift features, including objects, classes, inheritance, functions, methods and properties.

- Use NSDecimalNumbers to perform precise monetary calculations.

- Create locale-specific currency and percentage Strings with NSNumberFormatter.

- Use Text Fields and Sliders to receive user input.

- Programmatically manipulate UI components via outlets.

- Respond to user-interface events with actions.

- Understand the basics of automatic reference counting (ARC).

- Execute an interactive iOS app.

Outline

# 3.1 Introduction

The **Tip Calculator** app (Fig. 3.1(a))—which you test-drove in Section 1.17—calculates and displays possible tips and bill totals for a restaurant bill amount. As you enter each digit of an amount by touching the *numeric keypad*, the app calculates and displays the tip amount and total bill amount for a 15% tip and a custom tip (Fig. 3.1(b)). You specify the custom tip percentage by moving a **Slider**'s *thumb*—this updates the custom tip percentage **Labels** and displays the custom tip and bill total in the righthand column of yellow **Labels** below the **Slider** (Fig. 3.1(b). We chose 18% as the default custom percentage, because many restaurants in the U.S. add this tip percentage for parties of six people or more, but you can easily change this.

First, we'll overview the technologies used to build the app. Next, you'll build the app's UI using Interface Builder. As you'll see, Interface Builder's visual tools can be used to connect UI components to the app's code so that you can manipulate the corresponding UI components programmatically and respond to user interactions with them.

For this app, you'll write Swift code that responds to user interactions and programmatically updates the UI. You'll use Swift object-oriented programming capabilities, including objects, classes, inheritance, methods and properties, as well as various data types, operators, control statements and keywords. With our *app-driven approach*, we'll present the app's complete source code and do a detailed code walkthrough, introducing the Swift language features as we encounter them.

a) **Tip Calculator** when the
app first loads

b) **Tip Calculator** after the user enters the bill
amount and changes the custom tip percentage

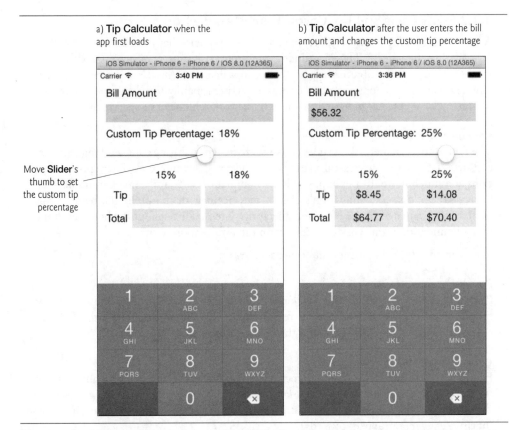

Move **Slider**'s
thumb to set
the custom tip
percentage

**Fig. 3.1** | **Tip Calculator** when the app first loads, then after the user enters the bill amount and changes the custom tip percentage.

## 3.2  Technologies Overview

This section introduces the Xcode, Interface Builder and Swift features you'll use to build the **Tip Calculator** app.

### 3.2.1 Swift Programming

Swift is Apple's programming language of the future for iOS and OS X development. The app's code uses Swift data types, operators, control statements and keywords, and other language features, including functions, overloaded operators, type inference, variables, constants and more. We'll introduce Swift object-oriented programming features, including objects, classes, inheritance, methods and properties. We'll explain each new Swift feature as we encounter it in the context of the app. Swift is based on many of today's popular programming languages, so much of the syntax will be familiar to programmers who use C-based programming languages, such as Objective-C, Java, C# and C++. For a detailed introduction to Swift, visit:

```
https://developer.apple.com/library/ios/documentation/Swift/
    Conceptual/Swift_Programming_Language/
```

### 3.2.2 Swift Apps and the Cocoa Touch® Frameworks

A great strength of iOS 8 is its rich set of prebuilt components that you can *reuse* rather than "reinventing the wheel." These capabilities are grouped into iOS's **Cocoa Touch frameworks**. These powerful libraries help you create apps that meet Apple's requirements for the look-and-feel of iOS apps. The frameworks are written mainly in Objective-C (some are written in C). Apple has indicated that new frameworks will be developed in Swift.

*Foundation Framework*

The Foundation framework includes classes for basic types, storing data, working with text and strings, file-system access, calculating differences in dates and times, inter-app notifications and much more. In this app, you'll use Foundation's NSDecimalNumber and NSNumberFormatter classes. Foundation's class names begin with the prefix NS, because this framework originated in the NextStep operating system. Throughout the book, we'll use many Foundation framework features—for more information, visit:

```
http://bit.ly/iOSFoundationFramework
```

*UIKit Framework*

Cocoa Touch's UIKit framework includes multi-touch UI components appropriate for mobile apps, event handling (that is, responding to user interactions with the UI) and more. You'll use many UIKit features throughout this book.

*Other Cocoa Touch Frameworks*

Figure 3.2 lists the Cocoa Touch frameworks. You'll learn features from many of these frameworks in this book and in *iOS 8 for Programmers: An App-Driven Approach, Volume 2*. For more information on these frameworks, see the *iOS Developer Library Reference* (http://developer.apple.com/ios).

**List of Cocoa Touch frameworks**

| | | | | |
|---|---|---|---|---|
| ***Cocoa Touch*** | AssetsLibrary | OpenAL | CoreLocation | Social |
| ***Layer*** | AudioToolbox | OpenGLES | CoreMedia | StoreKit |
| AddressBookUI | AudioUnit | Photos | CoreMotion | SystemConfig- |
| EventKitUI | CoreAudio | QuartzCore | CoreTelephony | uration |
| GameKit | CoreGraphics | SceneKit | EventKit | UIAutomation |
| MapKit | CoreImage | SpriteKit | Foundation | WebKit |
| MessageUI | CoreMIDI | | HealthKit | |
| Notification- | CoreText | ***Core Services*** | HomeKit | ***Core OS Layer*** |
| Center | CoreVideo | ***Layer*** | JavaScriptCore | Accelerate |
| PhotosUI | GLKit | Accounts | MobileCore- | CoreBluetooth |
| Twitter | GameController | AdSupport | Services | ExternalAccessory |
| UIKit | ImageIO | AddressBook | Multipeer- | LocalAuthen- |
| iAd | MediaAccess- | CFNetwork | Connectivity | tication |
| | ibility | CloudKit | NewsstandKit | Security |
| ***Media Layer*** | MediaPlayer | CoreData | PassKit | System |
| AVFoundation | Metal | CoreFoundation | QuickLook | |

**Fig. 3.2** | List of Cocoa Touch frameworks.

### 3.2.3 Using the UIKit and Foundation Frameworks in Swift Code

To use UIKit framework classes (or classes from any other existing framework), you must **import** the framework into each source-code file that uses it (as we do in Section 3.6.1). This exposes the framework's capabilities so that you can access them in Swift code. In addition to UIKit framework UI components, this app also uses various classes from the Foundation framework, such as `NSDecimalNumber` and `NSNumberFormatter`. We do not import the Foundation framework—its features are available to your code because the UIKit framework indirectly imports the Foundation framework.

### 3.2.4 Creating Labels, a Text Field and a Slider with Interface Builder

You'll again use Interface Builder and auto layout to design this app's UI, which consists of **Label**s for displaying information, a **Slider** for selecting a custom tip percentage and a **Text Field** for receiving the user input. Several **Label**s are configured identically—we'll show how to duplicate components in Interface Builder, so you can build UIs faster. **Label**s, the **Slider** and the **Text Field** are objects of classes `UILabel`, `UISlider` and `UITextField`, respectively, and are part the UIKit framework that's included with each app project you create.

### 3.2.5 View Controllers

Each *scene* you define is managed by a **view controller** object that determines what information is displayed. iPad apps sometimes use multiple view controllers in one scene to make better use of the larger screen size. Each scene represents a *view* that contains the UI components displayed on the screen. The view controller also specifies how user interactions with the scene are processed. Class `UIViewController` defines the basic view controller capabilities. Each view controller you create (or that's created when you base a new app on one of Xcode's app templates) inherits from `UIViewController` or one of its subclasses. In this app, Xcode creates the class `ViewController` to manage the app's scene, and you'll place additional code into that class to implement the **Tip Calculator**'s logic.

### 3.2.6 Linking UI Components to Your Swift Code

*Properties*
You'll use Interface Builder to generate *properties* in your view controller for programmatically interacting with the app's UI components. Swift classes may contain variable properties and constant properties. Variable properties are read/write and are declared with the **var** keyword. Constant properties, which cannot be modified after they're initialized, are read-only and are declared with **let**. These keywords can also be used to declare local and global variables and constants. A variable property defines a *getter* and a *setter* that allow you to obtain and modify a property's value, respectively. A constant property defines only a *getter* for obtaining its value.

*@IBOutlet Properties*
Each property for programmatically interacting with a UI component is prefixed with **@IBOutlet**. This tells Interface Builder that the property is an **outlet**. You'll use Interface Builder to *connect* a UI control to its corresponding outlet in the view controller using *drag-and-drop* techniques. Once connected, the view controller can manipulate the corresponding UI component programmatically. @IBOutlet properties are *variable* properties so they can be modified to refer to the UI controls when the storyboard creates them.

*Action Methods*

When you interact with a UI component (e.g., touching a **Slider** or entering text in a **Text Field**), a user-interface *event* occurs. The view controller handles the event with an **action**—an *event-handling method* that specifies what to do when the event occurs. Each action is annotated with **@IBAction** in your view controller's class. **@IBAction** indicates to Interface Builder that a method can respond to user interactions with UI components. You'll use Interface Builder to visually *connect* an action to a specific user-interface event using *drag-and-drop* techniques.

## 3.2.7 Performing Tasks After a View Loads

When a user launches the **Tip Calculator**:

- Its main storyboard is loaded.
- The UI components are created.
- An object of the app's initial view controller class is instantiated.
- Using information stored in the storyboard, the view controller's **@IBOutlets** and **@IBActions** are connected to the appropriate UI components.

In this app, we have only one view-controller, because the app has only one scene. After all of the storyboard's objects are created, iOS calls the view controller's **viewDidLoad** method—here you perform view-specific tasks that can execute only *after* the scene's UI components exits. For example, in this app, you'll call the method **becomeFirstResponder** on the **UITextField** to make it the active component—as if the user touched it. You'll configure the **UITextField** such that when it's the *active* component, the numeric keypad is displayed in the screen's lower half. Calling becomeFirstResponder from viewDidLoad causes iOS to display the keypad immediately after the view loads. (Keypads are *not* displayed if a Bluetooth keyboard is connected to the device.) Calling this method also indicates that the **UITextField** is the **first responder**—the first component that will receive notification when an event occurs. iOS's **responder chain** defines the order in which components are notified that an event occurred. For the complete responder chain details, visit:

```
http://bit.ly/iOSResponderChain
```

## 3.2.8 Financial Calculations with NSDecimalNumber

Financial calculations performed with Swift's **Float** and **Double** numeric types tend to be inaccurate due to rounding errors. For precise floating-point calculations, you should instead use objects of the Foundation framework class **NSDecimalNumber**. This class provides various methods for creating NSDecimalNumber objects and for performing arithmetic calculations with them. This app uses the class's methods to perform division, multiplication and addition.

*Swift Numeric Types*

Though this app's calculations use only NSDecimalNumbers, Swift has its own numeric types, which are defined in the Swift Standard Library. Figure 3.3 shows Swift's numeric and boolean types—each type name begins with a capital letter. For the integer types, each type's minimum and maximum values can be determined with its **min** and **max** properties—for example, Int.min and Int.max for type Int.

| Type | Description |
|------|-------------|
| *Integer types* | |
| Int | Default signed integer type—4 or 8 bytes depending on the platform. |
| Int8 | 8-bit (1-byte) signed integer. Values in the range −128 to 127. |
| Int16 | 16-bit (2-byte) signed integer. Values in the range −32,768 to 32767. |
| Int32 | 32-bit (4-byte) signed integer. Values in the range −2,147,483,648 to 2,147,483,647. |
| Int64 | 64-bit (8-byte) signed integer. Values in the range −9,223,372,036,854,775,808 to 9,223,372,036,854,775,807. |
| UInt8 | 8-bit (1-byte) unsigned integer. Values in the range 0 to 255. |
| UInt16 | 16-bit (2-byte) unsigned integer. Values in the range 0 to 65,535. |
| UInt32 | 32-bit (4-byte) unsigned integer. Values in the range 0 to 4,294,967,295. |
| UInt64 | 64-bit (8-byte) unsigned integer. Values in the range 0 to 18,446,744,073,709,551,615. |
| *Floating-point types (conforms to IEEE 754)* | |
| Float | 4-byte floating-point value. *Negative range:* −3.4028234663852886e+38 to −1.40129846432481707e−45 *Positive range:* 1.40129846432481707e−45 to 3.4028234663852886e+38 |
| Double | 8-byte floating-point value. *Negative range:* −1.7976931348623157e+308 to −4.94065645841246544e−324 *Positive range:* 4.94065645841246544e−324 to 1.7976931348623157e+308 |
| *Boolean type* | |
| Bool | true or false values. |

**Fig. 3.3** | Swift numeric and boolean types.

Swift also supports standard arithmetic operators for use with the numeric types in Fig. 3.3. The standard arithmetic operators are shown in Fig. 3.4.

| Operation | Operator | Algebraic expression | Swift expression |
|-----------|----------|----------------------|------------------|
| Addition | + | $f + 7$ | f + 7 |
| Subtraction | − | $p - c$ | p - c |
| Multiplication | * | $b \cdot m$ | b * m |
| Division | / | $x / y$ or $\frac{x}{y}$ or $x \div y$ | x / y |
| Remainder | % | $r \bmod s$ | r % s |

**Fig. 3.4** | Arithmetic operators in Swift.

### 3.2.9 Formatting Numbers as Locale-Specific Currency and Percentage Strings

You'll use Foundation framework class NSNumberFormatter's localizedStringFromNumber method to create locale-specific currency and percentage strings—an important part of internationalization. You could also add accessibility strings and internationalize the app using the techniques you learned in Sections 2.7—2.8.

### 3.2.10 Bridging Between Swift and Objective-C Types

You'll often pass Swift objects into methods of classes written in Objective-C, such as those in the Cocoa Touch classes. Swift's numeric types and its String, Array and Dictionary types can all be used in contexts where their Objective-C equivalents are expected. Similarly, the Objective-C equivalents (NSString, NSArray, NSMutableArray, NSDictionary and NSMutableDictionary), when returned to your Swift code, are automatically treated as their Swift counterparts. In this app, for example, you'll use class NSNumberFormatter to create locale-specific currency and percentage strings. These are returned from NSNumberFormatter's methods as NSString objects, but are automatically treated by Swift as objects of Swift's type String. This mechanism—known as bridging—is transparent to you. In fact, when you look at the Swift version of the Cocoa Touch documentation online or in Xcode, you'll see the Swift types, not the Objective-C types for cases in which this bridging occurs.

### 3.2.11 Swift Operator Overloading

Swift allows operator overloading—you can define your own operators for use with existing types. In Section 3.6.7, we'll define overloaded addition, multiplication and division operators to simplify the NSDecimalNumber arithmetic performed throughout the app's logic. As you'll see, you define an overloaded operator by creating a Swift function, but with an operator *symbol* as its name and a parameter list containing parameters that represent each operand. So, for example, you'd provide two parameters for an overloaded-operator function that defines an addition (+) *binary* operator—one for each operand.

### 3.2.12 Variable Initialization and Swift Optional Types

In Swift, every constant and variable you create (including a class's properties) must be initialized (or for variables, assigned to) before it's used in the code; otherwise, a compilation error occurs. A problem with this requirement occurs when you create @IBOutlet properties in a view controller using Interface Builder's drag-and-drop techniques. Such properties refer to objects that are not created in your code. Rather, they're created by the *storyboard* when the app executes, then the storyboard *connects* them to the view controller—that is, the storyboard assigns each UI component object to the appropriate property so that you can programmatically interact with that component.

For scenarios like this in which a variable receives its value at runtime, Swift provides optional types that can indicate the presence or absence of a value. A variable of an optional type can be initialized with the value nil, which indicates the *absence* of a value.

When you create an @IBOutlet with Interface Builder, it declares the property as an implicitly unwrapped optional type by following the type name with an exclamation point (!). Properties of such types are initialized *by default* to nil. Such properties must be declared as variables (with var) so that they can *eventually* be assigned actual values of the specified type. Using optionals like this enables your code to compile because the @IBOutlet properties *are*, in fact, initialized—just not to the values they'll have at runtime.

As you'll see in later chapters, Swift has various language features for testing whether an optional has a value and, if so, *unwrapping* the value so that you can use it—known as explicit unwrapping. With implicitly unwrapped optionals (like the @IBOutlet properties), you can simply assume that they're initialized and use them in your code. If an implicitly unwrapped optional is nil when you use it, a runtime error occurs. Also, an optional can be set to nil at any time to indicate that it no longer contains a value.

### 3.2.13 Value Types vs. Reference Types

Swift's types are either value types or reference types. Swift's numeric types, Bool type and String type are all values types.

#### Value Types

A value-type constant's or variable's value is *copied* when it's passed to or returned from a function or method, when it's assigned to another variable or when it's used to initialize a constant. Note that Swift's Strings are value types—in most other object-oriented languages (including Objective-C), Strings are reference types. Swift enables you to define your own value types as structs and enums (which we discuss in later chapters). Swift's numeric types and String type are defined as structs. An enum is often used to define sets of named constants, but in Swift it's much more powerful than in most C-based languages.

**Performance Tip 3.1**
*You might think that copying objects introduces a lot of runtime overhead. However, the Swift compiler optimizes copy operations so that they're performed only if the copy is modified in your code—this is known as copy-on-write.*

#### Reference Types

You'll define a class and use several existing classes in this chapter. All class types (defined with the keyword class) are reference types—all other Swift types are value types. A constant or variable of a reference type (often called a **reference**) is said to refer to an object. Conceptually this means that the constant or variable stores the object's *location*. Unlike Objective-C, C and C++, that location is not the *actual* memory address of the object, rather it's a *handle* that enables you to locate the object so you can interact with it.

Both structs and enums in Swift provide many of the same capabilities as classes. In many contexts where you'd use classes in other languages, Swift idiom prefers structs or enums. We'll say more about this later in the book.

#### Reference-Type Objects That Are Assigned to Constants Are Not Constant Objects

Initializing a constant (declared with let) with a reference-type object simply means that the constant always *refers to the same object*. You can still use a reference-type constant to access read/write properties and to call methods that modify the referenced object.

#### Assigning References

Reference-type objects are *not copied*. If you assign a reference-type variable to another variable or use it to initialize a constant, then both *refer to the same object* in memory.

*Comparative Operators for Value Types*

Conditions can be formed by using the **comparative operators** (==, !=, >, <, >= and <=) summarized in Fig. 3.5. These operators all have the same level of precedence and do not have associativity in Swift.

| Algebraic operator | Comparative operator | Sample condition | Meaning of condition |
|---|---|---|---|
| = | == | x == y | x is equal to y |
| ≠ | != | x != y | x is not equal to y |
| > | > | x > y | x is greater than y |
| < | < | x < y | x is less than y |
| ≥ | >= | x >= y | x is greater than or equal to y |
| ≤ | <= | x <= y | x is less than or equal to y |

**Fig. 3.5** | Comparative operators for value types.

*Comparative Operators for Reference Types*

One key difference between value types and reference types is comparing for equality and inequality. Only value-type constants and variables can be compared with the == (is equal to) and != (is not equal to) operators. In addition to the operators in Fig. 3.5, Swift also provides the === (**identical to**) and !== (**not identical to**) operators for comparing reference-type constants and variables to determine whether they *refer to the same object*.

## 3.2.14 Code Completion in the Source-Code Editor

As you type code in the source-code editor, Xcode displays *code-completion suggestions* (Fig. 3.6) for class names, method names, property names, and more. It provides one suggestion inline in the code (in gray) and below it displays a list of other suggestions (with the current inline one highlighted in blue). You can press *Enter* to select the highlighted suggestion or you can click an item from the displayed list to choose it. You can press the *Esc* key to close the suggestion list and press it again to reopen the list.

Inline code-completion suggestion      Recommended completion is highlighted      List of all suggestions

```
25        // select inputTextField so keypad displays when the view loads
26        inputTextField.becomeFirstResponder()
 M  UITextWritingDirection baseWritingDirectionForPosition(position: UITextPosition!, inDirect
 M            Bool becomeFirstResponder()
 V  UITextPosition! beginningOfDocument
 M            Bool beginTrackingWithTouch(touch: UITouch!, withEvent: UIEvent!)
 M         CGRect borderRectForBounds(bounds: CGRect)
 V  UITextBorderStyle borderStyle
 V         CGRect bounds
 M           Void bringSubviewToFront(view: UIView)
```

**Fig. 3.6** | Code-completion suggestions in Xcode.

## 3.3 Building the App's UI

In this section, you'll build the **Tip Calculator** UI using the techniques you learned in Chapter 2. Here, we'll show the detailed steps for building the UI—in later chapters, we'll focus on new UI features.

### 3.3.1 Creating the Project

As you did in Section 2.3, begin by creating a new **Single View Application** iOS project. Specify the following settings in the **Choose options for your new project** sheet:

- **Product Name:** TipCalculator.
- **Organization Name:** Deitel and Associates, Inc.—or you can use your own organization name.
- **Company Identifier:** com.deitel—or you can use your own company identifier or use edu.self.
- **Language**—Swift.
- **Devices: iPhone**—This app is designed for iPhones and iPod touches. The app will run on iPads, but it will fill most of the screen and be centered, as in Fig. 3.7.

After specifying the settings, click **Next**, indicate where you'd like to save your project and click **Create** to create the project.

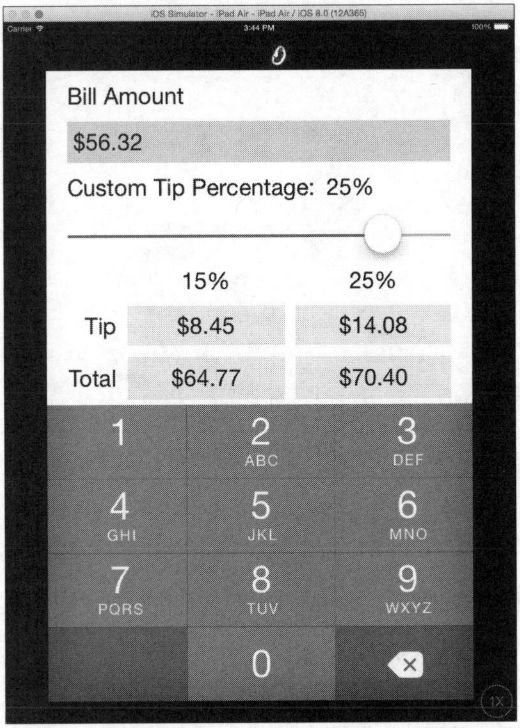

**Fig. 3.7** | **Tip Calculator** running in the iPad Air simulator.

*Configuring the App to Support Only Portrait Orientation*
In landscape orientation, the numeric keypad would obscure parts of the **Tip Calculator**'s UI. For this reason, this app will support only portrait orientation. In the project settings' **General** tab that's displayed in the Xcode **Editor** area, scroll to the **Deployment Info** section, then for **Device Orientation** ensure that only **Portrait** is selected. Recall from Section 2.5.1 that most iPhone apps should support *portrait, landscape-left* and *landscape-right* orientations, and most iPad apps should also support *upside down* orientation. You can learn more about Apple's *Human Interface Guidelines* at:

```
http://bit.ly/HumanInterfaceGuidelines
```

### 3.3.2 Configuring the Size Classes for Designing a Portrait Orientation iPhone App

In Chapter 2, we designed a UI that supported both portrait and landscape orientations for any iOS device. For that purpose, we used the default size class **Any** for the design area's width and height. In this section, you'll configure the *design area* (also called the *canvas*) for a tall narrow device, such as an iPhone or iPod touch in portrait orientation. Select Main.storyboard to display the design area—also known as the canvas. At the bottom of the canvas, click the **Size Classes** control to display the size classes tool, then click in the lower-left corner to specify the size classes **Compact Width** and **Regular Height** (Fig. 3.8).

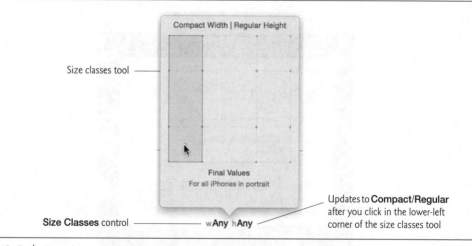

**Fig. 3.8** | Size classes tool with **Compact Width** and **Regular Height** selected.

### 3.3.3 Adding the UI Components

In this section, you'll add and arrange the UI components to create the basic design. In Section 3.3.4, you'll add auto layout constraints to complete the design.

*Step 1: Adding the "Bill Amount" Label*
First, you'll add the "**Bill Amount**" **Label** to the UI:

1. Drag a **Label** from the **Object** library to the scene's upper-left corner, using the blue guide lines to position the **Label** at the recommended distance from the

scene's top and left (Fig. 3.9). The ⊕ symbol indicates that you're adding a new component to the UI.

**Label** with placement guides for positioning

**Fig. 3.9** | Adding the "**Bill Amount**" **Label** to the scene.

2. Double click the **Label**, type Bill Amount, then press *Enter* to change its **Text** attribute.

*Step 2: Adding the Label That Displays the Formatted User Input*
Next, you'll add the blue **Label** that displays the formatted user input:

1. Drag another **Label** below the "**Bill Amount**" **Label**, such that the placement guides appear as shown in Fig. 3.10. This is where the user input will be displayed.

**Label** with placement guides for positioning

Placement guides help you position components so they're separated by the recommended amount of space as described in Apple's *Human Interface Guidelines*

**Fig. 3.10** | Adding the **Label** in which the formatted user input will be displayed.

2. Drag the middle sizing handle at the new **Label**'s right side until the blue guide line at the scene's right side appears (Fig. 3.11).

**Fig. 3.11** | Resizing the **Label** where the formatted user input will be displayed.

3. In the **Attributes** inspector, scroll to the **View** section and locate the **Label**'s **Background** attribute. Click the attribute's value, then select **Other...** to display the **Colors** dialog. This dialog has five tabs at the top that allow you to select colors different ways. For this app, we used the **Crayons** tab. On the bottom row, select the **Sky** (blue) crayon as the color (Fig. 3.12), then set the **Opacity** to 50%—this allows the scene's white background to blend with the **Label**'s color, resulting in a lighter blue color. The **Label** should now appear as shown in Fig. 3.13.

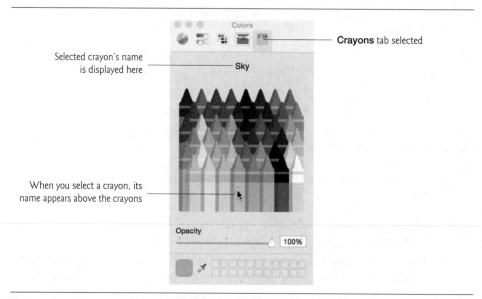

**Fig. 3.12** | Selecting the **Sky** crayon for the **Label**'s background color.

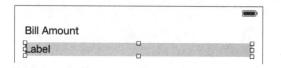

**Fig. 3.13** | Label with **Sky** blue background and 50% opacity.

4. A **Label**'s default height is 21 points. We increased this **Label**'s height to add space above and below its text to make it more readable against the colored background. To do so, drag the bottom-center sizing handle down until the **Label**'s height is 30 (Fig. 3.14).

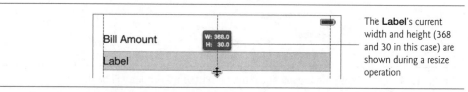

**Fig. 3.14** | Label with **Sky** blue background and 50% opacity.

5. With the **Label** selected, delete the value for its **Text** property in the **Attributes** inspector. The **Label** should now be empty.

***Step 3: Adding the "Custom Tip Percentage:" Label and a Label to Display the Current Custom Tip Percentage***
Next, you'll add the **Labels** in the UI's third row:

1. Drag another **Label** onto the scene and position it below the blue **Label** as shown in Fig. 3.15.

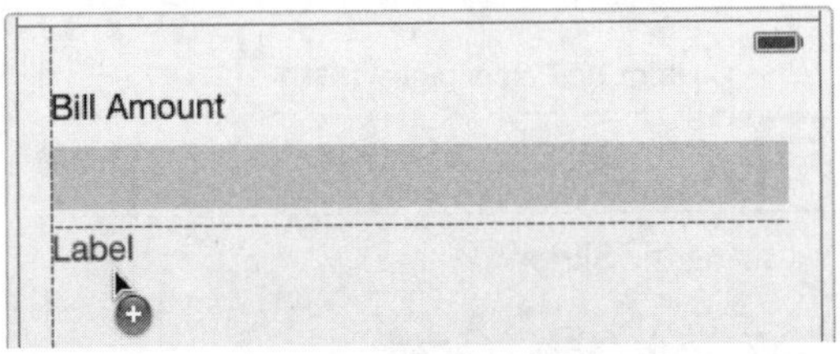

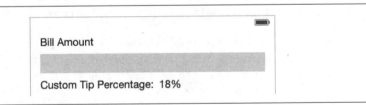

**Fig. 3.15** | Adding the "**Custom Tip Percentage:**" **Label** to the scene.

2. Double click the **Label** and set its text to Custom Tip Percentage:.

3. Drag another **Label** onto the scene and position it to the right of the "**Custom Tip Percentage:**" **Label** (Fig. 3.16), then set its text to **18%**—the initial custom tip percentage we chose in this app, which the app will update when the user moves the **Slider**'s thumb. The UI should now appear as shown in Fig. 3.17.

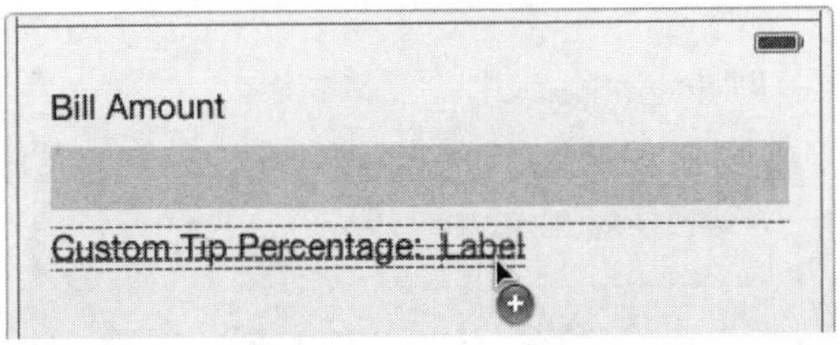

**Fig. 3.16** | Adding the **Label** that displays the current custom tip percentage.

**Fig. 3.17** | UI design so far.

### Step 4: Creating the Custom Tip Percentage *Slider*

You'll now create the **Slider** for selecting the custom tip percentage:

1. Drag a **Slider** from the **Object** library onto the scene so that it's the recommended distance from the "**Custom Tip Percentage:**" **Label**, then size and position it as shown in Fig. 3.18.

2. Use the **Attributes** inspector to set the **Slider**'s **Minimum** value to 0 (the default), **Maximum** value to 30 and **Current** value to 18.

Bill Amount
Custom Tip Percentage: 18%
W: 368.0
H: 30.0

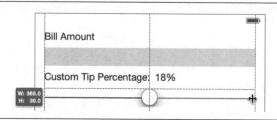

**Fig. 3.18** | Creating and sizing the **Slider**.

### *Step 5: Adding the "15%" and "18%" Labels*

Next, you'll add two more **Labels** containing the text **15%** and **18%** to serve as column headings for the calculation results. The app will update the "**18%**" **Label** when the user moves the **Slider**'s thumb. Initially, you'll position these **Labels** approximately—later you'll position them more precisely. Perform the following steps:

1. Drag another **Label** onto the scene and use the blue guides to position it the recommended distance below the **Slider** (Fig. 3.19), then set its **Text** to 15% and its **Alignment** to centered.

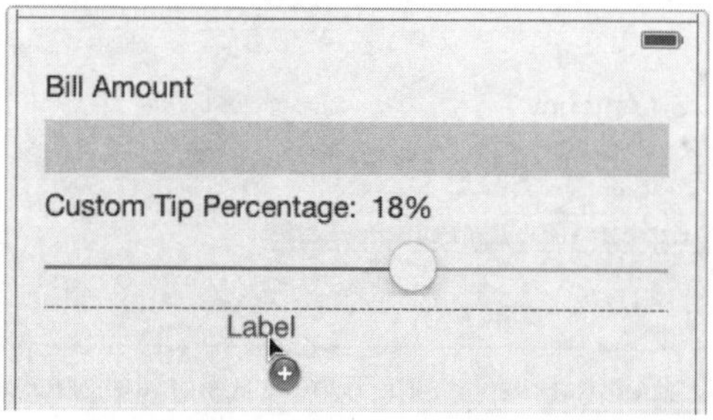

Bill Amount
Custom Tip Percentage: 18%
Label

**Fig. 3.19** | Adding the **Label** and right aligning it with the blue **Label**.

2. Next you'll duplicate the "**15%**" **Label**, which copies all of its settings. Hold the *option* key and drag the "**15%**" **Label** to the right (Fig. 3.20). You can also duplicate a UI component by selecting it and typing ⌘ + *D*, then moving the copy. Change the new **Label**'s text to 18%.

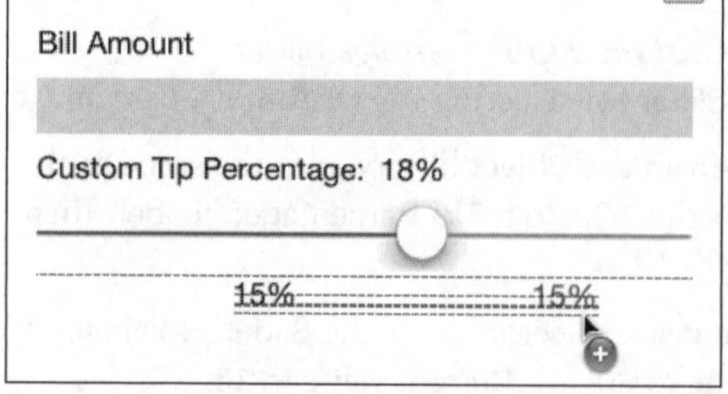

Bill Amount
Custom Tip Percentage: 18%
15%
15%

**Fig. 3.20** | Duplicating the "**15%**" **Label** so that you can create the "**18%**" **Label**.

*Step 6: Creating the* Labels *That Display the Tips and Totals*
Next, you'll add four Labels in which the app will display the calculation results:

1. Drag a Label onto the UI until the blue guides appear as in Fig. 3.21.

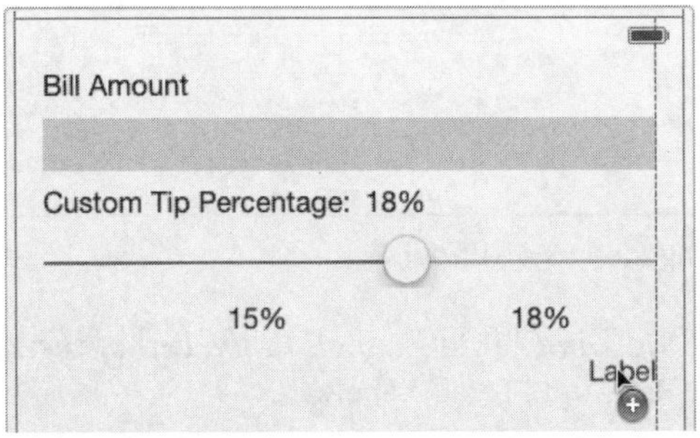

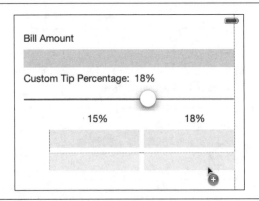

**Fig. 3.21** | Creating the first yellow Label.

2. Drag the Label's bottom-center sizing handle until the Label's **Height** is 30, and drag its left-center sizing handle until the Label's **Width** is 156.

3. Use the **Attributes** inspector to clear the **Text** attribute, set the **Alignment** so the text is centered and set the **Background** color to **Banana**, which is located in the **Color** dialog's **Crayons** tab in the second row from the bottom.

4. Set the **Autoshrink** property to **Minimum Font Scale** and change the value to .75— if the text becomes too wide to fit in the Label, this will allow the text to shrink to 75% of its original font size to accommodate more text. If you'd like the text to be able to shrink even more, you can choose a smaller value.

5. Next duplicate the yellow Label by holding the *option* key and dragging the Label to the left to create another Label below the "**15%**" Label.

6. Select both yellow Labels by holding the *Shift* key and clicking each Label. Hold the *option* key and drag any one of the selected Labels down until the blue guides appear as shown in Fig. 3.22.

**Fig. 3.22** | Creating the second row of yellow Labels.

7. Now you can center the "**15%**" and "**18%**" **Label**s over their columns. Drag the "**Tip**" **Label** so that the blue guide lines appear as shown in Fig. 3.23. Repeat this for the "**18%**" **Label** to center it over the right column of yellow **Label**s.

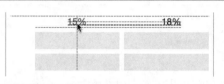

**Fig. 3.23** | Repositioning the "**15%**" **Label**.

***Step 7: Creating the "Tip" and "Total" Labels to the Left of the Yellow Labels***
Next you'll create the "**Tip**" and "**Total**" **Label**s:

1. Drag a **Label** onto the scene, change its **Text** to Total, set its **Alignment** to right aligned and position it to the left of the second row of yellow **Label**s as in Fig. 3.24.

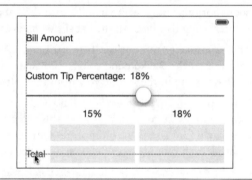

**Fig. 3.24** | Positioning the "**Total**" **Label**.

2. Hold the *option* key and drag the "**Total**" **Label** up until the blue guides appear as shown in Fig. 3.25. Change the new **Label**'s text to Tip, then drag it to the right so that the right edges of the "**Tip**" and "**Total**" **Label**s align.

**Fig. 3.25** | Duplicating the "**Total**" **Label** so that you can create the "**Tip**" **Label**.

*Step 8: Creating the Text Field for Receiving User Input*
You'll now create the **Text Field** that will receive the user input. Drag a **Text Field** from the **Object** library to the bottom edge of the scene, then use the **Attributes** inspector to set its **Keyboard Type** attribute to **Number Pad** and its **Appearance** to **Dark**. This **Text Field** will be *hidden* behind the numeric keypad when the app first loads. You'll receive the user's input through this **Text Field**, then format and display it in the blue **Label** at the top of the scene.

### 3.3.4 Adding the Auto Layout Constraints

You've now completed the **Tip Calculator** app's basic UI design, but have not yet added any auto layout constraints. If you run the app in the simulator or on a device, however, you'll notice that—depending on which simulator you use—some of the UI components extend beyond the trailing edge (Fig. 3.26). In this section, you'll add auto layout constraints so that the UI components can adjust to display properly on devices of various sizes and resolutions.

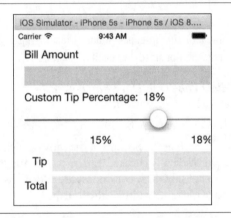

**Fig. 3.26** | App in the iPhone 5s simulator without auto layout constraints added to the UI— some components flow off the trailing edge (the right side in this screen capture).

In Chapter 2, you manually added the required auto layout constraints. In this section, you'll use Interface Builder to add missing constraints automatically, then run the app again to see the results. You'll then create some additional constraints so that the app displays correctly in the simulator or on a device.

*Step 1: Adding the Missing Auto Layout Constraints*
To add the missing auto layout constraints:

1. Click the white background in the design area or select **View** in the document outline window.

2. At the bottom of the canvas, click the **Resolve Auto Layout Issues** (⊢⊿⊣) button and under **All Views in View Controller** select **Add Missing Constraints**.

Interface Builder analyzes the UI components in the design and based on their sizes, locations and alignment, then creates a set of auto layout constraints for you. In some cases, these constraints will be enough for your design, but you'll often need to tweak the results. Figure 3.27 shows the UI in the iPhone 5s simulator after Interface Builder adds the missing constraints. Now, all of the UI components are completely visible, but some of them are not sized and positioned correctly. In particular, the yellow **Label**s should all be the same width.

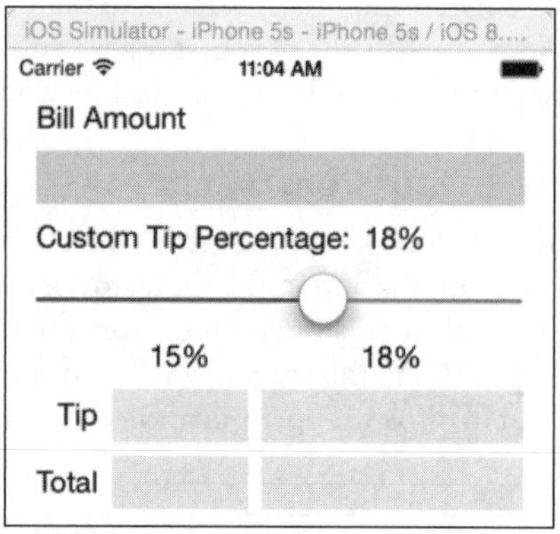

**Fig. 3.27** | App in the simulator after Interface Builder adds the missing auto layout constraints—some components are not sized and positioned correctly.

*Step 2: Setting the Yellow **Label**s to Have Equal Widths*
To set the yellow **Label**s to have equal widths:

1. Select all four yellow **Label**s by holding the *shift* key and clicking each one.

2. In the auto layout tools at the bottom of the canvas, click the **Pin** tools icon (⊢◻⊣). Ensure that **Equal Widths** is checked and click the **Add 3 Constraints** button, as shown in Fig. 3.28. Only three constraints are added, because three of the **Label**s will be set to have the same width as the fourth.

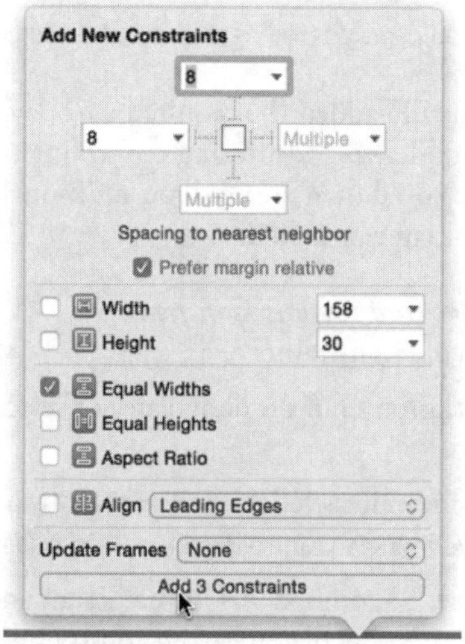

**Fig. 3.28** | Setting **Equal Widths** for the yellow **Label**s.

Figure 3.29 shows the UI in the simulator. Setting the yellow Labels to Equal Widths caused the 18% Label over the right column to disappear and the "Tip" and "Total" Labels to become too narrow to display.

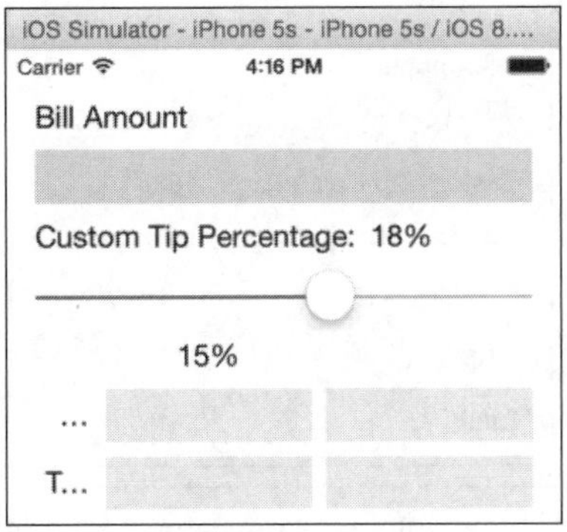

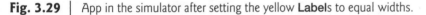

**Fig. 3.29** | App in the simulator after setting the yellow Labels to equal widths.

*Step 3: Debugging the Missing "18%" Label*
Based on the initial design, the missing "18%" Label should be centered over the right column of yellow Labels. If you select that Label in the canvas and select the Size inspector in the Utilities area, you can see the missing Label's complete set of constraints (Fig. 3.30).

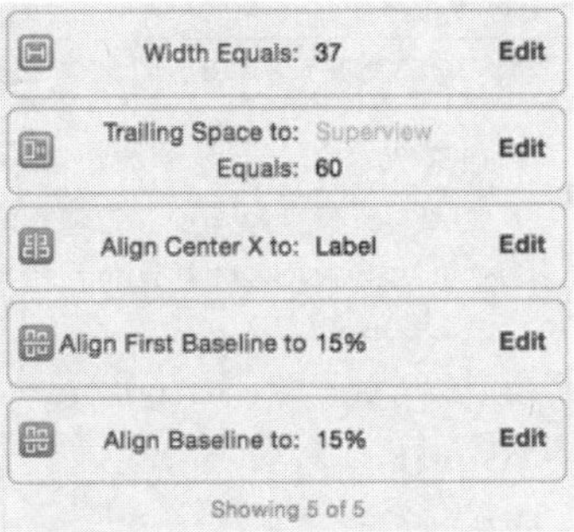

**Fig. 3.30** | "18%" Label's constraints.

There are two constraints on the "18%" Label's horizontal positioning:

- The Trailing Space to: Superview constraint specifies that this Label should be 60 points from the scene's trailing edge.

- The Align Center X to: Label constraint specifies that this Label should be centered horizontally over the specified Label.

These two constraints *conflict* with one another—depending on the yellow Label's width, the "18%" Label could appear different distances from the scene's trailing edge. By removing the Trailing Space to: Superview constraint, we can eliminate the conflict. To do so, simply click that constraint in the Size inspector and press the *delete* key. Figure 3.31

shows the final UI in the iPhone 5s simulator, but you can test the UI in other simulators to confirm that it works correctly in each.

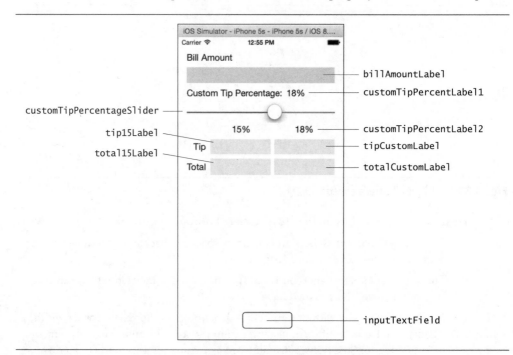

**Fig. 3.31** | App with its final UI running in the simulator.

## 3.4 Creating Outlets with Interface Builder

You'll now use Interface Builder to create the *outlets* for the UI components that the app interacts with programmatically. Figure 3.32 shows the outlet names that we specified when creating this app. A common naming convention is to use the UI component's class name without the UI class prefix at the end of an outlet property's name—for example,

**Fig. 3.32** | Tip Calculator's UI components labeled with their outlet names.

`billAmountLabel` rather than `billAmountUILabel`. (At the time of this writing, Apple had not yet published their Swift coding guidelines.) Interface Builder makes it easy for you to create outlets for UI components by *control* dragging from the component into your source code. To do this, you'll take advantage of the Xcode **Assistant** editor.

*Opening the **Assistant** Editor*

To create outlets, ensure that your scene's storyboard is displayed by selecting it in the **Project** navigator. Next, select the **Assistant** editor button (⊘) on the Xcode toolbar (or select **View > Assistant Editor > Show Assistant Editor**). Xcode's **Editor** area splits and the file `View-Controller.swift` (Fig. 3.33) is displayed to the right of the storyboard. By default, when viewing a storyboard, the **Assistant** editor shows the corresponding view controller's source code. However, by clicking **Automatic** in the jump bar at the top of the **Assistant** editor, you can select from options for previewing the UI for different device sizes and orientations, previewing localized versions of the UI or viewing other files that you'd like to view side-by-side with the content currently displayed in the editor. The comments in lines 1–7 are autogenerated by Xcode—later, we delete these comments and replace them with our own. Delete the method `didReceiveMemoryWarning` in lines 18–21 as we will not use it in this app. We'll discuss the details of `ViewController.swift` and add code to it in Section 3.6.

```
  Jump bar ──────┤ ⊞ ⟨ ⟩ ⊘ Automatic ⟩ ⩥ ViewController.swift ⟩ No Selection                    + ×
 1  //
 2  // ViewController.swift
 3  // TipCalculator
 4  //
 5  // Created by Paul Deitel on 9/3/14.
 6  // Copyright (c) 2014 Deitel & Associates, Inc. All rights reserved.
 7  //
 8
 9  import UIKit
10
11  class ViewController: UIViewController {
12
13      override func viewDidLoad() {
14          super.viewDidLoad()
15          // Do any additional setup after loading the view, typically
16      }
17
18      override func didReceiveMemoryWarning() {
19          super.didReceiveMemoryWarning()
20          // Dispose of any resources that can be recreated.
21      }
22
```

**Fig. 3.33** | `ViewController.swift` displayed in the **Assistant** editor.

*Creating an Outlet*

You'll now create an outlet for the blue **Label** that displays the user's input. You need this outlet to programmatically change the **Label**'s text to display the input in currency format. Outlets are declared as properties of a view controller class. To create the outlet:

1.  *Control* drag from the blue **Label** to below line 11 in `ViewController.swift` (Fig. 3.34) and release. This displays a popover for configuring the outlet (Fig. 3.35).

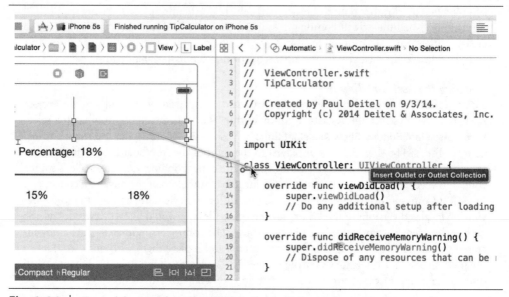

**Fig. 3.34** | *Control* dragging from the scene to the **Assistant** editor to create an outlet.

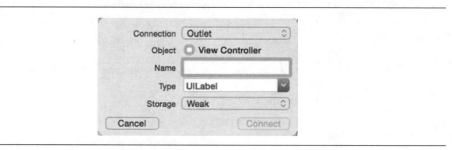

**Fig. 3.35** | Popover for configuring an outlet.

2. In the popover, ensure that **Outlet** is selected for the **Connection** type, specify the name billAmountLabel for the outlet's **Name** and click **Connect**.

Xcode inserts the following property declaration in class ViewController:

```
@IBOutlet weak var billAmountLabel: UILabel!
```

We'll explain this code in Section 3.6.3. You can now use this property to programmatically modify the **Label**'s text.

*Creating the Other Outlets*

Repeat the steps above to create outlets for the other labeled UI components in Fig. 3.32. Your code should now appear as shown in Fig. 3.36. In the gray margin to the left of each outlet property is a small bullseye (◉) symbol indicating that the outlet is connected to a UI component. Hovering the mouse over that symbol highlights the connected UI component in the scene. You can use this to confirm that each outlet is connected properly.

```
88  <  >  ⚙ Automatic ⟩ 📄 ViewController.swift ⟩ No Selection                            + ×
 1  //
 2  //  ViewController.swift
 3  //  TipCalculator
 4  //
 5  //  Created by Paul Deitel on 9/3/14.
 6  //  Copyright (c) 2014 Deitel & Associates, Inc. All rights reserved.
 7  //\
 8
 9  import UIKit
10
11  class ViewController: UIViewController {
12      @IBOutlet weak var billAmountLabel: UILabel!
13      @IBOutlet weak var customTipPercentLabel1: UILabel!
14      @IBOutlet weak var customTipPercentageSlider: UISlider!
15      @IBOutlet weak var customTipPercentLabel2: UILabel!
16      @IBOutlet weak var tip15Label: UILabel!
17      @IBOutlet weak var total15Label: UILabel!
18      @IBOutlet weak var tipCustomLabel: UILabel!
19      @IBOutlet weak var totalCustomLabel: UILabel!
20      @IBOutlet weak var inputTextField: UITextField!
21
22      override func viewDidLoad() {
23          super.viewDidLoad()
24          // Do any additional setup after loading the view, typically from a nib.
25      }
26  }
```

**Fig. 3.36** | Code after adding outlets for the programmatically manipulated UI components.

## 3.5 Creating Actions with Interface Builder

Now that you've created the outlets, you need to create actions (i.e., event handlers) that can respond to the user-interface events. A **Text Field**'s **Editing Changed** event occurs every time the user changes the **Text Field**'s contents. If you connect an action to the **Text Field** for this event, the **Text Field** will send a message to the view-controller object to execute the action each time the event occurs. Similarly, the **Value Changed** event repeatedly occurs for a **Slider** as the user moves the thumb. If you connect an action method to the **Slider** for this event, the **Slider** will send a message to the view controller to execute the action each time the event occurs.

In this app, you'll create one action method that's called for each of these events. You'll connect the **Text Field** and the **Slider** to this action using the **Assistant** editor. To do so, perform the following steps:

1. *Control* drag from the **Text Field** in the scene to ViewController.swift between the right braces (}) at lines 25 and 26 (Fig. 3.37), then release. This displays a popover for configuring an outlet. From the **Connection** list in the popover, select **Action** to display the options for configuring an action (Fig. 3.38).

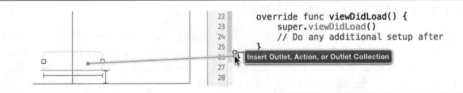

**Fig. 3.37** | *Control* dragging to create an action for the **Text Field**.

Fig. 3.38 shows a popover with the following fields:

```
Connection  Action
Object  ○ View Controller
Name  |
Type  AnyObject
Event  Editing Did End
Arguments  Sender
Cancel          Connect
```

**Fig. 3.38** | Popover for configuring an action.

**2.** In the popover, specify `calculateTip` for the action's **Name**, select **Editing Changed** for the **Event** and click **Connect**.

Xcode inserts the following empty method definition in the code:

```
@IBAction func calculateTip(sender: AnyObject) {
}
```

and displays a small bullseye (◉) symbol (Fig. 3.39) in the gray margin to the left of the method indicating that the action is connected to a UI component. Now, when the user edits the **Text Field**, a message will be sent to the `ViewController` object to execute `calculateTip`. You'll define the logic for this method in Section 3.6.6.

*Connecting the **Slider** to Method `calculateTip`*
Recall that `calculateTip` should also be called as the user changes the custom tip percentage. You can simply connect the **Slider** to this existing action to handle the **Slider**'s **Value Changed** event. To do so, select the **Slider** in the scene, then hold the *control* key and drag from the **Slider** to the `calculateTip:` method (Fig. 3.39) and release. This connects the **Slider**'s **Value Changed** event to the action. You're now ready to implement the app's logic.

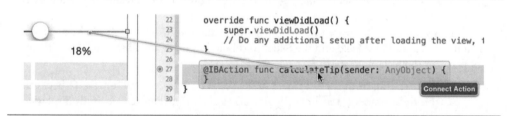

```
22    override func viewDidLoad() {
23        super.viewDidLoad()
24        // Do any additional setup after loading the view, 1
25    }
26
27    @IBAction func calculateTip(sender: AnyObject) {
28    }
29  }
30
```

18%

Connect Action

**Fig. 3.39** | *Control* dragging to connect an existing `@IBAction` to the **Slider**.

# 3.6 Class `ViewController`

Sections 3.6.1—3.6.7 present `ViewController.swift`, which contains class `ViewController` and several global utility functions that are used throughout the class to format `NSDecimalNumbers` as currency and to perform calculations using `NSDecimalNumber` objects. We modified the autogenerated comments that Xcode inserted at the beginning of the source code file.

### 3.6.1 import Declarations

Recall that to use features from the iOS 8 frameworks, you must *import* them into your Swift code. Throughout this app, we use the UIKit framework's UI component classes. In Fig. 3.46, line 3 is an import declaration indicating that the program uses features from the UIKit framework. All import declarations must appear *before* any other Swift code (except comments) in your source-code files.

```
1    // ViewController.swift
2    // Implements the tip calculator's logic
3    import UIKit
4
```

**Fig. 3.40** | import declaration in ViewController.swift.

### 3.6.2 ViewController Class Definition

In Fig. 3.41, line 5—which was generated by the IDE when you created the project—begins a **class definition** for class ViewController.

```
5    class ViewController: UIViewController {
```

**Fig. 3.41** | ViewController class definition and properties.

*Keyword class and Class Names*
The **class keyword** introduces a class definition and is immediately followed by the class name (ViewController). Class name *identifiers* use *camel-case* naming in which each word in the identifier begins with a capital letter. Class names (and other type names) begin with an initial uppercase letter and other identifiers begin with lowercase letters. Each new class you create becomes a new type that can be used to declare variables and create objects.

*Class Body*
A **left brace** (at the end of line 5), **{**, begins the body of every class definition. A corresponding **right brace** (at line 82 in Fig. 3.45), **}**, ends each class definition. By convention, the contents of a class's body are indented.

**Error-Prevention Tip 3.1**
*A class must be defined before you use it in a given source-code file. In an Xcode project, if you define a class in one* .swift *file, you can use it in the project's other source-code files— which is typical of other object-oriented languages, such as Objective-C, Java, C# and C++.*

*Inheriting from Class UIViewController*
The notation : UIViewController in line 5 indicates that class ViewController **inherits** from class UIViewController—the UIKit framework superclass of all view controllers. *Inheritance* is a form of software reuse in which a new class is created by absorbing an existing class's members and enhancing them with new or modified capabilities. This relationship indicates that a ViewController *is a* UIViewController. It also ensures that ViewController has the basic capabilities that iOS expects in all view controllers, including methods like

viewDidLoad (Section 3.6.5) that help iOS manage a view controller's lifecycle. The class on the left of the : in line 5 is the *subclass* (derived class) and one on the right is the *superclass* (base class). Every scene has its own UIViewController subclass that defines the scene's event handlers and other logic. Unlike some object-oriented programming languages, Swift classes are not required to directly or indirectly inherit from a common superclass.

### 3.6.3 ViewController's @IBOutlet Properties

Figure 3.42 shows class ViewController's nine @IBOutlet property declarations that were created by Interface Builder when you created the outlets in Section 3.4. Typically, you'll define a class's *properties* first followed by the class's *methods*, but this is not required.

```
 6    // properties for programmatically interacting with UI components
 7    @IBOutlet weak var billAmountLabel: UILabel!
 8    @IBOutlet weak var customTipPercentLabel1: UILabel!
 9    @IBOutlet weak var customTipPercentageSlider: UISlider!
10    @IBOutlet weak var customTipPercentLabel2: UILabel!
11    @IBOutlet weak var tip15Label: UILabel!
12    @IBOutlet weak var total15Label: UILabel!
13    @IBOutlet weak var tipCustomLabel: UILabel!
14    @IBOutlet weak var totalCustomLabel: UILabel!
15    @IBOutlet weak var inputTextField: UITextField!
16
```

**Fig. 3.42** | ViewController's @IBOutlet properties.

#### @IBOutlet *Property Declarations*
The notation @IBOutlet indicates to Xcode that the property references a UI component in the app's storyboard. When a scene loads, the UI component objects are created, an object of the corresponding view-controller class is created and the connections between the view controller's outlet properties and the UI components are established. The connection information is stored in the storyboard. @IBOutlet properties are declared as *variables* using the var keyword, so that the storyboard can assign each UI component object's reference to the appropriate outlet once the UI components and view controller object are created.

#### Automatic Reference Counting (ARC) and Property Attributes
Swift manages the memory for your app's reference-type objects using **automatic reference counting (ARC)**, which keeps track of how many references there are to a given object. The runtime can remove an object from memory only when its *reference count* becomes 0.

**Property attributes** can specify whether a class maintains an ownership or nonownership relationship with the referenced object. By default, properties in Swift create **strong references** to objects, indicating an ownership relationship. Every strong reference increments an object's reference count by 1. When a strong reference no longer refers to an object, its reference count decrements by 1. The code that manages incrementing and decrementing the reference counts is inserted by the Swift compiler.

The @IBOutlet properties are declared as **weak** references, because the view controller *does not own* the UI components—the view defined by the storyboard that created them does. A weak reference does *not* affect the object's reference count. A view controller does, however, have a strong reference to its view.

*Type Annotations and Implicitly Unwrapped Optional Types*
A **type annotation** specifies a variable's or constant's type. Type annotations are specified by following the variable's or constant's identifier with a colon (:) and a type name. For example, line 7 (Fig. 3.42) indicates that `billAmountLabel` is a `UILabel!`. Recall from Section 3.2.12 that the exclamation point indicates an implicitly unwrapped optional type and that variables of such types are initialized to `nil` by default. This allows the class to compile, because these `@IBOutlet` properties are initialized—they'll be assigned actual UI component objects once the UI is created at runtime.

### 3.6.4 Other `ViewController` Properties

Figure 3.43 shows class `ViewController`'s other properties, which you should add below the `@IBOutlet` properties. Line 18 defines the constant `decimal100` that's initialized with an `NSDecimalNumber` object. Identifiers for Swift constants follow the same camel-case naming conventions as variables. Class `NSDecimalNumber` provides many **initializers**—this one receives a `String` parameter containing the initial value (`"100.0"`), then returns an `NS-DecimalNumber` representing the corresponding numeric value. We'll use `decimal100` to calculate the custom tip percentage by dividing the slider's value by 100.0. We'll also use it to divide the user's input by 100.0 for placing a decimal point in the bill amount that's displayed at the top of the app. Initializers are commonly called constructors in many other object-oriented programming languages. Line 19 defines the constant `decimal15Percent` that's initialized with an `NSDecimalNumber` object representing the value 0.15. We'll use this to calculate the 15% tip.

```
17      // NSDecimalNumber constants used in the calculateTip method
18      let decimal100 = NSDecimalNumber(string: "100.0")
19      let decimal15Percent = NSDecimalNumber(string: "0.15")
20
```

**Fig. 3.43** | `ViewController` class definition and properties.

*Initializer Parameter Names Are Required*
When initializing an object in Swift, you must specify each parameter's name, followed by a colon (:) and the argument value. As you type your code, Xcode displays the parameter names for initializers and methods to help you write code quickly and correctly. Required parameter names in Swift are known as **external parameter names**.

*Type Inference*
Neither constant in Fig. 3.43 was declared with a type annotation. Like many popular languages, Swift has powerful **type inference** capabilities and can determine a constant's or variable's type from its initializer value. In lines 18–19, Swift infers from the initializers that both constants are `NSDecimalNumber`s.

### 3.6.5 Overridden `UIViewController` method `viewDidLoad`

Method `viewDidLoad` (Fig. 3.44)—which Xcode generated when it created class `ViewController`—is inherited from superclass `UIViewController`. You typically *override* it to define tasks that can be performed only *after* the view has been initialized. You should add lines 25–26 to the method.

```
21        // called when the view loads
22        override func viewDidLoad() {
23            super.viewDidLoad()
24
25            // select inputTextField so keypad displays when the view loads
26            inputTextField.becomeFirstResponder()
27        }
28
```

**Fig. 3.44** | Overridden `UIViewController` method `viewDidLoad`.

A method definition begins with the keyword **func** (line 22) followed by the function's name and parameter list enclosed in required parentheses, then the function's body enclosed in braces ({ and }). The parameter list optionally contains a comma-separated list of parameters with type annotations. This function does not receive any parameters, so its parameter list is empty—you'll see a method with parameters in Section 3.6.6. This method does not return a value, so it does not specify a return type—you'll see how to specify return types in Section 3.6.7.

When overriding a superclass method, you declare it with keyword **override** preceding the keyword `func`, and the first statement in the method's body typically uses the **super** keyword to invoke the superclass's version of the method (line 23). The keyword super references the object of the class in which the method appears, but is used to access members inherited from the superclass.

*Displaying the Numeric Keypad When the App Begins Executing*
In this app, we want `inputTextField` to be the selected object when the app begins executing so that the numeric keypad is displayed immediately. To do this, we use property `inputTextField` to invoke the `UITextField` method `becomeFirstResponder`, which programmatically makes `inputTextField` the *active component* on the screen—as if the user touched it. You configured `inputTextField` such that when it's selected, the numeric keypad is displayed, so line 26 displays this keypad when the view loads.

### 3.6.6 ViewController Action Method calculateTip

Method `calculateTip` (Fig. 3.45) is the *action* (as specified by `@IBAction` on line 31) that responds to the **Text Field**'s **Editing Changed** event and the **Slider**'s **Value Changed** event. Add the code in lines 32–81 to the body of `calculateTip`. (If you're entering the Swift code as you read this section, you'll get errors on several statements that perform NSDecimalNumber calculations using overloaded operators that you'll define in Section 3.6.7.) The method takes one parameter. Each parameter's name must be declared with a type annotation specifying the *parameter's type*. When a view-controller object receives a message from a UI component, it also receives as an argument a reference to that component—the event's **sender**. Parameter `sender`'s type—the Swift type **AnyObject**—represents *any* type of object and does not provide any information about the object. For this reason, the object's type must be determined at runtime. This **dynamic typing** is used for actions (i.e., event handlers), because many different types of objects can generate events. In action methods that respond to events from multiple UI components, the sender is often used to determine which UI component the user interacted with (as we do in lines 42 and 57).

```
29    // called when the user edits the text in the inputTextField
30    // or moves the customTipPercentageSlider's thumb
31    @IBAction func calculateTip(sender: AnyObject) {
32        let inputString = inputTextField.text // get user input
33
34        // convert slider value to an NSDecimalNumber
35        let sliderValue =
36            NSDecimalNumber(integer: Int(customTipPercentageSlider.value))
37
38        // divide sliderValue by decimal100 (100.0) to get tip %
39        let customPercent = sliderValue / decimal100
40
41        // did customTipPercentageSlider generate the event?
42        if sender is UISlider {
43            // thumb moved so update the Labels with new custom percent
44            customTipPercentLabel1.text =
45                NSNumberFormatter.localizedStringFromNumber(customPercent,
46                    numberStyle: NSNumberFormatterStyle.PercentStyle)
47            customTipPercentLabel2.text = customTipPercentLabel1.text
48        }
49
50        // if there is a bill amount, calculate tips and totals
51        if !inputString.isEmpty {
52            // convert to NSDecimalNumber and insert decimal point
53            let billAmount =
54                NSDecimalNumber(string: inputString) / decimal100
55
56            // did inputTextField generate the event?
57            if sender is UITextField {
58                // update billAmountLabel with currency-formatted total
59                billAmountLabel.text = " " + formatAsCurrency(billAmount)
60
61                // calculate and display the 15% tip and total
62                let fifteenTip = billAmount * decimal15Percent
63                tip15Label.text = formatAsCurrency(fifteenTip)
64                total15Label.text =
65                    formatAsCurrency(billAmount + fifteenTip)
66            }
67
68            // calculate custom tip and display custom tip and total
69            let customTip = billAmount * customPercent
70            tipCustomLabel.text = formatAsCurrency(customTip)
71            totalCustomLabel.text =
72                formatAsCurrency(billAmount + customTip)
73        }
74        else { // clear all Labels
75            billAmountLabel.text = ""
76            tip15Label.text = ""
```

**Fig. 3.45** | `ViewController` action method `calculateTip`. (Part 1 of 2.)

```
77                  total15Label.text = ""
78                  tipCustomLabel.text = ""
79                  totalCustomLabel.text = ""
80              }
81          }
82      }
83
```

**Fig. 3.45** | ViewController action method calculateTip. (Part 2 of 2.)

*Getting the Current Values of inputTextField and customTipPercentageSlider*
Line 32 stores the value of inputTextField's **text** property—which contains the user's input—in the local String variable inputString—Swift infers type String because UI-TextField's text property is a String.

Lines 35–36 get the customTipPercentageSlider's **value** property, which contains a Float value representing the **Slider's** *thumb position* (a value from 0 to 30, as specified in Section 3.3.3). The value is a Float, so we could get tip percentages like, 3.1, 15.245, etc. This app uses only whole-number tip percentages, so we convert the value to an Int before using it to initialize the NSDecimalNumber object that's assigned to local variable slider-Value. In this case, we use the NSDecimalNumber initializer that takes an Int value named integer.

Line 39 uses the overloaded division operator function that we define in Section 3.6.7 to divide sliderValue by 100 (decimal100). This creates an NSDecimalNumber representing the custom tip percentage that we'll use in later calculations and that will be displayed as a *locale-specific* percentage String showing the current custom tip percentage.

*Updating the Custom Tip Percentage Labels When the Slider Value Changes*
Lines 42–48 update customTipPercentLabel1 and customTipPercentLabel2 when the **Slider** value changes. Line 42 determines whether the sender *is a* UISlider object, meaning that the user interacted with the customTipPercentageSlider. The **is** operator returns true if an object's class is the same as, or has an *is a* (inheritance) relationship with, the class in the right operand.

We perform a similar test at line 57 to determine whether the user interacted with the inputTextField. Testing the sender argument like this enables you to perform *different* tasks, based on the component that caused the event.

Lines 44–46 set the customTipPercentLabel1's text property to a locale-specific percentage String based on the device's current locale. NSNumberFormatter class method localizedStringFromNumber returns a String representation of a formatted number. The method receives two arguments:

- The first is the NSNumber to format. Class NSDecimalNumber is a subclass of NSNumber, so you can use an NSDecimalNumber anywhere that an NSNumber is expected.

- The second argument (which has the external parameter name numberStyle) is a constant from the enumeration **NSNumberFormatterStyle** that represents the formatting to apply to the number—the PercentStyle constant indicates that the number should be formatted as a percentage. Because the second argument must be of type NSNumberFormatterStyle, Swift can infer information about the method's argument. As such, it's possible to write the expression `NSNumberFor-matterStyle.PercentStyle` with the shorthand notation:

```
.PercentStyle
```

Line 47 assigns the same `String` to `customTipPercentLabel2`'s `text` property.

### *Updating the Tip and Total Labels*

Lines 51–80 update the tip and total **Labels** that display the calculation results. Line 51 uses the Swift `String` type's **isEmpty** property to ensure that `inputString` is not empty—that is, the user entered a bill amount. If so, lines 53–72 perform the tip and total calculations and update the corresponding **Labels**; otherwise, the `inputTextField` is empty and lines 75–79 clear all the tip and total **Labels** and the `billAmountLabel` by assigning the empty `String` literal (`""`) to their `text` properties.

Lines 53–54 use `inputString` to initialize an `NSDecimalNumber`, then divide it by 100 to place the decimal point in the bill amount—for example, if the user enters 5632, the amount used for calculating tips and totals is 56.32.

Lines 57–66 execute only if the event's `sender` was a `UITextField`—that is, the user tapped keypad buttons to enter or remove a digit in this app's `inputTextField`. Line 59 displays the currency-formatted bill amount in `billAmountLabel` by calling the `formatAsCurrency` method (defined in Section 3.6.7). Line 62 calculates the 15% tip amount by using an overloaded multiplication operator function for `NSDecimalNumbers` (defined in Section 3.6.7). Then line 63 displays the currency-formatted value in the `tip15Label`. Next, lines 64–65 calculates and displays the total amount for a 15% tip by using an overloaded addition operator function for `NSDecimalNumbers` (defined in Section 3.6.7) to perform the calculation, then passing the result to the `formatAsCurrency` function. Lines 69–72 calculate and display the custom tip and total amounts based on the custom tip percentage.

### *Why an External Name Is Not Required for a Method's First Argument*

You might be wondering why we did not provide a parameter name for the first argument in the method call at lines 45–46. For method calls, Swift requires external parameter names for all parameters *after* the first parameter. Apple's reasoning for this is that they want method calls to read like sentences. A method's name should refer to the first parameter, and each subsequent parameter should have a name that's specified as part of the method call.

## 3.6.7 Global Utility Functions Defined in `ViewController.swift`

Figure 3.46 contains several global utility functions used throughout class `ViewController`. Add lines 84–103 after the closing right brace of class `ViewController`.

```
84  // convert a numeric value to localized currency string
85  func formatAsCurrency(number: NSNumber) -> String {
86      return NSNumberFormatter.localizedStringFromNumber(
87          number, numberStyle: NSNumberFormatterStyle.CurrencyStyle)
88  }
89
```

**Fig. 3.46** | `ViewController.swift` global utility and overloaded operator functions. (Part 1 of 2.)

```
90   // overloaded + operator to add NSDecimalNumbers
91   func +(left: NSDecimalNumber, right: NSDecimalNumber) -> NSDecimalNumber {
92      return left.decimalNumberByAdding(right)
93   }
94
95   // overloaded * operator to multiply NSDecimalNumbers
96   func *(left: NSDecimalNumber, right: NSDecimalNumber) -> NSDecimalNumber {
97      return left.decimalNumberByMultiplyingBy(right)
98   }
99
100  // overloaded / operator to divide NSDecimalNumbers
101  func /(left: NSDecimalNumber, right: NSDecimalNumber) -> NSDecimalNumber {
102      return left.decimalNumberByDividingBy(right)
103  }
```

**Fig. 3.46** | `ViewController.swift` global utility and overloaded operator functions. (Part 2 of 2.)

### Defining a Function—*formatAsCurrency*

Lines 85–88 define the function `formatAsCurrency`. Like a method definition, a function definition begins with the keyword `func` (line 85) followed by the function's name and parameter list enclosed in required parentheses, then the function's body enclosed in braces ({ and }). The primary difference between a method and a function is that a method is defined in the body of a class definition (or `struct` or `enum` definition). Function `formatAsCurrency` receives one parameter (number) of type `NSNumber` (from the Foundation framework).

A function may also specify a return type by following the parameter list with -> and the type the function returns—this function returns a `String`. A function that does not specify a return type does not return a value—if you prefer to be explicit, you can specify the return type `Void`. A function with a return type uses a **return** statement (line 86) to pass a result back to its caller.

We use `formatAsCurrency` throughout class `ViewController` to format `NSDecimalNumbers` as locale-specific currency `Strings`. `NSDecimalNumber` is a subclass of `NSNumber`, so any `NSDecimalNumber` can be passed as an argument to this function. An `NSNumber` parameter can also receive as an argument any Swift numeric type value—such types are automatically *bridged* by the runtime to type `NSNumber`.

Lines 86–87 invoke `NSNumberFormatter` class method `localizedStringFromNumber`, which returns a locale-specific `String` representation of a number. This method receives as arguments the `NSNumber` to format—`formatAsCurrency`'s number parameter—and a constant from the `NSNumberFormatterStyle` enum that specifies the formatting style—the constant `CurrencyStyle` specifies that a *locale-specific currency format* should be used. Once again, we could have specified the second argument as `.CurrencyStyle`, because Swift knows that the `numberStyle` parameter must be a constant from the `NSNumberFormatterStyle` enumeration and thus can infer the constant's type.

### Defining Overloaded Operator Functions for Adding, Subtracting and Multiplying *NSDecimalNumbers*

Lines 91–93, 96–98 and 101–103 create global functions that overload the addition (+), multiplication (*) and division (/) operators, respectively. **Global functions** (also called free functions or just functions) are defined outside a type definition (such as a class). These functions enable us to:

- add two NSDecimalNumbers with the + operator (lines 65 and 72 of Fig. 3.45)

- multiply two NSDecimalNumbers with the * operator (lines 62 and 69 of Fig. 3.45)

- divide two NSDecimalNumbers with the / operator (lines 39 and 54 of Fig. 3.45)

Overloaded operator functions are defined like other global functions, but the function name is the symbol of the operator being overloaded (Fig. 3.46lines 91, 96 and 101). Each of these functions receives two NSDecimalNumbers representing the operator's left and right operands.

The addition (+) operator function (lines 91–93) returns the result of invoking NSDec-imalNumber instance method **decimalNumberByAdding** on the left operand with the right operand as the method's argument—this adds the operands. The multiplication (*) oper-ator function (lines 96–98) returns the result of invoking NSDecimalNumber instance method **decimalNumberByMultiplyingBy** on the left operand with the right operand as the method's argument—this multiplies the operands. The division (/) operator function (lines 101–103) returns the result of invoking NSDecimalNumber instance method **decimalNum-berByDividingBy** on the left operand with the right operand as the method's argument—this divides the left operand by the right operand. Since each of these NSDecimalNumber instance methods receives only one parameter, the parameter's name is not required in the method call. Unlike initializers and methods, a global function's parameter names are not external parameter names and are not required in function calls unless they're are explicitly defined as external parameter names in the function's definition.

## 3.7 Wrap-Up

This chapter presented the **Tip Calculator** app that calculates and displays 15% and custom tip percentage tips and totals for a restaurant bill. The app uses **Text Field** and **Slider** UI components to receive user input and update suggested tips and bill totals in response to each user interaction.

We introduced Swift—Apple's programming language of the future—and several of its object-oriented programming capabilities, including objects, classes, inheritance, methods and properties. As you saw, the app's code required various Swift data types, operators, control statements and keywords.

You learned about strong and weak references and that only strong references affect an object's reference count. You also learned that iOS's automatic reference counting (ARC) removes an object from memory only when the object's reference count becomes 0.

You used Interface Builder to design the app's UI visually. We showed how to build your UI faster by duplicating UI components that had similar attribute settings. You learned that **Labels** (UILabel), **Sliders** (UISlider) and **Text Fields** (UITextField) are part of iOS's UIKit framework that's automatically included with each app you create.

We showed how to use import to give your code access to features in preexisting frameworks. You learned that a scene is managed by a view-controller object that deter-mines what information is displayed and how user interactions with the scene's UI are pro-cessed. Our view-controller class inherited from class UIViewController, which defines the base capabilities required by view controllers in iOS.

You used Interface Builder to generate `@IBOutlet` properties (outlets) in your view controller for programmatically interacting with the app's UI components. You used visual tools in Interface Builder to connect a UI control to a corresponding outlet in the view controller. Once a connection was made, the view controller was able to manipulate the corresponding UI component programmatically.

You saw that interacting with a UI component caused a user-interface event and sent a message from the UI component to an action (event-handling method) in the view controller. You learned that an action is declared in Swift code as an `@IBAction`. You used visual tools in Interface Builder to connect the action to specific user-interface events.

Next, you learned that after all the objects in a storyboard are created, iOS sends a `viewDidLoad` message to the corresponding view controller so that it can perform view-specific tasks that can be executed only after the UI components in the view exist. You also called the `UITextField`'s `becomeFirstResponder` method in `viewDidLoad` so that iOS would display this keypad immediately after the view loaded.

You used `NSDecimalNumbers` for precise financial calculations. You also used class `NSNumberFormatter` to create locale-specific currency and percentage string representations of `NSDecimalNumbers`. You used Swift's operator overloading capabilities to simplify `NSDecimalNumber` calculations.

In the next chapter, we present the **Twitter Searches** app, which allows you to save your favorite (possibly lengthy) Twitter search strings with easy-to-remember short tag names. You'll store the search strings and their short tag names in Foundation framework collections. You'll also use iCloud key–value pair storage so that you can sync your query between all your iOS devices that have the **Twitter Searches** app installed.

# Twitter® Searches App

### Master-Detail Applications, Split View Controllers, Navigation Controllers, Storyboard Segues, Social Framework Sharing, User Defaults, iCloud Key–Value Storage, Collections, Web Views, Alert Dialogs

iOS Simulator - iPhone 6 - iPhone 6 / iOS 8.0 (12A365)

| Carrier 🔆 | 11:30 AM | ▬ |
|---|---|---|
| Edit | Twitter Searches | + |

- Deitel
- iOSFP
- iOSLL
- SwiftFP
- SwiftLL
- JHTP
- LiveLessons
- AndroidFP
- CPPHTP
- IW3HTP
- VCSharpHTP
- VBHTP
- Swift
- iOS

## Objectives

In this chapter you'll:

- Store the user's Twitter searches on the device using `NSUserDefaults`.
- Use the Social Framework to allow users to share saved searches with friends.
- Synchronize key–value pair data across devices via iCloud.
- Test iCloud synchronization.
- Use the **Master-Detail Application** template.
- Use a `UISplitViewController` and `UINavigationController`s to support apps that display one or two view controllers based on the device and its orientation.
- Transition between view controllers with storyboard segues.
- Use Swift's `Array` and `Dictionary` collections.
- Create `UIActivityViewController`s to display dialogs in response to user interactions.
- Display web content in a `UIWebView`.

# 4.1 Introduction

Twitter's search mechanism makes it easy to follow the trending topics being discussed by the 270+ million monthly active Twitter users.[1] Searches can be fine tuned using Twitter's *search operators* (we overview several of these in Section 4.2), often resulting in lengthy search strings that are time consuming and cumbersome to enter on an iOS device. The **Twitter® Searches** app saves your favorite Twitter search queries with short tag names that are easy to remember (Fig. 4.1(a)). You can then touch the tag names representing these saved searches to view Twitter search results—enabling you to quickly and easily follow tweets on your favorite topics (Fig. 4.1(b)).

---

1. `https://about.twitter.com/company.`

a) App with tagged searches displayed in a `UITableView`    b) App after user touches the "**Deitel**" cell

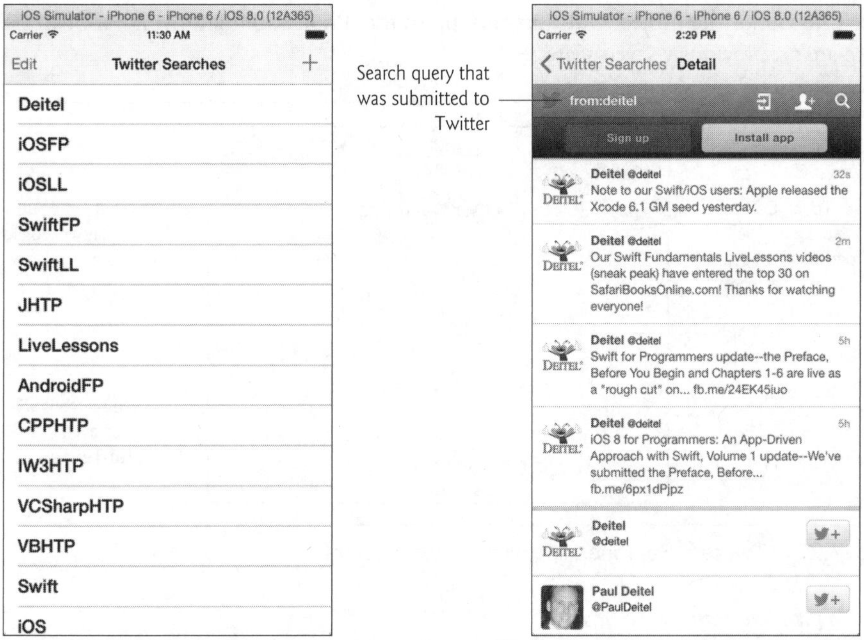

Search query that
was submitted to
Twitter

**Fig. 4.1** | Twitter® Searches app.

Your favorite searches are saved *locally* on the device, so they're available each time you launch the app. They're also saved to iCloud if you've configured an iCloud account on your device—you're prompted to do this when you first set up your device. **iCloud** allows you to store data such as app settings, music, photos, videos, documents and e-mail in the cloud and syncs the data to all of your iOS devices that use the same iCloud account. You can then access and modify that data from *any* of your iOS devices. You can also sync data with Mac OS X apps. The **Twitter® Searches** app uses iCloud to sync your favorite searches across your iOS devices.

First, you'll test-drive the app. Then we'll overview the technologies used to build it. Next, you'll design the static part of the app's UI using Interface Builder. This app also dynamically displays dialog boxes for adding, editing and sharing searches. We'll present the app's complete source code and walk through the code introducing additional Swift features.

# 4.2  Test-Driving the App

## *Opening the Completed Application*

Locate the folder on your Mac where you extracted the book's examples as specified in the Before You Begin section. Open the `TwitterSearches` folder and double click `Twit-terSearches.xcodeproj` to open the project in Xcode.

*Running the App*
Choose **iPhone 6 Simulator** from the **Scheme** selector on the Xcode toolbar, then run the app. This builds the project and runs the app in the iPhone Simulator (Fig. 4.2). Initially there are no previously saved searches.

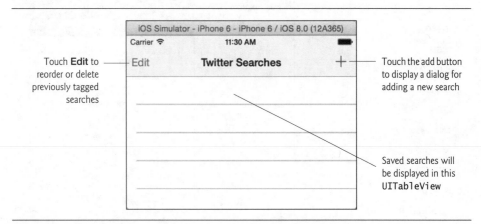

**Fig. 4.2** | **Twitter®** **Searches** app when it first executes.

*Adding a New Favorite Search*
To add a new search, touch the add (+) button in the app's top-right corner to display the **Add Search** dialog (Fig. 4.3). Touch its top text field, then enter `from:deitel` as the search query—the `from:` operator locates tweets from a specified Twitter account (`deitel` corresponds to the account `@deitel`). Figure 4.4 shows several popular Twitter search operators—a complete list can be found at

```
http://bit.ly/TwitterSearchOperators
```

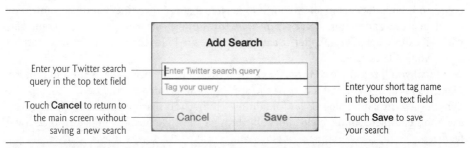

**Fig. 4.3** | **Add Search** dialog that appears when user touches the app's add (+) button.

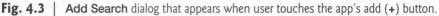

| Example | Finds tweets containing |
|---|---|
| `deitel iOS8` | Implicit logical and operator—finds tweets containing `deitel` *and* `iOS8`. |
| `deitel OR iOS8` | Logical `OR` operator—finds tweets containing `deitel` *or* `iOS8` *or both.* |

**Fig. 4.4** | Some Twitter search operators. (Part 1 of 2.)

| Example | Finds tweets containing |
|---|---|
| `"how to program"` | String in quotes("")—finds tweets containing the exact phrase "how to program". |
| `deitel ?` | ? (question mark)—finds tweets asking questions about `deitel`. |
| `deitel -eugene` | - (minus sign)—finds tweets containing `deitel` but not eugene. |
| `deitel :)` | :) (happy face)—finds *positive attitude* tweets containing `deitel`. |
| `deitel :(` | :( (sad face)—finds *negative attitude* tweets containing `deitel`. |
| `since:2012-08-12` | since:—finds tweets that occurred *on or after* the specified date, which must be in the form YYYY-MM-DD. |
| `from:deitel` | from:—finds tweets from the Twitter account @deitel. |
| `to:deitel` | to:—finds tweets to the Twitter account @deitel. |

**Fig. 4.4** | Some Twitter search operators. (Part 2 of 2.)

Touch the bottom text field, then enter `Deitel` as the tag for the search query. This will be the *short name* displayed in the master list of tags. The **Add Search** dialog should now appear as in Fig. 4.5. Next, touch **Save** to save the search. The app's main screen now appears as shown in Fig. 4.6. For simplicity, touching **Save** with either or both of the text fields empty simply dismisses the dialog.

Touch **Save** to save your search

**Fig. 4.5** | **Add Search** dialog after user enters a search query and a tag.

**Fig. 4.6** | Main screen after saving a search.

*Viewing Twitter Search Results*

To view the search results, touch the **Deitel** tag in the app's main screen. A new screen slides in from the right side of the simulator (or device) and displays the search results in a UIWebView, which acts like a web browser. The app assembles a URL that represents the search and submits it to Twitter's mobile search web page. Then, Twitter returns the results as a web page that's displayed in the UIWebView—Fig. 4.7 shows a portion of the results that match the specified query. When you're done viewing the results, touch **Twitter Searches** in the navigation bar at the top of the app to return to the app's main screen where you can save more searches, and edit, delete and share previously saved searches.

**Fig. 4.7** | A portion of the search results for the query from:deitel.

*Editing a Search*

You can choose to edit or share a search by *long pressing* (touching and holding your finger on) a search's tag, which displays the **Options** dialog in Fig. 4.8. Touch **Edit** to display the **Edit Search** dialog in Fig. 4.9(a). We allow you to edit only the query, so the tag name is displayed in light gray to indicate that it's not editable. Let's restrict our search to tweets since August 1, 2014. To do so, add since:2014-08-01 to the end of the query (Fig. 4.9(b)) in the top **Text Field**. The since: operator restricts the search results to tweets that occurred *on or after* the specified date (in the form yyyy-mm-dd). Touch **Save** to update the saved search, then view the updated results by touching **Deitel** in the main screen. By default, the results are returned in reverse chronological order, so the most recent tweets are displayed at the top of the web page. Figure 4.10 shows a portion of the results after scrolling to the tweets from August 2014.

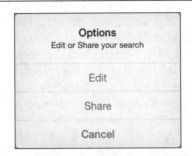

**Fig. 4.8** | **Options** dialog for choosing whether to edit or share an existing search.

a) **Edit Search** dialog showing search to edit    b) Edited search before saving

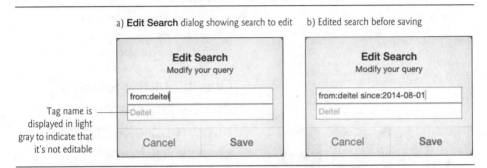

Tag name is displayed in light gray to indicate that it's not editable

**Fig. 4.9** | **Edit Search** dialog for editing an existing search.

**Fig. 4.10** | A portion of the search results for the query `from:deitel since:2014-08-01`.

*Sharing a Search*

The iOS Social Framework enables you to share information from an app via e-mail, SMS, AirDrop (other Apple devices nearby), various social networking sites and more. You can also copy information to the clipboard, print information and save an image to a contact in the **Contacts** app—when that contact calls you, the image will be displayed on the screen.

You can share a favorite search by *long pressing* a search's tag, then selecting **Share** from the **Options** dialog in Fig. 4.8. This displays a sheet of sharing options, which vary based on the content type you're sharing and your device. Fig. 4.11(a) shows the sharing sheet from the app running on our iPhone. The app shares a text representation of the search URL—on our device, this caused iOS to show options for **Message, Mail, Twitter, Facebook** and **Copy**. These options might vary—for example, in China the social network **Weibo** would be displayed. Figure 4.11(b) shows a prepopulated dialog for posting the shared search to Facebook. Facebook, Twitter and Weibo will be displayed only if the user has entered their account login information via the simulator's or device's **Settings** app.

a) Sheet of sharing options

b) Facebook share sheet for the **Deitel** search

**Fig. 4.11** | Sharing a search via Facebook.

### Deleting a Search and Reordering Searches

To delete a search or reorder the searches (perhaps to place your favorites first), touch **Edit** in the upper-left corner of the app's main screen (Fig. 4.2). This places the UITableView into edit mode. Figure 4.12 shows many saved searches in the UITableView in edit mode. If you want to delete a search, touch the ⊖ button to the left of the search's tag to reveal a **Delete** button, which you can then touch to delete the search. You may also delete a search when the UITableView is not in edit mode, by swiping right-to-left to reveal a **Delete** button, which you can then touch to delete the search. Drag the ≡ icon to the right of a search to move that search to a new location on the UITableView. Remove your finger from the screen (or release the mouse in the simulator) to complete the move operation. Touching **Done** exits edit mode for the UITableView.

**Fig. 4.12** | `UITableView` in edit mode.

### *Testing the App's iCloud Capabilities*

The iOS Simulator now supports iCloud, so you can test this app's iCloud synchronization capabilities either with the simulator or on actual devices. You must be a paid member of the iOS developer program to use the iCloud features and you'll need to build the project with a provisioning profile that supports iCloud. Xcode can set this up for you. Simply click the `TwitterSearches` node at the top of the **Project** explorer, then in the **General** tab of the app's settings, click the **Fix Issue** button in the Identity section.

To see the synchronization in action, sign into iCloud using the same Apple ID on each device or iOS Simulator you use for testing. Apple recommends setting up a separate Apple ID for testing purposes. To sign into iCloud:

1. Open the device's or simulator's **Settings** app and select **iCloud**.

2. Provide your Apple ID and password, then click **Sign In**.

When running the app on a device that's signed into iCloud, the app synchronizes with iCloud each time you add, modify or delete a search. If the app is running on another device that's signed into the same iCloud account, the app will be notified of the changes and update its list of searches accordingly. If the app is not running on another device, when it does so in the future it will be notified of any changes that occurred on other devices since the app last ran on a particular device. Because your app's iCloud changes travel over the Internet between Apple's servers and your devices, there's often a delay before changes on one device appear on another. When running the app in the iOS Simulator, you might need to manually initiate each iCloud sync operation by selecting **Debug > Trigger iCloud Sync**. Section 4.4.1 discusses how to enable iCloud's key–value storage capabilities in your apps.

# 4.3 Technologies Overview

This section introduces the Xcode, Interface Builder and Swift features you'll use to build the Twitter® Searches app.

## 4.3.1 Master-Detail Application Template

The **Master-Detail Application** template creates an app with a UI that displays a *master list* of items in a UITableView (Fig. 4.1(a)) from which a user can choose one item to see its *details* (Fig. 4.1(b))—similar to the built-in Mail and Contacts apps. The *master-list view* is managed by the MasterViewController and the *details view* is managed by the DetailsViewController—both classes are created for you by Xcode when you choose this application template.

For iPhones, the app initially displays the master list. When the user touches an item in the list, the app presents a separate view containing the details—in this app, the results of a Twitter search. For iPads, this template also includes a *split view* that displays differently based on the device's orientation:

- In portrait orientation, the app displays the detail view by default. Touching < Master in the upper-left corner of the screen displays the master list in a window that overlays part of the details view. Touching an item in the master list dismisses it and displays that item's details.

- In landscape orientation, the master list is always displayed at the left of the screen and the detail view is always displayed at the right (though it might be empty). Touching an item in the master list displays its details in the detail view.

The template is preconfigured such that touching the add (+) button in the master view adds to the view's UITableView a cell containing the current date and time—touching such a cell displays that date and time in the details view. After creating the project (Section 4.4.1), you can run the default app to see the template's predefined functionality. For more UITableView details, see Apple's *Table View Programming Guide* at

```
http://bit.ly/iOSTableViewGuide
```

## 4.3.2 Web View—Displaying Web Content in an App

This app uses a **Web View** (class UIWebView) to display the Twitter search results as a web page in the app. This enables the user to remain in the app to see the results, rather than switching to the device's Safari browser app.

## 4.3.3 Swift: Array and Dictionary Collections

This app uses Swift's **Array** and **Dictionary** collections and their Foundation framework counterparts (because most Cocoa Touch classes are written in Objective-C). An Array is a data structure consisting of related data items of the same type. A Dictionary is a collection of key–value pairs in which the keys are unique, but the values need not be, and the values are accessed by key.

We store in an Array the user's list of short tag names that identify saved searches. We use this Array to keep track of the user's preferred order for the searches on the device. When the user moves a search in the app's master list, the app moves the tag name in the Array accordingly.

We store in a `Dictionary` the user's favorite searches as key–value pairs. The keys are the tags the user entered, and the corresponding value for each key is the search-query `String` that the user enters. When the user touches a tag in the app's master list, we use that tag's index to look up the tag in the `Array`, then use the tag to look up the corresponding search query in the `Dictionary`.

### Array *Type Annotations*

A program can declare `Array`s of any type. Often the type can be inferred by the compiler based on the `Array`'s initializer, but you also can specify an `Array`'s type with a type annotation. For example,

```
var tags: Array<String>
```

defines the variable `tags` as type `Array<String>`, which is read as, "Array of `String`." The type in angle brackets (`<` and `>`) is the `Array`'s *element type*. Types like `Array` that specify the types they store or manipulate are **generic types**.

 **Error-Prevention Tip 4.1**

*Arrays are type safe—only values of the declared element type may be placed into the* `Array`*; values of other types result in compilation errors. Similarly, when you get a value from an* `Array`*, the value is guaranteed to be of the* `Array`*'s element type.*

### Shorthand Array *Type Annotations—The Preferred Idiom*

Swift also provides a shorthand for `Array` type annotations. For example,

```
var tags: [String]
```

declares the preceding `Array` `tags` with the element type specified in square brackets, which is the preferred idiom. For the rest of this book, we use this shorthand syntax.

### Dictionary *Type Annotations*

`Dictionary` is also a generic type. For example,

```
var searches: Dictionary<String, String>
```

defines the variable `searches` as type `Dictionary<String, String>`. The first type in angle brackets is the `Dictionary`'s *key type*, and the second is its *value type*—these types can be the same or different. There's also a shorthand for `Dictionary` type annotations. For example,

```
var searches: [String : String]
```

declares the `Dictionary` `searches` with the key and value types specified in square brackets separated by a colon, which is the preferred idiom. For the rest of this book, we use this shorthand syntax.

### Bridging Between Swift and Foundation Framework Types

Recall from Section 3.2.10 that Swift automatically *bridges* between its types and corresponding Foundation framework types. The **Twitter® Searches** app interacts with Cocoa Touch framework classes that manipulate Foundation framework collections **NSArray**, **NSMutableArray**, **NSDictionary** and **NSMutableDictionary**, which correspond to Swift's `Array` and `Dictionary` types.

### Swift's *AnyObject* Type

The Foundation framework collections are *not* generic types—they can store *any* object type, including many different types at the same time. For this reason, when the runtime bridges an NSArray or NSMutableArray to a Swift Array, the Array's type is [AnyObject]. The Swift type **AnyObject** represents an object of any Objective-C or Swift class. Similarly, a bridged NSDictionary's or NSMutableDictionary's type in Swift is [NSObject : AnyObject]. The key type NSObject is the superclass of all iOS Cocoa Touch framework classes. When you know that a Foundation framework collection contains values of a specific type, you can downcast the Swift Array or Dictionary accordingly. For example, if you know an Array of type [AnyObject] contains only NSStrings, you can *downcast* it to type [String], because NSStrings can be bridged to Swift Strings. We'll use such downcasting several times in this app's code. For more details on bridging between Swift and Objective-C types, see Apple's *Using Swift with Cocoa and Objective-C* at:

> http://bit.ly/UsingSwiftWithObjC

## 4.3.4 NSUserDefaults—Local Key–Value Pair Storage for App Settings

iOS contains a *defaults system* for storing a user's app preferences as *key–value pairs* in which each preference has a name (the key) and a corresponding value. Each app has an **NSUserDefaults** object in which the keys are NSStrings. Each key's value can be a built-in type (e.g., Int, Double, etc.), a URL, an object of type NSData, NSString, NSNumber, NSDate, NSArray or NSDictionary, or an object of any Swift type that can be bridged to these Foundation framework types. Swift's numeric and String types, for example, are bridged to NSNumber and NSString. Swift's Array and Dictionary types are bridged to NSArray and NSDictionary—or NSMutableArray and NSMutableDictionary if the context requires a modifiable collection. You'll use the app's NSUserDefaults object to store the user's favorite searches on the device. For more information on NSUserDefaults, see the *Preferences and Settings Programming Guide* in the iOS Developer Library:

> http://bit.ly/iOSPreferencesSettings

Secure data such as usernames and passwords should not be stored in NSUserDefaults—rather, such data should be stored in the keychain. For more information see

> http://bit.ly/iOSKeychain

## 4.3.5 iCloud Key–Value Pair Storage with NSUbiquitousKeyValue-Store

For users who configure iCloud accounts on their devices, this app stores their favorite searches to iCloud as key–value (tag–query) pairs. If they then install the app on other iOS devices that are signed into the same iCloud account, their favorite searches sync across their devices so that the favorite searches are available on every device. You'll use an object of class **NSUbiquitousKeyValueStore** to save each new tag–query pair to iCloud, to update modified tag–query pairs in iCloud and to remove deleted pairs. In addition, you'll register with **NSNotificationCenter** to receive notifications from iCloud when the user's favorite searches change on another device. For more information on iCloud, see the *iCloud Design Guide* in the iOS Developer Library:

> http://bit.ly/iCloudDesignGuide

According to Apple's documentation for class `NSUbiquitousKeyValueStore`, if the key–value pairs stored in iCloud are essential to your app's functionality when the user is offline, you should also store the key–value pairs locally using the defaults system. For this reason, we use both `NSUserDefaults` and `NSUbiquitousKeyValueStore` in this app.

### 4.3.6 Social Framework

The Social Framework allows you to build apps that integrate with social networking services, without using separate code or frameworks for each. You can use the Social framework to post status updates and images, and retrieve the user's *activity feeds*—the streams of updates the user receives from other people in a social network. For more information, see the *Social Framework Reference* in the iOS Developer Library at

```
http://bit.ly/iOSSocialFramework
```

Social functionality also is integrated in many built-in iOS apps (Fig. 4.13).

| App | Functionality |
|---|---|
| Safari | Share a web page. |
| Maps | Share location information. |
| Camera | Share photos. |
| Contacts | With your permission, contact information for Facebook friends can be added to the Contacts app. |
| Game Center | Post high scores. |
| Siri | Tell Siri to post to Facebook, Twitter, etc. |
| Notifications | Social network notices appear in Notifications. |

**Fig. 4.13** | Some social networking functionality in native iOS apps.

In this app, you'll use the Social Framework indirectly. When the user chooses to share a search, the app will create a `UIActivityViewController`, which presents a sheet of sharing options to the user (Fig. 4.11(a)). When the user selects a particular sharing option, the `UIActivityViewController` will display an appropriate user interface containing the search query that the user chose to share. When the user completes the sharing operation, the `UIActivityViewController` is dismissed and the app returns to the main screen.

### 4.3.7 Model-View-Controller (MVC) Design Pattern

Most iOS apps adhere to the **Model-View-Controller (MVC) design pattern**, which separates an app's data (contained in the model) from the graphical presentation (the view) and the app's logic (the controller). You'll create the **Twitter® Searches** app's views using Interface Builder; you'll construct the app's controllers in Swift. This app's data storage and retrieval is managed by a separate model class, which we call `Model` (Section 4.5). The model typically represents data in a database or in the cloud. In this app, it will represent data stored locally in the app's `NSUserDefaults` and on iCloud with `NSUbiquitousKeyValueStore`. A key benefit of the MVC design pattern is that you can modify the model, view and controller independently of each other. Some of this app's interactions between the model, view and controller include:

- When the user adds a new search through the UI (the view), the `MasterViewController` (the controller) receives events from the UI, then interacts with the model to store the search.

- When the user deletes a search, the `MasterViewController` receives events from the UI, then updates the view and the model accordingly.

- When the user edits a search, the `MasterViewController` receives events from the UI, then updates the model accordingly.

- When the user touches a tag to display the search results, the `MasterViewController` receives events from the UI, then gets the corresponding search from the model and passes that information to the `DetailViewController` for presentation on the screen.

- When the user attempts to share a search, the `MasterViewController` receives events from the UI, gets the corresponding search from the model and passes its URL to a `UIActivityViewController`, which displays the sharing options.

- When the model receives an external notification that changes occurred to the app's iCloud data, the model updates the data locally, then notifies the `MasterViewController`, which, in turn, updates the master list of searches in the view.

To learn more about MVC in iOS, see Apple's discussion at

```
http://bit.ly/iOSMVC
```

## 4.3.8 Swift: Conforming to Protocols

A **protocol** is similar to the concept of an "interface" in many other object-oriented languages. A Swift type can adopt (implement) a protocol and implement its requirements—any type that does so is said to *conform to* that protocol. A class can inherit from at most one superclass, but can adopt *many* protocols. After the colon (:) in a class's definition, you place a comma-separated list in which the superclass (if any) appears first (otherwise an error occurs), followed by the protocols to which the class conforms. Swift's `struct` and `enum` types do not support inheritance, but they can adopt protocols.

Swift protocols are more flexible than protocols in Objective-C and interfaces in other object-oriented languages. Swift protocols may contain instance properties and methods, type properties and methods (similar to `static` class members in other object-oriented languages), overloaded operators and subscripts (which allow a class to support subscripting like Swift's `Array` and `Dictionary` types).

In this app, when the model receives iCloud changes, it must notify the `MasterViewController` so that it can update the `UITableView`. Our model will define a protocol with a single method that the `MasterViewController` will adopt, then implement that method. When the iCloud changes occur, the model will call that `MasterViewController` method so that it can update the UI accordingly. As you'll see, when the `MasterViewController` creates the app's model object, we'll pass its initializer a reference to the `MasterViewController`, which the model will store and use to call the protocol's method.

We'll discuss protocol features in more detail as we encounter them. For additional information, see the Protocols chapter of Apple's *Swift Programming Language* book at

```
http://bit.ly/SwiftProtocols
```

### 4.3.9 Swift: Exposing Methods to Cocoa Touch Libraries

Many Cocoa Touch classes have methods that require as arguments other methods—for example, when you register for notifications, you provide a method to call in response to the notification. Such arguments are known as **selectors** (Section 4.5.3). A Swift method provided as a selector must be defined in a subclass of an Objective-C class or you must precede the Swift method with the **@objc** attribute, which you'll see in Fig. 4.22.

### 4.3.10 UIAlertController for Alert Dialogs

The app uses a **UIAlertController** (new in iOS 8) to display an appropriate dialog when the user

- touches the add (+) button to add a search
- *long presses* a tag to choose between editing and sharing a search
- decides to edit a search

As you'll see in Section 4.6.4, you can add **UIAlertActions** to a UIAlertController to display buttons and to specify what the app should do when the user touches them. You can also add UITextFields to a UIAlertController to accept user input, which you'll do to receive a new search from the user and to allow the user to edit an existing search.

### 4.3.11 UILongPressGestureRecognizer

iOS supports many gestures (Chapter 1). To recognize these gestures and respond to them in your app, you can use objects of various **UIGestureRecognizer** subclasses. When the user *long presses* a tag in the master-list view, this app responds by displaying options for editing and sharing the search. To respond to this event, the app registers a **UILongPress-GestureRecognizer** for every cell in the UITableView.

### 4.3.12 iOS Design Patterns Used in This App

This section discusses several commonly used iOS design patterns. To learn more about these design patterns, see

```
http://bit.ly/iOSDesignPatterns
```

*Delegation*
The design pattern described in Section 4.3.8 is known as the **Delegation design pattern** and is commonly used in iOS. In this pattern, one object performs a task on behalf of another—for iCloud notifications in this app, the MasterViewController updates the view *on behalf of* the model. For UIWebView notifications, the object that conforms to the UIWebViewDelegate protocol performs tasks on behalf of the UIWebView, such as responding when a web page starts and finishes loading.

*Target-Action*
The **Target-Action design pattern** is frequently used in event handling. The *target* is an object that will respond to an event that occurred. The *action* is the method that will be called on the target object to handle the event. For example, in the **Tip Calculator** app, the target of the UISlider and UITextField events was the ViewController and the action was its calculateTip method. The **Master-Detail Application** template used in this **Twitter®**

**Searches** app preconfigures various event handlers using this design pattern. We'll configure others programmatically to respond to actions the user takes in the app's dialogs.

*Observer*

We'll use the **Observer design pattern** to respond to notifications from iCloud when the app's data changes on another device. In this pattern, a **subject object** notifies **observer objects** based on state changes in the subject object. The listeners *observe* these state changes by *registering to listen for* the subject object's notifications. When such a notification occurs, the observer objects are notified via calls to observer methods that were specified when the observer registered to receive those notification. In this app, the Model listens for notifications of changes to the app's iCloud data. When such changes occur, the iCloud server (i.e., the subject object) sends notifications and the Model's updateSearches method (Section 4.5.8) is called. As you'll see in Section 4.5.3, we specify that this method should be called when the iCloud notifications occur.

### 4.3.13 Swift: External Parameter Names

By default, the parameter names you specify in a function definition are *local* to that function—they're used only in the body of that function to access the function's argument values. You can also define **external parameter names** that the caller is required to use when a function is called—recall from Section 3.6.6 that this is the case for all the arguments to an initializer and any arguments after the first argument in a method call. This can help make the meaning of each argument clear to the programmer calling the function.

For each parameter, you can specify both an external name and a local name by placing the external name before the local name as in

> *externalName localName*: *type*

or you can specify that the local parameter name should also be used as the external parameter name by placing a # before the local parameter name, as in

> # *localName*: *type*

We'll use both ways to specify external parameter names in the Model class (Section 4.5).

*Changing the Default External Parameter Names for an Initializer or Method*

By default, the names of an initializer's parameters and the names of a method's parameters for every parameter after the first are *both* local *and* external parameter names. You can customize a method's or initializer's external parameter names by specifying your own, using the syntax discussed above for functions.

*Requiring an External Parameter Name for a Method's First Argument*

You can require a method's caller to provide an external parameter name for the method's first argument. To do so, simply precede the parameter name with # to use the local parameter name as the external parameter name or specify an external parameter name.

*Passing Method Arguments Without Parameter Names*

You can allow a method to be called without labeling its arguments by using an underscore (_) for each parameter's external name, as in

> _ *localName*: *type*

## 4.3.14 Swift: Closures

A **closure** is an *anonymous function* (i.e., a function with no name)—a shorthand notation that's typically used to:

- pass a function to another function or method.

- return a function from a function or method.

- assign a function to a variable that can be used to call the function at a later time.

Closures support all the features of Swift functions. In fact, a function is actually a closure that has a name. As you'll see in this app, methods of various Cocoa Touch classes can receive as arguments the names of methods to execute (such as event handlers), and closures are a convenient and concise way to specify such arguments.

For cases in which a function's parameter types and return type can be inferred from the context in which it's called, you can define the function as an inline **closure expression**.

The rest of this section discusses basic closure expressions in the context of the Swift Array type's sorted method, which sorts an Array's elements into the order specified by its argument. The argument is a function or closure that receives two arguments of the Array's type and returns a Bool indicating whether they're in sorted order. Method sorted passes two Array elements at a time to this function and uses the result to determine the sort order for those elements. This process occurs repeatedly until the Array is sorted.

### Fully Typed Closure Expression

A *fully typed closure expression* is one in which the parameter types and return type (if there is one) are explicitly specified. The general syntax for such an expression is:

```
{(ParameterList) -> ReturnType in
    Statements
}
```

The in keyword introduces the closure's body. For example, if you have an Array of Strings, you could pass the following closure expression to Array method sorted:

```
{(s1: String, s2: String) -> Bool in
    return s1 < s2
}
```

The preceding closure expression determines whether s1 is *less than* s2, so that Array method sorted can sort the elements in *ascending* order.

If the closure expression contains only one statement, then you can write it as a single line:

```
{(ParameterList) -> ReturnType in Statement}
```

To define a closure expression with an empty parameter list, specify the parameter list as empty parentheses.

### Closure Expression with Inferred Types

Often, the compiler can infer a closure expression's parameter types and return types from the context in which the closure expression is defined. For an Array of Strings, if you pass the closure expression

```
{s1, s2 in return s1 < s2}
```

to sorted, the compiler infers the parameter types and return type from the context. For an Array of Strings, the argument that has the type

```
(String, String) -> Bool
```

The types of parameters s1 and s2 are inferred as String and the return type is inferred as Bool. When using type inference, the parentheses around the parameter list are not required.

***Closure Expression with Inferred Types and an Implicit* return**
When the closure expression's body contains *only* a return statement, the return keyword may be omitted, as in the closure expression:

```
{s1, s2 in s1 < s2}
```

In this case, the result of the expression s1 < s2 is *implicitly* returned. Again, the compiler infers the parameters' types and the return type from the context in which the closure is used.

***Closure Expression with Shorthand Argument Names***
You may omit a closure expression's parameter list by using Swift's *shorthand argument names*—$0 represents the first argument, $1 the second, etc. The closure expression:

```
{$0 < $1}
```

determines whether the first argument ($0) is *less than* the second ($1), so that Array method sorted can sort the elements in *ascending* order.

***Using an Operator Function as a Closure Expression***
The shortest form of closure is an *operator function*—a function that defines how an operator works for a given type. For example, the String type provides operator functions for the operators < and > to determine whether one String is less than or greater than another. These functions each take two String parameters (the left and right operands of the comparison operator) and return a Bool—exactly the type of function that Array method sorted requires as its argument that determines the sorting order. The closure < helps sort the elements in *ascending* order. Two elements of the Array at a time are used as the operands of the < operator, which returns true if they're in sorted order.

# 4.4  Building the App's UI

In this section, you'll create a **Master-Detail Application** project, then make some minor changes to the autogenerated UI.

## 4.4.1 Creating the Project

Begin by creating a new **Master-Detail Application** iOS project. Specify the following settings in the **Choose options for your new project** sheet:

- **Product Name:** TwitterSearches.

- **Organization Name:** Deitel and Associates, Inc.—for this app you should use your own organization name if you want to test the iCloud features.

- **Company Identifier:** com.deitel—To test this app's iCloud features, you'll need your own company identifier. You'll also need to be a paid member of the iOS Developer Program.

- **Language**—Swift.

- **Devices: Universal**—Recall that the **Master-Detail Application** template is designed to support iPhones and iPads in portrait and landscape orientation.

After specifying the settings, click **Next**, indicate where you'd like to save your project and click **Create** to create the project.

### iCloud Settings for Paid iOS Developer Program Members

In the project settings displayed in the Xcode **Editor** area, select the **Capabilities** tab, then under **iCloud**, click the **OFF** toggle to switch it to **ON** and enable iCloud support, then ensure that **Key-value storage** is checked and save the project. As you did in prior apps, specify the app's icons in the asset catalog (Section 2.5.2).

## 4.4.2 Examining the Default Master-Detail Application

When you use the **Master-Detail Application** template, Xcode creates classes for the master view (`MasterViewController`, Section 4.6) and the detail view (`DetailViewController`, Section 4.7) and generates default code for adding items to the master list and displaying the details of a given item when the user touches it. You should run the default app generated by Xcode to see its basic functionality. Xcode also creates a storyboard (Fig. 4.14) containing a scene for each of the view controllers and several other view controllers for managing how the master and detail views are presented, based on the device's size and orientation.

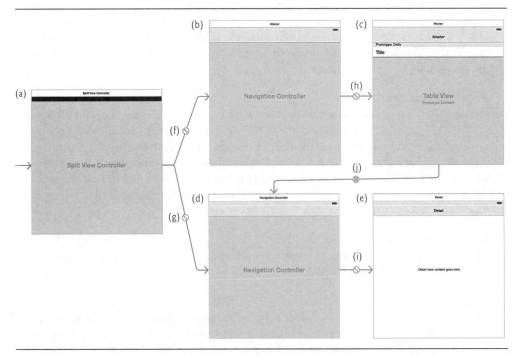

**Fig. 4.14** | Default storyboard (zoomed out 50%) for an app based on the **Master-Detail Application** template.

This section presents the autogenerated storyboard and its built-in navigation between the views. We've labeled elements of the screen capture with the letters *(a)* through *(j)* in Fig. 4.14 for discussion purposes. In Section 4.6, we discuss class `Master-ViewController`. As we encounter methods and statements that Xcode generated for the **Master-Detail Application** template, we discuss them and any modifications we made.

### *UISplitViewController*

Figure 4.14(a) is a `UISplitViewController`, which displays one or two view controllers, depending on the device and its orientation:

- On an iPhone—other than the iPhone 6 Plus in landscape orientation—either the master or detail view controller is displayed at a given time.

- On an iPhone 6 Plus or iPad in landscape orientation, the master view controller appears on the left in a 320-pixel-wide column and the detail view controller on the right, filling the remaining space.

- On an iPad in portrait orientation, the detail view controller fills the entire screen and when the master list is displayed it appears in a 320-pixel-wide popover window that partially covers the detail view controller.

The `UISplitViewController` manages all of this for you.

### *UINavigationController*

Figure 4.14(b) and (d) are `UINavigationControllers` that help users navigate between view controllers. Each `UINavigationController` manages a stack data structure of view controllers for easy navigation back to prior screens. When a new view controller is added to a `UINavigationController`, it's placed at the top of the stack. When the user navigates back to the prior screen, the `UINavigationController` removes the view controller from the screen and pops it from the stack.

### *UITableViewController*

Figure 4.14(c) is a `UITableViewController`, which consists of a `UITableView` for displaying a list of items. In the storyboard, the `UITableViewController` also contains a **prototype cell** that defines the layout of each cell's contents. The default prototype cell contains just a `UILabel` for displaying text. One of the prototype cell's properties is its **Reuse Identifier** (set to "Cell" by default), which is used in the code to create a new `UITableView` cell based on the prototype cell. A more complex `UITableView` can have multiple prototypes for different types of cells, each with its own **Reuse Identifier**.

### *UIViewController*

Figure 4.14(e) is a `UIViewController` that, by default, contains only a `UILabel`. You'll delete that and replace it with a `UIWebView` in Section 4.4.3.

### *Relationship Lines*

Figure 4.14(f)–(i) show the relationships between the view controllers. From the `UISplit-ViewController`, the line (f) leads to the `UINavigationController` that manages the master list view and the line (g) leads to the `UINavigationController` that manages the detail view. Similarly, there are relationship lines between the `UINavigationControllers` and the view controllers that they manage.

*Segues*

Figure 4.14(j) shows a **segue**, which indicates a transition from one view controller to another. Each segue has a case-sensitive **Identifier** property, which you can view in the **Attributes** inspector by selecting the segue. By default, the segue in this storyboard has the **Identifier** "showDetail". There can be many segues in a storyboard and each should have a different **Identifier**. Segue Strings are used in code to determine which segue is about to be performed so you can, for example, pass data to another view for display. They can also be used to programmatically initiate transitions.

### 4.4.3 Configuring the Master and Detail Views

In this section, you'll modify the default details view to remove the UILabel and add a UIWebView:

1. In the **Project** navigator, select Main.storyboard to display the storyboard.

2. In part (c) of Fig. 4.14, double click **Master** just above the **Prototype Cells** and type Twitter Searches.

3. In the storyboard, ensure that the **Document Outline** is displayed (Section 2.5.8).

4. In the **Document Outline**, expand the **Detail Scene** node and select **Detail**. The storyboard will scroll to the **Detail Scene**.

5. Within the **Detail Scene**, delete the UILabel containing "Detail view content goes here" and its corresponding @IBOutlet named detailDescriptionLabel in class DetailViewController.

6. In the **Utilities** area, drag a **Web View** (an object of class UIWebView) from the **Objects** library onto the **Detail Scene** and use the guide lines to ensure that it's centered horizontally and vertically in the scene.

7. Open the **Assistant** editor, then create an @IBOutlet for the **Web View** by *control* dragging from the **Web View** in the storyboard to between lines 11 and 12 in class DetailViewController. Name the outlet webView and click **Connect**.

### 4.4.4 Creating class Model

As we've mentioned, this app uses a class named Model to manage the app's locally stored data and its iCloud data. To create the file for this class:

1. In Xcode, select **File > New > File...** to display a sheet containing the file templates.

2. Under **iOS**, select the **Source** category, then select **Swift File** and click **Next**.

3. Name the file Model.swift and click **Create**.

The new file is placed in the project's TwitterSearches group (recall that this is Xcode's term for a folder) and opens immediately in the **Editor** area.

## 4.5  Class Model

In this section we discuss the app's Model class. The file Model.swift that you created in Section 4.4.4 initially contains code that was autogenerated by Xcode. You should replace that code with the code in Sections 4.5.1—4.5.10.

## 4.5.1 ModelDelegate Protocol

Lines 7–9 (Fig. 4.15) define the ModelDelegate protocol. A protocol definition begins with the keyword **protocol** followed by the protocol's type name and braces that delimit the protocol's body. In this case, the body describes only a modelDataChanged method with no parameters and no return value. In Section 4.6.1, class MasterViewController will define the method to update the UITableView. We'll define a property of type ModelDelegate in class Model and initialize it with a reference to the MasterViewController. When the model data changes, the Model will use this reference to call modelDataChanged on the MasterViewController.

```
1   // Model.swift
2   // Manages the Twitter Searches data
3   import Foundation
4
5   // delegate protocol that enables Model to
6   // notify controller when the data changes
7   protocol ModelDelegate {
8       func modelDataChanged()
9   }
10
```

**Fig. 4.15** | ModelDelegate protocol.

## 4.5.2 Model Properties

Figure 4.16 begins class Model's definition and defines its private properties. Swift provides three **access modifiers**—public, internal and private. Class members that are declared **public** can be reused in other apps—for example, you can use the Swift Standard Library's public features in your apps. Class members declared **internal** can be used only by other code in the *same project*—internal is the default access specifier if you do not provide one. Class members declared **private** can be used only in the *file* in which they're defined.

**Software Engineering Observation 4.1**

*If a type should be reusable in other apps, declare it* public. *If it's used only in the files of the project in which it's defined, use the default access* internal. *If it's used only in the file in which it's defined, declare it* private.

Swift's access modifiers are different from those in related object-oriented programming languages such as Java, C# and C++. For the complete rules of access modifiers, see the Access Control chapter of Apple's *Swift Programming Language* book at

http://bit.ly/SwiftAccessControl

```
11   // manages the saved searches
12   class Model {
13       // keys used for storing app's data in app's NSUserDefaults
14       private let pairsKey = "TwitterSearchesKVPairs" // for tag-query pairs
15       private let tagsKey = "TwitterSearchesKeyOrder" // for tags
```

**Fig. 4.16** | Model class properties. (Part 1 of 2.)

```
16
17    private var searches: [String: String] = [:] // stores tag-query pairs
18    private var tags: [String] = [] // stores tags in user-specified order
19
20    private let delegate: ModelDelegate // delegate is MasterViewController
21
```

**Fig. 4.16** | Model class properties. (Part 2 of 2.)

The constants pairsKey and tagsKey are used to store and retrieve copies of this app's searches and tags in the app's NSUserDefaults. Variable searches is a Dictionary with keys and values of type String—the keys are the user's short tag names and the values are the corresponding Twitter search queries. The Dictionary is initialized with the Dictionary literal [:], which represents an *empty* Dictionary. Variable tags is an Array of Strings that stores the user's short tag names in the order that they appear in the master list's UITableView. The Array is initialized with the Array literal [], which represents an *empty* Array. The constant delegate is a reference to the Model's ModelDelegate—the MasterViewController, as you'll see in Section 4.6.

### 4.5.3 Model Initializer and synchronize Method

Figure 4.17 defines class Model's initializer. Swift does not provide default values for a class's properties—you *must* initialize them before they're used. Lines 17–18 (Fig. 4.16) explicitly specify default values. Each class you declare can optionally provide one or more *initializers* that can be used to initialize a new object of a class. In fact, Swift requires an initializer call for *every* object that's created, so this is the ideal point to initialize an object's properties. For a class that does not explicitly define any initializers, the compiler defines a **default initializer** (with no parameters) that initializes the class's properties to the default values specified in their definitions. Initializers are like *constructors* in most other object-oriented programming languages.

```
22    // initializes the Model
23    init(delegate: ModelDelegate) {
24        self.delegate = delegate
25
26        // get the NSUserDefaults object for the app
27        let userDefaults = NSUserDefaults.standardUserDefaults()
28
29        // get Dictionary of the app's tag-query pairs
30        if let pairs = userDefaults.dictionaryForKey(pairsKey) {
31            self.searches = pairs as [String : String]
32        }
33
34        // get Array with the app's tag order
35        if let tags = userDefaults.arrayForKey(tagsKey) {
36            self.tags = tags as [String]
37        }
38
```

**Fig. 4.17** | Model initializer and synchronize method. (Part 1 of 2.)

```
39            // register to iCloud change notifications
40            NSNotificationCenter.defaultCenter().addObserver(self,
41                selector: "updateSearches:",
42                name: NSUbiquitousKeyValueStoreDidChangeExternallyNotification,
43                object: NSUbiquitousKeyValueStore.defaultStore())
44        }
45
46        // called by view controller to synchronize model after it's created
47        func synchronize() {
48            NSUbiquitousKeyValueStore.defaultStore().synchronize()
49        }
50
```

**Fig. 4.17** | Model initializer and synchronize method. (Part 2 of 2.)

### Initializer Definition

Each initializer's name is the keyword **init**, which is followed by an optional comma-separated list of parameters in parentheses and a body enclosed in braces. The parentheses enclosing the parameters are required, even if the initializer has no parameters. The argument values passed to the initializer's parameters initialize the properties for a particular object of the class. The initializer for class Model provides a delegate parameter of type ModelDelegate for initializing the class's private delegate property. Each parameter must be declared with a type annotation specifying the type of the expected argument.

### Parameters Are Local to Their Defining Initializer, Method or Function

Parameters are local to the initializer, method or function in which they're defined, as are any variables and constants defined in the body of an initializer, method or function. If a local variable or constant has the same name as a property, using the variable or constant in the body refers to the local variable or constant rather than the property—the local identifier *shadows* the property. You use the keyword **self** (like this in other popular object-oriented languages) to refer to the shadowed property explicitly, as shown on the left side of line 24, which stores the value of the parameter delegate in the class's property named delegate.

### There's No Default Initializer in a Class That Declares an Initializer

If you declare an initializer for a class, the compiler will *not* create a *default initializer* for that class. In that case, you will not be able to create a Model object with the expression Model()—unless the custom initializer you declare takes *no* parameters.

### Getting the App's *NSUserDefaults*—Optional Binding

Next, line 27 gets the app's default NSUserDefaults object by calling class method **standardUserDefaults**. The returned object is used to get the app's user defaults from the device. We store the user's favorite searches as a Dictionary in the NSUserDefaults object. Lines 30–32 use NSUserDefaults method **dictionaryForKey** to get an optional NSDictionary associated with the key pairsKey (line 14 of Fig. 4.16) and, if it exists, assign it to the class's searches property. The return type is an optional, because it's possible that there is no such key in the NSUserDefaults. The first time the app executes, the key pairsKey will not yet exist in the app's NSUserDefaults, so dictionaryForKey will return nil. On subsequent executions, a `Dictionary` of type [NSObject : AnyObject] will be returned.

Line 30 uses **optional binding** to determine whether a non-`nil` value was returned by `dictionaryForKey` and, if so, bind it to the constant `pairs` (defined with `let`). If `dictionaryForKey` returns `nil`, the optional does not contain a value and the `if` condition evaluates to `false`—in this case, the `searches` property maintains its default empty `Dictionary`. Otherwise, since we use only keys and values of type `String` in this app, line 31 uses the Swift cast operator **as** to cast the returned `NSDictionary` to a Swift `Dictionary` of type [String : String].

Lines 35–37 perform similar tasks to get an `NSArray` of the user's tags from the `NSUserDefaults`. Method **arrayForKey** returns an optional `Array` of type [AnyObject]. If the return value is non-`nil`, line 36 casts the result to a Swift `Array` of `String`s and assigns it to class `Model`'s `tags` property.

### Registering for iCloud Notifications

In an app that uses iCloud storage, you need to *register* to receive notifications when the app's data changes on another device (lines 40–43). Each iCloud-enabled app has a default `NSUbiquitousKeyValueStore`—returned by class method **defaultStore** (line 43)—for manipulating key–value pairs that iCloud should sync across devices.

To receive change notifications, you register the object that will respond to the notifications with the app's default `NSNotificationCenter` object, which is returned by `NSNotificationCenter` class method **defaultCenter** (line 40). `NSNotificationCenter` method **addObserver** registers an *observer* to receive notifications. Its arguments are:

- An `AnyObject` object—the observer object that will receive a method call when the specified notification occurs. In this case, we use `self`—i.e., the `Model`. Recall that the type `AnyObject` can represent an object of any class. An observer is similar to a delegate.

- A selector—specifies the observer's method that will receive notification messages. In this case, those messages will call method `updateSearches:`. In Objective-C, the keyword **@selector** is used to pass a method name as data in a method call. In Swift, you simply specify a `String` and Swift converts it to an object of Swift type **Selector** for you. The method that you specify as the selector must receive an `NSNotification`, and the colon following the method name indicates that the method receives one argument. For more information on selectors and interacting with classes implemented in Objective-C, see

```
http://bit.ly/SwiftSelectors
```

- An `NSString`—the name of the notification we're registering to receive—in this app, **NSUbiquitousKeyValueStoreDidChangeExternallyNotification**. This predefined `String` is the name of the iCloud notification for key–value store changes—iCloud can also store documents and database records.

- An `AnyObject` object representing the notification's sender—in this case, the `NSUbiquitousKeyValueStore` object returned by `defaultStore`, which represents the iCloud key–value store. If this argument is `nil`, you'll receive notifications from *any* object that posts a matching notification.

After registering to receive iCloud change notifications, Model's initializer returns to its caller—the MasterViewController in this app. The MasterViewController then uses its Model reference to call method synchronize (lines 47–49). This method calls NSUbiquitousKeyValueStore method **synchronize** on the default key–value store to ensure that the app's local tag–query pairs are in sync with those on the user's other devices.

We placed the call to method synchronize in a separate Model method to avoid a subtle bug that might occur as a result of asynchronous iCloud notifications. If you call NSUbiquitousKeyValueStore method synchronize in the Model's initializer, it's possible that the Model will receive iCloud notifications *before* the Model reference in the MasterViewController is assigned the new Model object. In that case, the Model would tell the MasterViewController (its delegate) that the Model data changed. This, in turn, would cause the MasterViewController to attempt to call Model methods using a Model reference that's nil and the program would crash.

### 4.5.4 Methods tagAtIndex, queryForTag and queryForTagAtIndex, and Property count

The methods and property in Fig. 4.18 are used by the MasterViewController to get various information from the model:

- Method tagAtIndex (lines 52–54) returns the String for the tag at the specified index in the tags Array.

- Method queryForTag (lines 57–59) returns a String? (an optional String) representing the query for the specified tag. The return value is an optional because it's possible that the searches Dictionary does not contain a query for a specific tag. Line 58 uses Dictionary subscripting notation in which you specify the key in square brackets following the Dictionary's name and the corresponding value is returned—or nil if the key is not in the Dictionary.

- Method queryForTagAtIndex (lines 62–64) returns a String? representing the query for the tag at the specified index in the tags Array.

- The computed property count (lines 67–69) returns number of items in the tags Array—this will be used by the MasterViewController to specify the number of rows in the UITableView. This is a computed property because it does not store any data; rather, it manipulates the data of a stored property.

```
51      // returns the tag at the specified index
52      func tagAtIndex(index: Int) -> String {
53          return tags[index]
54      }
55
56      // returns the query String for a given tag
57      func queryForTag(tag: String) -> String? {
58          return searches[tag]
59      }
60
```

**Fig. 4.18** | Methods tagAtIndex, queryForTag and queryForTagAtIndex, and property count. (Part 1 of 2.)

```
61      // returns the query String for the tag at a given index
62      func queryForTagAtIndex(index: Int) -> String? {
63          return searches[tags[index]]
64      }
65
66      // returns the number of tags
67      var count: Int {
68          return tags.count
69      }
70
```

**Fig. 4.18** | Methods tagAtIndex, queryForTag and queryForTagAtIndex, and property count. (Part 2 of 2.)

### 4.5.5 Method deleteSearchAtIndex

Method deleteSearchAtIndex (Fig. 4.19) deletes a search from the app's NSUserDefaults and the iCloud key–value store. The method first removes the deleted search from the searches Dictionary (line 74) by calling **removeValueForKey**. Next, line 75 removes the tag from the tags Array by calling **removeAtIndex**. Then line 76 calls our method updateUserDefaults (Section 4.5.7) to update both the tags and searches in the app's NSUserDefaults. Finally, lines 79–80 get the app's NSUbiquitousKeyValueStore object and use its **removeObjectForKey** method to remove the corresponding key–value pair from iCloud—if the user has this app installed on other devices that use the same iCloud account, those other devices will eventually receive a change notification.

```
71      // deletes the tag from tags Array, and the corresponding
72      // tag-query pair from searches iCloud
73      func deleteSearchAtIndex(index: Int) {
74          searches.removeValueForKey(tags[index])
75          let removedTag = tags.removeAtIndex(index)
76          updateUserDefaults(updateTags: true, updateSearches: true)
77
78          // remove search from iCloud
79          let keyValueStore = NSUbiquitousKeyValueStore.defaultStore()
80          keyValueStore.removeObjectForKey(removedTag)
81      }
82
```

**Fig. 4.19** | Method deleteSearchAtIndex.

### 4.5.6 Method moveTagAtIndex

Method moveTagAtIndex (Fig. 4.20) is called by MasterViewController when the user moves a search tag to a different position in the UITableView. Line 85 removes the tag from the tags Array, then line 86 inserts it at its new position and line 87 stores the updated tags Array in the app's NSUserDefaults. Note that method moveTagAtIndex uses a customized external parameter name (toDestinationIndex).

```
83    // reorders tags Array when user moves tag in controller's UITableView
84    func moveTagAtIndex(oldIndex: Int, toDestinationIndex newIndex: Int) {
85        let temp = tags.removeAtIndex(oldIndex)
86        tags.insert(temp, atIndex: newIndex)
87        updateUserDefaults(updateTags: true, updateSearches: false)
88    }
89
```

**Fig. 4.20** | Method moveTagAtIndex.

### 4.5.7 Method updateUserDefaults

Method updateUserDefaults (Fig. 4.21) stores updated versions of the tags Array and searches Dictionary in the app's NSUserDefaults. In some cases, only one or the other needs to be updated, so these updates are made only if the corresponding parameters are true. Line 92 gets the app's NSUserDefaults object. If the tags Array needs to be stored, line 95 calls NSUserDefaults method **setObject**, which receives as its first argument the object to store (tags) and as its second argument the key (tagsKey) that's used to store and retrieve that object. Line 99 performs the same task for the searches Dictionary if the searches need to be updated. Finally, line 102 calls NSUserDefaults method **synchronize** to immediately store the changes on the device. Note that method updateUserDefaults requires its first parameter to be named in method calls—as indicated by the # before the parameter name. We do this so the purpose of each Bool argument is clear.

```
90     // update user defaults with current searches and tags collections
91     func updateUserDefaults(# updateTags: Bool, updateSearches: Bool) {
92         let userDefaults = NSUserDefaults.standardUserDefaults()
93
94         if updateTags {
95             userDefaults.setObject(tags, forKey: tagsKey)
96         }
97
98         if updateSearches {
99             userDefaults.setObject(searches, forKey: pairsKey)
100        }
101
102        userDefaults.synchronize() // force immediate save to device
103    }
104
```

**Fig. 4.21** | Method updateUserDefaults.

#### *When to Synchronize NSUserDefaults*

In this app, we update the user defaults after every change to the tags Array or searches Dictionary—this guarantees that any changes are stored immediately. However, this is not necessary in most apps because synchronize is called periodically by the system. Instead you can call synchronize when the app is sent to the background—for example, when the user presses the device's home button or answers a phone call.

For application-level events, each app you create contains a class named **AppDelegate**, which is located in the project's AppDelegate.swift file. This class implements methods of the **UIApplicationDelegate** protocol, which are called by iOS in response to events such as the user launching the app, the app being placed into the background because another app is now in the foreground and the app returning from the background. Each method contains comments generated by Xcode that specify when the method is called and what it's typically used to accomplish.

When an app enters the background, there's a chance that it will never return to the foreground—for example, the user could terminate the app manually or iOS could terminate the app to free system resources for other apps to use. For this reason, you could place the call to the NSUserDefaults synchronize in the method **applicationDidEnterBackground**. This would ensure that the app saves the data to the device, just in case it never returns to the foreground.

### 4.5.8 Method updateSearches

Method updateSearches (Fig. 4.22) is called each time the Model receives an iCloud notification regarding key–value store changes. The NSNotification parameter contains an NSDictionary (bridged to a Dictionary) of information pertaining to the notification.

```
105     // update or delete searches when iCloud changes occur
106     @objc func updateSearches(notification: NSNotification) {
107         if let userInfo = notification.userInfo {
108             // check reason for change and update accordingly
109             if let reason = userInfo[
110                 NSUbiquitousKeyValueStoreChangeReasonKey] as NSNumber? {
111
112                 // if changes occurred on another device
113                 if reason.integerValue ==
114                     NSUbiquitousKeyValueStoreServerChange ||
115                     reason.integerValue ==
116                     NSUbiquitousKeyValueStoreInitialSyncChange {
117
118                     performUpdates(userInfo) // update searches
119                 }
120             }
121         }
122     }
123
```

**Fig. 4.22** | Method updateSearches.

In this app, the Dictionary contains a key–value pair representing the reason for the notification. Line 107 obtains the Dictionary from the notification via NSNotification property **userInfo**. Lines 109–110 use the expression:

```
userInfo[NSUbiquitousKeyValueStoreChangeReasonKey]
```

to get an AnyObject indicating the reason for the iCloud change—in this case, the AnyObject is an NSNumber. If this expression is not nil, we cast it to an NSNumber?. Next, lines 113–116 get the integer value of reason and determine whether the notification indicates a change in the app's key–value pairs in iCloud (NSUbiquitousKeyValueStoreServer-Change) or an initial synchronization request (NSUbiquitousKeyValueStoreInitialSync-

Change). In either case, line 118 calls method `performUpdates` (passing the `userInfo` `NSDictionary`) to update the app's locally stored key–value pairs accordingly.

### 4.5.9 Method performUpdates

Method `performUpdates` (Fig. 4.23) gets the iCloud changes and uses them to update the locally stored data. The `userInfo` `Dictionary` received from `updateSearches` also contains an `NSArray` of the keys that changed in iCloud. Changes occur when the user adds a new search, updates an existing search or deletes a search. Lines 127–128 get the changed keys object, then line 129 casts it to an `Array` of `String`s (the keys are `String`s) for use in this method. Line 132 gets the `NSUbiquitousKeyValueStore` object so we can locate the corresponding values, if any.

```
124     // add, update or delete searches based on iCloud changes
125     func performUpdates(userInfo: [NSObject : AnyObject?]) {
126         // get changed keys NSArray; convert to [String]
127         let changedKeysObject =
128             userInfo[NSUbiquitousKeyValueStoreChangedKeysKey]
129         let changedKeys = changedKeysObject as [String]
130
131         // get NSUbiquitousKeyValueStore for updating
132         let keyValueStore = NSUbiquitousKeyValueStore.defaultStore()
133
134         // update searches based on iCloud changes
135         for key in changedKeys {
136             if let query = keyValueStore.stringForKey(key) {
137                 saveQuery(query, forTag: key, syncToCloud: false)
138             } else {
139                 searches.removeValueForKey(key)
140                 tags = tags.filter{$0 != key}
141                 updateUserDefaults(updateTags: true, updateSearches: true)
142             }
143
144             delegate.modelDataChanged() // update the view
145         }
146     }
147
```

**Fig. 4.23** | Method `performUpdates`.

Next, lines 135–145 iterate through the changed keys. For each, line 136 obtains the key's corresponding value from the `NSUbiquitousKeyValueStore`. If the value (`query`) is not `nil`, then the key–value pair represents either a new search or an update of an existing search, so line 137 calls method `saveQuery` (Section 4.5.10) to store the key–value pair locally. The last argument is `false` because we don't need to sync this key–value pair to iCloud—we just received it from there.

If the key's value is `nil`, the search was deleted on another device, so we must delete it here, too. Line 139 removes the key from the `searches` `Dictionary`. Line 140 uses the `Array` method **filter** to remove the key from the `tags` `Array`. This method returns an `Array` containing only the elements that satisfy a condition, which is typically represented as a closure (Section 4.3.14). In this case, the only argument to the method is the closure, so we use Swift's trailing closure syntax, which eliminates the parentheses from the method call. Line 141 calls method `updateUserDefaults` (Section 4.5.7) to update the searches and tags in the app's `NSUserDefaults`. Finally, line 144 calls the `ModelDelegate`'s `model-DataChanged` method—as you'll see, this enables the `MasterViewController` to update its `UITableView` with any changes.

### 4.5.10 Method `saveQuery`

Method `saveQuery` (Fig. 4.24) first updates the `searches` `Dictionary` by calling method **`updateValue`** (line 153), which receives a value and a key. If the key exists, the method updates the value and returns the *old* value; otherwise, the method inserts the key–value pair and returns `nil`. For a new search, line 156 inserts its tag at index 0 of the `tags` `Array` and line 157 updates both the `tags` and `searches` in the `NSUserDefaults`. For an existing search, line 159 updates only the `searches` in the `NSUserDefaults`. Finally, if `saveQuery`'s sync argument is `true`, lines 164–165 use `NSUbiquitousKeyValueStore` method **`setOb-ject`** to store the new search in the app's iCloud key–value store.

```
148        // save a tag-query pair
149        func saveQuery(query: String, forTag tag: String,
150            syncToCloud sync: Bool) {
151
152            // Dictionary method updateValue returns nil if key is new
153            let oldValue = searches.updateValue(query, forKey: tag)
154
155            if oldValue == nil {
156                tags.insert(tag, atIndex: 0) // store search tag
157                updateUserDefaults(updateTags: true, updateSearches: true)
158            } else {
159                updateUserDefaults(updateTags: false, updateSearches: true)
160            }
161
162            // if sync is true, add tag-query pair to iCloud
163            if sync {
164                NSUbiquitousKeyValueStore.defaultStore().setObject(
165                    query, forKey: tag)
166            }
167        }
168    }
```

**Fig. 4.24** | Method `saveQuery`.

## 4.6  Class `MasterViewController`

Sections 4.6.1—4.6.9 discuss the app's `MasterViewController` class.

### 4.6.1 MasterViewController Properties and `modelDataChanged` Method

Figure 4.15 contains the beginning of class `MasterViewController`, its properties and its `modelDataChanged` method. Lines 6–7 begin the class definition. The class inherits from class `UITableViewController` and conforms to the `ModelDelegate` protocol (defined in

Fig. 4.15) and `UIGestureRecognizerDelegate` protocols. Conforming to the `ModelDelegate` protocol enables `MasterViewController` to perform a task when the model's data changes. Conforming to the `UIGestureRecognizerDelegate` protocol enables the `MasterViewController` to respond to the *long press* event that allows a user to choose between editing and sharing a search.

```
1   // MasterViewController.swift
2   // Handles user interactions with the master list view
3   // and interacts with the Model
4   import UIKit
5
6   class MasterViewController: UITableViewController,
7      ModelDelegate, UIGestureRecognizerDelegate {
8
9      // DetailViewController contains UIWebView to display search results
10     var detailViewController: DetailViewController? = nil
11     let twitterSearchURL = "http://mobile.twitter.com/search/?q="
12
13     var model: Model! = nil // manages the app's data
14
15     // conform to ModelDelegate protocol; updates view when model changes
16     func modelDataChanged() {
17         tableView.reloadData() // reload the UITableView
18     }
19
```

**Fig. 4.25** | `MasterViewController` properties and `modelDataChanged` method.

### *UITableViewController*

Superclass `UITableViewController` provides the basic functionality for a view containing a `UITableView` that displays a list of items. Throughout class `MasterViewController` are several overridden methods inherited from `UITableViewController`. These were autogenerated by Xcode when it created class `MasterViewController`, and we modified several of them to provide functionality specific to the **Twitter®** Searches app.

### *Properties*

The `detailViewController` property (line 10) was generated by code as part of the **Master-Detail Application** template. Code generated by Xcode in method `viewDidLoad` (Section 4.6.3) initializes this property. The `String` constant `twitterSearchURL` (line 11) contains the URL for Twitter's mobile search page. We'll concatenate the user's search query strings to this URL. The `Model` reference (line 13) enables the `MasterViewController` to communicate with the `Model` for managing the app's data. Recall that all Swift properties must be initialized. The `model` property is declared as an implicitly unwrapped optional because it needs to be initialized *after* the `MasterViewController` has already been created. An implicitly unwrapped optional can temporarily be initialized to `nil`, then assigned an actual object at a later time (as we'll do in `viewDidLoad`).

### *ModelDelegate Protocol and Method modelDataChanged*

Recall that the `ModelDelegate` protocol (Section 4.5.1) declares one method (`modelDataChanged`), which class `MasterViewController` implements at lines 16–18. Line 17 uses the inherited property `tableView` to invoke `UITableView` method `reloadData`, which updates the `UITableView` based on the list of tags currently stored in the `Model`.

### 4.6.2 Method awakeFromNib

Xcode autogenerated the method `awakeFromNib` (Fig. 4.26). It configures the popover that displays the `UITableView` when the app executes on an iPad in portrait orientation. Once a storyboard's objects have been created, method `awakeFromNib` is called on any of the objects that implement it, making this a good location to perform additional configuration when objects from a storyboard must already exist.

```
20      // configure size
21      override func awakeFromNib() {
22          super.awakeFromNib()
23          if UIDevice.currentDevice().userInterfaceIdiom == .Pad {
24              self.clearsSelectionOnViewWillAppear = false
25              self.preferredContentSize =
26                  CGSize(width: 320.0, height: 600.0)
27          }
28      }
29
```

**Fig. 4.26** | Method `awakeFromNib`.

Class **UIDevice** is used to determine information about the device on which an app is running. Line 23 determines whether the app is running on an iPad. `UIDevice` property **userInterfaceIdiom** is a value of enum type `UIUserInterfaceIdiom`, which contains constants `Pad` (for iPads) or `Phone` (for iPhones). Because Swift knows that the right operand of `==` must match the type on the left, it can infer that the right operand must be a constant of type `UIUserInterfaceIdiom`. The notation `.Pad` is shorthand for `UIUserInterfaceIdiom.Pad`.

Line 24 indicates that the `UITableViewController` will not clear the current selection in the `UITableView` when it's displayed, and lines 25–26 specify the preferred size of the `UITableView` when it's displayed on an iPad in portrait orientation.

### 4.6.3 Overridden UIViewController Method viewDidLoad and Method addButtonPressed

As you learned in Section 3.6.5, you typically override method `viewDidLoad` (Fig. 4.27) to define tasks that can be performed only *after* the view has been initialized. Xcode autogenerated most of the code in this method (with the exception of lines 47–48).

```
30      // called after the view loads for further UI configuration
31      override func viewDidLoad() {
32          super.viewDidLoad()
33
34          // set up left and right UIBarButtonItems
35          self.navigationItem.leftBarButtonItem = self.editButtonItem()
```

**Fig. 4.27** | Overridden `UIViewController` method `viewDidLoad`. (Part 1 of 2.)

```
36        let addButton = UIBarButtonItem(barButtonSystemItem: .Add,
37            target: self, action: "addButtonPressed:")
38        self.navigationItem.rightBarButtonItem = addButton
39
40        if let split = self.splitViewController {
41            let controllers = split.viewControllers
42            self.detailViewController =
43                controllers[controllers.count-1].topViewController as?
44                    DetailViewController
45        }
46
47        model = Model(delegate: self) // create the Model
48        model.synchronize() // tell model to sync its data
49    }
50
51    // displays a UIAlertController to obtain new search from user
52    func addButtonPressed(sender: AnyObject) {
53        displayAddEditSearchAlert(isNew: true, index: nil)
54    }
55
```

**Fig. 4.27** | Overridden UIViewController method viewDidLoad. (Part 2 of 2.)

Line 35 displays a preconfigured **Edit** UIBarButtonItem at the left side of the navigation bar above the UITableView. When the user touches **Edit**, the UITableView enters edit mode and the UIBarButtonItem's text changes to **Done**.

Lines 36–37 create an add (**+**) UIBarButtonItem that the user touches to add a new search. When you create an app using the **Master-Detail Application** template, Xcode configures the add button to call a method named insertNewItem. We renamed that method to addButtonPressed (lines 52–54) and reimplemented it to call a method that displays a dialog for adding a new search. The UIBarButtonItem initializer receives three arguments:

- a UIBarButtonSystemItem enum constant indicating which icon to display

- a target object that receives a method call when the user touches the UIBarButtonItem, and

- a String specifying the Selector—the method that will be called when the user touches the UIBarButtonItems.

Line 38 displays the add button at the right side of the navigation bar.

Lines 40–45 of the autogenerated code initialize MasterViewController's detailViewController property if the UISplitViewController is currently expanded—that is, both the MasterViewController and DetailViewController are displayed because the app is running on an iPad in landscape orientation. If so, line 41 gets the Array of UIViewControllers from the SplitViewController. When the UISplitViewController is expanded, the first element is the MasterViewController and the second is the DetailViewController. Lines 42–44 cast the second element to type DetailViewController.

*Creating the Model*
Line 47 creates the Model object that manages the app's data, passing self (the MasterViewController) as the Model's delegate argument. Recall that the Model notifies its

`ModelDelegate` when the data changes. After the `Model` is created, line 48 calls the `Model`'s `synchronize` method, which synchronizes the `Model` with the app's iCloud data.

### 4.6.4 Methods `tableViewCellLongPressed` and `displayLong-PressOptions`

In the test drive, you saw that you can *long press* a cell to choose whether to edit the corresponding search query or share the search. Method `tableViewCellLongPressed` (Fig. 4.28, lines 57–67) is called to respond to the *long press* gesture. As you'll see in Fig. 4.34, this method is registered as a gesture handler for each `UITableView` cell. Lines 59–60 determine whether the method was called because a *long press* gesture began and whether the `UITableView` is currently in editing mode. If it is, we do not want to process the *long press* gesture; otherwise, the dialog that allows the user to edit or share a search would be displayed when the user tries to move a cell. If the `UITableView` is not in editing mode, line 61 gets the `UITableViewCell` on which the user long pressed. Line 63 then gets the `NSIndexPath` for that cell and we pass the cell's index to method `displayLong-PressOptions`.

```
56    // handles long press for editing or sharing a search
57    func tableViewCellLongPressed(
58        sender: UILongPressGestureRecognizer) {
59        if sender.state == UIGestureRecognizerState.Began &&
60            !tableView.editing {
61            let cell = sender.view as UITableViewCell // get cell
62
63            if let indexPath = tableView.indexPathForCell(cell) {
64                displayLongPressOptions(indexPath.row)
65            }
66        }
67    }
68
69    // displays the edit/share options
70    func displayLongPressOptions(row: Int) {
71        // create UIAlertController for user input
72        let alertController = UIAlertController(title: "Options",
73            message: "Edit or Share your search",
74            preferredStyle: UIAlertControllerStyle.Alert)
75
76        // create Cancel action
77        let cancelAction = UIAlertAction(title: "Cancel",
78            style: UIAlertActionStyle.Cancel, handler: nil)
79        alertController.addAction(cancelAction)
80
81        let editAction = UIAlertAction(title: "Edit",
82            style: UIAlertActionStyle.Default,
83            handler: {(action) in
84                self.displayAddEditSearchAlert(isNew: false, index: row)})
85        alertController.addAction(editAction)
```

**Fig. 4.28** | Methods `tableViewCellLongPressed` and `displayLongPressOptions`. (Part 1 of 2.)

```
86
87              let shareAction = UIAlertAction(title: "Share",
88                  style: UIAlertActionStyle.Default,
89                  handler: {(action) in self.shareSearch(row)})
90              alertController.addAction(shareAction)
91              presentViewController(alertController, animated: true,
92                  completion: nil)
93          }
94
```

**Fig. 4.28** | Methods `tableViewCellLongPressed` and `displayLongPressOptions`. (Part 2 of 2.)

### Creating a *UIAlertController*

Method `displayLongPressOptions` (lines 70–93) uses class `UIAlertController` to create a dialog containing options to edit a search, share a search or cancel. Lines 72–74 create the `UIAlertController` with three arguments to its initializer:

- `title`—a `String` that's displayed at the top of the dialog.

- `message`—a `String` that's displayed above the dialog's options.

- `preferredStyle`—a `UIAlertControllerStyle` constant indicating what type of alert should be displayed—in this case, we use `Alert`, which displays a dialog box, but you can also specify an `ActionSheet` that slides over the view.

Lines 77–92 create three **UIAlertActions** that represent the options to display in the dialog and what to do if the user selects each option. The `UIAlertAction` initializer receives three arguments:

- `title`—the `String` to display for the option's `UIButton`.

- `style`—a `UIAlertActionStyle` constant indicating the style of the `UIButton`.

- `handler`—an event handler that receives a `UIAlertAction`.

### Creating the Cancel *UIAlertAction*

Lines 77–79 create the **Cancel** `UIAlertAction` and add it to the `UIAlertController`. This action automatically appears last in the dialog's list of option buttons. By default, touching the **Cancel** action (which has the style `UIAlertActionStyle.Cancel`) dismisses the dialog, so we specify this action's `handler` as `nil`.

### Creating the Edit *UIAlertAction*

Lines 81–85 create the **Edit** `UIAlertAction` with the style `UIAlertActionStyle.Default` (a standard button) and add it to the `UIAlertController`. For this option's `handler`, we provide a closure that receives one parameter, which Swift infers to be of type `UIAlertAction`, based on the context. When the user touches this action's `UIButton`, line 84 calls `MasterViewController`'s `displayAddEditSearch` method (Section 4.6.5). As you'll see, this method's first argument (`false`) indicates that we're editing an existing search. The second argument indicates the index of the search—for editing, we use this to look up the corresponding query. Note the use of `self` in line 84—this is required in a closure when referring to the containing class's members.

*Creating the Share `UIAlertAction`*
Lines 87–92 create the **Share** `UIAlertAction` with the style `UIAlertActionStyle.De-`
`fault` and add it to the `UIAlertController`. For this option's `handler`, we provide a closure that calls `MasterViewController`'s `shareSearch` method (Section 4.6.6), which
displays sharing options.

*Displaying the `UIAlertController`*
Lines 91–92 call inherited method `presentViewController` to display the `UIAlertCon-`
`troller`. The first argument is the `UIViewController` to display, the second indicates
whether iOS should use animation when displaying the `UIViewController`, and the last
specifies a method to execute once the `UIViewController` is displayed. This method (or
closure; Section 4.3.14) receives no parameters and does not return a value. Specifying `nil`
indicates that we don't need to perform an additional task once the `UIViewController` is
displayed.

## 4.6.5 Method `displayAddEditSearchAlert`

When the user chooses to add a new search or edit an existing one, method `displayAdd-`
`EditSearch` (Fig. 4.29) displays an appropriate `UIAlertController` based on the method's
first argument. This dialog provides `UITextFields` for receiving user input. Lines 98–101
create the `UIAlertController`. If the search is new, the dialog's `title` will be "Add Search"
(line 99) and the `message` will be empty (line 100) because we'll provide text in the `UIText-`
`Fields` with instructions for the user. If the search is being edited, the dialog's `title` will be
"Edit Search" (line 99) and the `message` will be "Modify your query" (line 100).

```
95     // displays add/edit dialog
96     func displayAddEditSearchAlert(# isNew: Bool, index: Int?) {
97         // create UIAlertController for user input
98         let alertController = UIAlertController(
99             title: isNew ? "Add Search" : "Edit Search",
100            message: isNew ? "" : "Modify your query",
101            preferredStyle: UIAlertControllerStyle.Alert)
102
103        // create UITextFields in which user can enter a new search
104        alertController.addTextFieldWithConfigurationHandler(
105            {(textField) in
106                if isNew {
107                    textField.placeholder = "Enter Twitter search query"
108                } else {
109                    textField.text = self.model.queryForTagAtIndex(index!)
110                }
111            })
112
113        alertController.addTextFieldWithConfigurationHandler(
114            {(textField) in
115                if isNew {
116                    textField.placeholder = "Tag your query"
117                } else {
118                    textField.text = self.model.tagAtIndex(index!)
```

**Fig. 4.29** | Method `displayAddEditSearchAlert`. (Part 1 of 2.)

```
119                         textField.enabled = false
120                         textField.textColor = UIColor.lightGrayColor()
121                     }
122                 })
123
124             // create Cancel action
125             let cancelAction = UIAlertAction(title: "Cancel",
126                 style: UIAlertActionStyle.Cancel, handler: nil)
127             alertController.addAction(cancelAction)
128
129             let saveAction = UIAlertAction(title: "Save",
130                 style: UIAlertActionStyle.Default,
131                 handler: {(action) in
132                     let query =
133                         (alertController.textFields?[0] as UITextField).text
134                     let tag =
135                         (alertController.textFields?[1] as UITextField).text
136
137                     // ensure query and tag are not empty
138                     if !query.isEmpty && !tag.isEmpty {
139                         self.model.saveQuery(
140                             query, forTag: tag, syncToCloud: true)
141
142                         if isNew {
143                             let indexPath =
144                                 NSIndexPath(forRow: 0, inSection: 0)
145                             self.tableView.insertRowsAtIndexPaths([indexPath],
146                                 withRowAnimation: .Automatic)
147                         }
148                     }
149             })
150             alertController.addAction(saveAction)
151
152             presentViewController(alertController, animated: true,
153                 completion: nil)
154         }
155
```

**Fig. 4.29** | Method displayAddEditSearchAlert. (Part 2 of 2.)

### Adding *UITextFields* to a *UIAlertController*

Lines 104–111 and 113–122 add UITextFields for receiving user input. UIAlertController method **addTextFieldWithConfigurationHandler**'s argument is a method or closure that receives a UITextField and does not return a value—this is called to configure the UITextField. In this case, we provide a closure. For a new search, we set the UITextField's **placeholder** text (line 107)—this appears in the UITextField and tells the user to enter a query. When the user enters text, the placeholder disappears. For an existing search, line 109 looks up the corresponding query and assigns it to the UITextField's text property.

In lines 113–122, for a new search we display placeholder text that tells the user to enter a tag. For an existing search, lines 118–120 look up the existing tag and assign it to the UITextField's text property, disable the UITextField (so the user cannot modify the tag's text) and set the UITextField's textColor property to light gray to indicate that the text is not editable. Notice the use of `self` in line 118—when accessing an enclosing class's members in a closure, you must precede each member with the `self` keyword and a dot. Also notice in line 118 the exclamation point in the expression `index!`, which explicitly unwraps the optional `Int` `index`—this will fail at runtime if the `index` parameter is `nil`.

### Creating the Dialog's `UIAlertActions`

Lines 125–127 configure and add this `UIAlertController`'s **Cancel** action. Lines 129–150 configure and add the **Save** action. The `handler` for this action gets the information from the `UITextFields` and stores it in the model, and if the search is new, inserts the new search's cell at the beginning of the `UITableView`.

Lines 132–135 use the `UIAlertController`'s `textFields` property to get references to the `UITextFields`, then obtain their `text` property values. Because `textFields` is an optional `Array` of `AnyObjects`, we must cast each reference to `UITextField` before accessing its `text` property. We also must follow the `textFields` property name with a question mark (?) to unwrap the optional `Array` before accessing its members—the `text-Fields` property is `nil` in `UIAlertControllers` that do not contain `UITextFields`. The expression `textFields?` ensures that the property is not `nil` before continuing. If it is, the entire expression (e.g, lines 133 or 135) evaluates to `nil`.

Line 138 ensures that both the `query` and `tag` `Strings` contain values. If so, lines 139–140 call the `Model`'s `saveQuery` method to save the new or edited search and sync the changes to iCloud.

If the search is new (line 142), we create a new `NSIndexPath` representing index 0 in the `UITableView`'s first (and only) section, then call `UITableView`'s **`insertRowsAtIndexPaths`** method to insert the new cell. This in turn calls a method discussed in Section 4.6.9 to create the cell and display the appropriate tag in it. Lines 152–153 display the `UIAlertController`.

### 4.6.6 Method `shareSearch`

When the user *long presses* a search, then chooses to share it, method `shareSearch` (Fig. 4.30) configures and displays a `UIActivityViewController`. Line 158 creates a message that will be included with the shared data. Lines 159–160 create a `String` representation of the Twitter search URL and query for the shared search. Line 161 places these into an `Array` that's used to initialize the `UIActivityViewController`.

```
156      // displays share sheet
157      func shareSearch(index: Int) {
158          let message = "Check out the results of this Twitter search"
159          let urlString = twitterSearchURL +
160              urlEncodeString(model.queryForTagAtIndex(index)!)
161          let itemsToShare = [message, urlString]
162
163          // create UIActivityViewController so user can share search
164          let activityViewController = UIActivityViewController(
165              activityItems: itemsToShare, applicationActivities: nil)
166          presentViewController(activityViewController,
167              animated: true, completion: nil)
168      }
169
```

**Fig. 4.30** | Method `shareSearch`.

Lines 164–165 create the `UIActivityViewController`. Its initializer receives a non-nil `Array` containing the items to share and an `Array` of `Strings` (possibly `nil`) representing the sharing activities to display—a complete list is located at:

```
http://bit.ly/BuiltInActivityTypes
```

If the second argument is `nil`, the `UIActivityViewController` chooses which activities to display based on the data in the first argument's `Array`. Lines 166–167 display the `UIActivityViewController`.

### 4.6.7 Overridden `UIViewController` Method `prepareForSegue`

Method `prepareForSegue` (Fig. 4.31) was generated by Xcode as part of the **Master-Detail Application** template. This method is called when the app is about to perform the segue from the `MasterViewController` to the `DetailViewController` (to show search results). We modified the method to set the `DetailViewController`'s `detailItem` property to the `NSURL` representing the Twitter search to perform (lines 182–187).

```
170    // called when app is about to seque from
171    // MasterViewController to DetailViewController
172    override func prepareForSegue(segue: UIStoryboardSegue,
173        sender: AnyObject?) {
174
175        if segue.identifier == "showDetail" {
176            if let indexPath = self.tableView.indexPathForSelectedRow() {
177                let controller = (segue.destinationViewController as
178                    UINavigationController).topViewController as
179                        DetailViewController
180
181                // get query String
182                let query =
183                    String(model.queryForTagAtIndex(indexPath.row)!)
184
185                // create NSURL to perform Twitter Search
186                controller.detailItem = NSURL(string: twitterSearchURL +
187                    urlEncodeString(query))
188                controller.navigationItem.leftBarButtonItem =
189                    self.splitViewController?.displayModeButtonItem()
190                controller.navigationItem.leftItemsSupplementBackButton =
191                    true
192            }
193        }
194    }
195
```

**Fig. 4.31** | Overridden `UIViewController` method `prepareForSegue`.

Because a storyboard may contain many segues, line 175 first checks which segue is about to be performed—in this case, the `showDetail` segue, which was configured and named by Xcode as part of the **Master-Detail Application** template. Line 176 gets the `NSIndexPath` for the `UITableView` row that the user touched. Next, lines 177–179 get a reference to the `DetailViewContoller` so we can use it to configure its `detailItem` property (the `NSURL` representing the search).

Lines 188–189 set the `DetailViewController` `navigationItem`'s `leftBarButton-`
`Item` to the result of the `UISplitViewController`'s `displayModeButtonItem` method.
This method returns a `UIBarButtonItem` that's managed by the `UISplitViewController`.
Lines 190–191 specify that the `UIBarButtonItem` configured in lines 188–189 should be
used in addition to a back button, not as a replacement for it. Together, lines 188–191
display different `UIBarButtonItems` based on the device and orientation:

- On an iPhone (except for the iPhone 6 Plus in landscape orientation), this item
displays the **< Twitter Searches** back button to indicate that touching the `UIBar-`
`ButtonItem` returns the user to the `MasterViewController`'s list of searches.

- On an iPad in portrait orientation, this displays the **< Master** back button to indicate that the touching the `UIBarButtonItem` displays the `MasterViewCon-`
`troller`'s list of searches in a popover.

- On an iPad in landscape orientation, nothing is displayed because both the `Mas-`
`terViewController` and the `DetailViewController` are always displayed.

- On an iPhone 6 Plus in landscape orientation, both the `MasterViewController`
and the `DetailViewController` are initially displayed. In this case, the `UIBarBut-`
`tonItem` displays an icon indicating that the user can expand the `DetailViewCon-`
`troller` to fill the entire screen width. At this point, the `UIBarButtonItem` displays
the back button **< Master** to allow the user to redisplay the `MasterViewCon-`
`troller`'s list of searches to the left of the `DetailViewController`.

## 4.6.8 Method `urlEncodeString`

We need to URL encode the query to ensure that special URL characters in the Twitter
query are passed properly to Twitter's search mechanism. This is necessary because the
query entered by the user might contain special URL characters (e.g., :, /, etc.). Method
`urlEncodeString` (Fig. 4.32) uses `NSString` method **stringByAddingPercentEncoding-**
**WithAllowedCharacters** to encode the special URL characters. The argument is an
`NSCharacterSet` containing the characters that should not be encoded—all others are
considered special characters and are encoded accordingly. In this case, the `NSCharacter-`
`Set` specifies the allowed characters in a URL's query substring.

```
196     // returns a URL encoded version of the query String
197     func urlEncodeString(string: String) -> String {
198         return string.stringByAddingPercentEncodingWithAllowedCharacters(
199             NSCharacterSet.URLQueryAllowedCharacterSet())!
200     }
201
```

**Fig. 4.32** | Method `urlEncodeString`.

## 4.6.9 `UITableViewDataSource` Callback Methods

Several inherited `UITableViewController` methods are called by the `UITableView` to populate its cells and determine other information about the corresponding data. These methods
(Figs. 4.33–4.36) are defined in the **UITableViewDataSource** protocol, which `UITable-`
`ViewController` (and thus `MasterViewController`) implements. A `UITableView` gets its

data from its *data source*—in this case, the Model. Xcode generated these methods as part of the **Master-Detail Application** template and we modified them to interact with our Model.

### Determining the Number of Sections and the Number of Rows in Each Section

A UITableView may contain many sections—for example, an alphabetical list might have separate sections for each letter of the alphabet. In this app, all the search tags are displayed in a single section, as specified by the return value (1) of the UITableViewDataSource protocol's **numberOfSectionsInTableView** method (Fig. 4.33, lines 203–206), which is optional for a UITableView with only one section. When the UITableView needs to know the number of rows in one of its sections, it calls the UITableViewDataSource protocol's **tableView** method that receives the UITableView and an Int specifying the section number as arguments (lines 209–212). We return the model's count property value in this case, since all of the saved searches are shown in one section of the table.

```
202    // callback that returns total number of sections in UITableView
203    override func numberOfSectionsInTableView(
204        tableView: UITableView) -> Int {
205        return 1
206    }
207
208    // callback that returns number of rows in the UITableView
209    override func tableView(tableView: UITableView,
210        numberOfRowsInSection section: Int) -> Int {
211        return model.count
212    }
213
```

**Fig. 4.33** | Determining the number of sections and the number of rows in each section.

### Configuring Cells in the UITableView

When the UITableView is about to display a new cell—perhaps because one is scrolling onto the screen or the user added a new item that needs to be displayed—the UITableView calls the **tableView** method in Fig. 4.34 that receives a UITableView and an **NSIndexPath**—an object that represents a cell's index in the UITableView. This method returns a **UITableViewCell** for the specified NSIndexPath. Lines 220–221 create call UITableView's **dequeueReusableCellWithIdentifier** method to get a UITableViewCell from the tableView (lines 220–221). The String "Cell" is the reuse identifier (Section 4.4.2) that specifies the type of cell we want to receive. This method attempts to reuse an existing UITableViewCell (with the specified identifier) which is not in use at the moment, possibly because it's not displayed on the screen—otherwise, it returns a new UITableViewCell. Line 224 sets the text of cell's UILabel to the tag at the corresponding index in the Model's tags Array. The argument to method tagAtIndex—indexPath.row—uses the NSIndexPath's **row** property to get the integer row number.

Lines 227–231 create and configure a UILongPressGestureRecognizer for the cell. Lines 227–228 indicate that when the user *long presses* this cell, the MasterViewController's (self) tableViewCellLongPressed method (Section 4.6.4) will be called. Line 229 specifies the *long press* gesture's minimum duration. Line 230 adds the gesture recognizer to the cell. Finally, line 232 returns the configured cell to the UITableView.

```
214    // callback that returns a configured cell for the given NSIndexPath
215    override func tableView(tableView: UITableView,
216       cellForRowAtIndexPath indexPath: NSIndexPath) ->
217       UITableViewCell {
218
219       // get cell
220       let cell = tableView.dequeueReusableCellWithIdentifier(
221          "Cell", forIndexPath: indexPath) as UITableViewCell
222
223       // set cell label's text to the tag at the specified index
224       cell.textLabel.text = model.tagAtIndex(indexPath.row)
225
226       // set up long press guesture recognizer
227       let longPressGestureRecognizer = UILongPressGestureRecognizer(
228          target: self, action: "tableViewCellLongPressed:")
229       longPressGestureRecognizer.minimumPressDuration = 0.5
230       cell.addGestureRecognizer(longPressGestureRecognizer)
231
232       return cell
233    }
234
```

**Fig. 4.34** | Configuring cells in the UITableView.

### Determining Whether *UITableView* Cells Are Editable and Deleting Cells

The user can enable edit mode for deleting and reordering searches by touching **Edit** above the UITableView. This calls the UITableViewDataSource protocol's **tableView** method at lines 236–239 (Fig. 4.35) that determines whether the cell at a given NSIndexPath is editable. In this app, all the cells are, so this method returns true. If some cells should be editable and others should not, this method can return true or false, accordingly.

```
235    // callback that returns whether a cell is editable
236    override func tableView(tableView: UITableView,
237       canEditRowAtIndexPath indexPath: NSIndexPath) -> Bool {
238       return true // all cells are editable
239    }
240
241    // callback that deletes a row from the UITableView
242    override func tableView(tableView: UITableView,
243       commitEditingStyle editingStyle: UITableViewCellEditingStyle,
244       forRowAtIndexPath indexPath: NSIndexPath) {
245       if editingStyle == .Delete {
246          model.deleteSearchAtIndex(indexPath.row)
247
248          // remove UITableView row
249          tableView.deleteRowsAtIndexPaths(
250             [indexPath], withRowAnimation: .Fade)
251       }
252    }
253
```

**Fig. 4.35** | Determining whether UITableView cells are editable and editing cells.

When the user chooses to delete a cell, the UITableView calls the UITableViewData-Source protocol's **tableView** method at lines 242–252 that receives the UITableView, a constant from the UITableViewCellEditingStyle enum and an NSIndexPath. If the given UITableViewCellEditingStyle is Delete (line 245), the user touched the **Delete** button, so line 246 calls the Model's deleteSearchAtIndex method to remove the tag at index-Path.row. Lines 249–250 then call UITableView's **deleteRowsAtIndexPaths** method to remove the deleted row from tableView.

*Determining Whether **UITableView** Cells Are Movable and Moving Cells*
In the test drive, you saw that when the UITableView is in edit mode, you can reorder the searches. When the user touches **Edit**, the UITableView calls the UITableViewDataSource protocol's **tableView** method at lines 255–258 (Fig. 4.36) to determine whether the cell at a given NSIndexPath is movable. If so, the UITableView displays the ≡ icon so the user can move the cell. In this app, all the cells are movable, so this method simply returns true, but you can return false if a particular cell should not be movable.

When the user chooses to move a cell, the UITableView calls the UITableViewData-Source protocol's **tableView** method at lines 261–267 that receives the UITableView and two NSIndexPaths indicating the cell's original and new locations. You use this method to notify the Model of the change (lines 265–266), so it can reorder the tags in its tags Array accordingly.

```
254      // callback that returns whether cells can be moved
255      override func tableView(tableView: UITableView,
256         canMoveRowAtIndexPath indexPath: NSIndexPath) -> Bool {
257         return true
258      }
259
260      // callback that reorders keys when user moves them in the table
261      override func tableView(tableView: UITableView,
262         moveRowAtIndexPath sourceIndexPath: NSIndexPath,
263         toIndexPath destinationIndexPath: NSIndexPath) {
264         // tell model to reorder tags based on UITableView order
265         model.moveTagAtIndex(sourceIndexPath.row,
266            toDestinationIndex: destinationIndexPath.row)
267      }
268   }
```

**Fig. 4.36** | Determining whether UITableView cells are movable and moving cells.

## 4.7 Class DetailViewController

Figure 4.37 defines class DetailViewController, which inherits from UIViewController and implements the UIWebViewDelegate protocol to respond to messages from the UIWebView that displays the search results. When you created this app using the **Master-Detail Application** template, Xcode autogenerated class DetailViewController and various properties and methods, which we modified or replaced with the code in Fig. 4.37. Line 6 defines the webView @IBOutlet that we used to interact with the UIWebView. We changed the type of the detailItem property to an optional NSURL that represents the Twitter search to perform.

```
1   // DetailViewController.swift
2   // Displays search results for selected query
3   import UIKit
4
5   class DetailViewController: UIViewController, UIWebViewDelegate {
6       @IBOutlet weak var webView: UIWebView! // displays search results
7       var detailItem: NSURL? // URL that will be displayed
8
9       // configure DetailViewController as the webView's delegate
10      override func viewDidLoad() {
11          super.viewDidLoad()
12          webView.delegate = self
13      }
14
15      // after view appears, load search results into webview
16      override func viewDidAppear(animated: Bool) {
17          super.viewDidAppear(animated)
18
19          if let url = self.detailItem {
20              webView.loadRequest(NSURLRequest(URL: url))
21          }
22      }
23
24      // stop page load and hide network activity indicator when
25      // returning to MasterViewController
26      override func viewWillDisappear(animated: Bool) {
27          super.viewWillDisappear(animated)
28          UIApplication.sharedApplication()
29              . networkActivityIndicatorVisible = false
30          webView.stopLoading()
31      }
32
33      // when loading starts, show network activity indicator
34      func webViewDidStartLoad(webView: UIWebView) {
35          UIApplication.sharedApplication()
36              . networkActivityIndicatorVisible = true
37      }
38
39      // hide network activity indicator when page finishes loading
40      func webViewDidFinishLoad(webView: UIWebView) {
41          UIApplication.sharedApplication()
42              . networkActivityIndicatorVisible = false
43      }
44
45      // display static web page if error occurs
46      func webView(webView: UIWebView,
47          didFailLoadWithError error: NSError) {
48          webView.loadHTMLString(
49              "<html><body><p>An error occurred when performing " +
50              "the Twitter search: " + error.description +
51              "</body></html>", baseURL: nil)
52      }
53  }
```

**Fig. 4.37** | DetailViewController private interface and class implementation.

### 4.7.1 Overridden `UIViewController` Method `viewDidLoad`

Method `viewDidLoad` (lines 10–13) is called *after* the view has been initialized. We added line 12, which specifies that the `UIWebView` delegate is `self`—the `DetailViewController` object that conforms to the `UIWebViewDelegate` protocol (line 5).

### 4.7.2 Overridden `UIViewController` Method `viewDidAppear`

Method `viewDidAppear` (lines 16–22) is called once the `DetailViewController` is added to the view hiearchy (the set of views on the screen). At this point, line 19 checks whether the `detailItem` is non-`nil` and, if so, line 20 calls the `UIWebView`'s `loadRequest` method to load the web page represented by the `NSURL`. This method requires an `NSURLRequest`, so line 20 passes the `NSURL` to the `NSURLRequest` initializer to before calling `loadRequest`.

### 4.7.3 Overridden `UIViewController` Method `viewWillDisappear`

Method `viewWillDisappear` (lines 26–31) is called when the `DetailViewController` is about to be removed from the view hierarchy—for example, when the user returns to the master list of searches. When the web page starts loading, we display a network activity indicator in the status bar at the top of the screen, so the user knows that the app is requesting information via the web. If the user returns to the master list of searches while the search results are still loading, we remove that network activity indicator (lines 28–29). Every app has one object of class `UIApplication` that can be used (among other things) to configure the status bar. That object is created for you (in `AppDelegate.swift`) when the app begins executing. Line 28 calls `UIApplication`'s class method `sharedApplication` to get the app's `UIApplication` object. We then set object's `Bool` property `networkActivityIndicator-Visible` property to `false` to remove the network activity indicator from the status bar. When this value is `true`, the network activity indicator spins in the status bar. Line 30 then calls `UIWebView` method `stopLoading` to terminate the current request (if any).

### 4.7.4 `UIWebViewDelegate` Protocol Methods

Line 5 of the class definition indicates that the class conforms to the `UIWebViewDelegate` protocol, which declares several methods:

- `webViewDidStartLoad` (lines 34–37) is called when a `UIWebView` begins loading a URL. Lines 35–36 display the network activity indicator to show that a request is in process.

- `webViewDidFinishLoad` (lines 40–43) is called when a `UIWebView` finishes loading a URL. When the Twitter search results page finishes loading, lines 41–42 remove the network activity indicator from the status bar.

- `webView` (lines 46–52), which receives an `NSError` as its second argument, is called when a web page fails to load properly into a `UIWebView`—for example, if there's no network connection when a request is made, the request will fail and an error will be passed to this method. If an error occurs in this app, we use the `UIWebView`'s `loadHTMLString` method to display HTML containing the `NSError`'s description.

There's also a fourth method that's called when a `UIWebView` is about to load a page. This method receives information indicating what caused the load request—for example, the user touched a hyperlink, submitted a form, touched a forward or back button, reloaded a page, etc.

## 4.8 Wrap-Up

In this chapter, you built the **Twitter® Searches** app for saving potentially lengthy Twitter search queries with short tag names and making it easy for a user to follow trending topics on Twitter.

You used the Xcode **Master-Detail Application** template to create an app containing master list and details views. In the details view, you used a **Web View** (class UIWebView) to display the Twitter search results as a web page in the app.

To store the user's favorite searches as app preferences on a device, you used iOS's defaults system. You learned that each app has an associated object of class NSUserDefaults that stores key–value pairs. You used that object to store a Dictionary containing the favorite and an Array with the search tags in the user's preferred order.

To sync the user's favorite searches across devices, you also stored the favorite searches in iCloud as key–value (tag–query) pairs using the app's NSUbiquitousKeyValueStore object. To receive notifications from iCloud when the user's favorite searches changed on other devices, you used NSNotificationCenter to register the model as a listener for changes in the app's key–value store.

During the app's execution, you stored the app's data using Swift's Array and Dictionary collections. We also discussed the bridging that occurs when objects of the Foundation framework's collections are returned to Swift code.

You used the Social framework to integrate sharing capabilities into the app. A UIActivityViewController presented a sheet of sharing options to the user, then displayed an appropriate sharing user interface based on the user's selection.

You used UIAlertControllers to display dialogs in which the user could add a new search and choose whether to edit or share an existing search. You also used UIAlertActions to define UIButtons the user could touch to dismiss the dialogs, either by canceling them or by performing a specific action.

We discussed Swift protocols. You learned that a protocol describes a set of capabilities that can be implemented by a class, enum or struct. You defined a protocol that the MasterViewController implemented so it could be notified when the Model's data changed. You also used UITableViewDelegate protocol to enable the MasterViewController to interact with the Model to update the app's UITableView, and the UIWebViewDelegate protocol to enable the DetailViewController to perform tasks when the UIWebView began loading a web page, finished loading a web page or encountered an error when attempting to load a web page.

In Chapter 5, you'll build the **Flag Quiz** app. You'll build a storyboard from scratch and you'll use new UI components to provide the answers that the user can select for each quiz question and to specify the quiz's settings. We'll demonstrate outlet collections for manipulating many controls of the same type and use view animations to provide visual indications of incorrect answers. Finally, you'll use iOS's Grand Central Dispatch to schedule tasks for future execution.

# 5

# Flag Quiz App

## UISegmentedControls, UISwitches, Outlet Collections, View Animations, UINavigationController, Segues, NSBundle, Scheduling Tasks with Grand Central Dispatch

### Objectives

In this chapter you'll:

- Use a storyboard, a `UINavigationController`, `UIViewController`s and a segue to design the app's flow through two scenes—the quiz and its settings.
- Display options to the user with `UISegmentedControl`s.
- Use `UISwitch`es to represent options with *on* and *off* states.
- Create outlet collections for interacting with a collection of UI controls of the same type.
- Use random-number generation to vary the flags and guess options displayed each time the app runs.
- Animate a view's `frame` and `alpha` property values to create "shake" and "fade" `UIView` animations.
- Use an `NSBundle` to get a list of the app's image filenames.
- Dynamically create a `UIImage` for each flag in a quiz and display it in a `UIImageView`.
- Schedule a task to execute in the future with Grand Central Dispatch.

# 5.1 Introduction

The **Flag Quiz** app (Fig. 5.1) tests your ability to correctly identify 10 country flags. Initially, the app presents a flag image and guess options representing the possible country answers—one matches the flag and the others are randomly selected, nonduplicated incorrect answers. The app displays your progress throughout the quiz, showing a `UILabel` containing the question number (out of 10) below the current flag image. The guess options are displayed on `UISegmentedControls` (two per control) below the quiz-progress label. Each `UISegmented-Control` presents mutually exclusive options, so only one segment per control can be selected at a time. In this app's logic, you'll allow only one segment to be selected across all the `UISegmentedControls`. By default, the app displays four guess options—Fig. 5.1 shows the app with eight. If you make an incorrect guess, the app uses view animations to shake the flag and gradually fade out the word "Incorrect" (at the bottom of the app) as visual indications of incorrect answers. When you make a correct guess, the app uses iOS's multithreading (to avoid hanging the UI thread) to display the next flag after a two-second delay.

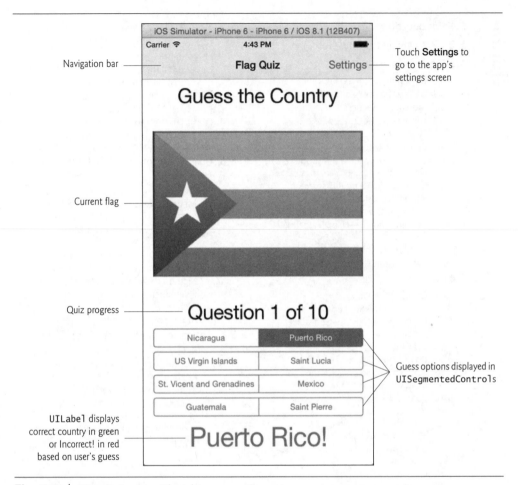

Navigation bar —

Touch **Settings** to
go to the app's
settings screen

Current flag —

Quiz progress —

Guess options displayed in
UISegmentedControls

UILabel displays
correct country in green
or Incorrect! in red
based on user's guess

**Fig. 5.1** | **Flag Quiz** app with eight guess options.

When you touch the **Settings** button on the app's navigation bar, the app presents a
**Settings** screen (Fig. 5.2). Here you can specify the quiz's difficulty by selecting whether
to display two, four, six or eight guess options, and by choosing the world regions whose
flags should be included in the quiz (only North America by default). A UISegmentedControl shows the possibilities for the number of guess options to display. UISwitches that
have "on" and "off" states enable you to select the world regions from which flags should
be selected.

Both the **Flag Quiz** and the **Settings** scenes have collections of controls—four UISegmentedControls and six UISwitches, respectively. In this app, you'll learn how to create
outlet collections containing multiple controls of the same type. As you'll see, these are
implemented as Arrays, so you can use these to iterate through controls, just as you do any
other collection.

First, you'll test-drive the app. Then we'll overview the technologies used to build it.
Next, you'll design the app's GUI. Finally, we'll present the app's complete source code
and walk through the code, emphasizing the app's new features in more detail.

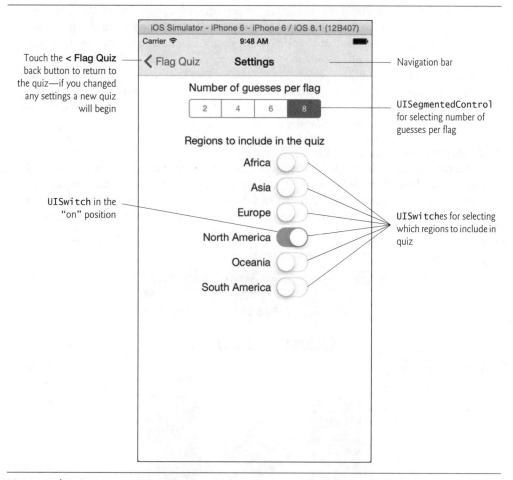

Touch the **< Flag Quiz** back button to return to the quiz—if you changed any settings a new quiz will begin

Navigation bar

`UISegmentedControl` for selecting number of guesses per flag

`UISwitch` in the "on" position

`UISwitch`es for selecting which regions to include in quiz

**Fig. 5.2** | Flag Quiz app **Settings** screen.

## 5.2 Test-Driving the Flag Quiz App

*Opening the Completed Application*
Locate the folder on your Mac where you extracted the book's examples as specified in the Before You Begin section. In the `FlagQuiz` folder, double click `FlagQuiz.xcodeproj` to open the project in Xcode.

*Running the App*
Choose **iPhone 6 Simulator** from the **Scheme** selector on the Xcode toolbar, then run the app. This builds the project and runs the app in the iPhone Simulator (Fig. 5.1).

*Configuring the Quiz*
When you first run the app, the quiz displays four guesses with each flag and selects flags from *only* North America. Touch the **Settings** button in the navigation bar to display the **Settings** screen (Fig. 5.2). To make the quiz more or less challenging, you can change the

number of guesses to display by touching the appropriate segment in the UISegmented-Control. You can touch the UISwitches next to **Africa**, **Asia**, **Europe**, **North America**, **Oceania** (Australia, New Zealand and various South Pacific island nations) and **South America** to toggle them "on" or "off"—only flags from the regions toggled "on" will be included in the quiz. When you complete your changes, touch **< Flag Quiz** in the navigation bar to return to the quiz. If you made any settings changes, a new quiz begins based on the new app settings; otherwise, the prior quiz continues. (This sample app does not inform the user that a new quiz begins—we leave that to you as an exercise.)

*Taking the Quiz: Making a Correct Selection*
Work through the quiz by touching the guess for the country that you think matches each flag. If the choice is correct (Fig. 5.3), the app disables all the guesses and displays the country name in green followed by an exclamation point at the bottom of the screen (Fig. 5.3(b)). After a short delay, the app loads the next flag and displays new guesses.

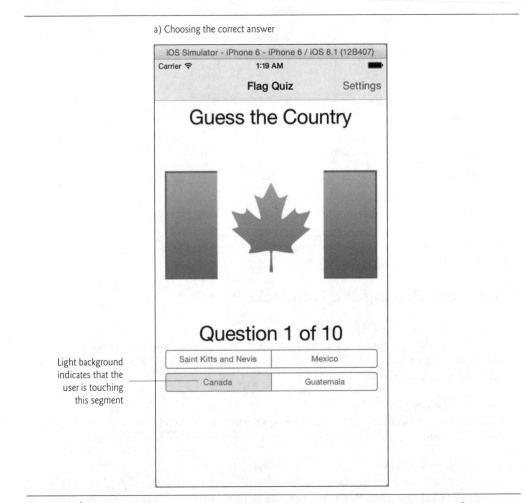

**Fig. 5.3** | User choosing the correct answer and the correct answer displayed. (Part 1 of 2.)

b) Correct answer displayed

Dark background
indicates a
selected segment

Correct answer
displayed in green

All segments are
disabled when the user
guesses correctly, but
the correct guess
remains selected

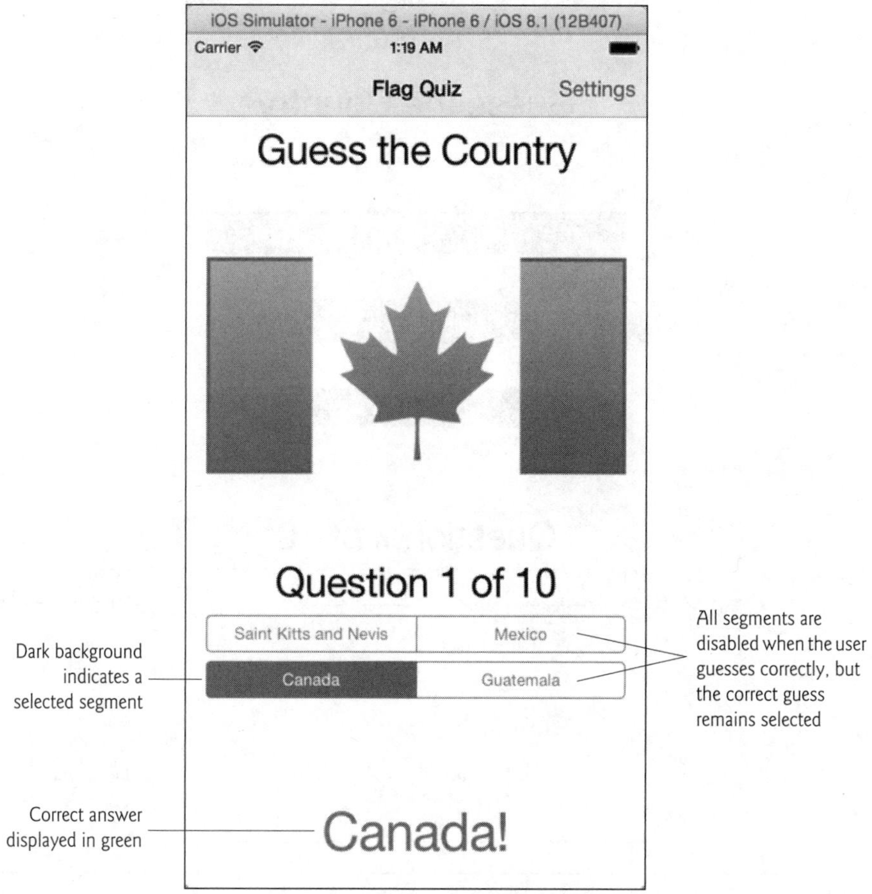

**Fig. 5.3** | User choosing the correct answer and the correct answer displayed. (Part 2 of 2.)

### *Taking the Quiz: Making an Incorrect Selection*

If you select incorrectly, the app disables the corresponding guess—see Jamaica grayed out in Fig. 5.4. As visual indications of the incorrect guess, the app uses a view animation to *shake* the flag left-to-right and displays **Incorrect** in red at the bottom of the screen. A separate view animation gradually fades out **Incorrect** so that it does not remain on the screen between guesses. Keep guessing until you get the correct answer for that flag.

### *Completing the Quiz*

After you've guessed every country name in the quiz, the app displays a UIAlert-Controller dialog showing your total number of guesses and your percentage of correct answers (Fig. 5.5). When you touch the dialog's **New Quiz** Button, the app schedules the next quiz to begin two seconds later.

Incorrect guess's
segment is disabled

**Incorrect**
displayed in red

**Fig. 5.4** | **Incorrect** displayed after an incorrect guess.

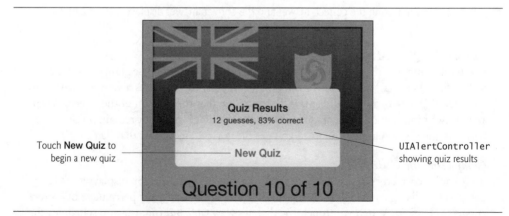

Touch **New Quiz** to
begin a new quiz

UIAlertController
showing quiz results

**Fig. 5.5** | Results displayed at end of quiz.

# 5.3  Technologies Overview

This section introduces the features you'll use to build the **Flag Quiz** app.

## 5.3.1 Designing a Storyboard from Scratch

For each app in Chapters 2–4, you used view controllers that were created by an Xcode app template and simply added controls to complete each app's UI. In this app, you'll start with the **Single View Application** template, then embed its view controller in a UINavigationController and design this app's flow through its scenes.

## 5.3.2 UINavigationController

In Chapter 4, you learned that a UINavigationController helps users navigate between view controllers. Each UINavigationController manages a stack of view controllers for easy navigation back to prior screens. When a new view controller is added to a UINavigationController, it's placed at the top of the stack and is displayed. When the user navigates to the prior screen, the UINavigationController removes the view controller from the screen and pops it from the stack, and the view controller at the top of the stack is redisplayed.

In Section 5.4.2, you'll embed the UIViewController created by the **Single View Application** template in a UINavigationController. That UIViewController will display the quiz and be set as the UINavigationController's **root view controller**—the first view controller that the UINavigationController displays.

## 5.3.3 Storyboard Segues

In Chapter 4, you saw that the **Master-Detail Application** template's storyboard included a predefined *segue*, representing a transition from one view controller to another. In Section 5.4.2, you'll add a second UIViewController to the storyboard, then create a segue between the root view controller and the second UIViewController. As you'll see, this will enable the app to transition from the quiz view controller to the settings view controller when the user touches the **Settings** button (Fig. 5.1) on the root view controller's navigation bar.

## 5.3.4 UISegmentedControls

This app uses **UISegmentedControls** (bottom of Fig. 5.1) to display the guess options to the user. Each UISegmentedControl consists of segments that represent a *mutually exclusive* set of options (similar to radio buttons in other UI technologies). We'll programmatically set each segment's text. When the user makes an incorrect guess, we'll disable that segment. When the user makes a correct guess, we'll disable all of the UISegmentedControls until the next question is displayed.

## 5.3.5 UISwitches

This app uses **UISwitches** (Fig. 5.2) to enable the user to choose which world regions to include in the quiz. Each UISwitch has two states—*on* and *off*. We'll programmatically set the UISwitch states based on the app's NSUserDefaults when the app first loads, and we'll update the NSUserDefaults when the user changes the state of a given UISwitch.

### 5.3.6 Outlet Collections

So far, to programmatically interact with UI controls, you've created outlet properties in your view controller classes. When you have many UI controls of the same type, you can manipulate them as an array known as an **outlet collection**. You'll use two outlet collections in this app. In the QuizViewController, you'll use an outlet collection to interact with the UISegmentedControls shown at the bottom of Fig. 5.1. In the SettingsView-Controller, you'll use an outlet collection to interact with the UISwitches shown in Fig. 5.2.

### 5.3.7 Using the App's Main NSBundle to Get a List of Image Filenames

This app's flag images are loaded into the app only when needed and are located in an images group (i.e., folder) that you'll create in the app's project. To add the flag images to the project, you'll drag each region's folder from the filesystem onto the images group (i.e., folder) in the **Project** navigator. The flag images[1] are located in the images/FlagQuizImages folder with the book's examples.

Foundation framework class **NSBundle** enables an app to access resources that are bundled with the app. Each app has a main bundle that provides access to the directory in which the app's executable is located. Groups that contain resources—like the images group you'll add to this app's project—are added to the app's main bundle by Xcode when you build your app. You'll use class NSBundle (Section 5.5.3) to query the app's bundle for a list of all the files ending in .png (PNG-format images). We do not place the flag images in an asset catalog, because there's no way to query one for a list of images.

### 5.3.8 Using Grand Central Dispatch to Perform a Task in the Future

Today's iOS devices have dual- or tri-core CPUs, and future CPUs will surely have more cores. Writing code that can take advantage of multicore CPUs is difficult, especially when you consider that your apps will run on various devices with different numbers of cores, and that multiple apps and services can be competing on those devices for CPU time. iOS's **Grand Central Dispatch (GCD)** consists of language features, libraries and operating system-features that help apps and the operating system use multicore processors more effectively. GCD is one of the key concurrent-programming technologies you'll use in iOS development.

In this app, when the user makes a correct guess, the app waits two seconds, then displays the next flag. To do this, we use the GCD function **dispatch_after** (Section 5.6.4), which schedules a task to be performed after a specified time interval expires. *Operations that interact with or modify the UI must be performed in the UI thread, because UI components are not thread safe.* For this reason, we'll specify that the future task must be performed in the same thread that displays the UI and responds to the user's interactions. For more details on GCD, see Apple's *Grand Central Dispatch (GCD) Reference* at

```
http://bit.ly/GCDReference
```

---

1. We obtained the images from http://www.free-country-flags.com.

### 5.3.9 Applying an Animation to a `UIView`

When the user makes an incorrect choice, the app shakes the flag by performing a series of view animations using methods of class `UIView`—the superclass of all UIKit controls. To shake the flag, we'll animate a `UIImageView`'s `frame` property (Section 5.6.5). We'll also animate a `UILabel`'s `alpha` property (Section 5.6.4) to transition it from opaque to transparent—this enables the word **Incorrect** to fade off the screen so it's displayed only briefly after an incorrect guess. Figure 5.6 shows the `UIView` properties that can be animated.

| Property | Description |
|---|---|
| `alpha` | Specifies a `UIView`'s transparency—0.0 (transparent) to 1.0 (opaque). |
| `backgroundColor` | Specifies a `UIView`'s background color. |
| `bounds` | Sizes a `UIView` relative to its center point. |
| `center` | Specifies a `UIView`'s center point with respect to its parent `UIView`. |
| `frame` | Sizes a `UIView` relative to its parent `UIView`. |
| `transform` | Scales, rotates or translates (moves) a `UIView` relative to its center point. |

**Fig. 5.6** | `UIView` properties that can be animated with view animations.

### 5.3.10 Darwin Module—Using Predefined C Functions

Just as your apps can reuse Cocoa Touch frameworks (written largely in Objective-C), they can also reuse C-based UNIX functions (such as `arc4random_uniform` in Sections 5.5.6– and 5.6.3) and C Standard Library functions (such as the C math functions) that are built into iOS. These and many other features of UNIX and C are available via the **Darwin module**, which provides access to the C libraries in Darwin—Apple's open-source UNIX-based core on which Apple's OS X and iOS operating systems are built. The `Darwin` module is imported by default into several Cocoa Touch frameworks—such as Foundation and UIKit—but you can also import it explicitly with following `import` declaration:

```
import Darwin
```

### 5.3.11 Random-Number Generation

You'll randomly select flags in this app by choosing random `Array` indices using the `arc4random_uniform` function (a C-based UNIX function from the `Darwin` module), which produces random unsigned 32-bit integers (Swift type `UInt32`) from 0 up to but not including an upper bound that you specify as an argument. There's also function `arc4random`, which takes no arguments and returns a random unsigned 32-bit integer in the range 0 (`UInt32.min`) to 4,294,967,295 (`UInt32.max`).

Both functions use the RC4 (also called ARCFOUR) random-number generation algorithm (`http://en.wikipedia.org/wiki/RC4`) and produce **nondeterministic random numbers** that cannot be predicted.

**Error-Prevention Tip 5.1**

*Functions* arc4random_uniform *and* arc4random *cannot produce repeatable random-number sequences. If you require repeatability for testing, use the* Darwin *module's C function* random *to obtain the random values and function* srandom *to seed the random-number generator with the same seed during each program execution. Once you've completed testing, use either* arc4random_uniform *or* arc4random *to produce random values.*

## 5.3.12 Swift Features Introduced

This section introduces the new Swift language features you'll see in this app's code.

### while *Statement*

In Section 5.5.6, you'll use Swift's **while** statement to perform statements repeatedly. The statement consists of the while keyword followed by a condition and a body delimited by required braces ({ and }), as in:

```
while condition {
    statements
}
```

### The for–in *Statement*

The **for–in** statement (first used in Section 5.5.3) iterates through a collection of values without using a counter, thus avoiding various common errors, such as off-by-one errors. The syntax of a for–in statement is:

```
for item in collection {
    statements
}
```

During each iteration, the for–in assigns to *item* the next value from the *collection* and the loop terminates when the entire collection has been processed. The type of *item* is inferred from the types of the collection's elements.

### Closed Ranges, Half-Open Ranges and the Global stride Functions

The for...in statement can be used with different types of collections, including Arrays and ranges of Int values produced by Swift's closed-range operator (...), the half-open range operator (..<) and the global stride functions.

You can use the for...in loop to iterate over a closed range of Int values, as in

```
for count in 1 ... 5 {
    statements
}
```

This iterates over the collection of five values containing 1 (the first value in the range), 2, 3, 4 and 5 (the last value in the range). The ... operator is known as the **closed-range operator** because it includes both the *starting* and *ending* values in the range. Each iteration of the loop assigns one value from the collection to count.

You can use the for...in loop to iterate over a half-open range of Int values, as in:

```
for count in 1 ..< 5 {
    statements
}
```

This iterates over the collection of *four* values containing 1 (the first value in the range), 2, 3 and 4 (the last value in the range, which is less than 5). The ..< operator is known as the **half-open range operator** because it includes the range's starting value but *not* its ending value.

The closed range and half-open range operators each produce ranges of values in *increasing* order that increment by *one*. You can use Swift's global stride functions to produce ranges with any increments or decrements. For example, the for...in loop

```
for count in stride(from: 11, through: 1, by: -2) {
    statements
}
```

uses the closed-range stride function to specify a *decreasing* closed range of values. This loop iterates over the collection of six values containing 11 (the from argument), 9, 7, 5, 3 and 1 (the through argument), decrementing by 2 (the by argument) each time.

A second version of function **stride** produces half-open ranges. The for...in loop

```
for count in stride(from: 10, to: 50, by: 10) {
    print("\(count) ")
}
```

uses the half-open range stride function to specify an *increasing* half-open range of values that terminates *before* 50 (the to argument). This loop iterates over the collection of *only* the values 10 (the from argument), 20, 30 and 40 (the largest value *less than* the to argument), incrementing by 10 (the by argument) each time.

### *Computed Properties*

In this app's Model (Section 5.5), you'll define both stored properties and computed properties. **Computed properties** do not store data—rather, they manipulate other properties. For example, a Circle class could have a stored property radius and computed properties diameter, circumference and area that would calculate the diameter, circumference and area, respectively, using the stored property radius in the calculations. Computed properties also can *modify* stored properties. We show the syntax of computed properties in Section 5.5.4.

### *Swift Standard Library Global Functions* swap, countElements *and* join

The Swift Standard Library defines over 70 global functions (including the stride functions introduced earlier in this section) for performing various tasks. In this app, you'll also use the following global functions:

- swap—This function receives two arguments and exchanges their values. We'll use this in Section 5.6.8 when we define a shuffle function for randomly ordering an Array's elements.

- **countElements**—This function receives a collection as an argument and returns its number of elements. We'll pass a String to this function (Section 5.6.3) to determine its length.

- **join**—In Section 5.6.3, we'll use this function to create a String by concatenating the elements of a String Array (the second argument), each separated from the next by a space (the first argument).

### *Swift extensions*

Extensions enable you to enhance existing types with new features, including computed properties, methods, initializers, subscripts (i.e., subscript operators like those used with Swift types Array and Dictionary), protocol conformance and more. Each extension begins with the keyword **extension** followed by the name of the type you're extending and a body in braces. We'll use an extension to create a shuffle method (Section 5.6.8) that can be called on any Array object and use the method to randomly order an Array of Strings. For more information on extensions, see the Extensions chapter of *The Swift Programming Language* at:

```
http://bit.ly/SwiftExtensions
```

## 5.4 Building the GUI

In this section, you'll create the project, design the storyboard, create the classes for the storyboard's view controllers and create the outlets and actions for various UI controls.

### 5.4.1 Creating the Project

Begin by creating a new **Single View Application** project. Specify the following settings in the **Choose options for your new project** sheet:

- **Product Name:** FlagQuiz.
- **Organization Name:** Deitel & Associates, Inc.—or use your own.
- **Company Identifier:** com.deitel—or use your own company identifier.
- **Language**—Swift.
- **Devices: Universal.**

After specifying the settings, click **Next**, indicate where you'd like to save your project and click **Create** to create the project.

### *Portrait Orientation*

This app is designed for only portrait orientation so that all its UI components can fit vertically on the screen. In the project settings' **General** tab that's displayed in the Xcode **Editor** area, scroll to the **Deployment Info** section, then for **Device Orientation** ensure that only **Portrait** is selected.

### *App Icons*

As you've done in the earlier apps, add app icons to the project's asset catalog.

## 5.4.2 Designing the Storyboard

For this app, you'll use the storyboard to design the flow through the app's scenes. You'll embed the app's default **View Controller** in a **Navigation Controller**. Doing so will automatically specify the view controller as the navigation controller's root view controller—the view controller at the bottom of the **Navigation Controller**'s stack. The **Navigation Controller** presents its root view controller to the user *first* when the app loads. In this app, the root view controller will display the quiz scene. You'll then add another **View Controller** for displaying the app's settings scene.

For this app's storyboard, you might find it helpful to zoom in and out so you can see all or part of the design. To do so, right click an empty space in the storyboard and select a zoom option.

### Step 1: Embedding a `UIViewController` in a `UINavigationController`
Perform the following steps:

1. Select `Main.storyboard` to display the storyboard in the **Editors** area.

2. In the storyboard, click **View Controller** then select **Editor > Embed In > Navigation Controller**.

Xcode adds to the storyboard a **Navigation Controller** and sets as its **Root View Controller** the app template's original **View Controller**. The **Root View Controller** is indicated by the relationship segue line (—⊘→). To the left of the **Navigation Controller**, notice the right pointing arrow ( ——→ ) indicating that the **Navigation Controller** is now the app's initial view controller—the one displayed when the storyboard first loads. When the initial view controller is a **Navigation Controller**, it displays its **Root View Controller** as the app's first scene.

### Step 2: Configuring the View Controller for the Quiz Scene
Next, you'll configure the **View Controller** for the **Flag Quiz**'s scene (Fig. 5.1):

1. Double click in the center of the navigation bar and type `Flag Quiz` (Fig. 5.7) as its title. You can also do this by selecting the navigation bar, then setting the **Title** property in the **Attributes** inspector.

**Fig. 5.7** | Setting the navigation bar's **Title** property.

2. From the **Objects** library, drag a **Bar Button Item** onto the right side of the navigation bar (as in Fig. 5.8), then double click the **Bar Button Item** and set its **Title** property to `Settings`. This **Bar Button Item** will initiate the segue from the quiz scene (the root view controller) to the settings scene.

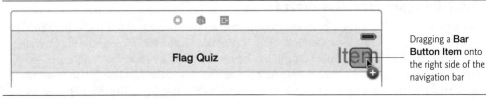

Dragging a **Bar Button Item** onto the right side of the navigation bar

**Fig. 5.8** | Adding a **Bar Button Item** to the navigation bar.

*Step 3: Adding the View Controller for the Settings Scene and Creating a Segue Between the Quiz and Settings Scenes*

Next, you'll add the settings scene's **View Controller** (Fig. 5.2) and create the segue that tells the **Navigation Controller** to display it:

1. From the **Utilities** area's **Objects** library, drag another **View Controller** to the right of the **Flag Quiz** one that you added in *Step 2*.

2. To create a segue from the **Flag Quiz** scene (Fig. 5.1) to the **Settings** scene (Fig. 5.2), *control* drag from **Settings** on the **Flag Quiz** scene's navigation bar to the new **View Controller** you just added and release the mouse. From the **segue popover** that appears (Fig. 5.9), select **show** under **Action Segue** to indicate that this segue performs the action of showing another view controller. Interface Builder configures the segue (displaying —⊕→ between the view controllers) and adds to the settings scene's view controller a navigation bar.

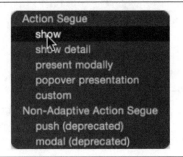

**Fig. 5.9** | Segue popover.

3. Select the segue line —⊕→ in the storyboard, then in the **Attributes** inspector set the segue's **Identifier** to showSettings. You'll use this in Section 5.6.7 to programmatically check which segue is being performed.

4. Click the settings scene's navigation bar then set its **Title** attribute to Settings.

*Running the App to Test the Storyboard Segues*

Run the app now in the iOS simulator to test the storyboard segues. Initially, an empty **Flag Quiz** scene is displayed with a **Settings** button at the navigation bar's right side. Touch **Settings** to perform the segue to the **Settings** scene. Notice that the **Navigation Controller** automatically adds a < **Flag Quiz** back button to the **Settings** scene's navigation bar so that you can navigate back to the **Flag Quiz** scene. Touch < **Flag Quiz** to return to the **Flag Quiz** scene.

### 5.4.3 Configuring the View Controller Classes

When you created this app's project, Xcode automatically generated the UIViewController subclass ViewController for the storyboard's original **View Controller**. In this section, you'll rename that class and designate it as the one that manages the root view controller (for the **Flag Quiz** scene), then create another subclass of UIViewController to manage the **Settings** scene. Perform the following steps:

1. Select ViewController.swift in the **Project** explorer, click the filename again to make it editable, then rename it QuizViewController.swift.

2. In the **Editors** area, change the class name from ViewController to QuizViewController and remove method didReceiveMemoryWarning.

3. In the **Project** explorer, select Main.storyboard to display the storyboard.

4. To indicate that the **Flag Quiz** scene is managed by class QuizViewController, use the storyboard's **Document Outline** to select **Flag Quiz** under **Flag Quiz Scene**, then in the **Identity** inspector under **Custom Class** set the **Class** property to QuizViewController. When the storyboard loads, it will automatically create an object of this class. It will also initialize any @IBOutlets that you create by *control* dragging from this scene's controls to class QuizViewController.

5. Next, you'll create the file SettingsViewController.swift. Select the FlagQuiz group, then select **File > New > File...**. In the sheet that appears, from the **iOS > Source** category, select **Cocoa Touch Class** and click **Next**. In the **Class** field, enter SettingsViewController. In the **Subclass of** field, select UIViewController. In the **Language** field, select **Swift** (it should be selected by default) then click **Next**. Click **Create** to create the file.

6. In the **Project** explorer, select Main.storyboard to display the storyboard.

7. To indicate that the **Settings Scene** is managed by class SettingsViewController, use the **Document Outline** to select **Settings** under **Settings Scene**, then in the **Identity** inspector under **Custom Class** set **Class** to SettingsViewController. When the storyboard loads, it will automatically create an object of this class. It will also initialize any @IBOutlets that you create by *control* dragging from this scene's controls to class SettingsViewController.

### 5.4.4 Creating the UI for the QuizViewController

This section presents the QuizViewController's UI. Figure 5.10 shows the QuizViewController's outlet and outlet collection names. Now that you've built several apps and their user interfaces, going forward we'll simply indicate which controls to add to the user interface and what their settings should be. Use the techniques you've learned previously to lay out the controls. In this UI, ensure that all of the controls snap to the recommended distance from the left and right edges of the screen—this is easiest to see in the screen capture for the **Image View** and **Segmented Controls**. Figure 5.11 shows (from top to bottom in the user interface) the property settings for the controls in Fig. 5.10. The next two sections discuss their auto layout settings and creating their outlets and actions.

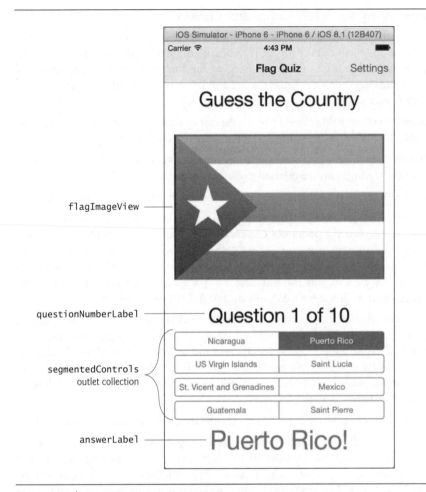

**Fig. 5.10** | **Flag Quiz** UI's components labeled with outlet names.

| GUI component | Property | Value |
|---|---|---|
| Label | Text | Guess the Country |
| | Alignment | Click the icon for center alignment |
| | Font | System 32.0 |
| | Autoshrink | Minimum Font Scale (with the default value 0.5) |
| | Height | Use the sizing handles to ensure that the **Label** is 36 points tall |
| Image View (flagImageView) | Mode | Aspect Fit |
| | Height | Use the sizing handles to ensure that the **Image View** is 219 points tall |

**Fig. 5.11** | Property values for the **Flag Quiz** UI's components. (Part 1 of 2.)

| GUI component | Property | Value |
|---|---|---|
| **Label**<br>(`questionNumberLabel`) | **Text** | `Question 1 of 10` |
| | **Alignment** | Click the icon for center alignment |
| | **Font** | `System 32.0` |
| | **Autoshrink** | `Minimum Font Scale` (with the default value 0.5) |
| | **Height** | Ensure that the **Label** is 36 points tall |
| **Segmented Controls**<br>(`segmentedControls`) | **Selected** | Uncheck the checkbox |
| **Label**<br>(`answerLabel`) | **Text** | `Correct!` |
| | **Alignment** | Click the icon for center alignment |
| | **Font** | `System 42.0` |
| | **Autoshrink** | `Minimum Font Scale` (with the default value 0.5) |
| | **Height** | Ensure that the **Label** is 50 points tall |

**Fig. 5.11** | Property values for the **Flag Quiz** UI's components. (Part 2 of 2.)

## 5.4.5 Auto Layout Settings for the `QuizViewController` UI

Set the auto layout constraints as follows:

- For each control, use the auto layout techniques that you learned in prior chapters to set the control's **Leading Space to Container Margin** and **Trailing Space to Container Margin** constraints. You can do this for all the controls at once by selecting them in the **Document Outline** window, then *control* dragging from one to the scene's **View** node.

- For the **Guess the Country** label, set its **Top Space to Top Layout Guide** constraint.

- For the other controls below the **Guess the Country** label, set each one's **Vertical Spacing** constraint between that control and the one immediately above it.

- For the **Correct!** label, set its **Bottom Space to Bottom Layout Guide** constraint.

- For the **Image View**, set its **Height** constraint. Initially, this creates a fixed height constraint based on the **Image View**'s current height in the design. We want this control's height to grow to occupy the remaining space in the UI. To enable this, you must modify the **Height** constraint. Select the **Image View**, then in the **Size** inspector click the **Height** constraint's **Edit** button. In the popover, change the equality constraint (=) to a greater than or equal to constraint (≥).

- Finally, with the **Flag Quiz** scene's **View** node selected in the **Document Outline** window, use the **Resolve Auto Layout Issues** (⊬) menu at the bottom of the storyboard to select **Add Missing Constraints**, then save the storyboard.

## 5.4.6 `QuizViewController` Outlets and Actions

Open the **Assistant Editor**, then create the following outlets and actions:

- Use the techniques you learned in earlier chapters to create @IBOutlets in class `QuizViewController` for the `flagImageView`, `questionNumberLabel` and `answerLabel` in Fig. 5.10.

- *Control* drag from the first **Segmented Control** to the QuizViewController as you normally do, but in the outlet popover that appears, for **Connection** select **Outlet Collection** and name the outlet collection segmentedControls. Also, since this action will be used only for **Segmented Controls**, choose UISegmentedControl for the **Type** (i.e., the type of the action's sender parameter). Next, *control* drag from the remaining **Segmented Controls** (in order from top to bottom) to the name of the outlet collection you just created to add each **Segmented Control** to the Array in the same order they appear on the UI. Dragging to the outlet collection's name enables you to connect to the existing outlet collection, rather than create a new one.

- Use the techniques you learned in earlier chapters to create the action submit-Guess for the first **Segmented Control**, then *control* drag from each remaining **Segmented Control** to that action's name in QuizViewController. Once again, dragging to the action's name enables you to connect to the existing action.

## 5.4.7 Creating the UI for the SettingsViewController

This section presents the SettingsViewController's UI. Figure 5.12 shows the SettingsViewController's outlet and outlet collection names. Figure 5.13 shows (from top-to-bottom and left-to-right in the user interface) property settings for the controls in Fig. 5.12. For this scene's auto layout constraints, you can simply select the scene's **View** in the storyboard, then use the **Resolve Auto Layout Issues** menu at the bottom of the storyboard to select **Add Missing Constraints**, then save the storyboard. The next section discusses creating the scene's outlets and actions.

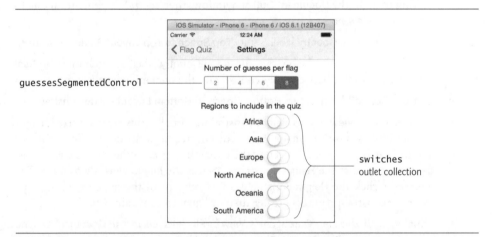

**Fig. 5.12** | **Settings** UI's components labeled with outlet names.

| GUI component | Property | Value |
|---|---|---|
| Label | Text | Number of guesses per flag |
| | Alignment | Click the icon for center alignment |

**Fig. 5.13** | Property values for the GUI components in fragment_quiz.xml. (Part 1 of 2.)

| GUI component | Property | Value |
|---|---|---|
| Segmented Control (guessesSegmentedControl) | Segments | 4 |
| | Segment > Segment 0 Title | 2 |
| [*Note:* Each segment has its own properties. To access them, use the **Segment** property to select the segment number (**Segment 0**, **Segment 1**, etc.).] | Segment > Segment 1 Title Selected | 4 Check the checkbox |
| | Segment > Segment 2 Title | 6 |
| | Segment > Segment 3 Title | 8 |
| Label | Text Alignment | Regions to include in the quiz Click the icon for center alignment |
| Switch | State | Off |
| Label | Text Alignment | Africa Click the icon for right alignment |
| Switch | State | Off |
| Label | Text Alignment | Asia Click the icon for right alignment |
| Switch | State | Off |
| Label | Text Alignment | Europe Click the icon for right alignment |
| Switch | State | Off |
| Label | Text Alignment | North America Click the icon for right alignment |
| Switch | State | On (the default) |
| Label | Text Alignment | Oceania Click the icon for right alignment |
| Switch | State | Off |
| Label | Text Alignment | South America Click the icon for right alignment |
| Switch | State | Off |

**Fig. 5.13** | Property values for the GUI components in `fragment_quiz.xml`. (Part 2 of 2.)

## 5.4.8 SettingsViewController Outlets and Actions

Open the **Assistant Editor**, then create the following outlets and actions:

- Use the techniques you learned previously to create the guessesSegmentedControl outlet (Fig. 5.12) in class SettingsViewController.

- *Control* drag from the first **Switch** (to the right of the **Africa** label) to the SettingsViewController as you normally do, but in the outlet popover that appears, for **Connection** select **Outlet Collection** and name the outlet collection switches. Next, *control* drag from the remaining **Switches** (in order from top to bottom) to the outlet collection's name to add each **Segmented Control** to the Array in the same order they appear on the UI.

- Use the techniques you learned in earlier chapters to create the action numberOf-GuessesChanged for the **Segmented Control**. Since this action will be used only for the **Segmented Control**, choose UISegmentedControl for the **Type** in the popover.

- Next, for the first **Switch** create the action switchChanged. Since this action will be used only for the **Switch**es, choose UISwitch for the **Type** in the popover. *Control* drag from each remaining **Switch** to the switchChanged action in QuizViewController. Later, you'll see how we distinguish among the **Switch**es in the action method.

### 5.4.9 Creating Class Model

As in Chapter 4, this app uses a class named Model to manage the app's locally stored data—in this case, the app's settings and the images. To create the file for this class:

1. In Xcode, select **File > New > File...** to display a sheet containing the file templates.

2. Under **iOS**, select the **Source** category, then select **Swift File** and click **Next**.

3. Name the file Model.swift and click **Create**.

The new file is placed in the project's FlagQuiz group (recall that this is Xcode's term for a folder) and opens immediately in the **Editor** area.

### 5.4.10 Adding the Flag Images to the App

The flag images are located with the book's examples in the images/FlagQuizImages folder. Perform the following steps to add these to the project:

1. In Xcode, right click the FlagQuiz group (folder) and select **New Group**.

2. Enter images as the new group's name.

3. Open the images/FlagQuizImages folder in Finder, then drag the subfolders for the six world regions (Africa, Asia, Europe, North America, Oceania and South America) onto the images group you just created in Xcode. In the sheet that appears, ensure that **Copy if needed** is checked.

## 5.5 Model Class

In this section we discuss the app's Model class. In the file Model.swift that you created in Section 5.4.9, enter the code in Sections 5.5.1—5.5.6.

### 5.5.1 ModelDelegate Protocol

Lines 6–8 (Fig. 5.14) define the ModelDelegate protocol that this app's QuizViewController adopts so it can be notified when the app's settings change. This protocol describes only a settingsChanged method with no parameters and no return value. In Section 5.6.2, class QuizViewController will define the method to reset the quiz based on the new app settings. We'll define a property of type ModelDelegate in class Model and initialize it with a reference to the QuizViewController. When the model data changes, the Model will use this reference to call settingsChanged on the QuizViewController.

```
 1   // Model.swift
 2   // Manages the app's settings and quiz data
 3   import Foundation
 4
 5   // adopted by delegate so it can be notified when settings change
 6   protocol ModelDelegate {
 7       func settingsChanged()
 8   }
 9
```

**Fig. 5.14** | ModelDelegate protocol.

## 5.5.2 Model Properties

Figure 5.15 begins class Model's definition and defines its properties:

- Lines 12–13 define private properties regionsKey and guessesKey. These are used by the Model to store and retrieve the settings in the app's NSUserDefaults.

- Line 16 defines the private property delegate as an implicitly unwrapped ModelDelegate optional. The Model uses this property to notify the QuizView-Controller to start a new quiz when the settings change.

- Line 18 defines the property numberOfGuesses with the default value 4. This is used by the QuizViewController to determine how many guesses to display with each flag and by the SettingsViewController to change the number of guesses.

- Lines 19–26 define the private Dictionary property enabledRegions, which represents the regions in the quiz and whether they're enabled.

```
10   class Model {
11       // keys for storing data in the app's NSUserDefaults
12       private let regionsKey = "FlagQuizKeyRegions"
13       private let guessesKey = "FlagQuizKeyGuesses"
14
15       // reference to QuizViewController to notify it when settings change
16       private var delegate: ModelDelegate! = nil
17
18       var numberOfGuesses = 4 // number of guesses to display
19       private var enabledRegions = [ // regions to use in quiz
20           "Africa" : false,
21           "Asia" : false,
22           "Europe" : false,
23           "North_America" : true,
24           "Oceania" : false,
25           "South_America" : false
26       ]
27
28       // variables for maintaining quiz data
29       let numberOfQuestions = 10
30       private var allCountries: [String] = [] // list of all flag names
31       private var countriesInEnabledRegions: [String] = []
32
```

**Fig. 5.15** | Model properties.

- Line 29 defines the constant `numberOfQuestions` representing the number of questions in the quiz. This is used by both the `Model` and the `QuizViewController`.

- Lines 30–31 define `String Array`s representing the filenames of all the flags bundled with the app (`allCountries`) and the names of all the flags for the countries in the enabled regions (`countriesInEnabledRegions`).

### 5.5.3 `Model` Initializer and `regionsChanged` Method

The `Model`'s initializer (Fig. 5.16, lines 34–63) receives its `ModelDelegate` as an argument and uses it to initialize the `delegate` property (line 35). Lines 38–49 get the app's `NSUserDefaults` and use it to obtain the stored number of guesses (lines 41–44) and region settings (lines 47–49). If this is the first time the app has been launched or if the user has never changed the app's default settings, then the default values specified in the definitions of properties `numberOfGuesses` and `enabledRegions` are used. Note that `NSUserDefaults` method `integerForKey` returns 0 if the key was not previously stored.

```
33    // initialize the Settings from the app's NSUserDefaults
34    init(delegate: ModelDelegate, numberOfQuestions: Int) {
35        self.delegate = delegate
36
37        // get the NSUserDefaults object for the app
38        let userDefaults = NSUserDefaults.standardUserDefaults()
39
40        // get number of guesses
41        let tempGuesses = userDefaults.integerForKey(guessesKey)
42        if tempGuesses != 0 {
43            numberOfGuesses = tempGuesses
44        }
45
46        // get Dictionary containing the region settings
47        if let tempRegions = userDefaults.dictionaryForKey(regionsKey) {
48            self.enabledRegions = tempRegions as [String : Bool]
49        }
50
51        // get a list of all the png files in the app's images group
52        let paths = NSBundle.mainBundle().pathsForResourcesOfType(
53            "png", inDirectory: nil) as [String]
54
55        // get image filenames from paths
56        for path in paths {
57            if !path.lastPathComponent.hasPrefix("AppIcon") {
58                allCountries.append(path.lastPathComponent)
59            }
60        }
61
62        regionsChanged() // populate countriesInEnabledRegions
63    }
64
```

**Fig. 5.16** | `Model` initializer and `regionsChanged` method. (Part 1 of 2.)

```
65        // loads countriesInEnabledRegions
66        func regionsChanged() {
67            countriesInEnabledRegions.removeAll()
68
69            for filename in allCountries {
70                let region = filename.componentsSeparatedByString("-")[0]
71
72                if enabledRegions[region]! {
73                    countriesInEnabledRegions.append(filename)
74                }
75            }
76        }
77
```

**Fig. 5.16** | Model initializer and regionsChanged method. (Part 2 of 2.)

### *Using NSBundle to Get Filenames*

Recall that Foundation framework class NSBundle enables an app to access resources that are bundled with the app. Lines 52–53 obtain an Array of Strings containing the paths to all of the PNG images stored in the app's main bundle. NSBundle method mainBundle returns the app's main bundle. NSBundle method pathsForResourcesOfType returns an NSArray containing NSString representations of the paths for every file with the type specified by the first argument in the directory specified by the second argument. If the second argument is nil (as in line 53), pathsForResourcesOfType searches for all matching files in the app's main bundle. We cast the returned NSArray of NSStrings to a Swift String Array—recall that this is allowed because the NSArray and NSString types are *bridged* to Swift's Array and String types by the runtime. Next, lines 56–60 obtain the PNG image filenames from each path by using NSString property lastPathComponent. For each one, line 57 uses String method hasPrefix to determine whether that filename starts with "AppIcon"—the name Xcode gives to the app icons when you drag them onto the app's asset catalog. Our app icons are also PNG images, so we add a filename to allCountries only if it does not start with "AppIcon". Finally, line 62 calls method regionsChanged to populate the countriesInEnabledRegions Array that's used by the QuizViewController to select guesses to display with each flag.

### *Method regionsChanged to Get Filenames*

The regionsChanged method (lines 66–76) is called by the Model's initializer and whenever the user changes the enabled quiz regions. Line 67 clears the Array, then lines 69–75 determine which filenames to add to the countriesInEnabledRegions Array by first checking whether a particular filename is for a country in an enabled region. Each country's filename begins with its region name and a dash, as in

```
North_America-United_States.png
```

Line 70 uses NSString method componentsSeparatedByString to break apart the filename at the dash. This method returns an NSArray of NSStrings containing the components. The element at index 0 in that NSArray is the region name. Line 72 determines whether that region is enabled and, if so, line 73 adds the filename to the Array countriesInEnabledRegions.

### 5.5.4 Model Computed Properties

Figure 5.17 defines the read-only computed properties `regions` and `enabledRegionCoun-tries`. The property `regions` returns a copy of the `enabledRegions` Dictionary. This is used by the `SettingsViewController` to determine which regions are enabled and con-figure its `UISwitches` accordingly. The property `enableRegionCountries` returns a copy of the `countriesInEnabledRegions` Array. This is used by the `QuizViewController` to display randomly chosen guesses for each flag in the quiz.

```
78      // returns Dictionary indicating the regions to include in the quiz
79      var regions: [String : Bool] {
80          return enabledRegions
81      }
82
83      // returns Array of countries for only the enabled regions
84      var enabledRegionCountries: [String] {
85          return countriesInEnabledRegions
86      }
87
```

**Fig. 5.17** | Model computed properties.

*Computed Property Syntax*
The general syntax of a computed property is:

```
var propertyName: Type {
    get {
        statements
    }
    set {
        statements
    }
}
```

The var keyword is required for all computed properties. A computed property's **get** ac-cessor returns a computed value, typically based on the values of other properties. A com-puted property's **set** accessor sets the values of other properties. If a computed property defines both accessors, it is a read–write property. If it defines only a **get** accessor, it is a read-only property. When defining a read-only computed property, you can eliminate the keyword `get` and the braces around the get accessor's statements, as we did for both read-only properties in Fig. 5.17.

### 5.5.5 Model Methods toggleRegion, setNumberOfGuesses and notifyDelegate

Figure 5.18 defines methods `toggleRegion`, `setNumberOfGuesses` and `notifyDelegate`. Method `toggleRegion` (lines 89–95) is called by the `SettingsViewController` when the user toggles a region's `UISwitch`. Line 90 toggles to corresponding value in the `enabled-Regions` Dictionary, then lines 91–93 store the dictionary in the app's `NSUserDefaults` to update the app's settings. Line 94 calls method `regionsChanged` (Section 5.5.3) to repopu-late the Array `countriesInEnabledRegions` based on the regions that are now enabled.

```
88      // toggles a region on or off
89      func toggleRegion(name: String) {
90          enabledRegions[name] = !(enabledRegions[name]!)
91          NSUserDefaults.standardUserDefaults().setObject(
92              enabledRegions as NSDictionary, forKey: regionsKey)
93          NSUserDefaults.standardUserDefaults().synchronize()
94          regionsChanged() // populate countriesInEnabledRegions
95      }
96
97      // changes the number of guesses displayed with each flag
98      func setNumberOfGuesses(guesses: Int) {
99          numberOfGuesses = guesses
100         NSUserDefaults.standardUserDefaults().setInteger(
101             numberOfGuesses, forKey: guessesKey)
102         NSUserDefaults.standardUserDefaults().synchronize()
103     }
104
105     // called by SettingsViewController when settings change
106     // to have model notify QuizViewController of the changes
107     func notifyDelegate() {
108         delegate.settingsChanged()
109     }
110
```

**Fig. 5.18** | Model methods toggleRegion, setNumberOfGuesses and notifyDelegate.

Method setNumberOfGuesses (lines 98–103) is called by the SettingsViewController when the user changes the number of guesses to display with each flag. Line 99 updates numberOfGuesses and lines 100–102 store the updated value in the app's NSUserDefaults.

Method notifyDelegate (lines 107–109) is called by the SettingsViewController if the user changes the number of guesses to display or the enabled regions. Line 108 calls the delegate's (that is, QuizViewController's) settingsChanged method, which resets the quiz based on the new app settings.

### 5.5.6 Model Method newQuizCountries

Each time a new quiz begins, the SettingsViewController calls method newQuizCountries (Fig. 5.19) to get an Array of randomly chosen filenames for the flags to include in the quiz. Line 113 creates an empty Array and lines 117–127 populate it. Lines 118–119 pick a random index, then line 120 uses it to get a filename. Line 123 calls Array method filter with the closure argument {$0 == filename} to determine whether the filename is already in the quizCountries Array. If not, line 124 adds the filename. Once the proper number of flag filenames have been chosen, line 129 returns a copy of quizCountries to the SettingsViewController.

```
111     // return Array of flags to quiz based on enabled regions
112     func newQuizCountries() -> [String] {
113         var quizCountries: [String] = []
```

**Fig. 5.19** | Model method newQuizCountries. (Part 1 of 2.)

```
114            var flagCounter = 0
115
116            // add 10 random filenames to quizCountries
117            while flagCounter < numberOfQuestions {
118                let randomIndex = Int(arc4random_uniform(
119                    UInt32(enabledRegionCountries.count)))
120                let filename = enabledRegionCountries[randomIndex]
121
122                // if image's filename is not in quizCountries, add it
123                if quizCountries.filter({$0 == filename}).count == 0 {
124                    quizCountries.append(filename)
125                    ++flagCounter
126                }
127            }
128
129            return quizCountries
130        }
131    }
```

**Fig. 5.19** | Model method newQuizCountries. (Part 2 of 2.)

## 5.6 QuizViewController Class

Class QuizViewController (Sections 5.6.1—5.6.8) implements the quiz's logic. In the file QuizViewController.swift replace the class definition with the code in Sections 5.6.1—5.6.8.

### 5.6.1 Properties

Figure 5.19 contains the beginning of class QuizViewController, which extends UIView-Controller. We modified the class to conform to the ModelDelegate protocol (line 5) so that the Model can notify the QuizViewController to reset the quiz when the app's settings change.

```
1    // QuizViewController.swift
2    // Manages the quiz
3    import UIKit
4
5    class QuizViewController: UIViewController, ModelDelegate {
6        @IBOutlet weak var flagImageView: UIImageView!
7        @IBOutlet weak var questionNumberLabel: UILabel!
8        @IBOutlet var segmentedControls: [UISegmentedControl]!
9        @IBOutlet weak var answerLabel: UILabel!
10
11        private var model: Model! // reference to the model object
12        private let correctColor =
13            UIColor(red: 0.0, green: 0.75, blue: 0.0, alpha: 1.0)
14        private let incorrectColor = UIColor.redColor()
15        private var quizCountries: [String]! = nil // countries in quiz
16        private var enabledCountries: [String]! = nil // countries for guesses
```

**Fig. 5.20** | QuizViewController class's properties. (Part 1 of 2.)

```
17        private var correctAnswer: String! = nil
18        private var correctGuesses = 0
19        private var totalGuesses = 0
20
```

**Fig. 5.20** | QuizViewController class's properties. (Part 2 of 2.)

### @IBOutlets
Lines 6–8 define the properties that enabled class QuizViewController to interact with
the UI. You created these @IBOutlets in Section 5.4.6. Line 8 is an outlet collection that's
implemented as an Array of UISegmentedControls. As you've seen, these display the
guesses below the flag.

### Other Properties
Lines 11–19 define QuizViewController's private properties that are used throughout
the quiz logic:

- Line 11 defines the Model reference that's used to get the app's settings and Arrays of Strings representing the flag image filenames.

- Lines 12–14 define two UIColors representing the correct and incorrect answer
  colors. Lines 12–13 use the UIColor initializer that receives as arguments values
  in the range 0.0–1.0 for the red, green, blue and alpha (transparency) components of a color, respectively. We use this initializer to create a medium green color for correct answers. Line 14 uses UIColor method redColor to get the built-
  in definition of red that's used for incorrect answers.

- Line 15 defines the quizCountries Array that will store the filenames for the
  flags to display in the current quiz.

- Line 16 defines the enabledCountries Array that will store the filenames for all
  countries in the app's currently enabled regions—again, these are used to provide
  guesses with each flag.

- Line 17 stores the correctAnswer for the currently displayed flag image.

- Lines 18–19 keep track of the correct guesses and total number of guesses so far.

## 5.6.2 Overridden UIViewController Method viewDidLoad, and Methods settingsChanged and resetQuiz
When the QuizViewController's scene loads, method viewDidLoad (Fig. 5.21, lines 22–
28) is called. We modified this autogenerated method to create the Model (line 26) and to
call method settingsChanged.

Method settingsChanged (lines 32–35), which is also called by the Model when the
user changes the settings, gets the current list of filenames for the enabled countries (line
33), then calls resetQuiz.

Method resetQuiz (lines 38–50) gets from the Model a new randomly selected set of
filenames for the images to include in the new quiz (line 39) and reinitializes properties
correctGuesses and totalGuesses to 0. Lines 44–47 iterate through the outlet collection
of UISegmentedControls and display only the ones necessary to support the total number
of guesses to display. Finally, line 49 calls method nextQuestion (Section 5.6.3).

```
21      // obtains the app
22      override func viewDidLoad() {
23          super.viewDidLoad()
24
25          // create Model
26          model = Model(delegate: self)
27          settingsChanged()
28      }
29
30      // SettingsDelegate: reconfigures quiz when user changes settings;
31      // also called when app first loads
32      func settingsChanged() {
33          enabledCountries = model.enabledRegionCountries
34          resetQuiz()
35      }
36
37      // start a new quiz
38      func resetQuiz() {
39          quizCountries = model.newQuizCountries() // countries in new quiz
40          correctGuesses = 0
41          totalGuesses = 0
42
43          // display appropriate # of UISegmentedControls
44          for i in 0 ..< segmentedControls.count {
45              segmentedControls[i].hidden =
46                  (i < model.numberOfGuesses / 2) ? false : true
47          }
48
49          nextQuestion() // display the first flag in quiz
50      }
51
```

**Fig. 5.21** | Overridden `UIViewController` method `viewDidLoad`, and methods `settingsChanged` and `resetQuiz`.

### 5.6.3 Methods nextQuestion and countryFromFilename

Method `nextQuestion` (Fig. 5.22) prepares the UI for the next flag in the quiz. Lines 54–55 display the next question number and line 56 clears the `answerLabel`. Line 57 removes Array `quizCountries`' first element and stores it as the `correctAnswer` for this quiz question. Line 58 uses the `UIImage` initializer that loads an image based on its filename and assigns the returned `UIImage` to the `flagImageView`'s image property to display the new flag. Lines 61–64 then iterate through the `segmentedControls` outlet collection, enabling each `UISegmentedControl` (by setting its `enabled` property to `true`) and removing its segments (by calling `UISegmentedControl` method **removeAllSegments**) to prepare to display the guesses.

```
52      // displays next question
53      func nextQuestion() {
54          questionNumberLabel.text = String(format: "Question %1$d of %2$d",
55              (correctGuesses + 1), model.numberOfQuestions)
```

**Fig. 5.22** | Methods `nextQuestion` and `countryFromFilename`. (Part 1 of 2.)

```
56              answerLabel.text = ""
57              correctAnswer = quizCountries.removeAtIndex(0)
58              flagImageView.image = UIImage(named: correctAnswer) // next flag
59
60              // re-enable UISegmentedControls and delete prior segments
61              for segmentedControl in segmentedControls {
62                  segmentedControl.enabled = true
63                  segmentedControl.removeAllSegments()
64              }
65
66              // place guesses on displayed UISegmentedControls
67              enabledCountries.shuffle() // use Array extension method
68              var i = 0
69
70              for segmentedControl in segmentedControls {
71                  if !segmentedControl.hidden {
72                      var segmentIndex = 0
73
74                      while segmentIndex < 2 { // 2 per UISegmentedControl
75                          if i < enabledCountries.count &&
76                              correctAnswer != enabledCountries[i] {
77
78                              segmentedControl.insertSegmentWithTitle(
79                                  countryFromFilename(enabledCountries[i]),
80                                  atIndex: segmentIndex, animated: false)
81                              ++segmentIndex
82                          }
83                          ++i
84                      }
85                  }
86              }
87
88              // pick random segment and replace with correct answer
89              let randomRow =
90                  Int(arc4random_uniform(UInt32(model.numberOfGuesses / 2)))
91              let randomIndexInRow = Int(arc4random_uniform(UInt32(2)))
92              segmentedControls[randomRow].removeSegmentAtIndex(
93                  randomIndexInRow, animated: false)
94              segmentedControls[randomRow].insertSegmentWithTitle(
95                  countryFromFilename(correctAnswer),
96                  atIndex: randomIndexInRow, animated: false)
97          }
98
99          // converts image filename to displayable guess String
100         func countryFromFilename(filename: String) -> String {
101             var name = filename.componentsSeparatedByString("-")[1]
102             let length: Int = countElements(name)
103             name = (name as NSString).substringToIndex(length - 4)
104             let components = name.componentsSeparatedByString("_")
105             return join(" ", components)
106         }
107
```

**Fig. 5.22** | Methods nextQuestion and countryFromFilename. (Part 2 of 2.)

The remainder of method `nextQuestion` displays randomly selected guesses on the `UISegmentedControls`, then places the correct answer. First line 67 calls method `shuffle` on the `enabledCountries` Array to randomly order its elements. Swift's Array type does not have a `shuffle` method. However, we used Swift's `extension` capability to define one that can be called directly on any Array—you'll see its definition in Section 5.6.8.

Lines 70–86 randomly place country names (other than the correct answer) onto the *displayed* `UISegmentedControls`—one to four `UISegmentedControls` are displayed, depending on the number of guesses in the app's settings (2, 4, 6 or 8, respectively). Lines 78–80 place each new segment by calling `UISegmentedControl` method `insertSegmentWithTitle`, which receives three arguments:

- the `String` to display on the segment,
- the segment's index number (segments are indexed from 0), and
- a `Bool` indicating whether to use animation when displaying the segment.

The first argument to `insertSegmentWithTitle` is the result of a call to method `countryFromFileName` (lines 100–106), which converts the filename into a displayable country name.

Lines 89–96 replace one of the segments created in lines 70–86 with the correct answer. Lines 89–91 pick a random index in the `segmentedControls` outlet collection and a random index in the specified `UISegmentedControl`, then lines 92–96 remove that segment and replace it with one containing the correct answer.

### *Method* `countryFromFileName`

The image filenames in `enabledCountries` have the format

> *regionName-countryName*`.png`

If a *regionName* or *countryName* contains multiple words, they're separated by underscores (_). Method `countryFromFileName` (lines 100–106) parses the country name from the image filename. First, line 101 gets the portion of the filename after the dash (-) that separates the region from the country name. Line 102 uses Swift global function `countElements` to get the length of the resulting `String`. We use this in line 103, which calls `NSString` method `substringToIndex` to get a substring that does not include the `.png` extension.[2] Next, line 104 separates the filename string at any underscores. Finally, line 105 uses Swift global function `join` to reassemble the words in the country name into a `String` with the words separated by spaces.

## 5.6.4 Method `submitGuess`

Figure 5.23 defines the `@IBAction` `submitGuess` (created in Section 5.4.6) which is called each time the user touches an enabled segment on one of this app's `UISegmentedControls`. Lines 111–112 use `UISegmentedControl` method `titleForSegmentAtIndex` to get the ti-

---

2. Note the use of the expression (`name as NSString`) in line 103, which casts the Swift `String` name to an `NSString` before calling method `substringToIndex`. We added this to eliminate a compilation error. This should not be required because Swift `Strings` are supposed to support all `NSString` methods provided that the Foundation framework is imported (it's imported indirectly here via UIKit).

tle text for the selected segment—this is the user's guess. Line 113 gets the displayable country name for the correctAnswer, then line 114 increments totalGuesses.

```
108        // called when the user makes a guess
109        @IBAction func submitGuess(sender: UISegmentedControl) {
110            // get the title of the bar at that segment, which is the guess
111            let guess = sender.titleForSegmentAtIndex(
112                sender.selectedSegmentIndex)!
113            let correct = countryFromFilename(correctAnswer)
114            ++totalGuesses
115
116            if guess != correct { // incorrect guess
117                // disable incorrect guess
118                sender.setEnabled(false,
119                    forSegmentAtIndex: sender.selectedSegmentIndex)
120                answerLabel.textColor = incorrectColor
121                answerLabel.text = "Incorrect"
122                answerLabel.alpha = 1.0
123                UIView.animateWithDuration(1.0,
124                    animations: {self.answerLabel.alpha = 0.0})
125                shakeFlag()
126            } else { // correct guess
127                answerLabel.textColor = correctColor
128                answerLabel.text = guess + "!"
129                answerLabel.alpha = 1.0
130                ++correctGuesses
131
132                // disable segmentedControls
133                for segmentedControl in segmentedControls {
134                    segmentedControl.enabled = false
135                }
136
137                if correctGuesses == model.numberOfQuestions { // quiz over
138                    displayQuizResults()
139                } else { // use GCD to load next flag after 2 seconds
140                    dispatch_after(
141                        dispatch_time(
142                            DISPATCH_TIME_NOW, Int64(2 * NSEC_PER_SEC)),
143                        dispatch_get_main_queue(), {self.nextQuestion()})
144                }
145            }
146        }
147
```

**Fig. 5.23** | Method submitGuess.

### Incorrect Guess

If the guess is incorrect, lines 118–119 disable that guess's segment in the UISegmented-Control (sender). Lines 120–122 set the answerLabel's textColor to red (incorrect-Color), text to "Incorrect" and alpha to 1.0 (opaque). Lines 123–124 begin a view animation with UIView method **animateWithDuration**. The method's first argument is the duration in seconds. The second argument is a closure that sets UIView properties that can be animated—in this case the answerLabel's alpha property. When the animation be-

gins, it automatically changes the property's value from its value before the animation began (1.0) to its value specified in the closure argument (0.0) over the duration specified
in the method's first argument (one second)—this causes the word "Incorrect" to fade
away over one second. Finally, line 125 calls shakeFlag (Section 5.6.5) to animate the flag
horizontally as another visual indication of an incorrect guess. Note that the call to animateWithDuration (and several others in this app) could use trailing closure syntax, as in:

```
UIView.animateWithDuration(1.0){self.answerLabel.alpha = 0.0}
```

### Correct Guess

If the guess is correct, lines 127–129 set the answerLabel's textColor to green (correct-
Color), text to the country name followed by an exclamation point and alpha to 1.0
(opaque). Line 130 increments correctAnswers. Next, lines 133–135 disable all of the
UISegmentedControls. If correctAnswers is model.numberOfQuestions (line 137), the
quiz is over and line 138 calls displayQuizResults (Section 5.6.6). Otherwise, lines 140–
143 use Grand Central Dispatch (GCD) function dispatch_after to display the next
quiz question from the UI thread after a delay of two seconds. Using the UI thread is important because controls are not thread safe, so all modifications to them must be performed on the same thread to prevent corrupting the UI.

The function dispatch_after receives three parameters:

- dispatch_time_t—A representation of the amount of time after which the task
  should execute. We use GCD function dispatch_time to create an object of this
  type—the DISPATCH_TIME_NOW argument indicates that the delay is relative to the
  current time and its second argument is a number of nanoseconds into the future
  as a 64-bit integer. The NSEC_PER_SEC constant is the number of nanoseconds per
  second and we multiply that by 2 to create the two-second delay.

- dispatch_queue_t—A non-nil argument indicating the queue (thread) on
  which to execute the delayed task. GCD function dispatch_get_main_queue
  returns the app's main queue, which is the thread of execution in which the app's
  UI is created and the user-interface events are processed.

- A function that takes no arguments and returns nothing—This argument is typically a closure (line 143) for conciseness. Here, we call our nextQuestion method.

### 5.6.5 Method shakeFlag

Figure 5.24 defines the shakeFlag method, which uses a series of view animations to move
the flag horizontally, creating a shake effect as a visual indication of an incorrect answer. Each
animation in lines 150–163 modifies the flagImageView's frame property, which specifies
the flagImageView's size and position with respect to its parent view. Within this property,
the origin property contains the $x$- and $y$-coordinates of the frame's upper-left corner. For
the shake effect, we modify the origin's x property. Lines 150–151 uses the UIView method
animateWithDuration that you learned in the preceding section to add 16 (the distance between the flag's right edge and the screen's right edge) to the x property. This animation lasts
1/10 of a second. Lines 152–163 use an overloaded version of UIView method animateWith-
Duration that performs animations after a delay. The five arguments are:

- The duration of the animation in seconds.

- delay—The delay in seconds before starting the animation.

- options—A bitmask of UIViewAnimationOptions. If nil (as in Fig. 5.24), the default animation options are used.

- animations—A closure containing the statements that specify the final values of the UIView properties being animated.

- completion—A closure that receives a Bool and does not return a value. If non-nil, this closure executes when the animation completes.

The animation in lines 152–154 starts after 1/10 of a second and subtracts 32 from the origin's x property to move the flag to the screen's left edge. The animation in lines 155–157 starts after 2/10 of a second and adds 32 to the origin's x property to move the flag to the screen's right edge. The animation in lines 158–160 starts after 3/10 of a second and subtracts 32 from the origin's x property to move the flag to the screen's left edge. Finally, the animation in lines 161–163 starts after 4/10 of a second and adds 16 to the origin's x property to move the flag back to its original position.

```
148        // shakes the flag to visually indicate incorrect response
149        func shakeFlag() {
150            UIView.animateWithDuration(0.1,
151                animations: {self.flagImageView.frame.origin.x += 16})
152            UIView.animateWithDuration(0.1, delay: 0.1, options: nil,
153                animations: {self.flagImageView.frame.origin.x -= 32},
154                completion: nil)
155            UIView.animateWithDuration(0.1, delay: 0.2, options: nil,
156                animations: {self.flagImageView.frame.origin.x += 32},
157                completion: nil)
158            UIView.animateWithDuration(0.1, delay: 0.3, options: nil,
159                animations: {self.flagImageView.frame.origin.x -= 32},
160                completion: nil)
161            UIView.animateWithDuration(0.1, delay: 0.4, options: nil,
162                animations: {self.flagImageView.frame.origin.x += 16},
163                completion: nil)
164        }
165
```

**Fig. 5.24** | Method shakeFlag.

## 5.6.6 Method displayQuizResults

When the user has answered all of the quiz questions, method submitGuess calls method displayQuizResults to display a dialog containing the results. Lines 168–170 creates a locale-specific percentage String (introduced in Section 3.6.6) containing the correct guesses and the total number of guesses. Lines 173–182 create and display a UIAlertController that shows the results to the user as an alert dialog. When the user touches the dialog's **New Quiz** button, the handler (line 179) calls method resetQuiz to begin a new quiz with a new set of randomly chosen flags.

```
166    // displays quiz results
167    func displayQuizResults() {
168        let percentString = NSNumberFormatter.localizedStringFromNumber(
169            Double(correctGuesses) / Double(totalGuesses),
170            numberStyle: NSNumberFormatterStyle.PercentStyle)
171
172        // create UIAlertController for user input
173        let alertController = UIAlertController(title: "Quiz Results",
174            message: String(format: "%1$i guesses, %2$@ correct",
175                totalGuesses, percentString),
176            preferredStyle: UIAlertControllerStyle.Alert)
177        let newQuizAction = UIAlertAction(title: "New Quiz",
178            style: UIAlertActionStyle.Default,
179            handler: {(action) in self.resetQuiz()})
180        alertController.addAction(newQuizAction)
181        presentViewController(alertController, animated: true,
182            completion: nil)
183    }
184
```

**Fig. 5.25** | Method displayQuizResults.

## 5.6.7 Overridden UIViewController Method prepareForSegue

Figure 5.26 defines the overridden UIViewController method prepareForSegue. As you learned in Section 4.6.7, this method is called when the app is about to segue from one view controller to another. In this app, the method is invoked when the user touches the **Settings** button on the navigation bar to display the SettingsViewController. Line 189 confirms that the "showSettings" segue is the one that's about to be performed and, if so, lines 190–191 cast the segue's destinationViewController to type SettingsViewController and store the result in controller. Then line 192 sets the SettingsViewController's model property so it can interact with the Model object created and maintained by the QuizViewController.

```
185    // called before seque from MainViewController to DetailViewController
186    override func prepareForSegue(segue: UIStoryboardSegue,
187        sender: AnyObject?) {
188
189        if segue.identifier == "showSettings" {
190            let controller =
191                segue.destinationViewController as SettingsViewController
192            controller.model = model
193        }
194    }
195 }
196
```

**Fig. 5.26** | Overridden UIViewController method prepareForSegue.

### 5.6.8 Array Extension shuffle

Figure 5.27 defines method shuffle as an extension to the Swift Array type. Extensions enable you to enhance existing types with new features. Each extension begins with the keyword extension followed by the name of the type you're extending and a body in braces. This extension defines a shuffle method (lines 199–205) that can be called on any Array object. The keyword **mutating** (line 199) is required here because the extension modifies the type's data—in this case, shuffle reorders the Array's elements. Lines 201–204 implement the Fisher-Yates shuffle algorithm. The extension accesses the Array's data via self—the Array object on which shuffle is called (line 65 of Fig. 5.22). For example, in line 201 self.count accesses the Array's count property. Line 203 uses Swift global function swap to exchange the elements at indices first and second. This function uses two inout parameters so it can modify its arguments—Swift requires each argument passed to an inout parameter to be preceded by an ampersand (&).

```
197  // Array extension method for shuffling elements
198  extension Array {
199      mutating func shuffle() {
200          // Modern Fisher-Yates shuffle: http://bit.ly/FisherYates
201          for first in stride(from: self.count - 1, through: 1, by: -1) {
202              let second = Int(arc4random_uniform(UInt32(first + 1)))
203              swap(&self[first], &self[second])
204          }
205      }
206  }
```

**Fig. 5.27** | Array extension shuffle.

## 5.7 SettingsViewController Class

Class SettingsViewController (Sections 5.7.1—5.7.4) is a subclass of UIViewController that enables the user to manage the number of guesses displayed with each flag and the regions from which the flags are chosen. In the file SettingsViewController.swift replace the class definition with the code in Sections 5.7.1—5.7.4.

### 5.7.1 Properties

Figure 5.28 contains the beginning of class SettingsViewController's definition and its properties:

- Line 6 defines the guessesSegmentedControl outlet for interacting with the UISegmentedControl that specifies the number of guesses to display. You created this outlet in Section 5.4.8.

- Line 7 defines the switches outlet collection for interacting with the UISwitches that indicate which regions' flags to include in the quiz. You created this outlet collection in Section 5.4.8.

- Line 9 defines the Model reference model, which is set by the QuizViewController before the segue to the SettingsViewController is performed.

- Lines 10–11 define regionNames—the Strings in this Array are listed in the same order as the corresponding UISwitches in the outlet collection switches.

- Line 12 defines the defaultRegionIndex—if the user turns off all of the regions, the North America UISwitch will be turned back on and flags from that region will be used by default.

- Line 15 defines the Bool settingsChanged—if a setting is changed this will be set to true and, when the user returns to the QuizViewController, the Model's notifyDelegate method will be called (Section 5.7.4) to tell QuizViewController to begin a new quiz with the new settings.

```
1   // SettingsViewController.swift
2   // Manages the app's settings
3   import UIKit
4
5   class SettingsViewController: UIViewController {
6       @IBOutlet weak var guessesSegmentedControl: UISegmentedControl!
7       @IBOutlet var switches: [UISwitch]!
8
9       var model: Model! // set by QuizViewController
10      private var regionNames = ["Africa", "Asia", "Europe",
11          "North_America", "Oceania", "South_America"]
12      private let defaultRegionIndex = 3
13
14      // used to determine whether any settings changed
15      private var settingsChanged = false
16
```

**Fig. 5.28** | SettingsViewController properties.

## 5.7.2 Overridden UIViewController Method viewDidLoad

When the QuizViewController's scene is displayed, overridden UIViewController method viewDidLoad (Fig. 5.29) configures the scene's UISegmentedControl and UISwitches based on the app's current settings. Lines 22–23 set the UISegmentedControl's selectedSegmentIndex based on the Model's numberOfGuesses property. Lines 26–28 iterate through the switches outlet collection and set each UISwitch's on property to the corresponding Bool value from the Model's regions Dictionary. We use the UISwitch's index in the outlet collection to get the corresponding region name in the regionNames Array, then use that as the key for the Dictionary lookup.

```
17      // called when SettingsViewController is displayed
18      override func viewDidLoad() {
19          super.viewDidLoad()
20
21          // select segment based on current number of guesses to display
22          guessesSegmentedControl.selectedSegmentIndex =
23              model.numberOfGuesses / 2 - 1
```

**Fig. 5.29** | Overridden UIViewController method viewDidLoad. (Part 1 of 2.)

```
24
25              // set switches based on currently selected regions
26              for i in 0 ..< switches.count {
27                  switches[i].on = model.regions[regionNames[i]]!
28              }
29          }
30
```

**Fig. 5.29** | Overridden UIViewController method viewDidLoad. (Part 2 of 2.)

### 5.7.3 Event Handlers and Method displayErrorDialog

Figure 5.30 contains the SettingsViewController's @IBActions that you created in Section 5.4.8. When the user changes the number of guesses, the @IBAction numberOf-GuessesChanged sets the number of guesses in the Model and assigns true to settings-Changed to indicate that the QuizViewController needs to start a new quiz (this Bool is used in Section 5.7.4).

```
31          // update guesses based on selected segment's index
32          @IBAction func numberOfGuessesChanged(sender: UISegmentedControl) {
33              model.setNumberOfGuesses(2 + sender.selectedSegmentIndex * 2)
34              settingsChanged = true
35          }
36
37          // toggle region corresponding to toggled UISwitch
38          @IBAction func switchChanged(sender: UISwitch) {
39              for i in 0 ..< switches.count {
40                  if sender === switches[i] {
41                      model.toggleRegion(regionNames[i])
42                      settingsChanged = true
43                  }
44              }
45
46              // if no switches on, default to North America and display error
47              if model.regions.values.filter({$0 == true}).array.count == 0 {
48                  model.toggleRegion(regionNames[defaultRegionIndex])
49                  switches[defaultRegionIndex].on = true
50                  displayErrorDialog()
51              }
52          }
53
54          // display message that at least one region must be selected
55          func displayErrorDialog() {
56              // create UIAlertController for user input
57              let alertController = UIAlertController(
58                  title: "At Least One Region Required",
59                  message: String(format: "Selecting %@ as the default region.",
60                      regionNames[defaultRegionIndex]),
61                  preferredStyle: UIAlertControllerStyle.Alert)
62
```

**Fig. 5.30** | Event handlers and method displayErrorDialog. (Part 1 of 2.)

```
63          let okAction = UIAlertAction(title: "OK",
64              style: UIAlertActionStyle.Cancel, handler: nil)
65          alertController.addAction(okAction)
66
67          presentViewController(alertController, animated: true,
68              completion: nil)
69      }
70
```

**Fig. 5.30** | Event handlers and method `displayErrorDialog`. (Part 2 of 2.)

When the user toggles a `UISwitch`, the `@IBAction switchChanged` toggles to the corresponding region in the `Model` (line 41) and assigns `true` to `settingsChanged`. Next, line 47 checks whether none of the `UISwitch`es are in the "on" position—in that case, we'll programmatically enable the North America `UISwitch`. First, we use the `Model`'s `regions` property to get the `Dictionary` that specifies the region settings, then invoke `Dictionary` read-only property `values`, which returns a collection of the values currently stored. Next, we use that collection's `array` property to get its `Array` representation, then call `Array` method `filter` with the closure argument `{$0 == true}` to locate only the `true` values (if any). Method `filter` returns an `Array` containing the results. If the `Array`'s `count` is 0, then none of the `UISwitch`es are "on," so line 48 toggles the North America region, line 49 sets the corresponding `UISwitch` to the "on" position and line 50 displays an error message dialog indicating that at least one region must be selected. Method `displayError-Dialog` (lines 55–69) uses the same `UIViewController` techniques you learned in Chapter 4.

### 5.7.4 Overridden `UIViewController` Method `viewWillDisappear`

When the user returns to the quiz by touching the **< Flag Quiz** back button in the navigation bar, overridden `UIViewController` method `viewWillDisappear` (Fig. 5.31) is called. This method enables the `SettingsViewController` to perform a task *before* the `QuizViewController` is redisplayed. Line 73 checks whether any settings were changed and, if so, line 74 calls `Model` method `notifyDelegate` (Section 5.5.5), which notifies its delegate (`QuizViewController`) that the settings changed.

```
71      // called when user returns to quiz
72      override func viewWillDisappear(animated: Bool) {
73          if settingsChanged {
74              model.notifyDelegate() // called only if settings changed
75          }
76      }
77  }
```

**Fig. 5.31** | Overridden `UIViewController` method `viewWillDisappear`.

## 5.8 Wrap-Up

In this chapter, you built a **Flag Quiz** app that tests the user's ability to correctly identify country flags. For this app's UI, you completely replaced the default storyboard's contents to specify the flow through the app's scenes. You used a `UINavigationController` to help users navigate between view controllers. We demonstrated how to designate the `UINavigationController` as the storyboard's initial view controller, how to specify its root view controller and how to create a segue from the root view controller (the quiz's scene) to another (the settings scene).

You used `UISegmentedControls` to display mutually exclusive options to the user. We demonstrated how to programmatically set the text in each segment and enable or disable each segment. You used `UISwitches` to allow the user to choose which world regions to include in the quiz and saw how to programmatically set a `UISwitch`'s state based on the app's settings.

In both of the app's scenes, you used several UI controls of the same type—`UISegmentedControls` in the quiz scene and `UISwitches` in the settings scene. We demonstrated how to connect several controls of the same type to an outlet collection (an `Array` of controls) so that you could iterate through them programmatically.

This app used images for hundreds of countries' flags. To obtain their filenames dynamically, you used the Foundation framework class `NSBundle` to get the list of PNG images from the app's main bundle. After the user completed a quiz question, you used Grand Central Dispatch (GCD) function `dispatch_after` to load the next question on the UI thread after a two-second delay. Using the UI thread was important because controls are not thread safe, so all modifications to them must be performed on the same thread to prevent corrupting the UI.

To provide a visual indication of an incorrect guess, we demonstrated `UIView` methods for animating a view's `alpha` and `frame` properties, and you learned that you may also animate a view's `backgroundColor`, `bounds`, `center` and `transform` properties. You used UNIX function `arc4random_uniform` to produce random numbers for choosing a quiz's flags, choosing a flag's incorrect guesses and shuffling `Arrays`.

Finally, you used many Swift programming language features, including the `while` loop, `for-in` loop, range operators (`...` and `..<`) for producing ranges of integer values, various global Swift Standard Library functions (`stride`, `swap`, `countElements`, and `join`), computed properties (for manipulating stored properties) and extensions (for adding capabilities to existing types).

In Chapter 6, you'll create a **Cannon** game using iOS's SpriteKit framework, which provides the primitives you need to build your game's elements, a game loop for rendering the game's animations frame-by-frame and a physics engine for simulating physical interactions between elements of your game, such as how colliding objects bounce off one another, how gravity and friction affects game elements, and more. You'll also handle touch events to fire a cannon.

# 6

# Cannon Game App

### Xcode Game Template, SpriteKit, Animation, Graphics, Sound, Physics, Collision Detection, Scene Transitions, Listening for Touches

## Objectives

In this chapter you'll:

- Use the SpriteKit framework and the Xcode **Game** template to create a simple game that's easy to code and fun to play.

- Create custom **SKScene** subclasses for displaying the game scene and the game-over scene.

- Create the game's graphical elements using **SKNode**s, **SKTextNode**s, **SKSpriteNode**s and **SKShapeNode**s.

- Use **SKPhysicsBody** objects to specify the physics attributes of game elements and to apply impulses that make the game elements move.

- Respond to game-element collisions by conforming to the **SKPhysicsContactDelegate** protocol.

- Add sound to your app using the AVFoundation framework's **AVAudioPlayer** class.

- Respond to touch events.

- Transition between **SKScene**s with an **SKTransition**.

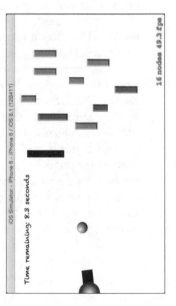

# 6.1 Introduction

This chapter introduces SpriteKit—one of iOS's powerful game-development frameworks. You'll use SpriteKit to build the **Cannon** game app—a landscape-only universal app that challenges you to destroy nine targets before time expires (Fig. 6.1). The game consists of several visual components—a *cannon*, a *cannonball*, the *targets* and a *blocker* that defends the targets. You aim and fire the cannon by *touching* the screen—the cannon then rotates to face the touched point and fires the cannonball in a straight line in that direction.

The game begins with a *10-second time limit*. Each time you destroy a target, you receive a time bonus that's *added* to your remaining time—smaller targets have larger time bonuses because they're harder to hit. Each time you hit the blocker, you receive a two-second time penalty that's *subtracted* from your remaining time. You win by destroying all the targets before running out of time. At the end of the game, the app displays a game-over scene indicating whether you won (Fig. 6.2) or lost (Fig. 6.3), and showing the elapsed time.

Time remaining          Blocker          Targets

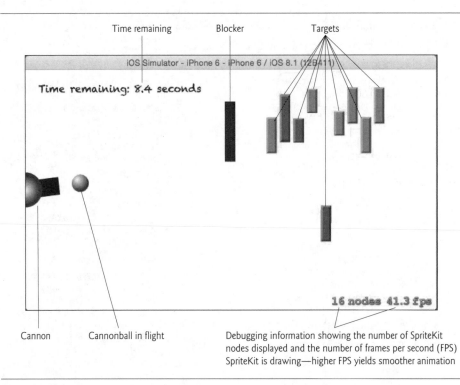

Cannon        Cannonball in flight          Debugging information showing the number of SpriteKit
                                            nodes displayed and the number of frames per second (FPS)
                                            SpriteKit is drawing—higher FPS yields smoother animation

**Fig. 6.1** | Completed **Cannon** game app.

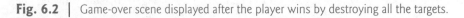

**Fig. 6.2** | Game-over scene displayed after the player wins by destroying all the targets.

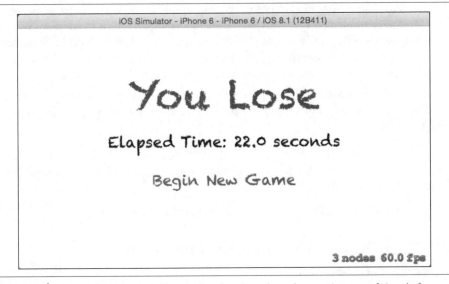

**Fig. 6.3** | Game-over scene displayed after the player loses by running out of time before destroying all the targets.

When you fire the cannon, the game plays a *firing sound*. When a cannonball hits a target piece, a *glass-breaking sound* plays and that target disappears. When the cannonball hits the blocker, a *hit sound* plays and the cannonball bounces off the blocker. The blocker cannot be destroyed. Initially, the targets and blocker move *vertically* at different speeds, reversing direction when they hit the top or bottom of the screen. When a cannonball hits the blocker, SpriteKit's physics capabilities cause the blocker to spin and move to the right, typically causing it to collide with the targets. Once that happens, chaos ensues as the blocker and targets bounce, move and spin, colliding with one another based on the physics properties that you'll set in code.

SpriteKit's features include:

- A hierarchy of classes for managing your game's scenes and for displaying elements in your game, such as text, images (known as **sprites**), shapes and more. These provide the primitives you need to build your game's elements.

- A **game loop** (also called a **rendering loop**) that drives your game, attempting to refresh the screen at 60 frames per second (FPS) for smooth animation. Before game-development frameworks like SpriteKit, you had to build your own game loop. You'd typically use multithreading to process each animation frame in one thread, then display the frame on the screen in the main UI thread. SpriteKit handles all this for you, enabling you to focus on the contents of each frame of your game's animation.

- A **physics engine** that simulates physical interactions between elements of your game, such as how colliding objects bounce off one another, how gravity and friction affect game elements, and more. Before game-development frameworks and physics engines, you had to write all the code that would handle collision detection and other physical effects yourself. Such interactions require complex calculations.

With frameworks like SpriteKit, you can simply specify the physics properties of your game elements and the physics engine handles the rest. In addition, you can have SpriteKit notify you of physics interactions, such as when specific elements collide, so that your game-specific logic can execute. You'll use this to handle interactions between the cannonball and the scene's edges, blocker and targets.

Xcode provides tools for designing SpriteKit scenes and special effects, though we do not use them in this chapter. For additional SpriteKit details, see Apple's SpriteKit Programming Guide at:

```
http://bit.ly/SpriteKitProgrammingGuide
```

For information about Xcode's SpriteKit scene-editing tools, see the *What's New in Sprite-Kit* WWDC session video at:

```
https://developer.apple.com/videos/wwdc/2014/
```

## 6.2 Test-Driving the Cannon Game App

*Opening the Completed Application*
Locate the folder where you extracted the book's examples as specified in the Before You Begin section. In the Cannon folder, double click Cannon.xcodeproj to open the project in Xcode, then run the app in the iOS simulator or on an iOS device.

*Playing the Game*
To aim and fire the cannon, tap anywhere on the screen in the direction in which you'd like to fire the cannon. The cannon then rotates toward that point and fires the cannonball along a line that starts at the end of the cannon's barrel and continues straight through the touch point. Figure 6.4 shows the cannonball in flight nearing a collision with a target.

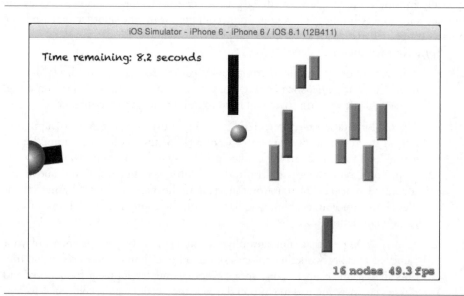

**Fig. 6.4** | Cannonball in flight nearing a collision with a target.

Figure 6.5 shows the targets and blocker after a cannonball collided with the blocker, causing it to collide with the targets. At this point SpriteKit's physics engine determines each element's velocity, direction and rotation. Further collisions between elements continuously change their direction and rotation.

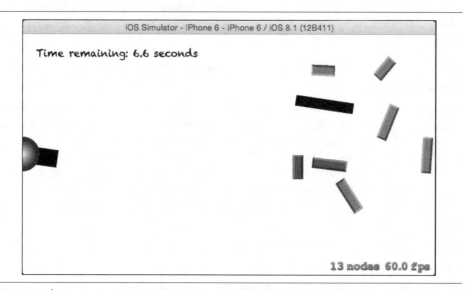

**Fig. 6.5** |  Targets and blocker after a cannonball collided with the blocker, causing the blocker to collide with the targets.

You can fire a cannonball only if there is not another cannonball on the screen. If you're running this in the iOS simulator, the mouse is your "finger." Your goal is to destroy all the targets in the least amount of time. You win if you destroy all the targets before time runs out; otherwise, you lose. When the game-over screen appears, you can tap anywhere on the screen to begin a new game.

## 6.3 Technologies Overview

This section introduces the new technologies that we use in the **Cannon** game app.

### 6.3.1 Xcode Game Template and SpriteKit

The Xcode **Game** template provides the starting point for developing games using one of several game technologies available in iOS:

- SpriteKit—A framework, rendering engine and physics engine for building high-performance, battery-efficient 2D games. You'll use SpriteKit in this chapter's app.

- SceneKit—A framework, rendering engine, physics engine and other capabilities for lighter-weight 3D games that do not have strict performance requirements.

- Metal—A framework for high-performance 3D games that require maximum performance (like the most complex games available on today's popular gaming consoles). This framework is optimized for Apple's A7, A8 and A8X processors.

- OpenGL ES—A low-level C-based library for 2D and 3D graphics that is the foundation of many other game frameworks.

SpriteKit games can contain SceneKit elements and vice versa. When you use the Xcode **Game** template and choose SpriteKit as the app's game technology, Xcode generates code that displays a rotating spaceship image each time you touch the screen. You'll replace this with your own game elements. You'll also use and customize some of the autogenerated code.

### 6.3.2 Adding Sound with the AVFoundation Framework and AVAudioPlayer

You can play sounds in your game using objects of class `AVAudioPlayer` from the AV-Foundation framework. After adding the sound files to your project, you'll load each sound into memory using the `AVAudioPlayer` initializer that receives an `NSURL` representing a sound file's location. Though you'll simply play each sound in this app by calling the corresponding `AVAudioPlayer`'s `play` method, `AVAudioPlayer` provides various properties and methods for controlling audio playback, and iOS supports many additional multimedia capabilities. For more information, see Apple's *Audio Video Starting Point* document at:

```
http://bit.ly/iOSAudioVideoStartingPoint
```

and Apple's *Multimedia Programming Guide* at

```
http://bit.ly/iOSMultimediaProgrammingGuide
```

### 6.3.3 SpriteKit Framework Classes

In this app, you'll work with various SpriteKit framework classes, including:

- `SKView`—An object of this class displays the game's scenes and runs the game loop.

- `SKScene`—The superclass of each scene in your game. This class provides the framework for a scene, including methods that are called by the game loop so you can specify changes to the scene's elements for each animation frame as well as any game logic required in each frame.

- `SKNode`—SKNodes are the fundamental building blocks for the items displayed in an SKScene. Each SKScene is the root SKNode in a tree of SKNodes that specify a scene's content. SKNode provides the base capabilities of a scene element, including its size, position, an `SKPhysicsBody` property that's used to specify the node's physics attributes and more. All SKNodes physics interactions are also dependent on the SKScene's `SKPhysicsWorld`. Each SKNode's location in the scene is specified relative to its parent node. In addition, any transformations you perform on a given node, such as rotating it, apply to that node and all of its children. We use this concept when building the Cannon, which is an SKNode containing the cannon's base and barrel—when we rotate the Cannon, the base and barrel rotate in unison.

- `SKLabelNode`—An SKNode subclass for displaying text.

- `SKSpriteNode`—An SKNode subclass for displaying sprites (images).

- **SKShapeNode**—An SKNode subclass for displaying rectangles, circles, ellipses, arbitrary shapes, etc.

- **SKTransition**—Defines an animated transition between SKScenes. Predefined transitions include cross fade, doors opening, doors closing, doorway, fade, flip, move in, push and reveal. We use the flip and doors-opening transitions in this app.

- **SKTexture**—Represents an image used to render a sprite. In this app, we'll use an SKSpriteNode initializer that creates an SKTexture from an image file.

- **SKAction**—Define tasks that SKNodes perform over time (and thus typically over many animation frames). SKActions are often used to perform animations that change SKNode properties like scale, rotation, alpha (transparency) and position. SKActions can also be used to play sounds, execute code, add new nodes and remove existing nodes.

## 6.3.4 SpriteKit Game Loop and Animation Frames

As we mentioned in Section 6.1, SpriteKit provides a game loop that renders your game's animation frames at a maximum rate of 60 frames per second (FPS) for the smoothest possible animation. The actual frame rate depends on the complexity of your game's logic and the number of nodes on the screen. Also, when running your app in the simulator, the frame rate might also depend on what you currently have running on your computer in addition to the simulator. For example, Fig. 6.1 showed the app running in the simulator at 41.3 frames per second, whereas when we tested the app on an actual device, the app executed at 58 FPS or higher. Note that the information regarding the number of nodes and the FPS displayed in this app is a debugging feature that's helpful for tuning your app. When you prepare your final app for submission to the App Store, you should remove the statements that display this information.

The game loop is defined by class SKScene. During each animation frame, the game loop performs the following tasks:

1. Calls the scene's **update** method—You can override this method to perform frame-by-frame game logic and updates to on-screen elements, such as manually managing element movements, rather than allowing the physics engine to do it. The method receives a **CFTimeInterval** (which is an alias for **Double**) representing the system time. By keeping track of the previous frame's time, you can determine the elapsed time between frames, then scale your updates of game elements accordingly. You'll use this technique in Section 6.9.7 to update the time remaining that's displayed to the user.

2. Executes the SKActions that you specified for the scene's SKNodes. Again, these SKActions might take many animation frames to complete.

3. Calls the scene's **didEvaluateActions** method—You can override this method to make changes after SKActions execute. For example, in a scrolling game that continues from left to right, as a node moves to the right, you might want to re-center the node on the scene and move the scene's background.

4. Executes physics simulations, based on the physics attributes you specified for the scene's nodes.

5. Calls the scene's `didSimulatePhysics` method—You can override this method to make changes after the physics engine updates the scene's nodes for the current animation frame. This method is used similarly to `didEvaluateActions`.

6. Applies `SKConstraints` for the scene's nodes—An `SKConstraint` defines a constraint on a node, such as the direction the node must face, the boundary in which the node must appear and the maximum distance between nodes.

7. Calls the scene's `didApplyConstraints` method—You can override this method to make changes after the nodes' `SKConstraints` are applied. This method is used similarly to `didEvaluateActions` and `didSimulatePhysics`.

8. Calls the scene's `didFinishUpdate` method—This method provides a final chance for you to make changes to a scene before the current animation frame is rendered.

At this point, the scene renders its nodes off the screen, then displays the entire frame. You can also define the methods discussed above in a class that implements the `SKSceneDelegate` protocol. If you set the `SKScene`'s `delegate` property to an `SKSceneDelegate`, then the methods discussed in this section are called on the `delegate`, rather than the `SKScene`.

### 6.3.5 Physics

A key benefit of using a game-development framework like SpriteKit is the built-in physics simulation capabilities, which require complex calculations. SpriteKit handles these for you, based on the scene's `SKPhysicsWorld` and the properties that you set on the nodes' `SKPhysicsBody` objects. SpriteKit supports two types of physics bodies—edge based and volume based. **Edge-based physics bodies** do not have mass and are not affected by physics interactions—these are used, for example, to define a scene's edges and immovable areas within a scene. **Volume-based physics bodies** have mass and are affected by physics interaction (unless you opt out on a node-by-node basis).

When you create an `SKNode`'s `SKPhysicsBody`, SpriteKit automatically calculates the node's mass based on its size—the larger the mass, the more force that's required to move the body and the more force that's applied to other bodies in a collision. You can also manually set each `SKPhysicsBody`'s `mass` so that you can specify the relative masses of your game's elements. This could be useful, for example, if you have projectiles that are the same size, but are meant to simulate items with different densities—denser items are heavier and thus have more mass. So, if you throw a hollow ball and a solid rock that are the same size at the same speed, the rock has greater density, thus it collides with other objects with more energy.

### 6.3.6 Collision Detection and the `SKPhysicsContactDelegate` Protocol

In earlier Android and iOS books, we coded every aspect of the game, from the game loop to the rendering of the game's elements. We manually performed simple collision detection based on rectangular shapes that enclosed the objects. This was complicated and inaccurate—sometimes resulting in collisions when the elements colliding were not actually touching one another. SpriteKit handles that complexity for you. Once you specify the `SKPhysicsBody` objects for the `SKScene`'s nodes, SpriteKit's physics engine handles collision detection for you. In addition, with iOS 8, SpriteKit now supports precise collision detection, based on a node's actual shape, rather than rectangular areas.

As you'll see, you can be notified when objects in your game collide by defining a class that conforms to the `SKPhysicsContactDelegate` protocol. You'll use the following SKPhysicsBody properties to define bit masks that the physics engine uses to determine which collisions result in calls to the SKPhysicsContactDelegate:

- `categoryBitMask`—Specifies up to 32 categories for a physics body (1 bit for each category). You define the categories and use this bit mask to help identify which physics bodies should participate in collisions. The default value for this bit mask is all bits on.

- `collisionBitMask`—When two nodes overlap, the `categoryBitMask` of one is bitwise ANDed with the `collisionBitMask` of the other and vice versa. If the result of these operations is nonzero, the physics bodies are colliding. The default value for this bit mask is all bits on. Because both `categoryBitMask` and `collisionBitMask` have all bits on by default, all nodes for which you create SKPhysicsBody objects participate in collision detection by default.

- `contactTestBitMask`—By default, your SKPhysicsContactDelegate is notified only for collisions you specify with this bit mask. When two nodes overlap, the `categoryBitMask` of one is bitwise ANDed with the `contactTestBitMask` of the other (and vice versa). If the result is nonzero, methods of the SKPhysicsContactDelegate are called by the game loop. This protocol provides methods `didBeginContact` and `didEndContact`—each receives an SKPhysicsContact object containing references to the two SKPhysicsBody objects participating in the collision. The default value for this bit mask is all bits off, so the SKPhysicsContactDelegate is notified only if you set an appropriate bit in `categoryBitMask`. We'll show how to do this in subsequent sections.

We discuss Swift bit manipulation in our book *Swift for Programmers*.

## 6.3.7 CGGeometry Structures and Functions

The ApplicationServices Framework contains CGGeometry `structs` and convenience functions for working with basic geometric types. In SpriteKit, many properties and method parameters are declared with CGGeometry types. We use several of these types and convenience functions thoughtout this app:

- `CGFloat`—Values in CGGeometry types are specified as this floating-point type. Swift does not allow implicit conversions, so you'll often need to convert Swift numeric values to type `CGFloat` for use with SpriteKit.[1]

- `CGPoint`—Contains properties x and y for an object's coordinates. You can create a CGPoint object by calling `CGPointMake` with arguments for *x*- and *y*-coordinates. You'll use CGPoints to specify the location of SpriteKit nodes. In UIKit, coordinates are measured from the upper-left corner of a view, with *x*-coordinates increasing from left to right and *y*-coordinates increasing from top to bottom. SpriteKit coordinates, however, are measured from the *lower-left corner* of a node's parent node with *x*-coordinates increasing from left to right and *y*-coordinates increasing from *bottom to top*.

---

1. According to the Apple Developer Forums, the Swift team is considering support for the CGFloat type directly in Swift so that such conversions are not necessary.

- **CGSize**—Contains properties `width` and `height` for the object's bounding box. You can create a `CGSize` object by calling **CGSizeMake** with width and height arguments.

- **CGRect**—Contains a `CGPoint` and a `CGSize` representing a rectangle's upper-left corner location, and its width and height. You can create a `CGRect` object by calling **CGRectMake** with arguments for the `CGPoint`'s *x*- and *y*-coordinates and the `CGSize`'s width and height.

- **CGVector**—Represents a vector with a direction and a magnitude. The vector is specified as *x* and *y* offsets (named `dx` and `dy`) from an object's existing location—the larger the offsets, the greater the vector's magnitude. You can create a `CGVector` object by calling **CGVectorMake** with arguments for `dx` (the change along the *x*-axis) and `dy` (the change along the *y*-axis). You'll use `CGVectors` to specify the direction in which a SpriteKit node should move and the magnitude of the force to apply to the node.

### 6.3.8 Overriding UIResponder Method touchesBegan

Class **UIResponder** defines the capabilities that enable on-screen elements to respond to events, such as the user touching the screen. Class `SKNode` is a subclass of `UIResponder`, so all `SKNodes` can respond to user-interface events. Users interact with this app by touching the device's screen. A *touch* aims the cannon at the touch point, then fires the cannon. To process simple touch events, you'll override `UIResponder` method `touchesBegan` (Section 6.9.6). In the next chapter, you'll learn more about touch-event handling—specifically, you'll handle and track multiple touches so the user can draw multiple lines at once by dragging more than one finger.

### 6.3.9 Game-Element Sizes and Velocities Based on Screen Size

In this example's classes, we define many constants that represent percentages for sizing and positioning the game's elements, based on the SKScene's width and height. For example, we use 50% of the SKScene's width to determine the location of the blocker, and the first target is at 60% of the SKScene's width. Similarly, the heights of the blocker and targets are percentages of the SKScene's height. You can change the constants we define to change the sizes and locations of the game's elements.

### 6.3.10 Swift Features

In this app, you'll use several more Swift programming-language features.

*Optional Chaining*
When manipulating a property that's defined with a Swift optional type, you can use optional chaining with ? to ensure that an expression continues executing only if the property is not `nil`. For example, in the statement:

```
self.physicsBody?.friction = 0.0
```

first `physicsBody?` is evaluated to determine whether `physicsBody` is `nil`. If not, the next operation in the chain—setting the `friction` property—is performed; otherwise, all other operations in the chain—that is, everything to the right of the ?—are ignored.

### struct *Types, Type Constants and* enum *Types*

In Section 3.2.13, you learned that Swift supports both references types (classes) and value types (structs and enums). Swift's struct and enum types are similar to classes, but are value types that do not support inheritance.

In this app, you'll define a struct type (Section 6.9.1) to represent the bit flags that SpriteKit uses to categorize physics bodies and test for collisions between them. The struct will contain several type constants—that is, constants associated with the type rather than with an individual object of the type. As you'll see, such constants are declared with the static keyword and accessed by following their type name with a dot (.) and the constant name—as in CollisionCategory.Target. Type constants (and similarly type variables declared with var) are like class variables in many other C-based object-oriented languages. For more details on Swift structs, see the Classes and Structures chapter of Apple's *Swift Programming Language* book at:

> http://bit.ly/SwiftClassesAndStructs

You'll also define enum types in Sections 6.6.1– and 6.7.1 to represent sets of named constants that you access like type constants—by following their type name with a dot (.) and the constant name. Swift's enum types (which we discuss in detail in our book *Swift for Programmers*) are much more flexible and powerful than their counterparts in many other C-based programming languages. For more details on Swift enums, see the Enumerations chapter of Apple's *Swift Programming Language* book at:

> http://bit.ly/SwiftEnums

### 6.3.11 NSLocalizedString

In Section 2.8, we demonstrated how to use Xcode and XLIFF files to internationalize the **Welcome** app and provide localized Strings in Spanish. All of the Strings were specified at *design time* in the app's storyboard. Most apps also define in their code Strings that are displayed to the user (or, in the case of the VoiceOver, spoken to the user)—such Strings must be localized at runtime. In Section 6.11, we'll show how to use Foundation framework function NSLocalizedString to specify localizable Strings in your source code.

## 6.4  Creating the Project and Classes

In this section you'll configure the **Cannon** game's project. Unlike prior apps, you will not build a UI in this chapter—Xcode's **Game** app template autogenerates the one view controller you'll need. The game's graphics will be displayed within an SKView that Xcode attaches to the view controller.

### *Creating the Project*

Begin by creating a new **Game** project. Specify the following settings in the **Choose options for your new project** sheet:

- **Product Name:** Cannon.
- **Organization Name:** Deitel & Associates, Inc.—or use your own organization name.
- **Company Identifier:** com.deitel—or use your own company identifier.

- **Language: Swift.**
- **Game Technology: SpriteKit**—iOS's 2D gaming framework.
- **Devices: Universal.**

After specifying the settings, click **Next**, indicate where you'd like to save your project and click **Create** to create the project.

### *Landscape Orientation*

This app is landscape-only—as most games are. In the project settings' **General** tab that's displayed in the Xcode **Editor** area, scroll to the **Deployment Info** section, then for **Device Orientation** ensure that only **Landscape Left** and **Landscape Right** are selected.

### *Hide Status Bar*

Most games use the device's full screen to display game content. By default, the **Game** app template is configured to hide the device's status bar that normally appears at the top of the screen. If you prefer to keep the status bar on the screen, in the project settings' **General** tab that's displayed in the Xcode **Editor** area, scroll to the **Deployment Info** section, then uncheck **Hide status bar**. We left this option checked for this app.

### *Add the App Icons to the Asset Catalog*

As you've done in the earlier apps, add app icons to the project's asset catalog.

### *Add the Game's Sprites (Images) to the Asset Catalog*

This app displays several sprites representing the cannon's base, cannonball, targets and blocker. These are located with the book's examples in the `images/CannonImages` folder. To add the images:

1. In the **Project** explorer, select the app's asset catalog (`Images.xcassets`).
2. In Finder, locate the folder containing the book's examples, then open its subfolder named `images/CannonImages`.
3. Drag the image files into the asset catalog's left column below **AppIcon**.

### *Adding the Sounds to the App*

This app's sound files—`blocker_hit.wav`, `target_hit.wav` and `cannon_fire.wav`—are located with the book's examples in the `sounds` folder. To add these files to your project:

1. In the **Project** explorer, right click the `Cannon` group, select **New Group** and name the group `sounds`.
2. In Finder, locate the folder containing the book's examples, then open its subfolder named `sounds`.
3. Drag the sound files onto the new `sounds` group you just created.
4. In the sheet that appears, ensure that **Copy items if needed** is checked.
5. Click **Finish**.

### *Add the Game's Other Classes*

Next, repeat the following steps to create the files for the classes `Blocker`, `Target`. `Cannon` and `GameOverScene`:

1. In the **Project** explorer, right click the Cannon group and select **New File…**

2. From the **iOS > Source** category, select **Cocoa Touch Class** and click **Next**.

3. For **Class**, enter the class name.

4. For **Subclass of**, select SKSpriteNode for the Blocker and Target classes, SKNode for the Cannon class and SKScene for the GameOverScene class.

5. For **Language**, ensure that **Swift** is selected (it should be by default), then click **Next**.

6. Click **Create** to create the file.

7. In the **Editor** area, change import UIKit to import SpriteKit and save the file.

## 6.5 Class GameViewController

Class GameViewController (Fig. 6.6) defines a view controller containing an SKView that displays an SKScene consisting of SpriteKit nodes. This class was autogenerated by Xcode when we created the **Game** project in Section 6.4, but we modified method viewDidLoad. We also deleted above classGameViewController the SKNode extension, which loads a pre-defined scene from an .sks file—in this app, we create the scene programmatically, rather than with Xcode's SpriteKit scene designer. Lines 8–10 declare global implicitly un-wrapped optional AVAudioPlayer variables that will be used to play the app's sounds when the cannon fires, when a cannonball hits a blocker and when the cannonball hits a target.

```
 1  // GameViewController.swift
 2  // Creates and presents the GameScene
 3  import AVFoundation
 4  import UIKit
 5  import SpriteKit
 6
 7  // sounds defined once and reused throughout app
 8  var blockerHitSound: AVAudioPlayer!
 9  var targetHitSound: AVAudioPlayer!
10  var cannonFireSound: AVAudioPlayer!
11
12  class GameViewController: UIViewController {
13      // called when GameViewController is displayed on screen
14      override func viewDidLoad() {
15          super.viewDidLoad()
16
17          // load sounds when view controller loads
18          blockerHitSound = AVAudioPlayer(contentsOfURL:
19              NSURL(fileURLWithPath: NSBundle.mainBundle().pathForResource(
20                  "blocker_hit", ofType: "wav")!), error: nil)
21          targetHitSound = AVAudioPlayer(contentsOfURL:
22              NSURL(fileURLWithPath: NSBundle.mainBundle().pathForResource(
23                  "target_hit", ofType: "wav")!), error: nil)
24          cannonFireSound = AVAudioPlayer(contentsOfURL:
25              NSURL(fileURLWithPath: NSBundle.mainBundle().pathForResource(
26                  "cannon_fire", ofType: "wav")!), error: nil)
27
```

**Fig. 6.6** │ Class GameViewController. (Part I of 2.)

```
28          let scene = GameScene(size: view.bounds.size) // create scene
29          scene.scaleMode = .AspectFill // resize scene to fit the screen
30
31          let skView = view as SKView // get GameViewController's SKView
32          skView.showsFPS = true // display frames-per-second
33          skView.showsNodeCount = true // display # of nodes on screen
34          skView.ignoresSiblingOrder = true // for SpriteKit optimizations
35          skView.presentScene(scene) // display the scene
36       }
37    }
```

**Fig. 6.6** | Class GameViewController. (Part 2 of 2.)

## 6.5.1 Overridden UIViewController Method viewDidLoad

When the view loads, method viewDidLoad creates an AVAudioPlayer for each sound (lines 18–26). The AVAudioPlayer initializer used here receives an NSURL representing the audio file's location in the app bundle and an NSErrorPointer object in which an error message is stored if the initializer fails to load the audio file. A nil second argument indicates that the app ignores the error if one occurs.

Lines 19–20 use the NSURL initializer that receives an NSPath specifying the audio file's location. We obtain the NSPath from the app's main NSBundle (as you did for image files in Section 5.5.3). NSBundle method **pathForResource** returns an optional NSPath—we know the audio file is included in the app's bundle, so we use Swift's ! operator to force unwrap the optional without checking whether it's nil.

The remaining code in viewDidLoad was autogenerated. Line 28 creates a GameScene object. This class (discussed in Section 6.9) is a subclass of SKScene that defines the game's elements and logic. A game, of course, can have many scenes, so the GameViewController is responsible for presenting the game's initial scene when the view controller first loads. The GameScene initializer receives a CGSize specifying the scene's width and height—in this case, the size of the view controller's root view. A scene could be larger than its containing scene if you intend to move the scene as the user moves through the game.

Line 29 sets scene's scaleMode property to the SKSceneScaleMode constant Aspect-Fill, which resizes the scene to fill the entire screen. Other options for this property are Fill, AspectFill and AspectFit. None of these options affects the **Cannon** game because the scene's size precisely matches its parent view's size.

In class GameViewController, the root view represented by the class's inherited view property is actually an SKView for displaying SpriteKit nodes. Line 31 casts this property to an SKView using Swift's as operator, so that lines 32–35 can use SKScene properties and an SKScene method. Lines 32–33 set the SKScene properties showsFPS and showsNode-Count to true, indicating that the scene should show the number of graphics frames-per-second being rendered and the number of SpriteKit nodes being displayed.

**Performance Tip 6.1**

*SKScene properties showsFPS and showsNodeCount help you understand your scene's performance. SpriteKit attempts to render scenes at 60 frames per second (FPS). If your scene renders significantly slower, you should tune your game's performance. The number of nodes can affect the frames per second, so you might need to reduce the total number of nodes.*

Line 34 sets the SKScene property `ignoresSiblingOrder` to `true` (the default is `false`). This is a performance optimization that enables SpriteKit to ignore parent–child relationships when rendering nodes on the screen. If such relationships are important in your app—for example, to ensure that a child node always appears in front of its parent—then you should remove this line of code.

Line 35 calls SKScene method `presentScene` to display the GameScene. As you'll see, this results in a call to the GameScene's overridden SKScene method `didMoveToView` (Section 6.9.3), which configures and starts the game.

### 6.5.2 Why Are the AVAudioPlayer Variables Global?

In other programming languages, we'd normally define the variables in lines 8–10 as `static` class variables in the classes Blocker (Section 6.6), Target (Section 6.7) and Cannon (Section 6.8), respectively, because these sounds are associated with objects of those classes and can be shared among those objects. Swift refers to class variables as type variables. At the time of this writing, type variables are supported only in structs and enums. Though the Swift documentation shows how to create type variables in classes, the Swift compiler currently reports an error if you use them. Unfortunately, we cannot use Swift's struct and enum types in this app to take advantage of type variables. The various classes we define must inherit from SpriteKit framework classes—struct and enum types do not support inheritance.

### 6.5.3 Autogenerated Methods That We Deleted from Class GameViewController

We deleted each of the following autogenerated overridden UIViewController methods from class GameViewController, as they're not necessary in this app:

- `shouldAutorotate`—Determines whether the view controller should autorotate when the user rotates the device. The autogenerated implementation returns `true`, which is the default, so this method is unnecessary. If an app should always remain in its initial orientation, you can keep this method and change it to return `false`.

- `supportedInterfaceOrientations`—Determines the view controller's supported orientations. You can specify these in the app's settings, as you did in Section 6.4, so this method is unnecessary. The autogenerated method, by default, specifies that the view controller should support all interface orientations except upside-down for an iPhone and all orientations for an iPad. You can also provide more complex logic in this method, based on your app's requirements.

- `prefersStatusBarHidden`—Determines whether the iOS status bar is displayed above the view controller. You can specify this in the app's settings, as you did in Section 6.4, so this method is unnecessary.

## 6.6  Class Blocker

Class Blocker (Sections 6.6.1—6.6.3) uses a rectangular sprite to define a blocker and configures the blocker's physicsBody. We create only one medium-sized blocker. The class enables you to add small, medium or large Blockers to make the game more challenging.

### 6.6.1 BlockerSize enum and Class Blocker's Properties

Recall that all of the game's on-screen elements are scaled, based on the scene's size. The BlockerSize enum (lines 6–10 of Fig. 6.7) defines three constants (Small, Medium and Large) that are used as multipliers in the calculations that determine a Blocker's height (as you'll see in Section 6.6.2). They're also used to determine the time penalty to subtract from the game's remaining time when a cannonball hits a Blocker—the BlockerSize constant's underlying value is used as the time penalty, so hitting a larger blocker results in a larger penalty.

```swift
 1   // Blocker.swift
 2   // Defines a blocker
 3   import AVFoundation
 4   import SpriteKit
 5
 6   enum BlockerSize: CGFloat {
 7       case Small = 1.0
 8       case Medium = 2.0
 9       case Large = 3.0
10   }
11
12   class Blocker : SKSpriteNode {
13       // constants for configuring a blocker
14       private let blockerWidthPercent = CGFloat(0.025)
15       private let blockerHeightPercent = CGFloat(0.125)
16       private let blockerSpeed = CGFloat(5.0)
17       private let blockerSize: BlockerSize
18
```

**Fig. 6.7** | BlockerSize enum and class Blocker's properties.

Line 12 indicates that Blocker is a subclass of SKSpriteNode—a node that displays a sprite. The constants in lines 14–15 are percentages that we use to calculate the Blocker's size based on the scene's size. The constant in line 16 helps determine the blocker's speed. The blockerSize is initialized to a BlockerSize constant (Small, Medium or Large) when the Blocker is initialized.

### 6.6.2 Blocker Initializers

Figure 6.8 presents class Blocker's initializers. The initializer at lines 20–39 receives two parameters—the scene's size (a GCSize) and the BlockerSize. Line 21 initializes the blockerSize property. Lines 22–27 invoke superclass SKSpriteNode's initializer that receives:

- an SKTexture representing the nodes sprite image (in this case, the "blocker"),
- an SKColor that can be used to tint the sprite (in this case nil to indicate that the sprite will not be tinted), and
- a CGSize specifying the node's width and height.

```
19        // initializes the Cannon, sizing it based on the scene's size
20        init(sceneSize: CGSize, blockerSize: BlockerSize) {
21            self.blockerSize = blockerSize
22            super.init(
23                texture: SKTexture(imageNamed: "blocker"),
24                color: nil,
25                size: CGSizeMake(sceneSize.width * blockerWidthPercent,
26                    sceneSize.height * blockerHeightPercent *
27                        blockerSize.rawValue))
28
29            // set up the blocker's physicsBody
30            self.physicsBody =
31                SKPhysicsBody(texture: self.texture, size: self.size)
32            self.physicsBody?.friction = 0.0
33            self.physicsBody?.restitution = 1.0
34            self.physicsBody?.linearDamping = 0.0
35            self.physicsBody?.allowsRotation = true
36            self.physicsBody?.usesPreciseCollisionDetection = true
37            self.physicsBody?.categoryBitMask = CollisionCategory.Blocker
38            self.physicsBody?.contactTestBitMask = CollisionCategory.Cannonball
39        }
40
41        // not called, but required if subclass defines an init
42        required init?(coder aDecoder: NSCoder) {
43            fatalError("init(coder:) has not been implemented")
44        }
45
```

**Fig. 6.8** | Blocker initializers.

*Configuring the Blocker's Physics Properties*
As we discussed in Section 6.3.5, each game element's physics properties are specified by creating an SKPhysicsBody and configuring its properties. Each SKNode has an optional SKPhysicsBody property named physicsBody. Lines 30–31 initialize the Blocker's physicsBody property with the initializer that creates a physics body from an SKTexture and a CGSize—in this case the Blocker's inherited texture and size properties that were initialized in the superclass initializer call. Lines 32–38 configure additional SKPhysics-Body properties that will be similarly configured for the app's other game elements. Because physicsBody is an optional, each reference to it uses optional chaining (that is, physicsBody is followed by a ?) to ensure that the properties in lines 32–38 will be set only if physicsBody is *not* nil:

- **friction**—A CGFloat value from 0.0 (smooth) to 1.0 (rough) indicating the roughness of the node's surface. The default value is 0.2. This property helps the physics world determine how physics bodies interact when nodes collide. For example, a car braking on a rough asphalt physics body would slow down faster than a car braking on a smooth ice physics body. In this app, we chose to set the friction to 0.0 for all of the physics bodies to they do not slow down as a result of friction. To replicate real-world surfaces, you'd set this value higher.

- **restitution**—A CGFloat value from 0.0 (not bouncy) to 1.0 (bouncy). The default value is 0.2. This property helps the physics world determine how much energy a physics body loses when it collides with other objects. In this app, we chose to set the `restitution` to `1.0` for all of the physics bodies.

- `linearDamping`—A `CGFloat` value from `0.0` to `1.0` that the physics world uses to simulate friction from air or fluids. The value `0.0` (used for all of this app's physics bodies) indicates that the physics world should not apply any linear damping. The default value is `0.1`.

- `allowsRotation`—A `Bool` value indicating whether the node can rotate. As you saw in the test drive, the blocker begins rotating when it's hit by a cannonball.

- `usePreciseCollisionDetection`—A `Bool` value indicating whether the physics world should use precise collision detection to determine when a node collides with other nodes. This should be set to `true` for fast-moving nodes; otherwise, nodes that should collide could appear to pass through one another.

**Performance Tip 6.2**

*The calculations for precise collision detection take more CPU time to complete and could affect your game's frame rate, so an `SKPhysicsBody`'s `usePreciseCollisionDetection` property should be set to `true` only for small, fast-moving game elements.*

- `categoryBitMask`—This app's categories are defined in the `CollisionCategory` struct in Section 6.9.1. Line 37 indicates that this physics body is a `Blocker`. You define your app's categories as unique bit values 1, 2, 4, 8, 16, 32, etc., up to a maximum of 32 categories.

- `contactTestBitMask`—Used by the physics world to determine when collisions occur between specific nodes and to notify an `SKPhysicsContactDelegate` about them. When two nodes overlap in the physics world, the `categoryBitMask` of one is bitwise ANDed with the `contactTestBitMask` of the other and vice versa. If the result is nonzero, the `SKPhysicsContactDelegate` is notified and passed an `SKPhysicsContact` object containing references to the nodes that collided and other information about the collision. Line 38 indicates that the physics world should test for `Blocker` collisions with a cannonball—that is, a node with its `categoryBitMask` set to `CollisionCategory.Cannonball`.

To see how each of the preceding properties affects the game's physics, experiment with different values for each property.

### Swift Required Initializers

The initializer in lines 42–44 is not used in this app and is provided only so that class `Blocker` will compile. This initializer is defined as `required` in the `NSCoding` protocol, which all `SKNode`s conform to—class `Blocker` is an indirect subclass of `SKNode`. If a class *conforms to a protocol* with a `required` initializer, the class must define that initializer.

Swift types must initialize all their properties—either in their declarations or via initializers. Swift initializers fall into two categories:

- Designated initializers which ensure that every property is initialized.

- Convenience initializers (declared with `convenience`) that each call a designated initializer, providing default values for some or all of the designated initializer's parameters.

When you define a subclass, if it does not provide any initializers, it inherits the superclass's initializers, including the required ones. However, if you explicitly define any subclass initializers, then:

- each must call a designated superclass initializer directly or indirectly, and
- if the superclass has any required initializers (indicating that they must be defined in every subclass), the subclass must explicitly define those required initializers (as we do in lines 42–44).

### Why Is There a Statement Before the Call to **super.init**?

We placed line 21 *before* the call to the superclass's initializer to prevent a compilation error that occurs when a designated initializer is called. In Swift, designated initializers are required to initialize *all* of a class's properties. However the superclass's designated initializer does not know about new properties added in the subclass. There are two ways you can deal with this:

1. Place the initialization statements for the subclass's properties before the call to the superclass's initializer, as we did in line 21.

2. Declare subclass properties as optional types (with ?) or implicitly unwrapped optional types (with !), then initialize them after the call to the superclass's initializer.

If a subclass property's initialization requires an inherited superclass property to be initialized first, then you must use the second option so that you can place the initialization statement after the call to the superclass's initializer.

### 6.6.3 Methods `startMoving`, `playHitSound` and `blockerTimePenalty`

Figure 6.9 contains class Blocker's other methods. Method startMoving (lines 47–50) uses SKPhysicsBody method **applyImpulse** to start the Blocker moving in a direction specified by its CGVector argument. In this case, the CGVector indicates that the Blocker should move up the *y*-axis at a speed determined by the Blocker's mass and the value calculated in line 49). We used the constant velocityMultiplier (passed to startMoving) to adjust element speeds, based on the screen size. Because an element's resulting speed also depends on its mass, we multiply by the blockerSize's rawValue (the underlying value of the BlockerSize enum constant); otherwise, larger blocker sizes move too slowly.

```
46      // applies an impulse to the blocker
47      func startMoving(velocityMultiplier: CGFloat) {
48          self.physicsBody?.applyImpulse(CGVectorMake(0.0,
49              velocityMultiplier * blockerSpeed * blockerSize.rawValue))
50      }
51
52      // plays the blockerHitSound
53      func playHitSound() {
54          blockerHitSound.play()
55      }
56
```

**Fig. 6.9** | Class Blocker. (Part I of 2.)

```
57    // returns time penalty based on blocker size
58    func blockerTimePenalty() -> CFTimeInterval {
59        return CFTimeInterval(BlockerSize.Small.rawValue)
60    }
61  }
```

**Fig. 6.9** | Class Blocker. (Part 2 of 2.)

Method playHitSound is called by the GameScene (Section 6.9.5) when a collision occurs between a cannonball and a blocker. Line 54 calls the AVAudioPlayer's play method to play the sound. Method blockerTimePenalty is called by the GameScene when a cannonball hits the blocker, in which case we subtract a penalty from the game's remaining time. The time penalty is the same as its BlockerSize value—since we use only a Medium blocker in this version of the app, the penalty is two seconds. The method returns the BlockerSize constant's rawValue as a CFTimeInterval, which you'll recall is a type alias for Double.

## 6.7 Class Target

Class Target (Sections 6.7.1—6.7.4) has many similarities to class Blocker, so in this section we focus on the differences.

### 6.7.1 TargetSize and TargetColor enums

Figure 6.10 contains the TargetSize and TargetColor enums. The TargetSize enum defines constants for three target sizes. These constants are used as multipliers in the calculations that determine each Target's actual size. They're also used to determine the time bonus to add to the game's remaining time when a cannonball hits a Target. The Target-Color enum defines constants representing the names of the sprites used to create Targets. Lines 22–23 and 24–25 create Arrays of the TargetColor and TargetSize constants, respectively. The Target initializer (Section 6.7.3) randomly chooses constants from these Arrays to pick a new Target's color and size. In other programming languages, we would have defined these Arrays as class variables (type variables in Swift), but as we mentioned in Section 6.5.2, Swift does not yet support this concept for classes.

```
1   // Target.swift
2   // Defines a target
3   import AVFoundation
4   import SpriteKit
5
6   // enum of target sizes
7   enum TargetSize: CGFloat {
8       case Small = 1.0
9       case Medium = 1.5
10      case Large = 2.0
11  }
12
```

**Fig. 6.10** | TargetSize and TargetColor enums. (Part 1 of 2.)

```
13   // enum of target sprite names
14   enum TargetColor: String {
15       case Red = "target_red"
16       case Green = "target_green"
17       case Blue = "target_blue"
18   }
19
20   // arrays of enum constants used for random selections;
21   // global because Swift does not yet support class variables
22   private let targetColors =
23       [TargetColor.Red, TargetColor.Green, TargetColor.Blue]
24   private let targetSizes =
25       [TargetSize.Small, TargetSize.Medium, TargetSize.Large]
26
```

**Fig. 6.10** | TargetSize and TargetColor enums. (Part 2 of 2.)

## 6.7.2 Class Target Properties

Figure 6.11 shows the beginning of class Target and its properties. Like class Blocker, class Target is a subclass of SKSpriteNode. The constants in lines 29–30 are the percentages we use to calculate the Target's size based on the scene's size. The constant in line 31 helps determine each Target's speed. The constants targetSize and targetColor are initialized to a TargetSize and TargetColor constants, respectively, by the initializer when a Target is created.

```
27   class Target : SKSpriteNode {
28       // constants for configuring a blocker
29       private let targetWidthPercent = CGFloat(0.025)
30       private let targetHeightPercent = CGFloat(0.1)
31       private let targetSpeed = CGFloat(2.0)
32       private let targetSize: TargetSize
33       private let targetColor: TargetColor
34
```

**Fig. 6.11** | Class Target's properties.

## 6.7.3 Target Initializers

Figure 6.12 presents class Target's initializer, which receives the scene's size (a GCSize). Lines 38–39 randomly select a TargetSize, and lines 40–41 randomly select a Target-Color. Next, lines 44–49 invoke superclass SKSpriteNode's initializer that receives an SK-Texture (for one of the target sprites), an SKColor (nil), and a CGSize, as we did in Section 6.6.2 for the Blocker. Lines 52–61 create the Target's physicsBody based on the Target's size, then configure its properties. For the Target, we set the categoryBitMask to CollisionCategory.Target and the contactTestBitMask to CollisionCategory.Cannonball. This enables the physics world to notify the SKPhysicsContactDelegate when a cannonball collides with a Target, so the target can be removed from the scene. Once again, as discussed in Section 6.6.2, we provide the initializer in lines 65–67 only because it's required for class Target to compile.

```
35    // initializes the Cannon, sizing it based on the scene's size
36    init(sceneSize: CGSize) {
37        // select random target size and random color
38        self.targetSize = targetSizes[
39            Int(arc4random_uniform(UInt32(targetSizes.count)))]
40        self.targetColor = targetColors[
41            Int(arc4random_uniform(UInt32(targetColors.count)))]
42
43        // call SKSpriteNode designated initializer
44        super.init(
45            texture: SKTexture(imageNamed: targetColor.rawValue),
46            color: nil,
47            size: CGSizeMake(sceneSize.width * targetWidthPercent,
48                sceneSize.height * targetHeightPercent *
49                    targetSize.rawValue))
50
51        // set up the target's physicsBody
52        self.physicsBody =
53            SKPhysicsBody(texture: self.texture, size: self.size)
54        self.physicsBody?.friction = 0.0
55        self.physicsBody?.restitution = 1.0
56        self.physicsBody?.linearDamping = 0.0
57        self.physicsBody?.allowsRotation = true
58        self.physicsBody?.usesPreciseCollisionDetection = true
59        self.physicsBody?.categoryBitMask = CollisionCategory.Target
60        self.physicsBody?.contactTestBitMask =
61            CollisionCategory.Cannonball
62    }
63
64    // not called, but required if subclass defines an init
65    required init?(coder aDecoder: NSCoder) {
66        fatalError("init(coder:) has not been implemented")
67    }
68
```

**Fig. 6.12** | Target initializers.

### 6.7.4 Methods startMoving, playHitSound and targetTimeBonus

Figure 6.13 contains class Target's other methods. Method startMoving (lines 70–74) uses SKPhysicsBody method applyImpulse to start the Blocker moving in a direction specified by its CGVector argument—for the Targets, we randomly vary their speeds using the calculation in lines 72–73. Initially, the Blocker and all Targets move only vertically, but when a cannonball collides with a Blocker, usually the Blocker collides with the Targets. Once that occurs, for the remainder of the game they all move around the scene, based on their physics collisions with one another and the scene's edges. Method playHitSound (lines 77–79) plays the targetHitSound. Method targetTimeBonus (lines 82–91) returns a CFTimeInterval, based on the Target's size. Smaller Targets are harder to hit so we give a three-second bonus for Small, two-second bonus for Medium and one-second bonus for Large.

```
69      // applies an impulse to the target
70      func startMoving(velocityMultiplier: CGFloat) {
71          self.physicsBody?.applyImpulse(CGVectorMake(0.0,
72              velocityMultiplier * targetSize.rawValue * (targetSpeed +
73                  CGFloat(arc4random_uniform(UInt32(targetSpeed) + 5)))))
74      }
75
76      // plays the targetHitSound
77      func playHitSound() {
78          targetHitSound.play()
79      }
80
81      // returns time bonus based on target size
82      func targetTimeBonus() -> CFTimeInterval {
83          switch targetSize {
84              case .Small:
85                  return 3.0
86              case .Medium:
87                  return 2.0
88              case .Large:
89                  return 1.0
90          }
91      }
92  }
```

**Fig. 6.13** | Methods startMoving, playHitSound and targetTimeBonus.

## 6.8 Class Cannon

Class Cannon (Sections 6.8.1—6.8.4) is a subclass of SKNode (Fig. 6.14, line 6) that aggregates an SKSpriteNode for the cannon's base and an SKShapeNode for the cannon's barrel. Class Cannon also rotates the cannon to face the point where the user touched the screen and fires a cannonball (an SKSpriteNode) in that direction.

### 6.8.1 Cannon Properties

Figure 6.14 shows class Cannon's properties. The constants in lines 8–11 are percentages that we use to determine the cannon base's size, cannonball size and cannon barrel's size, based on the scene's size. The constants at lines 12–13 help determine the cannonball's speed—cannonballSpeed is calculated in the initializer (Section 6.8.2). The constant in line 14 (also calculated in the initializer) specifies the barrel's actual length, which is used when positioning the cannonball before firing. The variable at line 16 (calculated when the user touches the screen) specifies the cannon barrel's angle, which is used to rotate the cannon. Line 17 is an implicitly unwrapped optional SKSpriteNode that refers to the cannonball when the cannon fires. The variable at line 18 is true when a cannonball is on the screen—this variable has internal access rather than private because its used by the GameScene to ensure that only one cannonball is on the screen at a time.

```
 1   // Cannon.swift
 2   // Defines the cannon and handles firing cannonballs
 3   import AVFoundation
 4   import SpriteKit
 5
 6   class Cannon : SKNode {
 7      // constants
 8      private let cannonSizePercent = CGFloat(0.15)
 9      private let cannonballSizePercent = CGFloat(0.075)
10      private let cannonBarrelWidthPercent = CGFloat(0.075)
11      private let cannonBarrelLengthPercent = CGFloat(0.15)
12      private let cannonballSpeed: CGFloat
13      private let cannonballSpeedMultiplier = CGFloat(0.25)
14      private let barrelLength: CGFloat
15
16      private var barrelAngle = CGFloat(0.0)
17      private var cannonball: SKSpriteNode!
18      var cannonballOnScreen = false
19
```

**Fig. 6.14** | Cannon properties.

## 6.8.2 Cannon Initializers

The Cannon initializer (Fig. 6.15) calculates the cannonballSpeed and barrelLength constants (lines 22–23), calls the superclass's designated initializer (line 24), then creates and configures the barrel and cannonBase. The barrel is an SKShapeNode (lines 27–28)—in this case, a rectangle shape as specified by the rectOfSize parameter. Class SKShapeNode also provides initializers for other shapes, including rounded rectangles, circles, ellipses and aribitrary shapes defined by paths or points. Line 29 sets the barrel's fillColor (an SK-Color) to black. SpriteKit can be used to develop games for both iOS and OS X. SKColor is an alias for UIColor on iOS and NSColor on OS X—this enables you to specify color independent of the underlying OS. Line 30 adds the barrel to the Cannon node.

```
20      // initializes the Cannon, sizing it based on the scene's size
21      init(sceneSize: CGSize, velocityMultiplier: CGFloat) {
22         cannonballSpeed = cannonballSpeedMultiplier * velocityMultiplier
23         barrelLength = sceneSize.height * cannonBarrelLengthPercent
24         super.init()
25
26         // configure cannon barrel
27         let barrel = SKShapeNode(rectOfSize: CGSizeMake(barrelLength,
28            sceneSize.height * cannonBarrelWidthPercent))
29         barrel.fillColor = SKColor.blackColor()
30         self.addChild(barrel)
31
32         // configure cannon base
33         var cannonBase = SKSpriteNode(imageNamed: "base")
34         cannonBase.size = CGSizeMake(sceneSize.height * cannonSizePercent,
35            sceneSize.height * cannonSizePercent)
```

**Fig. 6.15** | Cannon initializer. (Part 1 of 2.)

```
36          self.addChild(cannonBase)
37
38          // position barrel based on cannonBase
39          barrel.position = CGPointMake(cannonBase.size.width / 2.0, 0.0)
40       }
41
42       // not called, but required if subclass defines an init
43       required init?(coder aDecoder: NSCoder) {
44          fatalError("init(coder:) has not been implemented")
45       }
46
```

**Fig. 6.15** | Cannon initializer. (Part 2 of 2.)

Line 33 creates the cannonBase as an SKSpriteNode, then lines 34–35 calculate its size. The cannonBase is actually a circular image that we position halfway off the screen when we place the Cannon in the GameScene. When we rotate the Cannon, portions of the image that are located off the screen's left edge rotate onto the screen. Line 36 adds the cannonBase to the Cannon node.

By default, when you add the barrel and cannonBase to the Cannon node, they're centered horizontally and vertically on the node. However, we want the barrel (line 39) positioned so that its left end starts at the cannonBase's center. So, we set the x-coordinate of the barrel's position to half the cannonBase's width. The y-coordinate remains 0.0 to center the barrel vertically on the Cannon node.

### 6.8.3 Method rotateToPointAndFire

When the user touches the screen to aim and fire the Cannon, the GameScene passes the touch point (a CGPoint) to rotatePointAndFire (Fig. 6.16). This method calculates the barrelAngle based on deltaX and deltaY (lines 50–51)—the difference between the Cannon base's centerpoint coordinates and the touch point coordinates. Since the Cannon's x-coordinate is 0.0, the difference in the x-coordinates is simply the touch point's x-coordinate. Because the Cannon is positioned at the center of the scene's left edge, the difference between the y-coordinates will be a positive value if the touch point is above the Cannon's position and negative if the touch point is below—recall that y-coordinates are measured from the scene's lower-left corner. Line 52 calculates the angle in *radians* using the C Standard Library function atan2f (see en.wikipedia.org/wiki/Atan2 for a discussion of the math behind this calculation). The angle 0 radians represents the Cannon's x-axis and positive angles increase counter-clockwise.

```
47       // rotate cannon to user's touch point, then fire cannonball
48       func rotateToPointAndFire(point: CGPoint, scene: SKScene) {
49          // calculate barrel rotation angle
50          let deltaX = point.x
51          let deltaY = point.y - self.position.y
52          barrelAngle = CGFloat(atan2f(Float(deltaY), Float(deltaX)))
53
```

**Fig. 6.16** | Method rotateToPointAndFire. (Part 1 of 2.)

```
54            // rotate the cannon barrel to touch point, then fire
55            let rotateAction = SKAction.rotateToAngle(
56                barrelAngle, duration: 0.25, shortestUnitArc: true)
57
58            // perform rotate action, then call fireCannonball
59            self.runAction(rotateAction, completion: {
60                if !self.cannonballOnScreen {
61                    self.fireCannonball(scene)
62                }
63            })
64        }
65
```

**Fig. 6.16** | Method rotateToPointAndFire. (Part 2 of 2.)

*Specifying **SKActions** for an **SKNode** to Perform*

Lines 55–56 define an SKAction that rotates the Cannon's root SKNode to face the touch point. Recall that performing a transformation on an SKNode also performs that transformation on all of the node's children—in this case, the Cannon's base and barrel. SKAction type method **rotateToAngle** receives as parameters:

- the angle (barrelAngle) to which to rotate the cannon so that the barrel faces the touch point,

- the animation's duration (0.25 seconds) and

- a Bool indicating whether to perform the rotate animation in a direction that requires the smallest rotation arc—true here, so the cannon barrel always stays on the screen, rather than sometimes temporarily rotating in nearly a complete circle, which would result in the barrel temporarily rotating off the screen.

To execute an SKAction, you use the node's **runAction** method. The version used in lines 59–63 takes two parameters—the SKAction to perform and a completion handler (typically implemented as a closure in Swift) that's called *after* the SKAction completes. The game loop might require many animation frames to complete the rotation action, because it executes for 0.25 seconds and SpriteKit attempts to display 60 frames per second. After the action completes, the completion handler ensures that there is not a cannonball on the screen (line 60), then calls fireCannonball (line 61). Placing the call to fireCannonball in runAction's completion handler ensures that the cannonball does not appear on the screen until the cannon faces the touch point.

## 6.8.4 Methods fireCannonball and createCannonball

Once method rotateToPointAndFire finishes rotating the Cannon, method fireCannonball (Fig. 6.17, lines 67–85) is called to create the cannonball, place it on the screen, start it moving and play the cannonFireSound. Line 68 indicates that a cannonball is now on the screen, so that the GameScene can ensure that only one is on the screen at a time. Lines 72–73 use the C Standard Library functions cos (cosine) and sin (sine) and the current barrelAngle to determine the barrel's endpoint so we can fire the cannonball from the correct position on the screen—the *y*-coordinate will be positive if the barrel's endpoint is above the Cannon's *x*-axis. Next, line 74 calls method createCannonball (lines 88–108) to create an SKSpriteNode representing the cannonball. Then line 75 sets the cannonball's position based on the barrel's endpoint. Lines 78–79 create a velocityVector representing the cannonball's direction and speed. Line 82 attaches the cannonball to the scene, then line 83 uses the velocityVector to apply an impulse to the cannonball's physics-Body. Finally, line 84 plays the cannonFireSound.

```
66      // create cannonball, attach to scene and start it moving
67      private func fireCannonball(scene: SKScene) {
68          cannonballOnScreen = true
69
70          // determine starting point for cannonball based on
71          // barrelLength and current barrelAngle
72          let x = cos(barrelAngle) * barrelLength
73          let y = sin(barrelAngle) * barrelLength
74          let cannonball = createCannonball(scene.frame.size)
75          cannonball.position = CGPointMake(x, self.position.y + y)
76
77          // create based on barrel angle
78          let velocityVector =
79              CGVectorMake(x * cannonballSpeed, y * cannonballSpeed)
80
81          // put cannonball on screen, move it and play fire sound
82          scene.addChild(cannonball)
83          cannonball.physicsBody?.applyImpulse(velocityVector)
84          cannonFireSound.play()
85      }
86
87      // creates the cannonball and configures its physicsBody
88      func createCannonball(sceneSize: CGSize) -> SKSpriteNode {
89          cannonball = SKSpriteNode(imageNamed: "ball")
90          cannonball.size =
91              CGSizeMake(sceneSize.height * cannonballSizePercent,
92                  sceneSize.height * cannonballSizePercent)
93
94          // set up physicsBody
95          cannonball.physicsBody =
96              SKPhysicsBody(circleOfRadius: cannonball.size.width / 2.0)
97          cannonball.physicsBody?.friction = 0.0
98          cannonball.physicsBody?.restitution = 1.0
99          cannonball.physicsBody?.linearDamping = 0.0
100         cannonball.physicsBody?.allowsRotation = true
101         cannonball.physicsBody?.usesPreciseCollisionDetection = true
102         cannonball.physicsBody?.categoryBitMask =
103             CollisionCategory.Cannonball
104         cannonball.physicsBody?.contactTestBitMask =
105             CollisionCategory.Target | CollisionCategory.Blocker |
106             CollisionCategory.Wall
107         return cannonball
108     }
109 }
```

**Fig. 6.17** | Class Cannon.

Function createCannonball (lines 88–108) creates an SKSpriteNode representing the cannonball (line 89), sets its size (lines 90–92) and configures its physicsBody (lines 95–106), then returns the cannonball for display by method fireCannonball. Recall that the physics world uses a physicsBody's categoryBitMask and contactTestBitMask to check for collisions between bodies and notify the SKPhysicsContactDelegate. Lines 102–103 set the cannonball's categoryBitMask to CollisonCategory.Cannonball and lines 104–106 set its contactTestBitMask to the bitwise OR of CollisonCategory.Target and CollisonCategory.Wall. These values, combined with the corresponding Blocker, Target and GameScene physicsBody bit masks, enable the physics world to:

- Determine when the cannonball collides with a Blocker so that the GameScene can play the blocker-hit sound and apply a time penalty.

- Determine when the cannonball collides with a Target so that the GameScene can play the target-hit, apply a time bonus and remove the cannonball and Target from the scene.

- Determine when the cannonball collides with a wall so that the GameScene can remove the cannonball from the scene.

## 6.9 Class GameScene

Class GameScene (Sections 6.9.1—6.9.7) creates the game's elements, manages the game's state, responds to collisions, handles touch events for firing the Cannon and transitions to the GameOverScene (Section 6.10) when the game ends.

### 6.9.1 CollisionCategory struct

The CollisionCategory struct (Fig. 6.18) defines several type constants—i.e., constants that are associated with the type, rather than a specific object of the type. Recall that type constants are declared with static and accessed by following their type name with a dot (.) and the constant name—as in CollisionCategory.Target. To be used properly in the physics world's collision detection, the CollisionCategory constants should be *unique* bit values that can be combined in bitwise AND (&) and bitwise OR (|) operations. The values of the constants in lines 8–11 are 1, 2, 4 and 8, respectively.

```
1   // GameScene.swift
2   // Creates the scene, detects touches and responds to collisions
3   import AVFoundation
4   import SpriteKit
5
6   // used to identify objects for collision detection
7   struct CollisionCategory {
8       static let Blocker : UInt32 = 1
9       static let Target: UInt32 = 1 << 1 // 2
10      static let Cannonball: UInt32 = 1 << 2 // 4
11      static let Wall: UInt32 = 1 << 3 // 8
12  }
13
```

**Fig. 6.18** | CollisionCategory struct with constants that are used in collision detection.

## 6.9.2 GameScene Class Definition and Properties

Figure 6.18 contains the global private constant numberOfTargets, the beginning of the GameScene class definition and the class's properties.

```
14   // global because no type constants in Swift classes yet
15   private let numberOfTargets = 9
16
17   class GameScene: SKScene, SKPhysicsContactDelegate {
18       // game elements that the scene interacts with programmatically
19       private var secondsLabel: SKLabelNode! = nil
20       private var cannon: Cannon! = nil
21
22       // game state
23       private var timeLeft: CFTimeInterval = 10.0
24       private var elapsedTime: CFTimeInterval = 0.0
25       private var previousTime: CFTimeInterval = 0.0
26       private var targetsRemaining: Int = numberOfTargets
27
```

**Fig. 6.19** | Class GameScene and its properties.

### Constant *numberOfTargets*

The constant numberOfTargets is defined as a global constant (but private to this file) so that it can be used to initialize property targetsRemaining (line 26). Swift does not currently allow one property of a class to be initialized in its declaration with the value of another property of the class—an error occurs.

### Class *GameScene*

Line 17 indicates that class GameScene is a subclass of SKScene and conforms to the SKPhysicsContactDelegate protocol. An SKScene is an SKNode that represents a SpriteKit scene and is the root node for the scene's other SKNodes. Recall that this scene is presented by the GameViewController (Fig. 6.6) to begin the game. The class implements the SKPhysicsContactDelegate protocol so that the scene can be notified when certain objects collide with one another. The protocol's didBeginContact method (Section 6.9.5) is called when the collisions occur that you specified with the physics bodies' categoryBit-Masks and contactTestBitMasks.

### Properties

Line 19 declares an SKLabelNode that displays the number of seconds remaining on the scene. SKLabelNodes enable you to display text and configure the text's properties. Because Swift requires all properties to be initialized and class GameScene does not provide an initializer, we declared this property as an implicitly unwrapped optional so that its value can be set later. We could have defined an initializer for the GameScene and set the seconds-Label property there; however, an SKScene is normally configured in its didMoveToView method (Section 6.9.3). For the same reasons, line 20 declares the cannon as an implicitly unwrapped Cannon optional.

Lines 23–26 declare variables that we use to manage the game's state. Variable timeLeft maintains the time remaining in the game as a CFTimeInterval. If this becomes

0, the game ends. Variable elapsedTime tracks the total game time—recall that the player gets bonus time for each Target hit and a time penalty when the cannonball hits the Blocker. Variable previousTime is used when the game loop updates the scene so that we can accurately display the time in tenths of a second. The time between animation frames can vary based on the scene's complexity, so previousTime helps us account for those variations, as you'll see in Section 6.9.7. Variable targetsRemaining tracks the number of targets currently on the screen. If this becomes 0, the game ends.

### 6.9.3 Overridden SKScene Method didMoveToView

When an SKScene is presented, its didMoveToView method (Fig. 6.20) is called to enable you to configure the scene. The method receives as an argument a reference to the SKView that presented the scene—the view in the GameViewController that Xcode created for you when you used the **Game** app template to create this app. Line 30 sets the scene's background color to white.

```
28      // called when scene is presented
29      override func didMoveToView(view: SKView) {
30          self.backgroundColor = SKColor.whiteColor() // set background
31
32          // helps determine game element speeds based on scene size
33          var velocityMultiplier = self.size.width / self.size.height
34
35          if UIDevice.currentDevice().userInterfaceIdiom == .Pad {
36              velocityMultiplier = CGFloat(velocityMultiplier * 6.0)
37          }
38
39          // configure the physicsWorld
40          self.physicsWorld.gravity = CGVectorMake(0.0, 0.0) // no gravity
41          self.physicsWorld.contactDelegate = self
42
43          // create border for objects colliding with screen edges
44          self.physicsBody = SKPhysicsBody(edgeLoopFromRect: self.frame)
45          self.physicsBody?.friction = 0.0 // no friction
46          self.physicsBody?.categoryBitMask = CollisionCategory.Wall
47          self.physicsBody?.contactTestBitMask = CollisionCategory.Cannonball
48
49          createLabels() // display labels at scene's top-left corner
50
51          // create and attach Cannon
52          cannon = Cannon(sceneSize: size,
53              velocityMultiplier: velocityMultiplier)
54          cannon.position = CGPointMake(0.0, self.frame.height / 2.0)
55          self.addChild(cannon)
56
57          // create and attach medium Blocker and start moving
58          let blockerxPercent = CGFloat(0.5)
59          let blockeryPercent = CGFloat(0.25)
60          let blocker = Blocker(sceneSize: self.frame.size,
61              blockerSize: BlockerSize.Medium)
```

**Fig. 6.20** | Overridden SKScene method didMoveToView. (Part 1 of 2.)

```
62          blocker.position = CGPointMake(self.frame.width * blockerxPercent,
63             self.frame.height * blockeryPercent)
64          self.addChild(blocker)
65          blocker.startMoving(velocityMultiplier)
66
67          // create and attach targets of random sizes and start moving
68          let targetxPercent = CGFloat(0.6) // % across scene to 1st target
69          var targetX = size.width * targetxPercent
70
71          for i in 1 ... numberOfTargets {
72             let target = Target(sceneSize: self.frame.size)
73             target.position = CGPointMake(targetX, self.frame.height * 0.5)
74             targetX += target.size.width + 5.0
75             self.addChild(target)
76             target.startMoving(velocityMultiplier)
77          }
78       }
79
```

**Fig. 6.20** | Overridden SKScene method didMoveToView. (Part 2 of 2.)

*Managing Game-Element Speeds*

Lines 33–37 calculate the velocityMultiplier that we use to scale game elements' speeds based on the device's screen size. When the device is an iPad (line 35), we also multiply the velocityMultiplier by 6.0 to account for the larger screen size and larger element sizes. When you apply an impulse to a physics body, SpriteKit uses that physics body's mass to determine its speed. On larger screens, the game's elements are larger and thus considered to have more mass, so a harder push (i.e., larger impulse) is required to get an object moving at a faster speed.

*SKPhysicsWorld, Gravity and the SKPhysicsContactDelegate*

Every SKScene has an SKPhysicsWorld that simulates real-world physics in the scene. By default, the physicsWorld's gravity property (which is measured in meters per second) is initialized with CGVector dx and dy values of 0.0 (no gravity along the *x*-axis) and -9.8, respectively. The value -9.8 represents Earth's gravity. Line 40 eliminates gravity for this game by setting the dy component of the physicsWorld's gravity vector to 0.0. To see the effect of gravity on the game's elements, try commenting out this line in the final app. Line 41 indicates that the GameScene (self) is the SKPhysicsContactDelegate that will be notified when game elements collide.

*Configuring the Scene's SKPhysicsBody*

Lines 44–47 create and configure the scene's SKPhysicsBody. In this case, we use the SKPhysicsBody initializer that receives the edgeLoopFromRect parameter, which creates a physics body that defines the scene's edges so that other physics bodies can collide with those edges. This physics body has no friction (line 45). Line 46 sets the categoryBitMask to CollisionCategory.Wall. Line 47 sets sets the contactTestBitMask to Collision-Category.Cannonball to indicate that the SKPhysicsContactDelegate should be notified when a cannonball collides with the scene's edges, so we can remove the cannonball from the scene.

*Creating and Positioning the Game Elements*

Lines 49–77 create and display the game elements in the scene. Line 49 calls method `cre-ateLabels` (Section 6.9.4) to create the `SKTextNodes` that show the time remaining. Lines 52–55 create the `Cannon`, position it at the center of the scene's left edge and add it to the scene. Positions in the scene are measured from the *lower-left corner* with x-coordinates increasing from left to right and y-coordinates increasing from bottom to top.

Lines 58–65 create the `Blocker`, position it based on percentages of the screen's width and height (specified in lines 58–59), add it to the scene and call the `Blocker`'s `start-Moving` method to apply an impulse that starts the `Blocker` moving toward the scene's top edge. Lines 68–77 create and position the `Targets`, add them to the scene and call their `startMoving` methods to apply impulses that start them moving toward the scene's top edge. Recall from Section 6.7.4 that `Target`'s `startMoving` method uses random values so that the `Targets` move at different speeds.

### 6.9.4 Method `createLabels`

Method `createLabels` (Fig. 6.21) creates and attaches two `SKLabelNodes` to the scene—one that displays `"Time remaining:"` and one that we set dynamically to the number of seconds remaining. Line 88 creates the `timeRemainingLabel` using the `SKLabelNode` initializer that receives a font name as an argument. We used the Chalkduster font that was used in the sample code that Xcode generated when we created the project, but you can use any available iOS font (or even bundle fonts with your app). Lines 89–95 set the `time-RemainingLabel`'s `text`, `fontSize`, `fontColor`, `horizontalAlignmentMode` and `position` properties. By default, an `SKLabelNode`'s `horizontalAlignmentMode` is `Center`, so the node's text would be centered at the location specified by the node's `position` property. Setting `horizontalAlignmentMode` to `Left` (line 92) indicates that the left edge of the node's text should appear at the location specified by the `position` property. Lines 99–107 perform similar steps for the `secondsLabel`.

```
80      // create the text labels
81      func createLabels() {
82          // constants related to displaying text for time remaining
83          let edgeDistance = CGFloat(20.0)
84          let labelSpacing = CGFloat(5.0)
85          let fontSize = CGFloat(16.0)
86
87          // configure "Time remaining: " label
88          let timeRemainingLabel = SKLabelNode(fontNamed: "Chalkduster")
89          timeRemainingLabel.text = "Time remaining:"
90          timeRemainingLabel.fontSize = fontSize
91          timeRemainingLabel.fontColor = SKColor.blackColor()
92          timeRemainingLabel.horizontalAlignmentMode = .Left
93          let y = self.frame.height -
94              timeRemainingLabel.fontSize - edgeDistance
95          timeRemainingLabel.position = CGPoint(x: edgeDistance, y: y)
96          self.addChild(timeRemainingLabel)
97
```

**Fig. 6.21** | Method `createLabels`. (Part 1 of 2.)

```
 98            // configure label for displaying time remaining
 99       .    secondsLabel = SKLabelNode(fontNamed: "Chalkduster")
100            secondsLabel.text = "0.0 seconds"
101            secondsLabel.fontSize = fontSize
102            secondsLabel.fontColor = SKColor.blackColor()
103            secondsLabel.horizontalAlignmentMode = .Left
104            let x = timeRemainingLabel.calculateAccumulatedFrame().width +
105                edgeDistance + labelSpacing
106            secondsLabel.position = CGPoint(x: x, y: y)
107            self.addChild(secondsLabel)
108       }
109
```

**Fig. 6.21** | Method createLabels. (Part 2 of 2.)

### 6.9.5 SKPhysicsContactDelegate Method didBeginContact and Supporting Methods

SKPhysicsContactDelegate method didBeginContact (Fig. 6.22, lines 131–166) is called when a collision occurs between two physics bodies for which you've registered to receive collision notifications. The method receives an SKPhysicsContact that contains references to the two SKPhysicsBody objects that collided. We use methods isCannonball, isBlocker, isTarget and isWall (lines 111–128) to determine which objects the SKPhysicsContact references. Each method receives an SKPhysicsBody and returns a Bool indicating whether that SKPhysicsBody's categoryBitMask contains the corresponding CollisionCategory bit (Section 6.9.1). For example, to determine whether the SKPhysicsBody is a cannonball, line 112 bitwise ANDs (&) the categoryBitMask and CollisionCategory.Cannonball. If the result is nonzero, then the SKPhysicsBody is a cannonball.

```
110       // test whether an SKPhysicsBody is the cannonball
111       func isCannonball(body: SKPhysicsBody) -> Bool {
112           return body.categoryBitMask & CollisionCategory.Cannonball != 0
113       }
114
115       // test whether an SKPhysicsBody is a blocker
116       func isBlocker(body: SKPhysicsBody) -> Bool {
117           return body.categoryBitMask & CollisionCategory.Blocker != 0
118       }
119
120       // test whether an SKPhysicsBody is a target
121       func isTarget(body: SKPhysicsBody) -> Bool {
122           return body.categoryBitMask & CollisionCategory.Target != 0
123       }
124
125       // test whether an SKPhysicsBody is a wall
126       func isWall(body: SKPhysicsBody) -> Bool {
127           return body.categoryBitMask & CollisionCategory.Wall != 0
128       }
129
```

**Fig. 6.22** | Method didBeginContact responds to collisions. (Part 1 of 2.)

```
130    // called when collision starts
131    func didBeginContact(contact: SKPhysicsContact) {
132        var cannonball: SKPhysicsBody
133        var otherBody: SKPhysicsBody
134
135        // determine which SKPhysicsBody is the cannonball
136        if isCannonball(contact.bodyA) {
137            cannonball = contact.bodyA
138            otherBody = contact.bodyB
139        } else {
140            cannonball = contact.bodyB
141            otherBody = contact.bodyA
142        }
143
144        // cannonball hit wall, so remove from screen
145        if isWall(otherBody) || isTarget(otherBody) ||
146            isBlocker(otherBody) {
147            cannon.cannonballOnScreen = false
148            cannonball.node?.removeFromParent()
149        }
150
151        // cannonball hit blocker, so play blocker sound
152        if isBlocker(otherBody) {
153            let blocker = otherBody.node as Blocker
154            blocker.playHitSound()
155            timeLeft -= blocker.blockerTimePenalty()
156        }
157
158        // cannonball hit target
159        if isTarget(otherBody) {
160            --targetsRemaining
161            let target = otherBody.node as Target
162            target.removeFromParent()
163            target.playHitSound()
164            timeLeft += target.targetTimeBonus()
165        }
166    }
167
```

**Fig. 6.22** | Method didBeginContact responds to collisions. (Part 2 of 2.)

### Determining Which Object Is the Cannonball

In this app, one of the two SKPhysicsBody objects will always be the cannonball—due to how we configured the categoryBitMasks and contactTestBitMasks for the various game elements in earlier sections. Lines 136–142 uses the SKPhysicsContact's bodyA and bodyB properties and method isCannonball to determine which SKPhysicsBody is the cannonball and which is the otherBody.

### Removing the Cannonball from the Scene

Next, line 145 determines whether otherBody is a wall, a target or a blocker and, if so, removes the cannonball from the screen. Line 148 uses the cannonball SKPhysicsBody's node property to get the SKNode that represents the cannonball. We then invoke that SKNode's removeFromParent method to remove the node from the scene. The node property is an optional, so we once again use optional chaining (with ?) to ensure that remove-FromParent is called only if node is not nil.

### Handling Collisions with a *Blocker*
Line 152 determines whether otherBody is a Blocker. If so, line 153 casts its node property to Blocker, line 154 plays the Blocker's hit sound and line 155 subtracts the Blocker's time penalty from the timeLeft.

### Handling Collisions with a *Target*
Line 159 determines whether otherBody is a Target. If so:

- line 160 updates the number of targets remaining,
- line 161 casts otherBody's node property to Target,
- line 162 removes the Target from the scene,
- line 163 plays the Target's hit sound and
- line 164 adds the Target's time bonus to the timeLeft.

### *SKPhysicsContactDelegate* Method *didEndContact*
We did not define the SKPhysicsContactDelegate protocol's didEndContact method. The physics engine will call this protocol's methods only if they exist in the delegate's class.

## 6.9.6 Overridden UIResponder Method touchesBegan

Recall from Section 6.3.8 that class UIResponder defines the capabilities that enable on-screen elements to respond to events, such as the user touching the screen. Class SKNode is a subclass of UIResponder, so all SKNodes can respond to user-interface events. When you created the app using Xcode's **Game** template, the autogenerated GameScene class contained an override of UIResponder method touchesBegan. This method responded to each touch by creating a new SKSpriteNode at the touch point. Figure 6.23 contains our updated version of method touchesBegan. The method receives an NSSet of UITouches representing the touches (more than one finger could be touching the screen) and a UIEvent representing the event that occurred. NSSet is an unordered collection of objects. Lines 170–173 iterate through the touches. NSSet property **allObjects** returns an Array of AnyObjects, which we cast to an Array of UITouches. For each, line 171 calls its loca-tionInNode method with the GameScene (self) as an argument to determine the touch's location relative to the GameScene. Then, line 172 calls the Cannon's rotateToPointAnd-Fire method (Section 6.8.3) to aim the Cannon at that point and fire.

```
168    // fire the cannon if there is not a cannonball on screen
169    override func touchesBegan(touches: NSSet, withEvent event: UIEvent) {
170        for touch in touches.allObjects as [UITouch] {
171            let location = touch.locationInNode(self)
172            cannon.rotateToPointAndFire(location, scene: self)
173        }
174    }
175
```

**Fig. 6.23** | Overridden UIResponder method touchesBegan responds to touch events.

### 6.9.7 Overridden SKScene Method update and Method gameOver

Recall from Section 6.3.4 that SKScene method update (Fig. 6.24, lines 177–196) is called in the game loop once per animation frame so you can update scene elements and game state. In this app, we use it to update the scene's previousTime, elapsedTime and timeLeft properties and the secondsLabel's text property. Also, if there are no more Targets or time has expired we'll display the GameOverScene.

```
176      // updates to perform in each frame of the animation
177      override func update(currentTime: CFTimeInterval) {
178          if previousTime == 0.0 {
179              previousTime = currentTime
180          }
181
182          elapsedTime += (currentTime - previousTime)
183          timeLeft -= (currentTime - previousTime)
184          previousTime = currentTime
185
186          if timeLeft < 0 {
187              timeLeft = 0
188          }
189
190          secondsLabel.text = String(format: "%.1f seconds", timeLeft)
191
192          // check whether game is over
193          if targetsRemaining == 0 || timeLeft <= 0 {
194              runAction(SKAction.runBlock({self.gameOver()}))
195          }
196      }
197
198      // display the game over scene
199      func gameOver() {
200          let flipTransition = SKTransition.flipHorizontalWithDuration(1.0)
201          let gameOverScene = GameOverScene(size: self.size,
202              won: targetsRemaining == 0 ? true : false,
203              time: elapsedTime)
204          gameOverScene.scaleMode = .AspectFill
205          self.view?.presentScene(gameOverScene, transition: flipTransition)
206      }
207  }
```

**Fig. 6.24** | Overridden SKScene method update and method gameOver.

*Determining the Elapsed Time Between Animation Frames*
The number of frames per second displayed by SpriteKit can vary based on the complexity of your scene. For this reason, any changes you make to your game's state (such as property values or node locations) in method update are typically scaled by the amount of time that's passed between the last and the current animation frames. For example, if you're manually updating an element's position, you'd typically determine its new location based on its speed, direction and the amount of time that has passed since the last frame. The longer the time that has passed, the farther your element will move.

For this app, we determine the difference in times between frames so we can accurately reflect the time remaining and update the elapsedTime and timeLeft properties—the longer the time that has passed, the more we'll add to elapsedTime and subtract from timeLeft. In the first call to update, previousTime is 0.0. In this case, lines 178–180 set previousTime to currentTime for use in this first call to update. For all subsequent calls, previousTime contains the time from the last animation frame. Line 182 adds to the elapsedTime the difference between the currentTime and previousTime. Line 183 subtracts the same value from timeLeft. Then, line 184 stores currentTime in previousTime for use in the next call to update.

### Updating the secondsLabel
If timeLeft becomes negative, we set it back to 0, so that line 190 will not display a negative time remaining. Line 190 formats the timeLeft and assigns it to secondsLabel's text property to display the new time remaining on the scene.

### Displaying the GameOverScene
If there are no targets remaining or there is no time left, line 194 uses SKScene method runAction to execute an SKAction that calls our gameOver method (lines 199–206). Line 200 creates an SKTransition that's used to animate the transition between SKScenes. Method flipHorizontalWithDuration returns an SKTransition that flips the scene along the horizontal axis over the duration specified as an argument. Line 201 creates a GameOverScene, initializing it with the current scene's size, a Bool indicating whether the user won or lost, and the elapsedTime. Line 204 indicates that the GameScene should fill the screen. Finally, line 205 uses the GameScene's inherited view property—which refers to the SKView in the GameViewController—to call SKView's presentScene method that receives SKScene to present and the SKTransition to use to animate the transition.

## 6.10 Class GameOverScene
When the game is over, GameScene method gameOver (Section 6.9.7) creates a GameOverScene (Fig. 6.25) and initiates a transition to it.

```
1   // GameOverScene.swift
2   // Displays a game over scene with elapsed time
3   import SpriteKit
4
5   class GameOverScene: SKScene {
6       // configure GameOverScene
7       init(size: CGSize, won: Bool, time: CFTimeInterval) {
8           super.init(size: size)
9           self.backgroundColor = SKColor.whiteColor()
10          let greenColor =
11              SKColor(red: 0.0, green: 0.6, blue: 0.0, alpha: 1.0)
12
13          let gameOverLabel = SKLabelNode(fontNamed: "Chalkduster")
14          gameOverLabel.text = (won ? "You Win!" : "You Lose")
```

**Fig. 6.25** | GameOverScene displays when the game ends and enables the user to begin a new game. (Part 1 of 2.)

```
15              gameOverLabel.fontSize = 60
16              gameOverLabel.fontColor =
17                  (won ? greenColor : SKColor.redColor())
18              gameOverLabel.position.x = size.width / 2.0
19              gameOverLabel.position.y =
20                  size.height / 2.0 + gameOverLabel.fontSize
21              self.addChild(gameOverLabel)
22
23              let elapsedTimeLabel = SKLabelNode(fontNamed: "Chalkduster")
24              elapsedTimeLabel.text =
25                  String(format: "Elapsed Time: %.1f seconds", time)
26              elapsedTimeLabel.fontSize = 24
27              elapsedTimeLabel.fontColor = SKColor.blackColor()
28              elapsedTimeLabel.position.x = size.width / 2.0
29              elapsedTimeLabel.position.y = size.height / 2.0
30              self.addChild(elapsedTimeLabel)
31
32              let newGameLabel = SKLabelNode(fontNamed: "Chalkduster")
33              newGameLabel.text = "Begin New Game"
34              newGameLabel.fontSize = 24
35              newGameLabel.fontColor = greenColor
36              newGameLabel.position.x = size.width / 2.0
37              newGameLabel.position.y =
38                  size.height / 2.0 - gameOverLabel.fontSize
39              self.addChild(newGameLabel)
40          }
41
42      // not called, but required if you override SKScene's init
43      required init?(coder aDecoder: NSCoder) {
44          fatalError("init(coder:) has not been implemented")
45      }
46
47      // present a new GameScene when user touches screen
48      override func touchesBegan(touches: NSSet, withEvent event: UIEvent) {
49          let doorTransition =
50              SKTransition.doorsOpenHorizontalWithDuration(1.0)
51          let scene = GameScene(size: self.size)
52          scene.scaleMode = .AspectFill
53          self.view?.presentScene(scene, transition: doorTransition)
54      }
55  }
```

**Fig. 6.25** | GameOverScene displays when the game ends and enables the user to begin a new game. (Part 2 of 2.)

### Initializer

The GameOverScene's initializer (lines 7–40) configures the scene's background color (white), then creates and attaches three SKLabelNodes to the scene. Lines 13–21 create and add the gameOverLabel, which displays "You Win!" in green or "You Lose" in red, based on the initializer's won argument. Lines 23–30 create and add the elapsedTimeLabel to display the total time that the user played the game before winning or losing. Lines 32–39 create and add the newGameLabel that displays "Begin New Game" in green.

*Initializer*
As with earlier classes in this app, when you define any initializers in a subclass of SKScene, you do not inherit the superclass's initializers. For this reason, we must provide the `required` initializer at lines 43–45, even though it's never called.

*Overridden Method **touchesBegan***
The user can begin a new game by touching anywhere in the scene. This invokes method `touchesBegan` (lines 48–54). When a touch occurs, this method creates a door-opening transition (lines 49–50), creates a new `GameScene` (line 51), specifies that the scene should fill the screen (line 52) and uses `SKView` method `presentScene` (line 53) to transition from the `GameOverScene` to the new `GameScene`.

# 6.11 **Programmatic Internationalization**

Section 2.8 showed how to use Xcode and XLIFF files to internationalize the **Welcome** app and provide localized Spanish `Strings` for the app's UI. Most apps also contain `String` literals or dynamically generated `Strings` that are displayed to the user (or, in the case of VoiceOver, spoken to the user). Such `Strings` must be localized at runtime. For example, the **Cannon** game's text is displayed in `SKLabelNodes` by the app's code.

In this section, you'll *programmatically* specify localizable `Strings` and, once again, provide Spanish translations. You'll use the same techniques you learned in Section 2.8 to extract the `Strings` from the source-code files into XLIFF files for translation, translate the `Strings` and incorporate the translations into your project.

Before proceeding, *make a copy of your working **Cannon** app.* (We provide the final Spanish localized version of this app in the `CannonNSLocalizedString` folder with the book's examples.)

*Localizing **Strings** in Code with **NSLocalizedString***
The Foundation framework's **NSLocalizedString** function (and several other similarly named functions) specify `Strings` that should be loaded dynamically, based on the device's language settings. The first step in localizing `Strings` in code is to look at every `String` literal and determine which ones are *user facing*—that is, displayed or spoken to the user. For each one, you then use `NSLocalizedString` to define a key–value pair:

- The key (which must be unique) is used to load a localized `String` at runtime.
- The value is a comment that Xcode places in the XLIFF file as a `<note>` element. This comment explains the `String`'s purpose to the human translator.

For example, to specify that the `timeRemainingLabel`'s text (line 89, Fig. 6.21) should be localized, replace

```
timeRemainingLabel.text = "Time remaining:"
```
with

```
timeRemainingLabel.text = NSLocalizedString("Time remaining:",
    comment: "Text of the timeRemainingLabel")
```

Here, we used the English (base-language) `String` "Time remaining:" as the key. For a `String` that includes format specifiers, using the base-language `String` as the key helps the translator understand the format specifiers' contexts. Based on the language, these often need to be placed in different locations within the translated Strings, so the context is important information for the translator to have.

Figure 6.26 shows the code changes we made in the CannonNSLocalizedString project for the **Cannon** game's localizable Strings. Though we did not use locale-specific numeric formatting in this app, you should do so in localized versions of apps that you intend to submit to the App Store. Recall that you can use class NSNumberFormatter for locale-specific numeric formatting.

---

**NSLocalizedString replacements for the Cannon game**

In class GameScene, replace line 89 in Fig. 6.21 with:

```
timeRemainingLabel.text = NSLocalizedString("Time remaining:",
    comment: "Text of the timeRemainingLabel")
```

In class GameScene, replace line 190 in Fig. 6.24 with:

```
secondsLabel.text =
    String(format: NSLocalizedString("%.1f seconds",
        comment: "Formatted number of seconds remaining"), timeLeft)
```

In class GameOverScene, replace line 14 in Fig. 6.25 with:

```
gameOverLabel.text = (won ?
    NSLocalizedString("You Win!", comment: "String indicating that the user won") :
    NSLocalizedString("You Lose", comment: "String indicating that the user lost"))
```

In class GameOverScene, replace lines 24–25 in Fig. 6.25 with:

```
elapsedTimeLabel.text =
    String(format: NSLocalizedString("Elapsed Time: %.1f seconds",
        comment: "String displaying formatted elapsed time"), time)
```

In class GameOverScene, replace line 33 in Fig. 6.25 with:

```
newGameLabel.text = NSLocalizedString("Begin New Game",
    comment: "String for a simulated new game button")
```

---

**Fig. 6.26** | NSLocalizedString replacements for the **Cannon** game.

### *Exporting the String Resources*

After making the code changes in Figure 6.26, perform the steps you learned in Section 2.8.2 to create the XLIFF file containing the app's String resources. Recall that you provide a copy of this file—renamed to indicate the locale it represents—to the translator.

### *Translating the String Resources*

After generating the XLIFF file, make a copy of the en.xliff file and rename it es.xliff (recall that es is the language ID for Spanish). Open the file and add the target-language attribute for Spanish to the <file> element as you did in Section 2.8.3. Next, locate each <source> element shown in Figure 6.27, then add below it the corresponding <target> element (also shown in the figure). [*Note:* If you prefer to use a completed XLIFF file, we provide our es.xliff file in the Localizations folder with the book's examples.]

<target> elements to insert in the es.xliff file

```
<source>%.1f seconds</source>
<target>%.1f segundos</target>

<source>Begin New Game</source>
<target>Comience Nuevo Juego</target>

<source>Elapsed Time: %.1f seconds</source>
<target>Comience Nuevo Juego: %.1f segundos</target>

<source>Time remaining:</source>
<target>Tiempo restante:</target>

<source>You Lose</source>
<target>Perdió</target>

<source>You Win!</source>
<target>¡Ganó!</target>
```

**Fig. 6.27** | <target> elements to insert in the es.xliff file.

### Importing the Translated *String* Resources

Next, perform the steps in Section 2.8.4 to import the es.xliff file. Xcode extracts the translated Spanish Strings and, for NSLocalizedStrings in your code, creates the file Localizable.strings (Figure 6.28) in the project's Supporting Files group. Each comment you specified in the calls to NSLocalizedString appears as a comment in the file. Below each comment is a key–value pair containing a key that you specified in a call to NSLocalizedString and the corresponding Spanish-language String.

```
 1  /* Formatted number of seconds remaining */
 2  "%.1f seconds" = "%.1f seconds";
 3
 4  /* String for a simulated new game button */
 5  "Begin New Game" = "Comience Nuevo Juego";
 6
 7  /* String displaying formatted elapsed time */
 8  "Elapsed Time: %.1f seconds" = "Tiempo transcurrido: %.1f segundos ";
 9
10  /* Text of the timeRemainingLabel */
11  "Time remaining:" = "Tiempo restante:";
12
13  /* String indicating that the user lost */
14  "You Lose" = "Perdió";
15
16  /* String indicating that the user won */
17  "You Win!" = "¡Ganó!";
```

**Fig. 6.28** | Localizable.strings file that Xcode creates when you import the es.xliff file.

*Testing the App in Spanish*

You can now perform the steps in Section 2.8.5 to test the app in Spanish. Figure 6.29 shows the Spanish version of the game-over screen for a win.

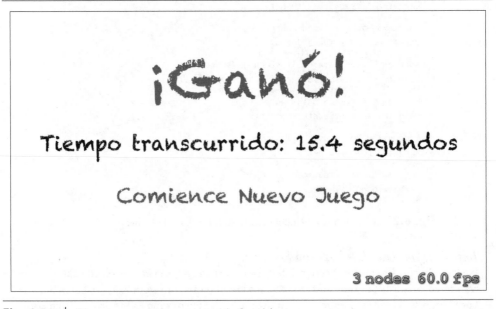

**Fig. 6.29** | Cannon app game-over screen in Spanish.

## 6.12 Wrap-Up

In this chapter, you created the **Cannon** game app, which challenges the player to destroy nine targets before time expires. You used the Xcode **Game** template as the starting point for developing this SpriteKit-based game. You learned that iOS also provides other game-development frameworks—SceneKit, Metal and OpenGL ES. You played sounds in your game using objects of class `AVAudioPlayer` from the AVFoundation framework.

This app required various SpriteKit framework classes. You used `SKView` to display the game's scenes and run the game loop. The game's two scenes were defined as subclasses of `SKScene`, which provides the framework for a scene. As we discussed, you override `SKScene` methods that are called by the game loop so you can specify changes to the scene's elements for each animation frame as well as any game logic required in each frame.

You learned that `SKNode`s are the fundamental building blocks for the items displayed in an `SKScene`, and that an `SKScene` is the root `SKNode` in a tree of `SKNode`s that specify a scene's content. You used `SKNode` properties to specify each node's size, position and `SKPhysicsBody` (for defining its physics attributes). You learned that physics interactions between `SKNode`s are dependent on the `SKScene`'s `SKPhysicsWorld`.

You positioned nodes with respect to the scene's lower-left corner, and saw that transformations performed on a given node (such as rotating the cannon) apply to that node and all of its children. You used `SKLabelNode`s to display text, `SKSpriteNode`s to display sprites (images) and an `SKShapeNode` to display a rectangle.

When the game ended, you switched from the game scene to the game-over scene, using an SKTransition to animate the presentation of the new scene. You used an SKAction with a completion handler to rotate the Cannon, then fire it. You learned that SKActions are often used to perform animations that change SKNode properties like scale, rotation, alpha (transparency) and position, and that they can also be used to play sounds, execute code, add new nodes and remove existing nodes.

We discussed SpriteKit's game loop (defined in class SKScene) that attempts to render your game's animation frames at a maximum rate of 60 frames per second (FPS) for the smooth animations. We also discussed that the actual frame rate depends on the complexity of your game's logic and the number of nodes on the screen.

One of the key benefits of using a game-development framework like SpriteKit is the built-in physics simulation capabilities, which encapsulate complex calculations. You let SpriteKit handle these for you by configuring properties of the scene's SKPhysicsWorld and the game nodes' SKPhysicsBody objects. SpriteKit's physics engine then used those settings to perform collision detection, to determine how elements should bounce off one another and to notify the app's SKPhysicsContactDelegate when specific collisions occurred. To specify the values of many of the SpriteKit class's properties, you used various CGGeometry types (CGFloat, CGPoint, CGSize, CGRect and CGVector) and functions (CGPointMake, CGSizeMake, CGRectMake and CGVectorMake).

Class UIResponder defines the capabilities that enable on-screen elements to respond to events, such as the user touching the screen. You learned that SKNode is a subclass of UIResponder, so all SKNodes can respond to user-interface events. You overrode UIResponder method touchesBegan to aim and fire the cannon at the location where the user touched the screen.

We used several additional Swift capabilities to build this app. When manipulating a property of a Swift optional type, you used optional chaining with ? to ensure that an expression continued executing only if the optional property was not nil. We mentioned that Swift's struct and enum value types are similar to classes (which are reference types), but do not support inheritance. You defined a struct containing type constants to represent the bit flags that SpriteKit used to test for collisions between physics bodies. You also defined enum types to represent sets of named constants for use with the Blocker and Target classes. Finally, you used NSLocalizedString to define localizable Strings in your source code.

In Chapter 7, we present the **Doodlz** app, which uses iOS's graphics capabilities and multitouch event handling to turn a device's screen into a *virtual canvas*. You'll learn how to handle and track multiple touches for drawing several lines at once by dragging more than one finger across the screen. In addition, we'll show how to convert the drawing to a UIImage then pass it to a UIActivityViewController, which will automatically display share, save, copy and print options.

# 7

# Doodlz App

Multi-Touch Event Handling, Graphics, UIBezierPaths, Drawing with a Custom UIView Subclass, UIToolbar, UIBarButtonItem, Accelerometer Sensor and Motion Event Handling

## Objectives

In this chapter you'll:

- Override **UIResponder** touch event-handling methods to process multi-touch events, allowing the user to draw lines by dragging multiple fingers across the screen.

- Store each line the user draws as a **UIBezierPath**.

- Use a **UIToolbar** to display **UIBarButtonItem**s containing the app's options.

- Create a **UIView** subclass and override its **drawRect** method to perform custom drawing with **UIBezierPath**s.

- Override a **UIResponder** motion event-handling method to process accelerometer events, allowing the user to erase a drawing by shaking the device.

- Use a **UIActivityViewController** to display options for sharing, saving, copying and printing an image.

- Override the UIView initializer that's called when an object in a storyboard is recreated at runtime.

**Outline**

# 7.1 Introduction

With the **Doodlz** app (Fig. 7.1), you can create a doodle (i.e., a drawing) by dragging one or more fingers across the screen to draw lines. The app's options—displayed at the bottom of the screen as `UIBarButtonItems` in a `UIToolbar`—enable you to set the drawing color and stroke width, undo lines one at a time and clear the entire doodle. You can also display a `UIActivityViewController` with options for sharing your doodle, saving it to the device, copying it to the clipboard or printing it (if an AirPrint-enabled printer is available).

In this app, you'll track multiple touch events simultaneously and associate each (a `UITouch`) with a specific line. You'll use a custom `UIBezierPath` subclass to store the lines' information, then draw them in a custom `UIView`'s `drawRect` method. You'll also process events from the accelerometer sensor to allow the user to erase the drawing by shaking the device. Finally, you'll capture a `UIView`'s contents (your drawing) as a `UIImage`, which you'll pass to a `UIActivityViewController` for sharing, saving, copying and printing.

**Fig. 7.1** | Doodlz app with a completed drawing.

## 7.2 Test-Driving the Doodlz App

In this section, you'll test-drive the **Doodlz** app, using it to draw a flower in the rain.

*Opening the Completed Application*
Locate the folder where you extracted the book's examples as specified in the Before You Begin section. In the Doodlz folder, double click Doodlz.xcodeproj to open the project in Xcode, then run the app in the iOS simulator or on your iOS device.

*Understanding the App's Options*
Figure 7.2 shows the UIToolbar containing the app's options. Touching **Color** displays a GUI for changing the drawing color. Touching **Stroke** displays a GUI for changing the thickness of the lines that you'll draw. Each time you touch **Undo**, the app removes the line you most recently completed. Touching **Clear** or shaking the device displays a dialog asking whether you'd like to delete the entire drawing, giving you an opportunity to cancel the operation. Touching the action icon (⬆) displays a UIActivityViewController for sharing, saving, copying or printing your doodle. You'll explore each of these options momentarily.

Color  Stroke  Undo  Clear                                    ⬆

**Fig. 7.2** | Doodlz app options displayed in a UIToolbar.

*Changing the Drawing Color to Red*

To change the brush color, first touch **Color** on the toolbar to display the **Choose Drawing Color** dialog (Fig. 7.3). Colors are defined using the *ARGB color scheme* in which the *alpha* (i.e., *transparency*), red, green and blue components are specified by floating-point values in the range 0.0–1.0. For alpha, 0.0 means *completely transparent* and 1.0 means *completely opaque*. For red, green and blue, 0.0 means *none* of that color and 1.0 means the *maximum amount* of that color. The GUI consists of **Alpha**, **Red**, **Green** and **Blue** UISliders that allow you to select the amounts of transparency and each color in the drawing color. You drag the UISliders' thumbs to change the color. As you do, the app continuously displays the new color by setting a UIView's background color. Select a red color now by dragging the **Red** UISlider to the right as in Fig. 7.3. Touch the **Done** button to return to close the dialog and return to the drawing area.

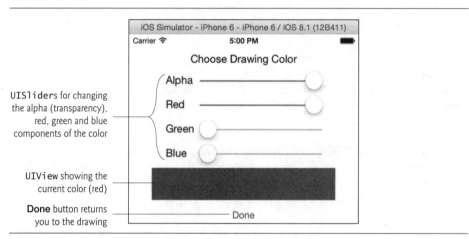

UISliders for changing the alpha (transparency), red, green and blue components of the color

UIView showing the current color (red)

**Done** button returns you to the drawing

**Fig. 7.3** | Changing the drawing color to red.

*Changing the Stroke Width*

To change the line thickness, touch **Stroke** on the toolbar to display the **Choose Stroke Width** dialog (Fig. 7.4). Drag the UISlider to the right to thicken the line. Touch the **Done** button to return to the drawing area.

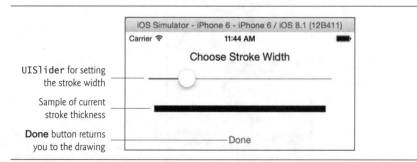

UISlider for setting the stroke width

Sample of current stroke thickness

**Done** button returns you to the drawing

**Fig. 7.4** | Changing the stroke thickness.

*Drawing the Flower Petals*

Drag your finger—or the mouse when using the simulator—on the screen to draw flower petals (Fig. 7.5).

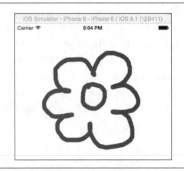

**Fig. 7.5** | Drawing flower petals.

*Changing the Brush Color to Dark Green*

Touch **Color** to display the **Choose Drawing Color** dialog. Select a dark green color by dragging the **Green** UISlider's thumb to the middle and ensuring that the **Red** and **Blue** UISliders are at the far left.

*Changing the Stroke Width and Drawing the Stem and Leaves*

Touch **Stroke** to display the **Choose Stroke Width** dialog. Drag the UISlider's thumb to the right to thicken the line, then draw the flower stem and leaves. Next, select a lighter green color and thinner line, then draw the grass (Fig. 7.6).

**Fig. 7.6** | Drawing the stem and grass.

*Changing the Brush Color to a Semitransparent Blue*
Change the drawing color to a semitransparent blue as shown in Fig. 7.7 and select a narrower line, then draw the raindrops to complete your doodle so that it appears similar to Fig. 7.1.

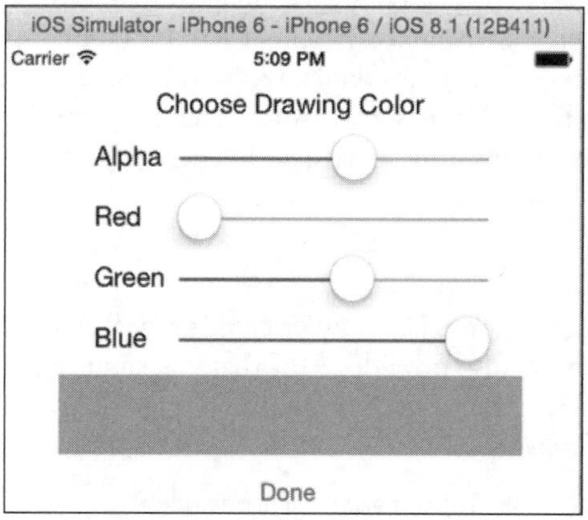

**Fig. 7.7** | Changing the line color to blue and narrowing the line.

*Actions You Can Perform with Your Image*
Touch the toolbar's action icon (⬆) to display a `UIActivityViewController` showing activities that can perform tasks with images (Fig. 7.8).

**Fig. 7.8** | `UIActivityViewController` showing activities for an image.

The tasks displayed vary based on the apps installed on your device and the social networks for which you've provided login credentials. Sometimes there are more options than can be displayed in each row of icons—you can swipe right-to-left to see additional options, if any. The bottom row contains options for saving the image (which you can then view in the **Photos** app or other apps with access to the devices's stored photos), copying to the clipboard (so you can paste the image into another app) and printing to an AirPrint-enabled printer. Experiment with these activities on your device or in the Simulator. If you save the image in the simulator, recall that you can use the **Hardware** menu's **Home** option to return to the home screen—from there you can launch the **Photos** app to view your image. When attempting to save an image for the first time, iOS will first ask for your permission to do so.

### Saving and Printing APIs

For this app, we let the `UIActivityViewController` deal with the details of saving or printing the image, but iOS also provides APIs that you can use in your apps to work with the file system and AirPrint. For more information on the file system APIs see Apple's *File System Programming Guide* at:

```
http://bit.ly/iOSFileSystemProgramming
```

For more information on the printing APIs see Apple's *Drawing and Printing Guide for iOS* at:

```
http://bit.ly/iOSDrawingAndPrinting
```

### Shake to Erase

As we mentioned previously, you can shake your device to display the confirmation dialog (Fig. 7.9) for deleting a doodle. In the simulator, you can test this with the **Hardware** menu's **Shake Gesture** option. Touching **Delete** erases the drawing—touching **Cancel** keeps it.

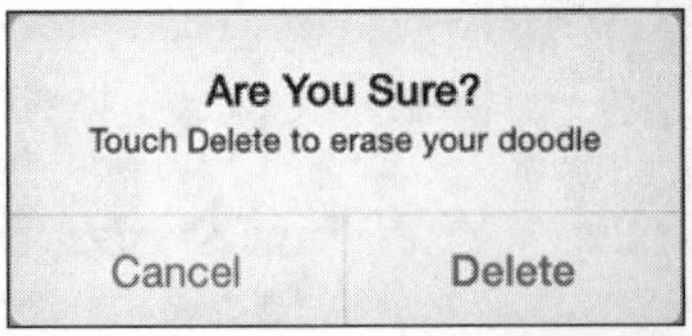

**Are You Sure?**
Touch Delete to erase your doodle

Cancel | Delete

**Fig. 7.9** | Dialog for deleting the current drawing.

### Simulating Multi-Touch

As we mentioned, you can draw with one or more fingers at a time. In the iOS simulator, you can test multi-touch for two touches at a time. To do so, hold the *option* key while dragging the mouse to draw. The simulator shows two circles representing the simulated touch points (Fig. 7.10). The mouse cursor appears over one, which follows the mouse's movement. The other circle mirrors the mouse's movement. You can move the two touch points together by holding the *shift* key and moving the mouse.

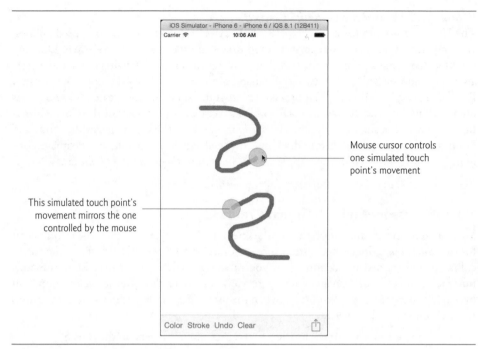

**Fig. 7.10** | Multi-touch in the iOS simulator.

# 7.3 Technologies Overview

This section introduces the new technologies that we use in the **Doodlz** app.

### 7.3.1 Drawing with UIView Subclasses, Method drawRect, UIBezierPaths and the UIKit Graphics System

iOS provides several drawing technologies (OpenGL, Quartz, UIKit and Core Animation) that are described in detail in Apple's *Drawing and Printing Guide for iOS* at:

```
http://bit.ly/DrawingAndPrintingGuide
```

OpenGL is an open-source graphics framework available for many operating systems. Quartz and Core Animation are specific to iOS and OS X. UIKit is iOS specific, but many UIKit features have corresponding ones in OS X's AppKit framework. In this app, you'll use the UIKit graphics system's higher-level, built-in drawing capabilities, which all UIViews support via their drawRect methods (discussed below). You'll also use some UIKit graphics-related functions to capture your doodle as an image (discussed in Section 7.3.4).

#### *UIView Method drawRect*

To perform custom drawing, you create your own UIView subclass and override its **drawRect** method, as you'll do in Sections 7.7.4— and 7.9.1. When present, iOS calls this method to draw the UIView. Method drawRect receives a CGRect object representing portion of the UIView that needs to be redrawn—the entire UIView the first time it's displayed, but possibly a smaller portion in subsequent drawRect calls. For example, if the user draws a short line, only the rectangular area that contains the line needs to be redrawn.

*UIBezierPaths and the Graphics Context*

The UIKit framework provides class `UIBezierPath` to represent shapes composed of lines, arcs and curves. This class's `stroke` method draws the specified `UIBezierPath`. Drawing is performed using a graphics context that provides the current drawing color and a rectangular region in which to draw—coordinates are measured from the upper-left corner. For a subclass of `UIView`, the graphics context that `drawRect` uses is created for you and is used to draw into the `UIView`'s `CALayer` object. Class `CALayer` is part of the Core Animation framework (a subset of the the Quartz Core framework) and manages the rendering of image content, such as custom drawings. It can also be used to animate the image content. For more information, see Apple's *Core Animation Programming Guide* at:

```
http://bit.ly/CoreAnimationProgrammingGuide
```

## 7.3.2 Processing Multiple Touch Events

You can drag one or more fingers across the screen to draw. The app stores the information for each *individual* finger in a custom subclass of `UIBezierPath` that also stores the path's color. As you learned in Section 6.3.8, you process touch events by overriding methods inherited from class `UIResponder` into your view controller class. In the **Cannon** app, you overrode `touchesBegan` to be notified when the user touched the screen to fire the cannon. In this app, you'll also override:

- `touchesMoved` to track touches as the user moves fingers on the screen.

- `touchesEnded` to complete a `Squiggle` (a `UIBezierPath` subclass that also stores a line's color) when the user removes the corresponding finger from the screen.

- `touchesCancelled` to remove in-progress `Squiggle`s if iOS cancels the touch events—for example, when the user receives a phone call.

As the user moves a given finger, that finger's touch events will be maintained in the same `UITouch` object from the time that finger touches the screen to the time the user removes it. We'll use the `UITouch` objects that are passed to `touchesBegan`, `touchesMoved` and `touchesEnded` as keys in a `Dictionary` that keeps track of the in-progress `Squiggle`s.

## 7.3.3 Listening for Motion Events

In this app, you can shake the device to erase your doodle—iOS devices have an accelerometer that allows apps to detect movement. Other sensor information currently supported in iOS (but not by all iOS devices) includes proximity, light, moisture, gyroscope, GPS, magnetometer, altimeter and barometer. In Section 7.5.4, we'll override the `UIResponder` class's `motionEnded` method to handle a shake event. iOS's Core Motion framework provides additional motion event-handling capabilities. For more information, see Apple's *Core Motion Framework Reference* at:

```
http://bit.ly/CoreMotionFramework
```

## 7.3.4 Rendering the Drawing as a UIImage

As you saw in this app's test drive, touching the toolbar's action icon (⬆️) displays a `UIActivityViewController` showing options for sharing, saving, copying and printing your drawing. All of these options require that the app first obtain a UIImage representing the drawing.

Drawing operations are always performed using the current graphics context. iOS maintains graphics contexts in a stack. When you perform custom drawing in a UIView subclass's drawRect method, a graphics context is created for you and placed at the top of the stack. You also can use UIKit functions to create your own graphics contexts—each new one you create is placed at the top of the graphics-context stack and becomes the current graphics context when you perform drawing operations.

In Section 7.7.6, you'll create a computed property (introduced in Section 5.5.4) that renders the contents of the app's DoodleView (the custom UIView subclass for drawing) as a UIImage and returns it. The UIImage will be used to initialize a UIActivity-ViewController that shows options for sharing, saving, copying and printing the image. You'll use UIKit functions to create a drawing context that enables the app to draw into an image (as opposed to drawing onto the screen), draw the DoodleView's contents into that image, obtain the image as a UIImage and return the graphics context's resources back to the system.

### 7.3.5 Storyboard Loading Initialization

As you've seen, you can design app UIs in storyboards. When you do, Xcode serializes each view controller's views into archive files that contain the settings for those views. When a view controller object is created, the view controller's initializer that receives an NSCoder

```
    required init(coder aDecoder: NSCoder)
```

is called to load and deserialize the archive, which recreates the view controller with the settings you specified in the storyboard. The same initializer is also called for each view that was serialized with its parent view controller. For several classes in this app, you'll override the default version of this initializer to perform additional tasks.

## 7.4 Building the App's UI and Adding Its Custom Classes

In this section, you'll create the project, design the storyboard, create the classes for the storyboard's view controllers and create the outlets and actions for various UI controls.

### 7.4.1 Creating the Project

Begin by creating a new **Single View Application** project. Specify the following settings in the **Choose options for your new project** sheet:

- **Product Name:** Doodlz.
- **Organization Name:** Deitel & Associates, Inc.—or use your own.
- **Company Identifier:** com.deitel—or use your own company identifier.
- **Language**—Swift.
- **Devices:** Universal.

After specifying the settings, click **Next**, indicate where you'd like to save your project and click **Create** to create the project.

*Portrait Orientation*

This app is designed for only portrait orientation. In the project settings' General tab that's displayed in the Xcode Editor area, scroll to the Deployment Info section, then for Device Orientation ensure that only Portrait is selected.

*App Icons*

As you've done in the earlier apps, add app icons to the project's asset catalog.

## 7.4.2 Creating the Initial View Controller's User Interface

In this section, you'll build the initial view controller's user interface that's managed by class ViewController (Section 7.5). You'll also create the custom DoodleView subclass of UIView, then designate DoodleView as the type of the view in which the user will draw. Figure 7.11 shows the completed user interface.

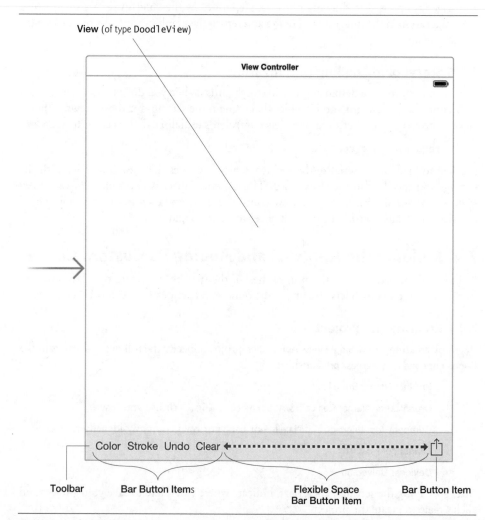

**Fig. 7.11** | User interface for the initial view controller.

Open the storyboard and perform the following steps:

1. Drag a **Toolbar** from the **Objects** library to the **View Controller**'s bottom-center. Initially, the **Toolbar** contains one **Bar Button Item** with the title **Item**.

2. Drag five additional **Bar Button Items** from the **Objects** library onto the **Toolbar**. Interface Builder automatically positions them left-to-right with the recommended amount of space between them.

3. Select the first **Bar Button Item** and set its **Title** to **Color**. Note that when you initially click the **Bar Button Item** the **Toolbar** is selected—click the **Bar Button Item** until it's highlighted by a white box and the rest of the **View Controller** is grayed out.

4. Select the second **Bar Button Item** and set its **Title** to **Stroke**.

5. Select the third **Bar Button Item** and set its **Identifier** to **Undo**. Notice that Xcode provides many predefined **Identifier** values for commonly used **Bar Button Items**. Some are displayed as text and others as icons (as you'll see momentarily).

6. Select the fourth **Bar Button Item** and set its **Title** to **Clear**.

7. Select the fifth **Bar Button Item** and set its **Identifier** to **Flexible Space**. This inserts a resizable space that pushes the last **Bar Button Item** to the **Toolbar**'s right side.

8. Select the last **Bar Button Item** and set its **Identifier** to **Action**. This displays the action icon (⬆️).

9. Next, drag a **View** onto the **View Controller** and center it horizontally and vertically in the remaining space—this will be the drawing area. Interface Builder automatically sizes the **View** to fill the remaining space.

### Configuring the Auto Layout Constraints

For this the initial **View Controller**'s auto layout constraints, you can simply select the scene's **View** in the **Document Outline**, then use the **Resolve Auto Layout Issues** menu at the bottom of the storyboard to select **Add Missing Constraints** under **All Views in View Controller**, then save the storyboard.

### Adding Class `DoodleView` and Specifying It as a View's Class

The **View** you added in *Step 9* is the app's drawing area. This should be an object of our `DoodleView` custom subclass of `UIView` (Section 7.7), which you have not yet created. Use the techniques you've learned previously to create a new Cocoa Touch class named `DoodleView` that inherits from `UIView`. Next, select the **View** you added in *Step 9* above, then in the **Identity Inspector**, set its **Class** property to `DoodleView`. When the storyboard is loaded to create the user interface, this **View** will be created as a `DoodleView` object.

### Configuring Class `ViewController`'s `@IBOutlet` and `@IBActions`

Using the **Assistant** editor, create in class `ViewController` a `DoodleView` `@IBOutlet` named `doodleView`. Then, create the following `@IBActions`:

- `undoButtonPressed` for the **"Undo"** Bar Button Item.
- `clearButtonPressed` for the **"Clear"** Bar Button Item.
- `actionButtonPressed` for the **Bar Button Item** that displays the action icon (⬆️).

You'll see the completed implementations of these methods in Sections 7.5.3– and 7.5.5.

### 7.4.3 Creating the Color View Controller's User Interface

Figure 7.12 shows the completed user interface for the ColorViewController (Section 7.8) that allows the user to set the drawing color.

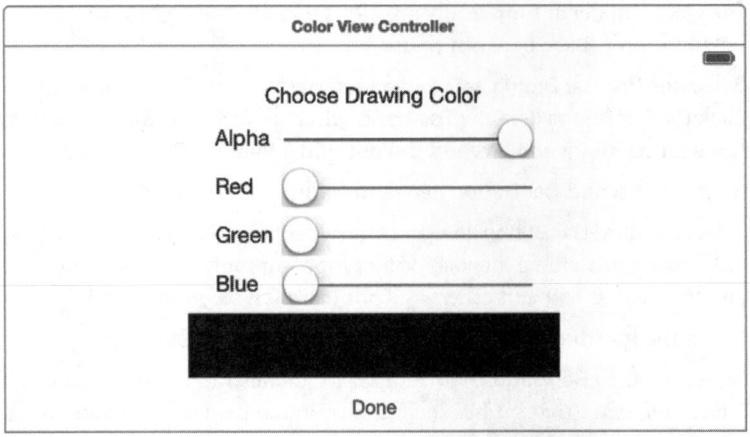

**Fig. 7.12** | User interface for class ColorViewController.

In the storyboard, perform the following steps to build the user interface:

1. Drag a **View Controller** onto the storyboard.

2. Create a segue to this new **View Controller** by *control* dragging from the **"Color"** **Bar Button Item** in the initial **View Controller** to the new **View Controller**. From the segue popover that appears, select **popover presentation** under **Action Segue**. Select the segue line in the storyboard, then in the **Attributes** inspector set the segue's **Identifier** to showColorChooser.

3. Use **Labels**, **Sliders**, a **View** and a **Button** to design the user interface in Fig. 7.12. Be sure to set the **View**'s background color to black. Each **Slider**'s range of values should be 0.0–1.0 and the **Alpha Slider** should have an initial value of 1.0.

*Configuring the Auto Layout Constraints*
For this **View Controller**'s auto layout constraints:

1. Select the colored **View** in the **Document Outline**, then in the **Resolve Auto Layout Issues** menu at the bottom of the storyboard, select **Add Missing Constraints** under **All Views in View Controller**. You'll remove three of these constraints and add others to ensure that the user interface displays correctly across devices.

2. Select the **"Alpha"** **Label** and in the **Size** inspector, remove its **Leading Space** constraint.

3. Select the nested **View** and in the **Size** inspector, remove its **Leading Space** constraint.

4. Select the **"Done"** **Button** and in the **Size** inspector, remove its **Bottom Space** constraint.

5. For the **Alpha, Red, Green** and **Blue Labels** and the **View**, *control* drag from each to the **"Choose Drawing Color" Label** and set the **Left** constraint.

6. Select the nested **View** and in the auto layout **Pin** menu, set its **Height** constraint.

*Adding Class* **ColorViewController** *and Specifying It as the View Controller's Class*
Create a Cocoa Touch class named `ColorViewController` that inherits from `UIViewController`. Next, select the new view controller you added in this section, then in the **Identity Inspector**, set **Class** to `ColorViewController`.

*Configuring Class* **ColorViewController**'s *@IBOutlet and @IBActions*
Using the **Assistant** editor, create the following `@IBOutlets` in class `ColorViewController`:

- `alphaSlider` for the **Slider** to the right of the **"Alpha" Label**.
- `redSlider` for the **Slider** to the right of the **"Red" Label**.
- `greenSlider` for the **Slider** to the right of the **"Green" Label**.
- `blueSlider` for the **Slider** to the right of the **"Blue" Label**.
- `colorView` for the **View** below the **Sliders**.

Next, create the following `@IBActions`:

- `colorChanged` for the **Sliders**—recall that you can *control* drag from one **Slider** to create the `colorChanged` method, then *control* drag from the other **Sliders** to the existing method.
- `done` for the **"Done" Button**.

You'll see the completed implementations of these methods in Section 7.8.3.

## 7.4.4 Creating the Stroke View Controller's User Interface

Figure 7.13 shows the completed user interface for the `StrokeViewController` (Section 7.8) that allows the user to set the stroke thickness.

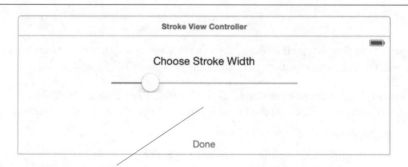

**Fig. 7.13** | UI for class `StrokeViewController`.

In the storyboard, perform the following steps to build the user interface:

1. Drag a **View Controller** onto the storyboard.

2. Create a segue to this new **View Controller** by *control* dragging from the **"Stroke"** **Bar Button Item** in the initial **View Controller** to the new **View Controller**. From the segue popover that appears, select **popover presentation** under **Action Segue**. Select the segue line in the storyboard, then in the **Attributes** inspector set the segue's **Identifier** to showStrokeWidthChooser.

3. Use a **Label**, a **Slider**, a **View** and a **Button** to design the user interface in Fig. 7.13. The **Slider**'s range of values should be 1–50 and should have an initial value of 10. The **View**'s height should be 50.

### Configuring the Auto Layout Constraints
For this **View Controller**'s auto layout constraints:

1. Select the scene's **View** in the **Document Outline**, then in the **Resolve Auto Layout Issues** menu at the bottom of the storyboard, select **Add Missing Constraints** under **All Views in View Controller**.

2. Select the **"Done" Button**, then in the **Size** inspector remove its **Bottom Space** constraint.

3. Select the **View** below the **Slider**, then in the auto layout **Pin** menu set the **Height** constraint.

### Adding Class *StrokeViewController* and Specifying It as the View Controller's Class
Create a Cocoa Touch class named StrokeViewController that inherits from UIViewController. Next, select the new view controller you added in this section, then in the **Identity Inspector**, set **Class** to StrokeViewController.

### Adding Class *SampleLineView* and Specifying It as the View's Class
In the StrokeViewController, the **View** below the **Slider** will be used to display a sample line using the current stroke width. For this purpose, you'll create a custom subclass of UIView named SampleLineView. In the file StrokeViewController.swift, add the following code above class StrokeViewController:

```
class SampleLineView: UIView {
}
```

Next, select the **View** below the **Slider**, then in the **Identity Inspector**, set **Class** to SampleLineView. You'll complete this class's definition in Section 7.9.1.

### Configuring Class *StrokeViewController*'s *@IBOutlet* and *@IBActions*
Using the **Assistant** editor, create the following @IBOutlets in class StrokeViewController:

- strokeWidthSlider for the **Slider**.
- strokeWidthView for the **View** below the **Slider**.

Next, create the following @IBActions:

- lineWidthChanged for the **Slider**.
- done for the **"Done" Button**.

You'll see the completed implementations of these methods in Section 7.9.4.

### 7.4.5 Adding the Squiggle Class

The lines that the user draws in this app are stored as Squiggle objects. Use the techniques you've learned previously to create a Cocoa Touch class named Squiggle that inherits from UIBezierPath. You'll see the completed class definition in Section 7.6.

## 7.5 ViewController Class

Class ViewController (Sections 7.5.1—7.5.5) manages the **Doodlz** app's UI. The class provides @IBActions that respond to the UIToolbar's UIBarButtonItem events, overrides UIResponder method motionEnded to respond to the shake gesture and is the delegate for the ColorViewController (Section 7.8) and StrokeViewController (Section 7.9) that enable the user to change the color and stroke thickness, respectively.

### 7.5.1 ViewController Class Definition, Property and Delegate Methods

Figure 7.14 shows the beginning of class ViewController's definition. Lines 6–7 indicate that the class inherits from UIViewController and conforms to the protocols ColorView-ControllerDelegate (defined in Section 7.8.1) and StrokeViewControllerDelegate (defined in Section 7.9.2). We added the protocols to the comma-separated list following superclass UIViewController and provided their implementations (lines 11–18). Recall from Section 7.4.2 that the @IBOutlet doodleView refers to an object of UIView subclass DoodleView that you configured in the storyboard.

```
 1   // ViewController.swift
 2   // Handles the UIBarButtonItems' events and motion events;
 3   // also sets DoodleView properties when user changes settings
 4   import UIKit
 5
 6   class ViewController: UIViewController, ColorViewControllerDelegate,
 7       StrokeViewControllerDelegate {
 8       @IBOutlet var doodleView: DoodleView!
 9
10       // called by ColorViewController when user changes the drawing color
11       func colorChanged(color: UIColor) {
12           doodleView.drawingColor = color
13       }
14
15       // called by StrokeViewController when user changes the stroke width
16       func strokeWidthChanged(width: CGFloat) {
17           doodleView.strokeWidth = width
18       }
19
```

**Fig. 7.14** | ViewController class definition, property and delegate methods.

#### *ColorViewControllerDelegate method colorChanged*

Lines 11–13 implement the ColorViewControllerDelegate method colorChanged, which is called by the ColorViewController when the user sets a new drawing color. Line 12 sets the doodleView's drawingColor property, which you'll define in Section 7.7.1.

***StrokeViewControllerDelegate*** *method* **strokeWidthChanged**
Lines 16–18 implement the StrokeViewControllerDelegate method strokeWidth-Changed, which is called by the StrokeViewController when the user sets a new stroke thickness. Line 17 sets the doodleView's strokeWidth property, which you'll define in Section 7.7.1.

## 7.5.2 Overridden UIViewController Method prepareForSeque

As you've seen in prior apps, UIViewController method prepareForSegue (Fig. 7.15) is called when the app is about to segue from one view controller to another. You specified two segue identifiers in this app's storyboard:

- "showColorChooser" for the segue to the ColorViewController, and
- "showStrokeWidthChooser" for the segue to the StrokeViewController.

The segue's destinationViewController property contains a reference to the view controller that's about to be presented. If the app is about to segue to the ColorViewController (line 24), then lines 25–26 cast the destinationViewController to a Color-ViewController so that we can set its color and delegate properties (lines 27–28). This enables us to pass information to the ColorViewController so that it can configure its UI to display the current drawing color (doodleView.drawingColor). ColorViewController uses its delegate property to call the colorChanged method (from the protocol Color-ViewControllerDelegate). If the app is about to segue to the StrokeViewController (line 29), then lines 30–31 cast the destinationViewController to a StrokeViewController so that we can set its strokeWidth (line 32) and delegate (line 33) properties. This enables the StrokeViewController to display a sample line representing the current stroke width and to call the StrokeViewControllerDelegate's strokeWidthChanged method when the user sets a new stroke width.

```
20      // set color or stroke width before presenting view controller
21      override func prepareForSegue(segue: UIStoryboardSegue,
22          sender: AnyObject?) {
23          // determine which segue is being performed
24          if segue.identifier == "showColorChooser" {
25              let destination = (segue.destinationViewController
26                  as ColorViewController)
27              destination.color = doodleView.drawingColor
28              destination.delegate = self
29          } else if segue.identifier == "showStrokeWidthChooser" {
30              let destination = (segue.destinationViewController
31                  as StrokeViewController)
32              destination.strokeWidth = doodleView.strokeWidth
33              destination.delegate = self
34          }
35      }
36
```

**Fig. 7.15** | Overridden UIViewController method prepareForSeque.

### 7.5.3 ViewController Methods undoButtonPressed, clearButtonPressed and displayEraseDialog

Figure 7.16 presents the completed @IBActions that you created in Section 7.4.2 for the **Undo** and **Clear** UIBarButtonItems. When the user touches **Undo**, method undoButton-Pressed (lines 38–40) calls the DoodleView's undo method (Section 7.7.3) to remove the most recent line. When the user touches **Clear**, method clearButtonPressed (lines 43–45) calls the displayEraseDialog method (lines 48–67) to confirm whether the drawing should be discarded. Method displayEraseDialog uses techniques you learned in prior chapters to display a UIAlertController with a **Cancel** and a **Delete** button. If the user touches **Cancel**, the dialog is dismissed. If the user touches **Delete**, the deleteAction's handler (lines 61–63) executes and calls the DoodleView's clear method (Section 7.7.3) to remove all the lines in the drawing.

```
37    // remove last Squiggle from DoodleView
38    @IBAction func undoButtonPressed(sender: AnyObject) {
39        doodleView.undo()
40    }
41
42    // confirm then clear current drawing
43    @IBAction func clearButtonPressed(sender: AnyObject) {
44        displayEraseDialog()
45    }
46
47    // displays a dialog asking for confirmation before deleting drawing
48    func displayEraseDialog() {
49        // create UIAlertController for user input
50        let alertController = UIAlertController(title: "Are You Sure?",
51            message: "Touch Delete to erase your doodle",
52            preferredStyle: UIAlertControllerStyle.Alert)
53
54        // create Cancel action
55        let cancelAction = UIAlertAction(title: "Cancel",
56            style: UIAlertActionStyle.Cancel, handler: nil)
57        alertController.addAction(cancelAction)
58
59        let deleteAction = UIAlertAction(title: "Delete",
60            style: UIAlertActionStyle.Default,
61            handler: {(action) in
62                self.doodleView.clear()
63            })
64        alertController.addAction(deleteAction)
65        presentViewController(alertController, animated: true,
66            completion: nil)
67    }
68
```

**Fig. 7.16** | ViewController methods undoButtonPressed, clearButtonPressed and displayEraseDialog.

### 7.5.4 Overridden UIResponder Method motionEnded

As we discussed in Section 7.2, the user can also shake the device to erase a drawing. Figure 7.17 shows the overridden method motionEnded, which class UIViewController inherits indirectly from class UIResponder. The method receives two parameters:

- a UIEventSubtype constant representing the subtype of the event, and
- a UIEvent representing the event that occurred.

Each UIEvent has a type property with a value from the **UIEventType enum**—Touches, Motion or RemoteControl. The UIEventSubtype enum provides constants that help you further categorize events. The constant MotionShake indicates a motion event in which the user shook the device. UIEventSubtype also provides various constants for remote-control events—for example, many headphones have an integrated remote control that enables the user to interact with the iOS Music app to play, pause, stop and more. Line 72 determines whether the event represents a shake gesture. If so, line 73 calls method displayEraseDialog (Fig. 7.16) to display the same confirmation dialog that's displayed when the user touches app's **Clear** button.

```
69    // handles shake-to-erase
70    override func motionEnded(motion: UIEventSubtype,
71        withEvent event: UIEvent) {
72        if motion == UIEventSubtype.MotionShake {
73            displayEraseDialog()
74        }
75    }
76
```

**Fig. 7.17** | Overridden UIResponder method motionEnded.

### 7.5.5 ViewController Method actionButtonPressed

Figure 7.18 presents the completed @IBAction that you created in Section 7.5.5 for the action (📤) UIBarButtonItem. When the user touches this button, the app displays a UIActivityViewController (as we did in Section 4.6.6) with options for sharing, saving, copying and printing the doodle. In this case, the Array itemsToShare contains a String and a UIImage returned by the DoodleView's image property (Section 7.7.6)—when sharing the doodle, the String and the UIImage are both included in the message or post.

```
77    // display UIActivityViewController for saving, printing, sharing
78    @IBAction func actionButtonPressed(sender: AnyObject) {
79        let itemsToShare = ["Check out my doodle!", doodleView.image]
80        let activityViewController = UIActivityViewController(
81            activityItems: itemsToShare, applicationActivities: nil)
82        presentViewController(activityViewController,
83            animated: true, completion: nil)
84    }
85    }
```

**Fig. 7.18** | ViewController method actionButtonPressed.

## 7.6 Squiggle Class

Class Squiggle (Fig. 7.19) is a subclass of UIBezierPath that stores a given line's color (line 6) in addition to path information, such as the points that compose the path. The class's initializer at lines 9–15 sets the Squiggle's color, calls the superclass's initializer, then configures the inherited properties lineWidth, lineCapStyle and lineJoinStyle. The **lineWidth** is a CGFloat representing the path's thickness. The **lineCapStyle** is a CGLineCap contact that specifies the appearance of the path's endpoints—the constant kCGLineCapRound indicates that they should be rounded. The **lineJoinStyle** is a CGLineJoin constant that specifies how the path's components are joined together—the constant kCGLineJoinRound indicates that they should be rounded. For the complete sets of constants for line caps and line joins, see the *CGPath Reference* at:

```
http://bit.ly/CGPathReference
```

The initializer at lines 18–20 is provided because it's required to enable the class to compile (as discussed in Section 6.6).

```
 1  // Squiggle.swift
 2  // UIBezierPath subclass that also stores the drawing color
 3  import UIKit
 4
 5  class Squiggle : UIBezierPath {
 6      var color: UIColor
 7
 8      // configure the Squiggle's properties
 9      init(color: UIColor, strokeWidth: CGFloat) {
10          self.color = color
11          super.init()
12          self.lineWidth = strokeWidth
13          self.lineCapStyle = kCGLineCapRound
14          self.lineJoinStyle = kCGLineJoinRound
15      }
16
17      // required initializer
18      required init(coder aDecoder: NSCoder) {
19          fatalError("init(coder:) has not been implemented")
20      }
21
22      // set Squiggle's color before drawing it
23      override func stroke() {
24          color.setStroke() // set the drawing color
25          super.stroke() // call superclass method to draw the UIBezierPath
26      }
27  }
```

**Fig. 7.19** | UIBezierPath subclass that also stores the drawing color.

### *Overridden UIBezierPath Method* stroke

UIBezierPath method **stroke** uses the current drawing color to display the path in the current graphics context—in this app, the DoodleView's graphics context. Lines 23–26 override `stroke` so that it first calls the `UIColor` method **setStroke** on the `color` property to set the drawing color in the current graphics context, then calls the superclass's version of `stroke` to display the path. As you'll see in Section 7.7.4, the `DoodleView`'s `drawRect` method uses this overridden method to display the `Squiggles` using the `DoodleView`'s graphics context.

## 7.7 DoodleView Class

As you learned in Section 7.3, custom drawing in iOS is typically performed in a subclass of `UIView` in which you override method `drawRect` to specify your custom drawing. The `DoodleView` class (Sections 7.7.1—7.7.6) is a subclass of `UIView` that manages collections of `Squiggles` and draws them. The class also overrides the `UIResponder` methods for touch event handling.

### 7.7.1 DoodleView Properties

Figure 7.20 shows class `DoodleView`'s properties. The `strokeWidth` and `drawingColor` properties are not declared `private`—this allows the `ViewController` to set them when the user changes the stroke width or drawing color. The property `finishedSquiggles` stores the finished lines as an `Array` of `Squiggle` objects. The property `currentSquiggles` is a `Dictionary` with `UITouch` keys and `Squiggle` values. When the user touches the screen to draw, a separate `UITouch` object represents each finger from the time the finger touches the screen until the user removes it from the screen. We use each `UITouch` to identify the corresponding `Squiggle` object for a given finger, so that we can add new line segments to the correct `Squiggles`.

```
1   // DoodleView.swift
2   // UIView subclass for drawing Squiggles and handling touch events
3   import UIKit
4
5   class DoodleView: UIView {
6       var strokeWidth: CGFloat = 10.0
7       var drawingColor: UIColor = UIColor.blackColor()
8       private var finishedSquiggles: [Squiggle] = []
9       private var currentSquiggles: [UITouch : Squiggle] = [:]
10
```

**Fig. 7.20** | DoodleView properties.

### 7.7.2 DoodleView Initializer

Figure 7.20 shows class `DoodleView`'s initializer. Recall from Section 7.3.5 that this initializer is used by the storyboard to initialize a view object that was created in the storyboard. Line 14 sets the inherited `UIView` property **multipleTouchEnabled** to `true` to enable the `UIView` to respond to multi-touch events (Section 7.7.5). By default, this property is `false`, so the view can respond to only one touch at a time.

```
11    // initializer
12    required init(coder aDecoder: NSCoder) {
13        super.init(coder: aDecoder)
14        self.multipleTouchEnabled = true // track multiple fingers
15    }
16
```

**Fig. 7.21** | DoodleView initializer.

### 7.7.3 DoodleView Methods undo and clear

Figure 7.22 shows DoodleView's undo and clear methods that are called by class View-Controller when the user touches the **Undo** and **Clear** UIBarButtonItems. Method undo (lines 18–23) ensures that finishedSquiggles is not empty (line 19), then removes the last Squiggle from the Array by calling method **removeLast**. Note that every UITouch represents a separate line. So, even if you draw several lines at the same time by dragging multiple fingers, those lines are stored independently in the finishedSquiggles collection. Whichever line was completed last will be the first removed by method undo.

```
17    // called by ViewController to remove last Squiggle
18    func undo() {
19        if finishedSquiggles.count > 0 {
20            finishedSquiggles.removeLast()
21            self.setNeedsDisplay()
22        }
23    }
24
25    // called by ViewController to remove all Squiggles
26    func clear() {
27        finishedSquiggles.removeAll()
28        self.setNeedsDisplay()
29    }
30
```

**Fig. 7.22** | DoodleView methods undo and clear.

Line 21 calls UIView inherited method setNeedsDisplay to tell iOS that the Doo-dleView needs to be redrawn. This results in a call to method drawRect (Section 7.7.4) to redisplay the remaining lines. Method clear (lines 26–29) empties the finishedSquig-gles Array by calling method **removeAll**, then calls UIView method setNeedsDisplay to tell iOS that the DoodleView needs to be redrawn.

### 7.7.4 Overridden UIView Method drawRect

Custom drawing in a UIView is performed in method drawRect (Fig. 7.23), which is called by iOS whenever a view needs to be displayed or redisplayed. Lines 33–35 iterate through the finishedSquiggles Array and call method stroke on each to draw it on the Doo-dleView. Next, lines 37–39 iterate through the currentSquiggles Dictionary's values—the Squiggles that are currently being drawn—and call method stroke on each to draw it.

```
31      // draws the completed and in-progress Squiggles
32      override func drawRect(rect: CGRect) {
33          for squiggle in finishedSquiggles {
34              squiggle.stroke()
35          }
36
37          for squiggle in currentSquiggles.values {
38              squiggle.stroke()
39          }
40      }
41
```

**Fig. 7.23** | Overridden `UIView` method `drawRect`.

### 7.7.5 Overridden UIResponder Methods for Touch Handling

Recall that class `UIView` inherits from class `UIResponder`, which provides methods and properties for handling touch, motion and remote-control events. Figure 7.24 shows class `DoodleView`'s overridden `UIResponder` methods for touch event handling.

```
42      // adds new Squiggles to Dictionary currentSquiggles
43      override func touchesBegan(touches: NSSet, withEvent event: UIEvent) {
44          for touch in touches.allObjects as [UITouch] {
45              let squiggle =
46                  Squiggle(color: drawingColor, strokeWidth: strokeWidth)
47              squiggle.moveToPoint(touch.locationInView(self))
48              currentSquiggles[touch] = squiggle
49          }
50      }
51
52      // updates existing Squiggles in Dictionary currentSquiggles
53      override func touchesMoved(touches: NSSet, withEvent event: UIEvent) {
54          for touch in touches.allObjects as [UITouch] {
55              currentSquiggles[touch]?.addLineToPoint(
56                  touch.locationInView(self))
57              setNeedsDisplay()
58          }
59      }
60
61      // adds finalized Squiggles to Array finishedSquiggles
62      override func touchesEnded(touches: NSSet, withEvent event: UIEvent) {
63          for touch in touches.allObjects as [UITouch] {
64              if let squiggle = currentSquiggles[touch] {
65                  finishedSquiggles.append(squiggle)
66              }
67              currentSquiggles[touch] = nil // delete touch from Dictionary
68          }
69      }
70
```

**Fig. 7.24** | Overridden `UIResponder` methods for touch handling. (Part 1 of 2.)

```
71      // if touches interruped by iOS, removes in-progress Squiggles
72      override func touchesCancelled(touches: NSSet!,
73          withEvent event: UIEvent!) {
74          currentSquiggles.removeAll()
75      }
76
```

**Fig. 7.24** | Overridden UIResponder methods for touch handling. (Part 2 of 2.)

### Method *touchesBegan*

Recall from Section 6.9.6 that when one or more new touches begin, iOS calls method touchesBegan (lines 43–50) and passes in an NSSet containing UITouch objects representing each new touch point. The method iterates through the UITouches and for each one:

- creates a new Squiggle (lines 45–46) with the current drawingColor and strokeWidth,

- calls Squiggle's **moveToPoint** method (inherited from UIBezierPath) to specify the Squiggle's starting point, and

- inserts a new key–value pair into the currentSquiggles Dictionary, using the UITouch as the key and the Squiggle as the value—the UITouch subsequently will be used in the touchesMoved and touchesEnded methods to look up the corresponding Squiggle.

Each UITouch contains a point representing where the touch event occurred. When setting the starting point of a Squiggle, line 47 uses UITouch method **locationInView** to determine the touch point's location with respect to the upper-left corner of self (i.e., the DoodleView).

### Method *touchesMoved*

When one or more touches move—that is, the user drags one or more fingers—iOS calls method touchesMoved (lines 53–59) and passes in an NSSet containing UITouch objects representing the new locations of the touches. The method iterates through the UITouches and for each one:

- gets the Squiggle that corresponds to the UITouch and updates it (lines 55–56) by calling the Squiggle's **addLineToPoint** method (inherited from UIBezierPath) to add a line from the Squiggle's prior point to the current point and

- calls inherited UIView method setNeedsDisplay to indicate that the DoodleView needs to be redrawn.

Line 55 uses the Dictionary's subscript operator to look up the Squiggle for a given UITouch. Recall that the subscript operator returns an optional of the Dictionary's value type (Squiggle in this app). For this reason, we use optional chaining to ensure that the returned value is not nil, before calling method addLineToPoint.

### Method *touchesEnded*

When one or more touches end—that is, the user removes one or more fingers from the screen—iOS calls method touchesEnded (lines 62–69) and passes in an NSSet containing

UITouch objects representing the new touch points. The method iterates through the UITouches and for each one:

- gets the corresponding Squiggle from the Dictionary (line 64) and adds it to the finishedSquiggles Array (line 65), then

- removes the key–value pair from the Dictionary by setting the value to nil for the given key (line 67).

*Method* **touchesCancelled**

When the user is drawing lines, it's possible that the touch events could be interrupted by external sources, such as a telephone call. In such cases, iOS calls method touchesCancelled (lines 72–75) so the app can decide how to handle cancelled touch events. For this app, we cancel all in-progress Squiggles by calling the Dictionary's removeAll method to discard all key–value pairs in the Dictionary.

### 7.7.6 DoodleView Computed Property image

When the user touches the action icon (⬆) to display a UIActivityController for sharing, saving, copying or printing the drawing, class ViewController accesses the DoodleView's computed property image (Fig. 7.25), which returns a UIImage containing the drawing. This property uses several UIKit functions to manage a graphics context for an image in which the DoodleView will draw its Squiggles.

```
77      // computed property that returns UIImage of DoodleView's contents
78      var image: UIImage {
79          // begin an image graphics context the size of the DoodleView
80          UIGraphicsBeginImageContextWithOptions(
81              self.bounds.size, true, 0.0)
82
83          // render DoodleView's contents into the image graphics context
84          self.layer.renderInContext(UIGraphicsGetCurrentContext())
85
86          // get the UIImage from the image graphics context
87          let newImage = UIGraphicsGetImageFromCurrentImageContext()
88          UIGraphicsEndImageContext() // end the image graphics context
89          return newImage
90      }
91  }
```

**Fig. 7.25** | DoodleView computed property image.

UIKit function **UIGraphicsBeginImageContextWithOptions** (lines 80–81) creates the graphics context. The first argument is the size of the bitmap image that will be created—in this case, the size of the DoodleView (self.bounds.size). The second argument specifies whether the bitmap image is opaque (true) or transparent (false). The last argument allows you to scale the image by specifying the number of pixels per point. Specifying 0.0 indicates that the image should have the same scale as the screen.

Next, line 84 accesses the DoodleView's inherited layer property—a CALayer object in which the DoodleView's custom drawing appears. CALayer method **renderInContext** receives as its argument a graphics context and renders the contents of the UIView (in this case the DoodleView) into that graphics context. UIKit function **UIGraphicsGetCurrent-Context** returns the current graphics context that you created in lines 80–81.

Line 87 calls UIKit function **UIGraphicsGetImageFromCurrentContext**, which returns a UIImage containing the drawing. Line 88 calls UIKit function **UIGraphicsEndImageContext**, which terminates the graphics context created in lines 80–81 and returns its resources to the system. Finally, line 89 returns the UIImage. For additional details of the UIKit functions used here and others, see Apple's *UIKit Function Reference* at:

```
http://bit.ly/UIKitFunctionReference
```

# 7.8 ColorViewController Class
Sections 7.8.1—7.8.3 present class ColorViewController, which enables the user to choose the drawing color for lines that the user subsequently draws.

### 7.8.1 ColorViewControllerDelegate Protocol and the Beginning of Class ColorViewController
In Fig. 7.26, lines 6–8 define the protocol ColorViewControllerDelegate. Class ViewController conforms to this protocol so that it can update the DoodleView's drawingColor property when the user changes the color. Line 10 begins class ColorViewController's definition. You created the @IBOutlet properties (lines 11–15) in Section 7.4.3. Lines 17–18 define the color and delegate properties that class ViewController sets when the segue to ColorViewController is about to be performed (Section 7.5.2). Once again, the delegate is declared as an optional (?) because it needs to be set *after* the ColorViewController object is initialized.

```
 1   // ColorViewController.swift
 2   // Manages UI for changing the drawing color
 3   import UIKit
 4
 5   // delegate protocol that class ViewController conforms to
 6   protocol ColorViewControllerDelegate {
 7       func colorChanged(color:UIColor)
 8   }
 9
10   class ColorViewController: UIViewController {
11       @IBOutlet weak var alphaSlider: UISlider!
12       @IBOutlet weak var redSlider: UISlider!
13       @IBOutlet weak var greenSlider: UISlider!
14       @IBOutlet weak var blueSlider: UISlider!
15       @IBOutlet weak var colorView: UIView!
16
17       var color: UIColor = UIColor.blackColor()
18       var delegate: ColorViewControllerDelegate? = nil
19
```

**Fig. 7.26** | ColorViewControllerDelegate protocol and the beginning of class ColorViewController.

### 7.8.2 Overridden `UIViewController` Method `viewDidLoad`

When the `ColorViewController` is displayed, method `viewDidLoad` (Fig. 7.27) configures the UI for setting the color. Lines 25–28 define `CGFloat` variables for the red, green, blue and alpha components of a color. Next, we get the color components from the `color` property, which was set by class `ViewController` when preparing to perform the segue (Section 7.5.2). The variables from lines 25–28 are passed by reference to `UIColor` method **getRed** (line 29), which receives four parameters in which the `UIColor`'s components will be stored. This method extracts the red, green, blue and alpha components from the `UIColor` and assigns them to the arguments in the caller. In Swift, when a variable is passed by reference, you must precede it with an ampersand (**&**); otherwise, a compilation error occurs. Lines 31–34 use the values obtained in line 29 to set the sliders' `value` properties. Line 35 then sets the `colorView`'s `backgroundColor` property to the current drawing color.

```
20       // when view loads, set UISliders to current color component values
21       override func viewDidLoad() {
22           super.viewDidLoad()
23
24           // get components of color and set UISlider values
25           var red: CGFloat = 0.0
26           var green: CGFloat = 0.0
27           var blue: CGFloat = 0.0
28           var alpha: CGFloat = 0.0
29           color.getRed(&red, green: &green, blue: &blue, alpha: &alpha)
30
31           redSlider.value = Float(red)
32           greenSlider.value = Float(green)
33           blueSlider.value = Float(blue)
34           alphaSlider.value = Float(alpha)
35           colorView.backgroundColor = color
36       }
37
```

**Fig. 7.27**  |  Overridden `UIViewController` method `viewDidLoad`.

### 7.8.3 `ColorViewController` Methods `colorChanged` and `done`

Figure 7.28 presents the completed @IBActions that you created in Section 7.4.3 for the `ColorViewController`'s `UISlider`s and `UIButton`. When the user moves the `UISlider`s' thumbs, method `colorChanged` (lines 39–46) sets the `colorView`'s `backgroundColor` property by assigning it a `UIColor` initialized with the red, green, blue and alpha color components (lines 40–44). Line 45 then stores the current color. `UIView` property `backgroundColor` is an optional `UIColor` that's `nil` by default (indicating that a `UIView` is transparent). We use ! to explicitly unwrap the optional—the `colorView`'s `backgroundColor` will not be `nil` because its value is set in method `viewDidLoad` when the `ColorViewController` is initially displayed. When the user touches the **Done** button, method `done` (lines 49–54) calls the delegate's `colorChanged` method, which then updates the drawing color for subsequent lines the user draws in the `DoodleView`.

```
38      // updates colorView's backgroundColor based on UISlider values
39      @IBAction func colorChanged(sender: AnyObject) {
40          colorView.backgroundColor = UIColor(
41              red: CGFloat(redSlider.value),
42              green: CGFloat(greenSlider.value),
43              blue: CGFloat(blueSlider.value),
44              alpha: CGFloat(alphaSlider.value))
45          color = colorView.backgroundColor!
46      }
47
48      // returns to ViewController
49      @IBAction func done(sender: AnyObject) {
50          self.dismissViewControllerAnimated(true) {
51              self.delegate?.colorChanged(self.color)
52              return
53          }
54      }
55  }
```

**Fig. 7.28** | `ColorViewController` methods `colorChanged` and `done`.

## 7.9 StrokeViewController Class

Sections 7.9.1—7.9.4 present class `StrokeViewController`, which enables the user to choose the stroke width for lines that the user subsequently draws.

### 7.9.1 SampleLineView Subclass of UIView

Just as we needed a custom `UIView` subclass to allow the user to draw, the `StrokeViewController` needs a custom `UIView` subclass to display a sample line showing the current line thickness. Class `SampleLineView` (Fig. 7.29) is a subclass of `UIView` that contains a `UIBezierPath` (line 7) to represent the sample line.

```
1   // StrokeViewController.swift
2   // Manages the UI for changing the stroke width
3   import UIKit
4
5   // UIView subclass for drawing the sample line
6   class SampleLineView : UIView {
7       var sampleLine = UIBezierPath()
8
9       // configures UIBezierPath for sample line
10      required init(coder aDecoder: NSCoder) {
11          super.init(coder: aDecoder)
12          let y = frame.height / 2
13          sampleLine.moveToPoint(CGPointMake(10, y))
14          sampleLine.addLineToPoint(CGPointMake(frame.width - 10, y))
15      }
16
```

**Fig. 7.29** | `SampleLineView` subclass of `UIView`. (Part 1 of 2.)

```
17      // draws the UIBezierPath representing the sample line
18      override func drawRect(rect: CGRect) {
19          UIColor.blackColor().setStroke()
20          sampleLine.stroke()
21      }
22  }
23
```

**Fig. 7.29** | SampleLineView subclass of UIView. (Part 2 of 2.)

In the storyboard, you defined a SampleLineView object as part of the ColorViewController's UI. Recall that such an object is initialized with a call to its class's initializer that receives an NSCoder. Line 12 determines the *y*-coordinate where the UIBezierPath should be displayed—half the SampleLineView's height so the sample line is centered vertically. Next, line 13 specifies the sample line's starting point, then line 14 adds a line from the starting to the ending point. Overridden UIView method drawRect (lines 18–21) sets the drawing color to black (line 18), then calls sampleLine's stroke method to display the UIBezierPath.

### 7.9.2 StrokeViewControllerDelegate Protocol and the Beginning of Class StrokeViewController

In Fig. 7.30, lines 25–27 define the protocol StrokeViewControllerDelegate. Class ViewController conforms to this protocol so that it can update the DoodleView's strokeWidth property when the user changes the stroke thickness. Line 29 begins class StrokeViewController's definition. You created the @IBOutlet properties (lines 30–31) in Section 7.4.4. Lines 32–33 define the delegate and strokeWidth properties that class ViewController sets when the segue to StrokeViewController is about to be performed (Section 7.5.2).

```
24  // delegate protocol that class ViewController conforms to
25  protocol StrokeViewControllerDelegate {
26      func strokeWidthChanged(width: CGFloat)
27  }
28
29  class StrokeViewController: UIViewController {
30      @IBOutlet weak var strokeWidthSlider: UISlider!
31      @IBOutlet weak var strokeWidthView: SampleLineView!
32      var delegate: StrokeViewControllerDelegate? = nil
33      var strokeWidth: CGFloat = 10.0
34
```

**Fig. 7.30** | StrokeViewControllerDelegate protocol and the beginning of class StrokeViewController.

### 7.9.3 Overridden UIViewController Method viewDidLoad

When the StrokeViewController is displayed, method viewDidLoad (Fig. 7.31) configures the UI for setting the stroke width. Line 38 sets the strokeWidthSlider's value property to the current strokeWidth, which was set by class ViewController when preparing to perform the segue (Section 7.5.2). Line 39 sets the `lineWidth` property of the `strokeWidthView`'s `sampleLine`, then calls `UIView` method `setNeedsDisplay` on the `strokeWidthView`. This indicates that `strokeWidthView` needs to be redrawn and results in a call to class `SampleLineView`'s overridden `drawRect` method to update the sample line.

```
35          // configure strokeWidthSlider and redraw strokeWidthView
36          override func viewDidLoad() {
37              super.viewDidLoad()
38              strokeWidthSlider.value = Float(strokeWidth)
39              strokeWidthView.sampleLine.lineWidth = strokeWidth
40              strokeWidthView.setNeedsDisplay()
41          }
42
```

**Fig. 7.31** | Overridden `UIViewController` method `viewDidLoad`.

### 7.9.4 StrokeViewController Methods lineWidthChanged and done

Figure 7.32 presents the completed `@IBActions` that you created in Section 7.4.4 for the `StrokeViewController`'s `UISlider` and `UIButton`. When the user moves the `UISlider`'s thumb, method `lineWidthChanged` (lines 44–47) sets the `strokeWidth`, sets the `line-Width` property of the `strokeWidthView`'s `sampleLine`, then calls `UIView` method `set-NeedsDisplay` on the `strokeWidthView` so that the sample line will be redisplayed. When the user touches the **Done** button, method `done` (lines 51–56) calls the delegate's `strokeWidthChanged` method, which then updates the stroke thickness for subsequent lines the user draws in the `DoodleView`.

```
43          // updates strokeWidth and redraws strokeWidthView
44          @IBAction func lineWidthChanged(sender: UISlider) {
45              strokeWidth = CGFloat(sender.value)
46              strokeWidthView.sampleLine.lineWidth = strokeWidth
47              strokeWidthView.setNeedsDisplay()
48          }
49
50          // returns to ViewController
51          @IBAction func done(sender: AnyObject) {
52              dismissViewControllerAnimated(true) {
53                  self.delegate?.strokeWidthChanged(self.strokeWidth)
54                  return
55              }
56          }
57      }
```

**Fig. 7.32** | StrokeViewController methods `lineWidthChanged` and done.

## 7.10 Wrap-Up

In this chapter, you built the **Doodlz** app, which enabled you to create a doodle by dragging one or more fingers across the screen to draw lines and shapes. The app provided options—displayed at the bottom of the screen as `UIBarButtonItems` in a `UIToolbar`—enabling you to set the drawing color and stroke width, undo lines one at a time and clear the entire doodle. The app also provided an option to display a `UIActivityViewController` for sharing your doodle, saving it to the device, copying it to the clipboard or printing it.

We mentioned that iOS provides several drawing technologies (OpenGL, Quartz, UIKit and Core Animation). In this app, you used the UIKit graphics system's higher-level, built-in drawing capabilities, which all `UIViews` support via their `drawRect` methods. You learned that when a `UIView` needs to be displayed, iOS calls the `UIView`'s `drawRect` method, and that to perform custom drawing, you create your own `UIView` subclass and override `drawRect`.

To store the lines drawn by the user, we subclassed the UIKit framework's `UIBezierPath` class, which can represent shapes composed of lines, arcs and curves. You learned that drawing is performed using a graphics context, which provides the current drawing color and a rectangular region in which to draw. For a subclass of `UIView`, the graphics context that `drawRect` used was created for you.

You enabled multi-touch events for the `DoodleView` subclass of `UIView`, then overrode `UIResponder` methods `touchesBegan`, `touchesMoved`, `touchesEnded` and `touchesCancelled` to respond to multi-touch events. We showed that as the user moves a given finger, that finger's touch events are maintained in the same `UITouch` object from the time the finger touches the screen to the time the user removes it. You used the `UITouch` objects as keys in a `Dictionary` that kept track of the in-progress `Squiggles`.

This app allowed you to shake the device to erase your doodle. We showed how to use iOS's accelerometer sensor to detect device movement and mentioned other sensors iOS supports. You overrode the `UIResponder` class's `motionEnded` method to handle the shake event.

You learned how to use UIKit functions to create a graphics context for rendering a `UIView`'s contents into an image. You then obtained the image as a `UIImage` and used it to initialize a `UIActivityViewController` that showed options for sharing, saving, copying and printing the image.

We explained that when you design a UI in a storyboard, Xcode serializes each view controller's views into archive files that contain the settings for those views. You learned that when a view controller object is created, each view controller and each view receives a call to its initializer with an `NSCoder` argument, which deserializes the object from the archive. For several classes in this app, you overrode the default version of this initializer to perform additional tasks.

In Chapter 8, you'll build the database-driven **Address Book** app, which provides quick and easy access to stored contact information and the ability to add contacts, delete contacts and edit existing contacts. Though the data will be stored in a traditional relational database, you'll use Xcode tools, Xcode-generated data-access code and the Core Data framework to design a data model and manipulate the data as so-called managed objects. Core Data will automatically map those objects to the underlying relational database, hiding from you the details of interacting with the database.

# Address Book App

Core Data Framework, Master-Detail Template with Core Data Support, Xcode Data Model Editor, UITableView with Static Cells, Programmatically Scrolling UITableViews

## Objectives

In this chapter you'll:

- Use the Core Data framework to store data in a database.
- Create a **Master-Detail Application** with Core Data support.
- Create a custom data model with Xcode's Data Model editor.
- Understand and customize Xcode's autogenerated Core Data code to work with the **Address Book**'s data model.
- Create UITableViewController with static cells containing UITextFields for user input.
- Listen for iOS notifications indicating when the keyboard will be shown or hidden.
- Programmatically scroll a UITableView so that a cell being edited is not hidden behind a keyboard.

**Outline**

## 8.1  Introduction

The **Address Book** app (Fig. 8.1) provides convenient access to contact information that's stored via the Core Data framework in a database on the device. You can add, edit and delete contacts. You can also scroll through an alphabetical master list of contacts and touch a specific contact name to view its details.

In this app, you'll use the Core Data framework to store data in a database. You'll once again use the **Master-Detail Application** template, but you'll choose to add Core Data support. Xcode will then autogenerate the code necessary to interact with the Core Data database. You'll use Xcode's data model editor to create the **Address Book**'s data model. We'll discuss the autogenerated Core Data code and modify it to use the **Address Book**'s data model.

In Chapter 4, you used a `UITableViewController`, which dynamically created cells based on a `UITableViewCell` prototype. You'll do that again in this app for the master contact list, but you'll choose a cell format that contains two `UILabel`s. In addition, you'll create a `UITableViewController` that displays a predesigned `UITableView` with static cells containing `UITextField`s that enable a user to edit a contact's data. You'll learn how to listen for notifications that indicate when a keyboard will be shown or hidden. When a keyboard is shown, you'll programmatically position the `UITableViewCell` containing the the `UITextField` the user touched so that it's positioned above the keyboard.

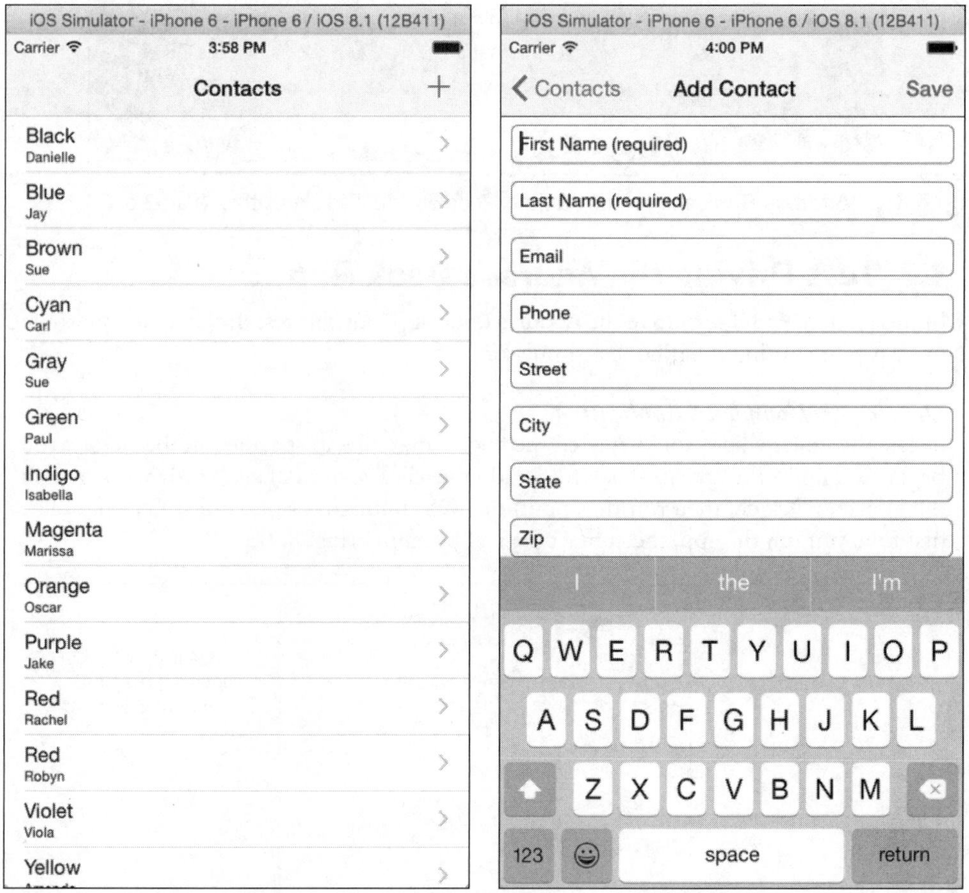

**Fig. 8.1** | **Address Book** app running on the iPhone 6 and iPad simulators. (Part 1 of 2.)

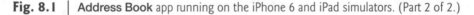

**Fig. 8.1** | Address Book app running on the iPhone 6 and iPad simulators. (Part 2 of 2.)

## 8.2 Test-Driving the Address Book App

In this section, you'll test-drive the **Address Book** app. For this test drive, we demonstrate the capabilities using the iPhone 6 simulator.

### Opening the Completed Application

Locate the folder where you extracted the book's examples as specified in the Before You Begin section. In the AddressBook folder, double click AddressBook.xcodeproj to open the project in Xcode, then run the app in the iOS simulator or on your iOS device. The first time you run the app, the contact list will be empty (Fig. 8.2).

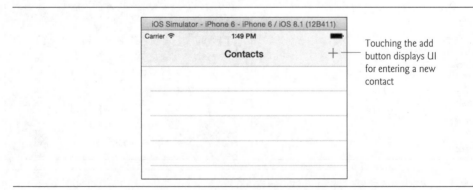

Touching the add button displays UI for entering a new contact

**Fig. 8.2** | Empty contact list shown in the iPhone 6 simulator.

*Adding a Contact*

Touch the add button (+) at the top of the master list to display the screen for adding a new entry (Fig. 8.3(a)). After adding the contact's information, touch the **Save** button to store the contact in the database and update the list of contacts. When you touch each UITextField, an appropriate keyboard is displayed. The **Email** UITextField displays a keyboard for entering e-mail addresses, the **Phone** UITextField displays a numeric keyboard and the others display the default keyboard. The first name and last name are required for each contact, so if one or both UITextFields are empty when you touch **Save**, the app displays an error. Add more contacts if you wish.

a) Empty **Add Contact** screen before entering data

b) Adding the contact **Paul Green**

**Fig. 8.3** | Empty **Add Contact** screen before the user touches any of the UITextFields and after the user fills in the fields.

*Viewing a Contact*

Once you've added contacts, they appear in the master contacts list in alphabetical order by last name. For this app, we chose a standard `UITableViewCell` format that displays a second line in each cell—we use this to show the contact's first name. In the contacts list, touch the name of the contact you just added (Fig. 8.4(a)) to view that contact's details (Fig. 8.4(b)).

a) Contact list with **Paul Green** selected

b) Details for the contact **Paul Green**

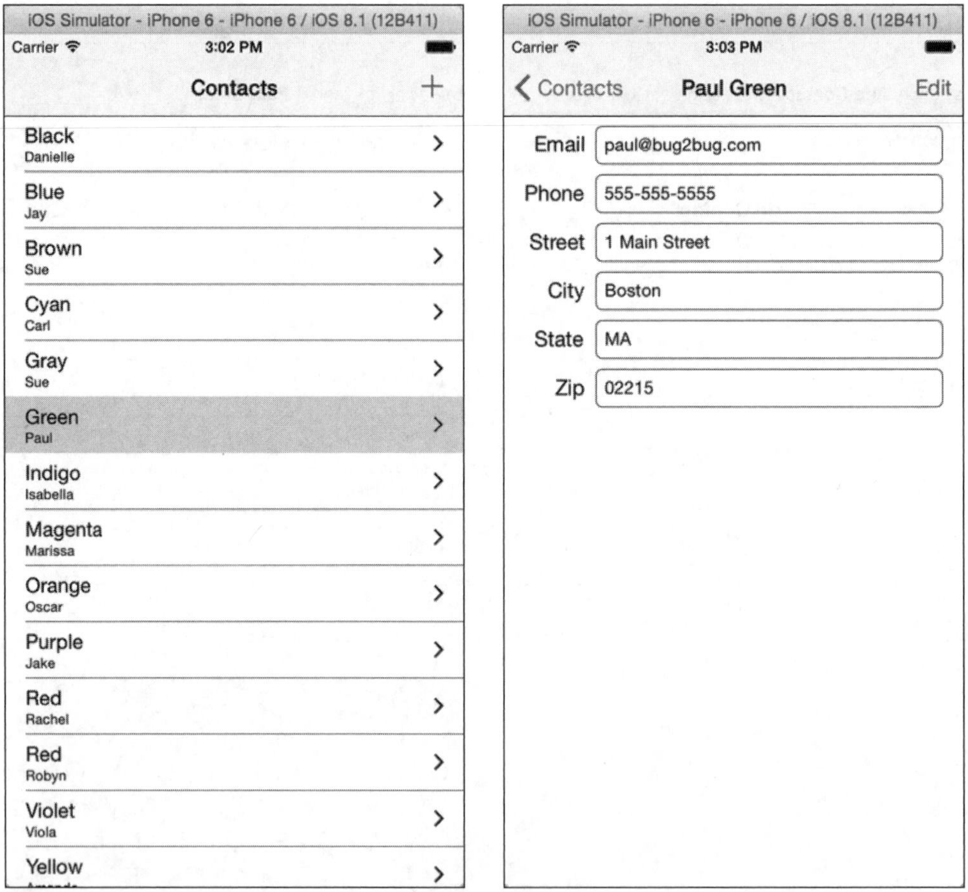

**Fig. 8.4** | Contact list with several contacts and the app showing Paul Green's details.

*Editing a Contact*

While viewing the contact's details, touch **Edit** on the navigation bar to display a screen containing `UITextFields` populated with the contact's data (Fig. 8.5(a)). Edit the data as necessary, then touch the **Save** button to update the contact information in the database. After editing a contact, the new contact's details are displayed (Fig. 8.5(a)).

a) The **Paul Green** contact before editing the phone number    b) Details for the **Paul Green** contact after edits were saved

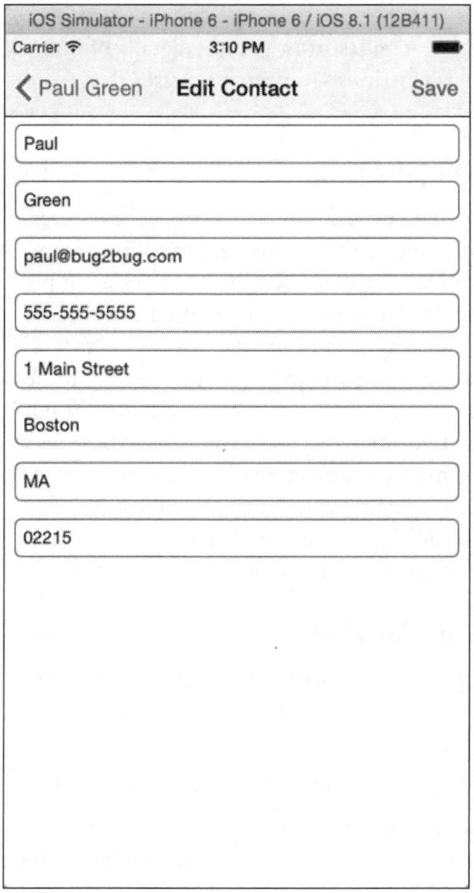

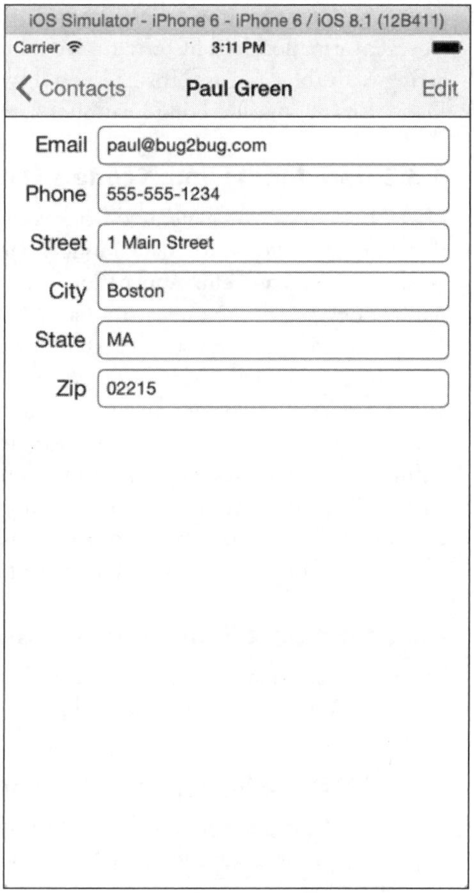

| iOS Simulator - iPhone 6 - iPhone 6 / iOS 8.1 (12B411) | | iOS Simulator - iPhone 6 - iPhone 6 / iOS 8.1 (12B411) |

Carrier 🛜          3:10 PM                    ▬          Carrier 🛜          3:11 PM                    ▬

‹ Paul Green    **Edit Contact**        Save        ‹ Contacts      **Paul Green**          Edit

Paul

Green

paul@bug2bug.com

555-555-5555

1 Main Street

Boston

MA

02215

Email    paul@bug2bug.com

Phone    555-555-1234

Street    1 Main Street

City    Boston

State    MA

Zip    02215

**Fig. 8.5** |   **Edit Contact** screen before editing Paul Green's phone number, and Paul Green's details after saving the edited phone number.

### Deleting a Contact

While viewing the contact list, swipe right-to-left on a contact's name to reveal a **Delete** button, which you can then touch to delete the contact. The app removes the contact from the database and updates the contact list.

## 8.3  Technologies Overview

This section presents the new technologies that we use in the **Address Book** app.

### 8.3.1 Enabling Core Data Support

When creating a **Single View Application** or **Master-Detail Application**, the project's options sheet contains a **Use Core Data** checkbox (Section 8.4.1) that you can select to add Core

Data support. When you use this option in this chapter's **Master-Detail Application**, Xcode generates all the code necessary for using Core Data to manage interactions with the app's persistent **data store** (i.e., where the app's data is stored on the device). Though Core Data stores information in a SQLite relational database, it hides from you the details of interacting with the database. Instead you'll work with **entities**—objects of classes that Core Data maps to an underlying relational database.

## 8.3.2 Data Model and Xcode's Data Model Editor

Core Data entities are generated from your app's **data model**, which describes the entities, their attributes and—for data models with multiple entities—the relationships among them. In a **Master-Detail Application** with Core Data support, Xcode generates a simple data model containing one entity named Event that has one attribute named timeStamp. It also generates all the code necessary for manipulating Event entities.

The data model's description is stored in a file with your app's project name and the .xcdatamodeld extension. Selecting that file displays Xcode's Data Model editor. You'll use this editor (Section 8.4.2) to replace the Event entity with a Contact entity. You'll also define attributes representing a Contact's first name, last name, e-mail, phone, street, city, state and zip code. After defining the Contact entity and its attributes, you'll use Xcode's **Editor** menu to autogenerate a Contact class containing properties for each of the Contact entity's attributes. This class will be used to create and interact with Contact entities.

## 8.3.3 Core Data Framework Classes and Protocols

In the **Address Book** app's classes, you'll work with various Core Data framework classes and protocols. We introduce several here—most are used in the autogenerated Core Data support code:

- **NSEntityDescription**—Represents an entity's description in the data model.

- **NSManagedObject**—Represents an entity in the app's data model. As you'll see, you can autogenerate NSManagedObject subclasses from your data model's entities.

- **NSManagedObjectModel**—Contains the data model's NSEntityDescriptions and maps between the NSManagedObjects and the underlying data store.

- **NSPersistentStoreCoordinator**—Associates the NSManagedObjectModel with an actual database file. Core Data typically uses a SQLite database to store the app's entities.

- **NSManagedObjectContext**—Manages the app's entities as NSManagedObjects in memory. This object interacts with the NSPersistentStoreCoordinator to access the data store.

- **NSFetchedResultsController**—Manages the data that's used to populate the MasterViewController's UITableView in a **Master-Detail Application.**

- **NSFetchedResultsControllerDelegate**—Specifies the methods that NSFetchedResultsController calls to update the UITableView in response to changes in the underlying data store.

- **NSFetchRequest**—Retrieves entities from the data store as NSManagedObjects, potentially ordering them based on a collection of NSSortDescriptors that specify the attributes used to determine the sorting order.

## 8.3.4 UITableViewController Cell Styles

In Chapter 4, you used a UITableViewController with *dynamic prototypes*—cells were created dynamically, based on a prototype cell defined in the storyboard. When designing a UITableViewController's cells, you can choose from several styles. In Chapter 4, we used the default **Basic** style in which each UITableViewCell contains one UILabel. In Section 8.5.1, for the MasterViewController's UITableView, we'll use the **Subtitle** style in which each UITableViewCell contains two UILabels—one with larger text for the cell's primary content (the Contact's last name) and one with smaller text (the Contact's first name) that's displayed below the primary content. You'll programmatically set the UILabels' contents in Section 8.6.8. We'll also design another UITableViewController (Section 8.5.3) that uses the **Custom** style, so that we can provide our own design for each cell.

## 8.3.5 UITableViewController with Static Cells

The UITableViewController in Chapter 4 dynamically generated UITableViewCells as necessary to display the app's master-list content—we'll use the same technique in this app. When you know exactly how many cells a UITableViewController needs to display, you can specify predefined *static cells*. We'll use this technique in Section 8.5.3 to define the UITableViewController for adding and editing contacts.

## 8.3.6 Listening for Keyboard Show and Hide Notifications

This app can be used on a variety of iOS devices. When the user is editing a Contact's data, depending on the device size, the keyboard could hide the UITextField in which the user is entering data. In Chapter 4, you learned how to register your app with NSNotificationCenter to receive iCloud notifications when the app's data changed on another device. In Section 8.8.3, you'll use the same technique to register for iOS keyboard notifications that occur when a keyboard is about to appear on the screen or disappear from the screen.

## 8.3.7 Programmatically Scrolling a UITableView

When you tap a UITextField to enter text in it, a keyboard is displayed—assuming that you do not have a hardware keyboard connected to your device. This app responds to the notifications discussed in Section 8.3.6 to ensure that the UITextField currently being edited is not displayed behind the keyboard. You'll use a UIView animation (Section 8.8.5) to modify the UITableView so that its content scrolls above the keyboard when it appears, then you'll restore the UITableView's prior settings when the keyboard disappears.

## 8.3.8 UITextFieldDelegate Methods

When the user is done editing a UITextField, the app should hide the corresponding keyboard. In this app, the AddEditViewController (Section 8.8) conforms to the UITableViewDelegate protocol and implements its textFieldShouldReturn method. We implemented this method (Section 8.8.6) to dismiss the keyboard if the user touches the keyboard's **Return** key.

## 8.4  Creating the Project and Configuring the Data Model

In this section, you'll create the **Address Book** app's project with Core Data support, then you'll customize the default data model that Xcode generates.

### 8.4.1 Creating the Project

Begin by creating a new **Master-Detail Application** iOS project. Specify the following settings in the **Choose options for your new project** sheet:

- **Product Name**: AddressBook.

- **Organization Name**: Deitel and Associates, Inc.—or your own organization name.

- **Company Identifier**: com.deitel—or your own company identifier.

- **Language**—Swift.

- **Devices: Universal**—Recall that the **Master-Detail Application** template is designed to support iPhones and iPads in portrait and landscape orientation.

- *Important:* Ensure that **Use Core Data** is *checked*—this tells Xcode to generate the Core Data support code that enables the app to interact with the database.

After specifying the settings, click **Next**, indicate where you'd like to save your project and click **Create** to create the project. As in Chapter 4, Xcode generates a project that's preconfigured with a MasterViewController and a DetailViewController and corresponding classes. You'll customize the app's storyboard in Section 8.5.

### 8.4.2 Editing the Data Model

When you add Core Data support to a **Master-Detail Application**, Xcode generates a basic data model in a file with the same name as the project and with the filename extension .xcdatamodeld—Addressbook.xcdatamodeld for this app. Select this file in the **Project** navigator to see the default data model's definition (Fig. 8.6). By default, the data model contains one entity named Event with one attribute named timeStamp. Xcode also generates the source code necessary for using Core Data to manipulate the database. We'll use most of that code as is and make some changes to support our customized data model. Most of the Core Data code is located in the MasterViewController (Section 8.6) and AppDelegate (Section 8.9) classes.

*Editing the Data Model*
This app's data model consists of a single entity named Contact containing first name, last name, e-mail address, phone number, street, city, state and zip code attributes. Though we will not do so in this app, you can use the Data Model editor to create many entities and model the relationships among them. Perform the following steps to modify the default data model:

1. In the Data Model editor's outline under **ENTITIES**, double click Event and change its name to Contact, then press *return*.

2. With the Contact entity selected, remove the timeStamp attribute by selecting it, then clicking the minus (–) icon below the **Attributes** section.

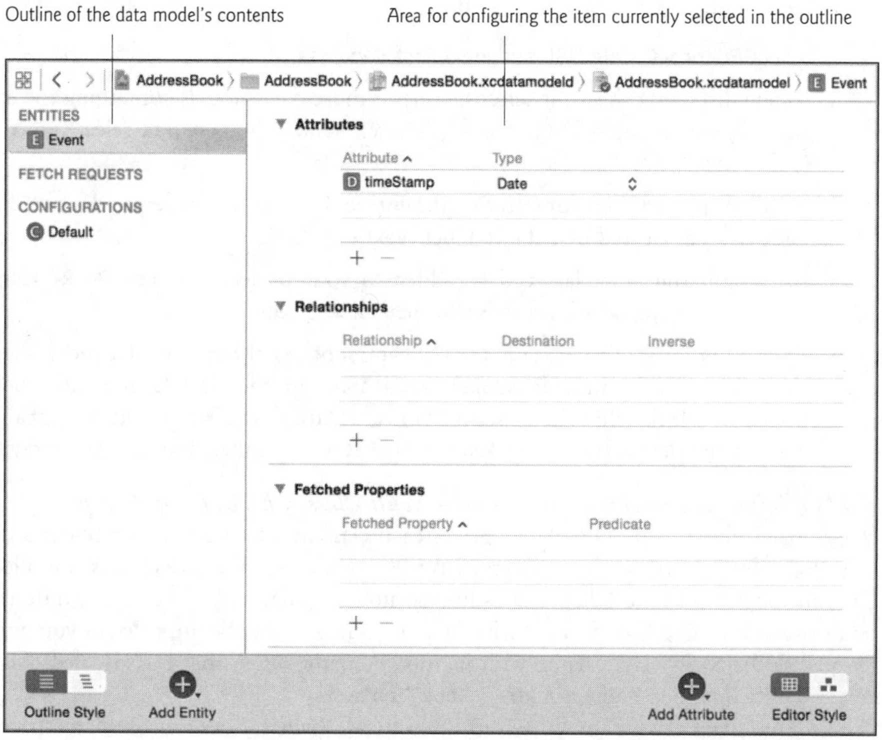

Outline of the data model's contents          Area for configuring the item currently selected in the outline

**Fig. 8.6** | Data Model editor showing the default data model containing the Event entity.

3. Next, add a `firstname` attribute by clicking the plus (+) icon below the **Attributes** section, then entering `firstname`.

4. In the **Type** column to the right of `firstname`, select `String` as the attribute's type.

5. Repeat *Steps 3* and *4* to create attributes named `lastname`, `email`, `phone`, `street`, `city`, `state` and `zip`.

6. By default, each attribute is optional, meaning that it's not required to have a value in the underlying database. In this app, we require the `firstname` and `lastname` to have values. Select the `firstname` attribute, then in the **Data Model** inspector (in the **Utilities** area), uncheck the **Optional** checkbox. Repeat this step for the `lastname` attribute and save the data model.

## 8.4.3 Generating the Contact Subclass of NSManagedObject

The project's autogenerated Core Data code manipulates entities as `NSManagedObjects` containing key–value pairs in which the entities' attribute names (`Strings`) are the keys. Though we'll use this technique to manipulate `Contacts` in one of this app's classes, you can also use Xcode to generate an `NSManagedObject` subclass for each entity type. The class that Xcode creates contains one property for each entity attribute. Perform the following steps to generate class `Contact`:

1. Select AddressBook.xcdatamodeld in the **Project** explorer to display the Data Model editor (if it's not already displayed).

2. Select **Editor > Create NSManagedObject Subclass…**.

3. Xcode displays a sheet for selecting one or more data models containing the entities for which you'd like to generate classes. AddressBook will be selected by default. Click **Next**.

4. Xcode displays a sheet for selecting the entities for which to generate classes. Contact will be selected by default. Click **Next**.

5. By default the new class will be added to your project's AddressBook group. Ensure that **Language** is set to **Swift**, then click **Create**.

6. At this point, Xcode generates the Contact subclass of NSManagedObject. Select the Contact entity in AddressBook.xcdatamodeld, then look at the **Data Model** inspector. Notice that Xcode set the Contact entity's **Class** attribute to Contact. Modify the **Class** attribute to AddressBook.Contact, then save the data model.

### *Fully Qualifying the Entity Class's Name—Swift Classes, Modules and Scope*

*Step 6* is particularly important. Swift places each class in a *namespace* that restricts the class's scope. By default, Swift class's scope is the module in which the class is compiled, such as an app project's module or a class-library module. To use a Swift class in a different module or in Objective-C code, the Swift class's module needs to be imported or you must fully qualify the Swift class's name with its module name when that class is used. Class Contact's fully qualified name is AddressBook.Contact.

The Core Data classes are written in Objective-C (which does not use namespaces) and, because the Core Data classes already exist, we cannot modify them to import our AddressBook project's module. For this reason, when you try to use the new Contact class with Core Data classes, they cannot see class Contact—it's hidden in the scope of this project's module. Changing the Contact entity's **Class** attribute from Contact to the fully qualified name AddressBook.Contact enables the Core Data classes to use class Contact.

### *Autogenerated **Contact** Class*

Figure 8.7 shows the autogenerated Contact class. Each property is qualified with @NSManaged to indicate that the property corresponds to an attribute in the data model. We slightly modified the autogenerated class. A Contact entity's email, phone, street, city, state and zip attributes are optional in the database. For this reason, we changed the corresponding properties to type String?. This enables our app's code to use optional binding and optional chaining to ensure that these properties are non-nil before using their values. Otherwise, runtime errors occur when you try to access those attributes.

```
1   // Contact.swift
2   // Xcode generated class for interacting with a Contact; we edited
3   // this class to make all but the lastName and firstName optionals
4   import Foundation
5   import CoreData
```

**Fig. 8.7** | Autogenerated Contact class (which we edited slightly) for interacting with the database's Contact entities. (Part 1 of 2.)

```
6
7   class Contact: NSManagedObject {
8       @NSManaged var city: String?
9       @NSManaged var email: String?
10      @NSManaged var firstname: String
11      @NSManaged var lastname: String
12      @NSManaged var phone: String?
13      @NSManaged var state: String?
14      @NSManaged var street: String?
15      @NSManaged var zip: String?
16  }
```

**Fig. 8.7** | Autogenerated `Contact` class (which we edited slightly) for interacting with the database's `Contact` entities. (Part 2 of 2.)

## 8.5 Building the GUI

In this section, you'll customize the **Address Book** app's storyboard and add classes for the new view controllers. In prior chapters, we presented all the capabilities you need to customize this app's storyboard, so we provide generalized instructions here and point out key changes and steps. As you work through this section, keep in mind that sometimes it's easier to select an object in the **Document Outline** rather than in the storyboard.

### 8.5.1 Customizing the `MasterViewController`

In the view controller titled **Master**, double click the title **Master** in the navigation bar and change it to **Contacts**. Add a **Bar Button Item** to the navigation bar's right side and set its **Identifier** property to **Add**—the add (+) button icon should now be displayed. In Section 8.5.3, you'll create a segue to perform when the user touches this button.

### 8.5.2 Customizing the `DetailViewController`

In the view controller titled **Detail**, delete the default **Label**, then create the user interface of **Labels** and **Text Fields** shown in Fig. 8.8.

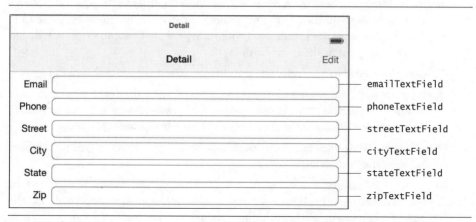

**Fig. 8.8** | `DetailViewController` UI labeled with their `@IBOutlet` property names.

Add @IBOutlets with the specified names to class DetailViewController. Rename the segue from the Master view controller to the **Detail** view controller from "showDetail" to "showContactDetails". Note that we did not provide for the Contact's first or last name—in Section 8.7.3, you'll programmatically display the Contact's name as the navigation bar's title. Add a **Bar Button Item** to the navigation bar's right side and set its **Identifier** property to **Edit**. In Section 8.5.3, you'll create a segue to perform when the user touches this button.

### 8.5.3 Adding the AddEditViewController

When the user chooses to add or edit a contact the app displays an AddEditViewController. You'll create this in the storyboard as a **Table View Controller** with static cells—i.e., cells that you predefine at design time, rather than created them dynamically from a UITableView's data source. Add a new subclass of UITableViewController named AddEditViewController to the project—you'll set this class as the new **Table View Controller**'s class and you'll add @IBOutlets and an @IBAction to it. Perform the following steps:

1. Drag a **Navigation Controller** onto the storyboard—recall that this also creates a **Table View Controller**.

2. Select the **Table View Controller**, then use the **Identity** inspector to set the **Class** attribute to the new AddEditTableViewController class you just created.

3. Create a **Show Detail** segue named "showAddContact" from the **Master** view controller's add (+) button to the new **Navigation Controller**. This will display the AddEditViewController when the user taps the add (+) button to create a new Contact.

4. Create a **Show Detail** segue named "showEditDetails" from the **Detail** view controller's **Edit** button to the new **Navigation Controller**. This will display the AddEditViewController when the user taps the **Edit** button to view a Contact's details.

5. With the new **Table View Controller**'s **Table View** selected, use the **Attributes** inspector set the **Content** attribute to **Static Cells** and the **Selection** attribute to **No Selection**, which prevents highlighting a cell when the user taps it.

6. In the **Document Outline** for the new **Table View Controller**, select the **Table View**'s **Table View Section**, then in the **Attributes** inspector, set the **Rows** attribute to 8. This displays eight static cells, each with its **Style** set to **Custom**, so you can design the cell's content in the storyboard.

7. Add a **Text Field** to each cell and set its **Placeholder** attribute as shown in Fig. 8.9.

8. For each **Text Field**, set auto-layout constraints between the **Text Field** and its cell's **View** for the **Leading Space to Container Margin**, **Trailing Space to Container Margin**, **Top Space to Container Margin** and **Bottom Space to Container Margin**.

9. Select the **Table View** and set its **Separator** property to **None** to remove the lines between the **Text Field**s.

10. Using the **Assistant** editor, create an @IBAction named saveButtonPressed for the **Save** button, then create an outlet collection named inputFields for the eight **Text Field**s, using the techniques we discussed in Section 5.4.4.

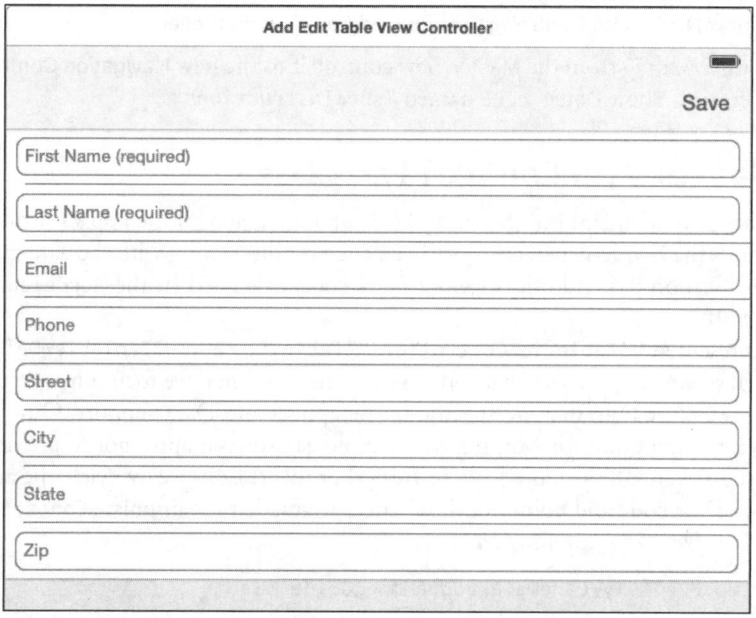

**Fig. 8.9** | AddEditViewController UI.

## 8.5.4 Adding the InstructionsViewController

When the app first loads and there are no Contacts (or if the user deletes the last Contact), the app displays a simple InstructionsViewController. You'll create this in the storyboard as a **View Controller** containing just a centered **Label**, then designate it as the **Split View Controller**'s detail view controller (rather than the **Detail View Controller**). The app will then programmatically determine whether an InstructionsViewController or a DetailViewController should be displayed at a given time when the app executes on an iPhone 6 Plus in landscape orientation or on an iPad. Add a new subclass of UIViewController named InstructionsViewController to the project—you'll set this class as the new **Table View Controller**'s class. We do not show this class's code in the chapter, because we did not add any functionality to the class that Xcode generates. Perform the following steps:

1. Drag a **Navigation Controller** onto the storyboard then delete the corresponding **Table View Controller** that's also created.

2. Drag a **View Controller** onto the storyboard then *control* drag from the new **Navigation Controller** to the new **View Controller** and set the **View Controller** as the **root view controller**.

3. Select the new **View Controller**, then use the **Identity** inspector to set the **Class** attribute to the new InstructionsViewController class.

4. Drag a **Label** onto the **View Controller**, set its text to "Touch a contact to display its details" and center it vertically and horizontally. Use the auto layout **Align** menu to set the **Horizontal Center in Container** and **Vertical Center in Container** constraints.

5. *Control* drag from the **Split View Controller** at the left side of the storyboard to the new **Navigation Controller** and select **detail view controller**.

6. *Control* drag from the **Master** view controller to the new **Navigation Controller** and create a **Show Detail** segue named "showInstructions".

# 8.6 `MasterViewController` Class

Class `MasterViewController` (Sections 8.6.1—8.6.9) manages the app's list of contacts and contains the Xcode-generated Core Data code for interacting with the data model you created in Section 8.4. Additional Core Data code is located in the `AppDelegate` class (Section 8.9).

We presented `UITableViewController`, `UITableView` and `UITableViewDelegate` in Chapter 4, so we do not cover that code in detail here. Rather, we focus on aspects of class `MasterViewController` that are specific to the app's Core Data support. Our goal is to give you a starting point for working with simple data-driven apps, not to provide an in-depth discussion of all the Core Data features. For this reason, we overview the autogenerated Core Data code and point out the changes we made to manipulate `Contact` entities. Apple's *Core Data Programming Guide* at:

```
http://bit.ly/CoreDataProgrammingGuide
```

describes Core Data in detail. Be sure to read this guide, if you intend to build substantial data-driven apps with complex entity relationships.

## 8.6.1 `MasterViewController` Class, Properties and `awakeFromNib` Method

Figure 8.10 shows the beginning of class `MasterViewController`, which inherits from `UITableViewController` and implements the following protocols:

- `NSFetchedResultsControllerDelegate` so the `NSFetchedResultsController`, which manages the interactions with the data model, can notify the `MasterViewController` when the underlying data changes (e.g., when a `Contact` is added, updated or deleted).

- `AddEditTableViewControllerDelegate` (defined in Section 8.8.1) so the `AddEditTableViewController` can notify the `MasterViewController` to save the `NSManagedObjectContext` when the user saves a new `Contact`.

- `DetailViewControllerDelegate` (defined in Section 8.7.1) so the `DetailViewController` can notify the `MasterViewController` to save the `NSManagedObjectContext` when the user saves an edited `Contact`.

Lines 12–13 were generated by Xcode to store references to the `DetailViewController` that shows a `Contact` and the `NSManagedObjectContext` that's defined by the app's `AppDelegate` (Section 8.9) and used to manage loading and storing the app's `Contact` entities. Method `awakeFromNib` (lines 16–23) was autogenerated by Xcode. It configures the popover that displays the `MasterViewController`'s `UITableView` when the app executes on an iPad in portrait orientation. Recall that once a storyboard's objects have been created, method `awakeFromNib` is called on any of the objects of classes that implement it.

```
 1   // MasterViewController.swift
 2   // Manages the contact list and contains various autogenerated Core Data
 3   // code, some of which we modified to use the Contact class
 4   import UIKit
 5   import CoreData
 6
 7   class MasterViewController: UITableViewController,
 8       NSFetchedResultsControllerDelegate,
 9       AddEditTableViewControllerDelegate,
10       DetailViewControllerDelegate {
11
12       var detailViewController: DetailViewController? = nil
13       var managedObjectContext: NSManagedObjectContext? = nil
14
15       // configure popover for UITableView on iPad
16       override func awakeFromNib() {
17           super.awakeFromNib()
18           if UIDevice.currentDevice().userInterfaceIdiom == .Pad {
19               self.clearsSelectionOnViewWillAppear = false
20               self.preferredContentSize =
21                   CGSize(width: 320.0, height: 600.0)
22           }
23       }
24
```

**Fig. 8.10** | MasterViewController class, properties and awakeFromNib.

## 8.6.2 Overridden UIViewController Method viewWillAppear and Method displayFirstContactOrInstructions

Recall from Chapter 4 that for an iPad in portrait orientation a UISplitViewController displays the DetailViewController and allows the user to tap a button to view the Master-ViewController in a popover. For this app, we show how to ensure that the MasterView-Controller is always displayed to the left of the DetailViewController if there's enough room—similar to the iOS Settings app on an iPad. As you'll see in Section 8.9, we added a statement in class AppDelegate to enable this functionality. When both are displayed as the app loads, if there are no contacts, the InstructionsViewController (Section 8.5.4) should be displayed to the MasterViewController's right; otherwise, the first Contact should be selected and displayed in a DetailViewController to the MasterViewController's right.

To make this decision, we override UIViewController method **viewWillAppear** (Fig. 8.11, lines 26–29), which iOS calls when a view controller is about to appear. In this app, we call method displayFirstContactOrInstructions (lines 33–50), which determines whether the UISplitViewController is collapsed. If it is, then only the Master-ViewController is on the screen and the method terminates. Otherwise, line 37 checks whether there's at least one Contact. If so, line 38 creates an NSIndexPath representing the first Contact (row 0 and section 0) in the UITableView, then lines 39–41 call UITableView method **selectRowAtIndexPath** to programmatically select the first Contact. Unlike when the user taps a Contact to display its details, programmatically selecting a cell does *not* fire the selection event. So lines 42–43 then perform the "showContactDetail" segue to display the selected Contact. If there are no Contacts, lines 45–46 perform the "show-Instructions" segue, which displays the InstructionsViewController.

```
25        // called just before MasterViewController is presented on the screen
26        override func viewWillAppear(animated: Bool) {
27            super.viewWillAppear(animated)
28            displayFirstContactOrInstructions()
29        }
30
31        // if the UISplitViewController is not collapsed,
32        // select first contact or display InstructionsViewController
33        func displayFirstContactOrInstructions() {
34            if let splitViewController = self.splitViewController {
35                if !splitViewController.collapsed {
36                    // select and display first contact if there is one
37                    if self.tableView.numberOfRowsInSection(0) > 0 {
38                        let indexPath = NSIndexPath(forRow: 0, inSection: 0)
39                        self.tableView.selectRowAtIndexPath(indexPath,
40                            animated: false,
41                            scrollPosition: UITableViewScrollPosition.Top)
42                        self.performSegueWithIdentifier(
43                            "showContactDetail", sender: self)
44                    } else { // display InstructionsViewController
45                        self.performSegueWithIdentifier(
46                            "showInstructions", sender: self)
47                    }
48                }
49            }
50        }
51
```

**Fig. 8.11** | Overridden UIViewController method viewWillAppear and method display-FirstContactOrInstructions.

### 8.6.3 Overridden UIViewController Method viewDidLoad

Figure 8.12 presents the autogenerated viewDidLoad method, which initializes Master-ViewController's detailViewController property as discussed in Section 4.6.3. We removed the autogenerated statements that programmatically displayed an add (+) button—recall from Section 8.5.1 that we added one to the MasterViewController's navigation bar that segues to the AddEditViewController.

```
52        // called after the view loads for further UI configuration
53        override func viewDidLoad() {
54            super.viewDidLoad()
55
56            if let split = self.splitViewController {
57                let controllers = split.viewControllers
58                self.detailViewController =
59                    controllers[controllers.count-1].topViewController as?
60                    DetailViewController
61            }
62        }
63
```

**Fig. 8.12** | Overridden UIViewController method viewDidLoad.

## 8.6.4 Overridden UIViewController Method prepareForSegue

Figure 8.13 shows method prepareForSegue, which configures either the DetailView-Controller or the AddEditContactViewController, based on the user's actions.

```
64        // configure destinationViewController based on segue
65        override func prepareForSegue(segue: UIStoryboardSegue,
66           sender: AnyObject?) {
67           if segue.identifier == "showContactDetail" {
68              if let indexPath = self.tableView.indexPathForSelectedRow() {
69                 // get Contact for selected cell
70                 let selectedContact =
71                    self.fetchedResultsController.objectAtIndexPath(
72                       indexPath) as Contact
73
74                 // configure DetailViewController
75                 let controller = (segue.destinationViewController as
76                    UINavigationController).topViewController as
77                    DetailViewController
78                 controller.delegate = self
79                 controller.detailItem = selectedContact
80                 controller.navigationItem.leftBarButtonItem =
81                    self.splitViewController?.displayModeButtonItem()
82                 controller.navigationItem.leftItemsSupplementBackButton =
83                    true
84              }
85           } else if segue.identifier == "showAddContact" {
86              // create a new Contact object that is not yet managed
87              let entity =
88                 self.fetchedResultsController.fetchRequest.entity!
89              let newContact = Contact(entity: entity,
90                 insertIntoManagedObjectContext: nil)
91
92              // configure the AddEditTableViewController
93              let controller = (segue.destinationViewController as
94                 UINavigationController).topViewController as
95                 AddEditTableViewController
96              controller.navigationItem.title = "Add Contact"
97              controller.delegate = self
98              controller.editingContact = false // adding, not editing
99              controller.contact = newContact
100          }
101       }
102
```

**Fig. 8.13** | Overridden UIViewController method prepareForSegue.

*Configuring the "showContactDetail" Segue*

When the user selects a Contact to display, line 68 gets UITableView method indexPath-ForSelectedRow to get the selected Contact's NSIndexPath, then lines 70–72 use the objectAtIndexPath method of the autogenerated NSFetchResultsController to get the Contact from the database. When Xcode generated this statement, it cast the returned object to an NSManagedObject. In this app, we know that each NSManagedObject is a Contact, so we changed the cast to type Contact (and changed the name of the constant in line 70). Lines 75–83 configure the DetailViewController, specifying that its delegate is the MasterViewController (self; line 78) and its detailItem is the selectedContact obtained in lines 70–72. The other statements configure the navigation bar items as discussed in Section 4.6.7.

*Configuring the "showAddContact" Segue*

When the user touches the add (+) button to add new Contact, lines 87–99 create a new Contact entity object that's not yet managed by Core Data—because the user could decide not to add the Contact—and configure the AddEditTableViewController. To create the Contact entity object, lines 87–88 use the autogenerated NSFetchResultsController (Section 8.6.9) to get the NSEntityDescription that describes the Contact entity in the data model. Lines 89–90 then create a new Contact object using an intializer that was inherited into the class from NSManagedObject. The initializer uses the NSEntityDescription to determine which entity object type to create. In this case, we specify nil for the insertIntoManagedObjectContext argument because the new Contact should be added to the NSManagedObjectContext only when the user touches the **Save** button in the AddEditTableViewController. Lines 93–99 configure the AddEditTableViewController:

- line 96 sets the navigationItem's title (i.e., the title in the navigation bar),
- line 97 sets the MasterViewController as the delegate (self),
- line 98 indicates that the AddEditTableViewController will be used to add (not edit) a Contact, and
- line 99 specifies the newContact object as the Contact to manipulate.

## 8.6.5 AddEditTableViewControllerDelegate Method didSaveContact

When the user saves a new Contact, the AddEditTableViewController calls method didSaveContact (Fig. 8.14) to add the Contact to the NSManagedObjectContext and save it, which updates the database. Line 106 uses the autogenerated NSFetchResultsController to get the NSManagedObjectContext that manages the Contact entities. Only objects that are managed can be added to, updated in and removed from the database. In Section 8.6.4 we created the new Contact as an *unmanaged* object in case the user decided not to add it. Line 107 calls NSManagedObjectContext method insertObject to make the new Contact a *managed* object so that it can be saved. Line 108 then pops the AddEditViewController from the UINavigationController's stack so it's no longer displayed on the screen. Notice that we did not add a new row to the UITableView for the new Contact—the autogenerated Core Data support code in Section 8.6.9 handles that for you.

```
103    // called by AddEditViewController after a contact is added
104    func didSaveContact(controller: AddEditTableViewController) {
105       // get NSManagedObjectContext and insert new contact into it
106       let context = self.fetchedResultsController.managedObjectContext
107       context.insertObject(controller.contact!)
108       self.navigationController?.popToRootViewControllerAnimated(true)
```

**Fig. 8.14** | AddEditTableViewControllerDelegate method didSaveContact. (Part 1 of 2.)

```
109
110          // save the context to store the new contact
111          var error: NSError? = nil
112          if !context.save(&error) { // check for error
113              displayError(error, title: "Error Saving Data",
114                  message: "Unable to save contact")
115          } else { // if no error, display new contact details
116              let sectionInfo =
117                  self.fetchedResultsController.sections![0] as
118                      NSFetchedResultsSectionInfo
119              if let row = find(sectionInfo.objects as [NSManagedObject],
120                  controller.contact!) {
121                  let path = NSIndexPath(forRow: row, inSection: 0)
122                  tableView.selectRowAtIndexPath(path,
123                      animated: true, scrollPosition: .Middle)
124                  performSegueWithIdentifier("showContactDetail",
125                      sender: nil)
126              }
127          }
128      }
129
```

**Fig. 8.14** | AddEditTableViewControllerDelegate method didSaveContact. (Part 2 of 2.)

### Saving the *NSManagedObjectContext*

When you attempt to save an NSManagedObjectContext so that it updates the database with any changes to the managed objects in memory, it's possible that an error might occur. For example, you could attempt to add an entity to the database that does not meet the entity's description, such as missing a required field. If an error occurs, the NSManaged-ObjectContext stores the error in an NSError (declared at line 111). Line 112 calls the NSManagedObjectContext's **save** method to attempt to store the new Contact entity. The error variable is passed by reference so the method can assign it an NSError if a problem occurs—in which case, lines 113–114 would call method displayError (Section 8.6.7).

### Saving the *NSManagedObjectContext*

If no error occurs, we programmatically select the new object and display it (if the UISplit-ViewController is not collapsed). First, we need to locate the new Contact. In a Core Data app, when a UITableViewController has more than one section, the corresponding NSFetchResultsController's sections Array contains NSFetchedResultsSectionInfo objects that you use when implementing section-related UITableViewDelegate methods. In this app, there's only one section in the UITableView, so lines 116–118 get the NSFetched-ResultsSectionInfo object at index 0 in the NSFetchResultsController's sections Array. Lines 119–120 then use Swift's global find function to locate the new Contact in the NSFetchedResultsSectionInfo's objects collection containing all the NSManagedOb-jects in that section. Function find receives a collection as its first argument and the object to locate as its second argument, and returns the object's index or nil if the object is not found. The index in this case corresponds to the Contact's row in the UITableView. Line 121 creates an NSIndexPath for that row, then lines 122–125 programmatically select that row and perform the "showContactDetail" segue to show the new Contact's details.

### 8.6.6 `DetailViewControllerDelegate` Method `didEditContact`

When the user edits then saves, an existing `Contact`, the `DetailViewController` calls method `didEditContact` (Fig. 8.15) to save the `NSManagedObjectContext` (line 134), which updates the `Contact` in the database.

```
130    // called by DetailViewController after a contact is edited
131    func didEditContact(controller: DetailViewController) {
132        let context = self.fetchedResultsController.managedObjectContext
133        var error: NSError? = nil
134        if !context.save(&error) {
135            displayError(error, title: "Error Saving Data",
136                message: "Unable to save contact")
137        }
138    }
139
```

**Fig. 8.15** | `DetailViewControllerDelegate` method `didEditContact`.

### 8.6.7 Method `displayError`

Figure 8.16 presents method `displayError`, which is called by several methods in class `MasterViewController` to display error messages in a `UIAlertController`.

```
140    // indicate that an error occurred when saving database changes
141    func displayError(error: NSError?, title: String, message: String) {
142        // create UIAlertController to display error message
143        let alertController = UIAlertController(title: title,
144            message: String(format: "%@\nError:\(error)\n", message),
145            preferredStyle: UIAlertControllerStyle.Alert)
146        let okAction = UIAlertAction(title: "OK",
147            style: UIAlertActionStyle.Cancel, handler: nil)
148        alertController.addAction(okAction)
149        presentViewController(alertController, animated: true,
150            completion: nil)
151    }
152
```

**Fig. 8.16** | Method `displayError`.

### 8.6.8 `UITableViewDelegate` Methods

The `UITableViewDelegate` methods (Fig. 8.17) were first introduced in Chapter 4. Here we discuss only the highlighted Core Data features that Xcode added to these methods (and our changes) for managing the interactions between the data model and the `UITableView`.

```
153    // UITableViewDelegate methods
154    // callback that returns total number of sections in UITableView
155    override func numberOfSectionsInTableView(
156        tableView: UITableView) -> Int {
```

**Fig. 8.17** | `UITableViewDelegate` methods. (Part I of 3.)

```
157          return self.fetchedResultsController.sections?.count ?? 0
158      }
159
160      // callback that returns number of rows in the UITableView
161      override func tableView(tableView: UITableView,
162          numberOfRowsInSection section: Int) -> Int {
163          let sectionInfo =
164              self.fetchedResultsController.sections![section] as
165                  NSFetchedResultsSectionInfo
166          return sectionInfo.numberOfObjects
167      }
168
169      // callback that returns a configured cell for the given NSIndexPath
170      override func tableView(tableView: UITableView,
171          cellForRowAtIndexPath indexPath: NSIndexPath) -> UITableViewCell {
172          let cell = tableView.dequeueReusableCellWithIdentifier(
173              "Cell", forIndexPath: indexPath) as UITableViewCell
174          self.configureCell(cell, atIndexPath: indexPath)
175          return cell
176      }
177
178      // callback that returns whether a cell is editable
179      override func tableView(tableView: UITableView,
180          canEditRowAtIndexPath indexPath: NSIndexPath) -> Bool {
181          return true
182      }
183
184      // callback that deletes a row from the UITableView
185      override func tableView(tableView: UITableView,
186          commitEditingStyle editingStyle: UITableViewCellEditingStyle,
187          forRowAtIndexPath indexPath: NSIndexPath) {
188          if editingStyle == .Delete {
189              let context =
190                  self.fetchedResultsController.managedObjectContext
191              context.deleteObject(
192                  self.fetchedResultsController.objectAtIndexPath(
193                      indexPath) as Contact)
194
195              var error: NSError? = nil
196              if !context.save(&error) {
197                  displayError(error, title: "Unable to Load Data",
198                      message: "AddressBook unable to acccess database")
199              }
200
201              displayFirstContactOrInstructions()
202          }
203      }
204
205      // called by line 174 to configure a cell
206      func configureCell(cell: UITableViewCell,
207          atIndexPath indexPath: NSIndexPath) {
208          let contact = self.fetchedResultsController.objectAtIndexPath(
209              indexPath) as Contact
```

**Fig. 8.17** | UITableViewDelegate methods. (Part 2 of 3.)

| | |
|---|---|
| 210 | `cell.textLabel!.text = contact.lastname` |
| 211 | `cell.detailTextLabel!.text = contact.firstname` |
| 212 | `}` |
| 213 | |

**Fig. 8.17** | `UITableViewDelegate` methods. (Part 3 of 3.)

### *Method* ***numberOfSectionsInTableView***
Line 157 returns the autogenerated `NSFetchedResultsController`'s number of sections (discussed in Section 8.6.5). The expression

`self.fetchedResultsController.sections?.count`

returns an optional because the `sections` property could be `nil`. For this reason, line 157 uses Swift's **nil coalescing operator ??**, which unwraps the optional in its left operand if it contains a value; otherwise, the expression evaluates to the right operand's value.

### *Method* ***tableView:numberOfRowsInSection***
Lines 163–166 use the `NSFetchedResultsSectionInfo` object to determine the number of rows in the data model's corresponding section (discussed in Section 8.6.5).

### *Method* ***tableView:commitEditingStyle:forRowAtIndexPath***
When the user deletes a row from the `UITableView`, lines 189–193 get the autogenerated `NSFetchedResultsController`'s `NSManagedObjectContext`, then call its `deleteObject` method to remove the corresponding `Contact` entity. The method receives as its argument the `Contact` to delete, which is returned by the `NSFetchedResultsController`'s `objectAtIndexPath` method—we modified this statement to cast the resulting object to type `Contact`. Removing the object from the `NSManagedObjectContext` does *not* remove it from the database until the `NSManagedObjectContext` is saved (line 196).

### *Method* ***configureCell***
Recall from Section 8.5.1 that we changed the `MasterViewController`'s `UITableViewCell` format to **Subtitle** so that the `UITableView` shows each `Contact`'s last name and first name. We modified the autogenerated `configureCell` method (lines 208–211) to display a `Contact`'s last name in the cell's `textLabel` and the `Contact`'s first name in the `detailTextLabel`.

## 8.6.9 Autogenerated `NSFetchedResultsController` and `NSFetchedResultsControllerDelegate` Methods
Recall from Section 8.3.3 that an `NSFetchedResultsController` (Fig. 8.18) manages the data for the master list's `UITableView`. All of the necessary `NSFetchedResultsController` code is autogenerated by Xcode when you create a **Master-Detail Application** with Core Data support:

- The computed property `fetchedResultsController` (lines 216–257) manages the stored property `_fetchedResultsController` (line 258). If the stored property is not `nil` the computed property returns the existing `NSFetchedResults-`

Controller (line 218); otherwise, the computed property creates a new one, configures it, then returns the new NSFetchedResultsController.

- The NSFetchedResultsControllerDelegate methods (lines 260–310) update the UITableView in response to changes in the underlying data store. We kept the autogenerated comment in lines 312–325, which describes potential performance issues with NSFetchedResultsControllerDelegate methods updating the UITableView in response to many changes at once. Though this is not a problem in the **Address Book** app, the comment contains an NSFetchedResultsControllerDelegate method that you can use to replace the ones in lines 260–310 for apps in which this performance problem occurs.

We made only three changes to this autogenerated code to update it for use with our Contact entities:

- The default app generated by Xcode manipulates Event entities. In line 224, we changed "Event" to "Contact" to manipulate Contact entities.

- The default app sorted the Event entities in *ascending* order by their timeStamps. When an NSFetchRequest gets entities from the database, it uses the NSSortDescriptors to determine their sort order. We'd like to sort Contacts by last name, then first name. Lines 233–236 create two NSSortDescriptors for sorting Contacts in *ascending* order by their lastname and firstname attributes. We placed both in an Array and assigned it to the NSFetchRequest's sortDescriptors Array property. Initially, the NSFetchRequest sorts the entities it returns by the first NSSortDescriptor in the Array—the one for lastnames in this case. If there are two or more entities with the same lastname, then the NSFetchRequest sorts those entities by the next NSSortDescriptor in the Array—the one for firstnames in this case.

- Finally, we replaced the abort method call in the autogenerated code with a call to our own displayError method (lines 252–253).

```
214    // Core Data autogenerated code for interacting with the data model;
215    // sightly modified to work with the Contact entity
216    var fetchedResultsController: NSFetchedResultsController {
217        if _fetchedResultsController != nil {
218            return _fetchedResultsController!
219        }
220
221        let fetchRequest = NSFetchRequest()
222
223        // edited to use the Contact entity
224        let entity = NSEntityDescription.entityForName("Contact",
225            inManagedObjectContext: self.managedObjectContext!)
226        fetchRequest.entity = entity
227
228        // Set the batch size to a suitable number.
229        fetchRequest.fetchBatchSize = 20
```

**Fig. 8.18** | Autogenerated NSFetchedResultsController and NSFetchedResultsControllerDelegate methods. (Part 1 of 3.)

```
230
231        // edited to sort by last name, then first name;
232        // both using case insensitive comparisons
233        let lastNameSortDescriptor = NSSortDescriptor(key: "lastname",
234            ascending: true, selector: "caseInsensitiveCompare:")
235        let firstNameSortDescriptor = NSSortDescriptor(key: "firstname",
236            ascending: true, selector: "caseInsensitiveCompare:")
237
238        fetchRequest.sortDescriptors =
239            [lastNameSortDescriptor, firstNameSortDescriptor]
240
241        // Edit the section name key path and cache name if appropriate.
242        // nil for section name key path means "no sections".
243        let aFetchedResultsController = NSFetchedResultsController(
244            fetchRequest: fetchRequest,
245            managedObjectContext: self.managedObjectContext!,
246            sectionNameKeyPath: nil, cacheName: "Master")
247        aFetchedResultsController.delegate = self
248        _fetchedResultsController = aFetchedResultsController
249
250        var error: NSError? = nil
251        if !_fetchedResultsController!.performFetch(&error) {
252            displayError(error, title: "Error Fetching Data",
253                message: "Unable to get data from database")
254        }
255
256        return _fetchedResultsController!
257    }
258    var _fetchedResultsController: NSFetchedResultsController? = nil
259
260    func controllerWillChangeContent(
261        controller: NSFetchedResultsController) {
262        self.tableView.beginUpdates()
263    }
264
265    func controller(controller: NSFetchedResultsController,
266        didChangeSection sectionInfo: NSFetchedResultsSectionInfo,
267        atIndex sectionIndex: Int,
268        forChangeType type: NSFetchedResultsChangeType) {
269        switch type {
270        case .Insert:
271            self.tableView.insertSections(NSIndexSet(index: sectionIndex),
272                withRowAnimation: .Fade)
273        case .Delete:
274            self.tableView.deleteSections(NSIndexSet(index: sectionIndex),
275                withRowAnimation: .Fade)
276        default:
277            return
278        }
279    }
280
```

**Fig. 8.18** | Autogenerated NSFetchedResultsController and
NSFetchedResultsControllerDelegate methods. (Part 2 of 3.)

```
281        func controller(controller: NSFetchedResultsController,
282            didChangeObject anObject: AnyObject,
283            atIndexPath indexPath: NSIndexPath?,
284            forChangeType type: NSFetchedResultsChangeType,
285            newIndexPath: NSIndexPath?) {
286            switch type {
287            case .Insert:
288                tableView.insertRowsAtIndexPaths(
289                    [newIndexPath!], withRowAnimation: .Fade)
290            case .Delete:
291                tableView.deleteRowsAtIndexPaths(
292                    [indexPath!], withRowAnimation: .Fade)
293            case .Update:
294                self.configureCell(
295                    tableView.cellForRowAtIndexPath(indexPath!)!,
296                    atIndexPath: indexPath!)
297            case .Move:
298                tableView.deleteRowsAtIndexPaths(
299                    [indexPath!], withRowAnimation: .Fade)
300                tableView.insertRowsAtIndexPaths(
301                    [newIndexPath!], withRowAnimation: .Fade)
302            default:
303                return
304            }
305        }
306
307        func controllerDidChangeContent(
308            controller: NSFetchedResultsController) {
309            self.tableView.endUpdates()
310        }
311
312        /*
313        // Implementing the above methods to update the table view in response
314        // to individual changes may have performance implications if a large
315        // number of changes are made simultaneously. If this proves to be an
316        // issue, you can instead just implement controllerDidChangeContent:
317        // which notifies the delegate that all section and object changes
318        // have been processed.
319
320        func controllerDidChangeContent(
321            controller: NSFetchedResultsController) {
322            // In the simplest, most efficient, case, reload the table view.
323            self.tableView.reloadData()
324        }
325        */
326 }
```

**Fig. 8.18** | Autogenerated NSFetchedResultsController and NSFetchedResultsControllerDelegate methods. (Part 3 of 3.)

# 8.7 DetailViewController Class

Class DetailViewController (Sections 8.7.1—8.7.5) displays one Contact's data, prepares for the segue to the AddEditTableViewController (Section 8.8) when the user chooses to edit the Contact, updates the user interface after the user edits a Contact and notifies the MasterViewController if the Contact was edited.

## 8.7.1 DetailViewControllerDelegate Protocol

Figure 8.19 declares the protocol DetailViewControllerDelegate containing the method didEditContact that MasterViewController implements to be notified when the user saves changes to an edited Contact.

```
1   // DetailViewController.swift
2   // Shows the details for one Contact
3   import CoreData
4   import UIKit
5
6   // MasterViewController conforms to be notified when contact edited
7   protocol DetailViewControllerDelegate {
8       func didEditContact(controller: DetailViewController)
9   }
10
```

**Fig. 8.19** | DetailViewControllerDelegate protocol.

## 8.7.2 DetailViewController Properties

Class DetailViewController (Fig. 8.20) inherits from UIViewController and conforms to the AddEditTableViewControllerDelegate protocol to update the UI when the user saves changes to an edited contact. Lines 15–20 declare the @IBOutlets for the UIText-Fields in which a contact's data will be displayed—the Contact's name will be placed in the DetailViewController's navigation bar.

```
11   class DetailViewController: UIViewController,
12       AddEditTableViewControllerDelegate {
13
14       // outlets for UITextFields that display contact data
15       @IBOutlet weak var emailTextField: UITextField!
16       @IBOutlet weak var phoneTextField: UITextField!
17       @IBOutlet weak var streetTextField: UITextField!
18       @IBOutlet weak var cityTextField: UITextField!
19       @IBOutlet weak var stateTextField: UITextField!
20       @IBOutlet weak var zipTextField: UITextField!
21
22       var delegate: DetailViewControllerDelegate!
23       var detailItem: Contact!
24
```

**Fig. 8.20** | DetailViewController properties.

The delegate property (which is set by the MasterViewController) refers to the DetailViewControllerDelegate that's notified when the user edits the Contact. In this case, the AddEditTableViewController notifies the DetailViewController so that it can update the Contact's details on the screen, then the DetailViewController notifies its delegate (the MasterViewController) so that it can save the changes into the database.

The contact property represents the Contact that the DetailViewController displays. When Xcode generated the DetailViewController class, it declared the detailItem as an NSManagedObject!. As we discussed in Section 8.4.3, the Contact subclass of NSManagedObject contains properties to interact with a Contact entity's attributes. In this app, we know that each NSManagedObject is a Contact and we want to use class Contact's properties (as you'll see in the next section) to access the data so we changed the type to Contact.

### 8.7.3 Overridden UIViewController Method viewDidLoad and Method displayContact

When the DetailViewController loads, iOS calls method viewDidLoad (Fig. 8.21) to configure the UI. If the detailItem is not nil (line 29), line 30 calls method displayContact (lines 35–47) to display the Contact's data—we placed this code in a separate method so it also can be called to update the UI after the user edits a Contact. Method displayContact uses class Contact's autogenerated properties to access each piece of data. Lines 37–38 set the DetailViewController navigationItem's title to the Contact's firstname and lastname separated by a space. Lines 41–46 use the Contact's email, phone, street, city, state and zip properties to set the corresponding UITextFields' text properties. Recall from Section 8.4.3 that these properties are declared as String? because the corresponding attributes in the database are optional and thus could be nil when retrieved from the database. Each of these statements performs the assignment only if the corresponding property is non-nil.

```
25      // when DetailViewController is presented, display contact's data
26      override func viewDidLoad() {
27          super.viewDidLoad()
28
29          if detailItem != nil {
30              displayContact()
31          }
32      }
33
34      // show selected Contact's data
35      func displayContact() {
36          // display Contact's name in navigation bar
37          self.navigationItem.title =
38              detailItem.firstname + " " + detailItem.lastname
39
40          // display other attributes if they have values
41          emailTextField.text = detailItem.email?
42          phoneTextField.text = detailItem.phone?
43          streetTextField.text = detailItem.street?
44          cityTextField.text = detailItem.city?
45          stateTextField.text = detailItem.state?
46          zipTextField.text = detailItem.zip?
47      }
48
```

**Fig. 8.21** | Overridden UIViewController method viewDidLoad and method displayContact.

### 8.7.4 AddEditTableViewControllerDelegate Method didSaveContact

When the user edits a Contact with the AddEditTableViewController (Section 8.8), then presses the **Save** button, the AddEditTableViewController calls its delegate's did-SaveContact method (Fig. 8.22) to update the UI with any new Contact data (line 51). Recall that the DetailViewController is embedded in a UINavigationController that maintains a stack of view controllers—when didSaveContact is called, the AddEdit-TableViewController is at the top of the stack. Line 52 pops the top view controller so the app returns to the DetailViewController. The DetailViewController then calls its delegate's didEditContact method (line 53)—this tells the MasterViewController to save the edited Contact into the database.

```
49      // called by AddEditTableViewController when edited contact is saved
50      func didSaveContact(controller:AddEditTableViewController) {
51          displayContact() // update contact data on screen
52          self.navigationController?.popViewControllerAnimated(true)
53          delegate?.didEditContact(self)
54      }
55
```

**Fig. 8.22** | AddEditTableViewControllerDelegate method didSaveContact.

### 8.7.5 Overridden UIViewController Method prepareForSegue

When the user taps the DetailViewController's **Edit** button, method prepareForSegue (Fig. 8.23) is called to configure the AddEditTableViewController. Lines 62–64 get a reference to the AddEditTableViewController, then lines 65–71 configure it. The key lines for this app (lines 65–68), set the title in the AddEditTableViewController's navigation bar, specify that the DetailViewController (self) is the delegate, indicate that the Add-EditTableViewController is being used to edit an existing Contact and specify the Contact to edit.

```
56      // called when user taps Edit button
57      override func prepareForSegue(segue: UIStoryboardSegue,
58          sender: AnyObject?) {
59
60          // configure destinationViewController for editing current contact
61          if segue.identifier == "showEditContact" {
62              let controller = (segue.destinationViewController as
63                  UINavigationController).topViewController as
64                  AddEditTableViewController
65              controller.navigationItem.title = "Edit Contact"
66              controller.delegate = self
67              controller.editingContact = true
68              controller.contact = detailItem
69              controller.navigationItem.leftBarButtonItem =
70                  self.splitViewController?.displayModeButtonItem()
```

**Fig. 8.23** | Overridden UIViewController method prepareForSegue. (Part 1 of 2.)

```
71                    controller.navigationItem.leftItemsSupplementBackButton = true
72            }
73        }
74  }
```

**Fig. 8.23** | Overridden UIViewController method prepareForSegue. (Part 2 of 2.)

## 8.8 AddEditTableViewController Class

The AddEditTableViewController (Sections 8.8.1—8.8.7) provides the UI for adding new contacts or editing existing ones.

### 8.8.1 AddEditTableViewControllerDelegate Protocol

Figure 8.24 declares the protocol AddEditTableViewControllerDelegate containing the method didSaveContact that MasterViewController and DetailViewController implement to be notified when the user saves a new Contact or saves changes to an existing one.

```
 1   // AddEditTableViewController.swift
 2   // Manages editing an existing contact or editing a new one.
 3   import CoreData
 4   import UIKit
 5
 6   // MasterViewController and DetailViewController conform to this
 7   // to be notified when a contact is added or edited, respectively
 8   protocol AddEditTableViewControllerDelegate {
 9       func didSaveContact(controller: AddEditTableViewController)
10   }
11
```

**Fig. 8.24** | AddEditTableViewControllerDelegate protocol.

### 8.8.2 AddEditTableViewController Properties

Figure 8.25 shows the beginning of class AddEditTableViewController, which inherits from UITableViewController—required so that we can use static UITableViewCells in Interface Builder—and conforms to the UITextFieldDelegate protocol. Lines 14–23 define the class's properties:

- The Array inputFields is the outlet collection that you created in Section 8.5.3 to programmatically access the UITextFields in this view controller's UI.

- In the DetailViewController, you manipulated each contact via the generated Contact class's properties. In the AddEditTableViewController, we'll use methods inherited into class Contact from class NSManagedObject for demonstration purposes. The Array fieldNames is used in loops to get and set Contact attribute values via NSManagedObject methods valueForKey and setValue, respectively.

- The delegate property refers to the AddEditTableViewControllerDelegate that's notified when the user clicks the **Save** button in this view controller's navigation bar.

- The contact property represents the current Contact being manipulated.

- The editingContact property enables us to determine whether the Contact is being edited or added—when editing, we need to display the existing Contact's data.

The delegate, contact and editingContact properties are set by either the MasterView-Controller's or DetailViewController's prepareForSegue method.

```
12   class AddEditTableViewController: UITableViewController,
13      UITextFieldDelegate {
14      @IBOutlet var inputFields: [UITextField]!
15
16      // field names used in loops to get/set Contact attribute values via
17      // NSManagedObject methods valueForKey and setValue
18      private let fieldNames = ["firstname", "lastname", "email",
19         "phone", "street", "city", "state", "zip"]
20
21      var delegate: AddEditTableViewControllerDelegate?
22      var contact: Contact? // Contact to add or edit
23      var editingContact = false // differentiates adding/editing
24
```

**Fig. 8.25** | AddEditTableViewController properties.

### 8.8.3 Overridden UIViewController Methods viewWillAppear and viewWillDisappear

When the AddEditTableViewController is about to appear on the screen, iOS invokes the UIViewController method viewWillAppear (Fig. 8.26, lines 26–38). When the user taps a UITextField in a UITableViewController, it's supposed to scroll itself so that the selected UITextField appears above the keyboard. At the time of this writing, this does not work across all devices and orientations. For this reason, we used viewWillAppear to register this view controller with NSNotificationCenter to receive the notifications UIKeyboardWill-ShowNotifications (lines 30–33) and UIKeyboardWillHideNotifications (lines 34–37). (We introduced notifications in Chapter 4.) When the keyboard is about to appear, method keyboardWillShow (Section 8.8.5) is called to scroll the UITableView so the selected UITextField above the keyboard. When the keyboard is about to be hidden, method keyboard-WillHide (Section 8.8.5) is called to scroll the UITableView back to its original position. When the AddEditTableViewController is about to disappear from the screen, iOS invokes the UIViewController method **viewWillDisappear** (Fig. 8.26, lines 41–49), which we use to unregister the keyboard notifications—this ensures that the AddEditTableViewController is not notified when the keyboard shows and hides in other view controllers. *Note:* You can unregister for all notifications simply by defining a **deinitializer** for this class, as in:

```
deinit {
    NSNotificationCenter.defaultCenter().removeObserver(self)
}
```

```
25      // called when AddEditTableViewController about to appear on screen
26      override func viewWillAppear(animated: Bool) {
27          super.viewWillAppear(animated)
28
29          // listen for keyboard show/hide notifications
30          NSNotificationCenter.defaultCenter().addObserver(self,
31              selector: "keyboardWillShow:",
32              name: UIKeyboardWillShowNotification,
33              object: nil)
34          NSNotificationCenter.defaultCenter().addObserver(self,
35              selector: "keyboardWillHide:",
36              name: UIKeyboardWillHideNotification,
37              object: nil)
38      }
39
40      // called when AddEditTableViewController about to disappear
41      override func viewWillDisappear(animated: Bool) {
42          super.viewWillDisappear(animated)
43
44          // unregister for keyboard show/hide notifications
45          NSNotificationCenter.defaultCenter().removeObserver(self,
46              name: UIKeyboardWillShowNotification, object: nil)
47          NSNotificationCenter.defaultCenter().removeObserver(self,
48              name: UIKeyboardWillHideNotification, object: nil)
49      }
50
```

**Fig. 8.26** | Overridden UIViewController methods viewWillAppear and viewWillDisappear.

### 8.8.4 Overridden UIViewController Method viewDidLoad

When the AddEditTableViewController appears on the screen, the method viewDidLoad (Fig. 8.27) sets the AddEditTableViewController as the delegate for each of the UIText-Fields (lines 56–58), so that it can respond to UITextField interactions and programmatically hide the keyboard. If the user is editing an existing contact (line 61), lines 62–68 use NSManagedObject's **valueForKey** method to get the contact object's value for each key in the fieldNames Array. Method valueForKey returns an AnyObject? that's nil if the value does not exist for the given key in the NSManagedObject, so lines 64–65 use optional binding to ensure that the value is not nil before setting the corresponding UITextField's text property (line 66).

```
51      // if editing an existing Contact, display its info
52      override func viewDidLoad() {
53          super.viewDidLoad()
54
55          // set AddEditTableViewController as the UITextFieldDelegate
56          for textField in inputFields {
57              textField.delegate = self
58          }
```

**Fig. 8.27** | Overridden UIViewController method viewDidLoad. (Part 1 of 2.)

```
59
60            // if editing a Contact, display its data
61            if editingContact {
62                for i in 0..<fieldNames.count {
63                    // query Contact object with valueForKey
64                    if let value: AnyObject =
65                        contact?.valueForKey(fieldNames[i]) {
66                        inputFields[i].text = value.description
67                    }
68                }
69            }
70        }
71
```

**Fig. 8.27** | Overridden `UIViewController` method `viewDidLoad`. (Part 2 of 2.)

### 8.8.5 Methods keyboardWillShow and keyboardWillHide

When the keyboard is about to appear on the screen, `NSNotificationCenter` sends the `AddEditTableViewController` the `UIKeyboardWillShowNotification` and calls method `keyboardWillShow` (Fig. 8.28, lines 73–89), which we registered in Section 8.8.3. For such a notification, the `NSNotification`'s `userInfo` Dictionary contains the key `UIKeyboardFrameEndUserInfoKey` (line 75) with a corresponding `NSValue` representing the keyboard's size and location on the screen. Line 76 gets a `CGRect` value from the `NSValue`, then obtains its `size` (a `CGSize` containing the keyboard's `width` and `height`). To ensure that the `AddEditTableViewController`'s scroll animation has the same duration as the keyboard's slide-up animation, we get the duration of the keyboard's animation (lines 79–80), which is stored in the `NSNotification`'s `userInfo` Dictionary under the key `UIKeyboardAnimationDurationUserInfoKey`. Lines 83–88 then perform an `UIView` animation that gets the `UITableView`'s current `contentInset`, then adjusts it—recall that `UIView` method `animateWithDuration` automatically interpolates between the original and new values that you set on the `tableView`.

```
72        // called when app receives UIKeyboardWillShowNotification
73        func keyboardWillShow(notification: NSNotification) {
74            let userInfo = notification.userInfo!
75            let frame = userInfo[UIKeyboardFrameEndUserInfoKey] as NSValue!
76            let size = frame.CGRectValue().size // keyboard's size
77
78            // get duration of keyboard's slide-in animation
79            let animationTime =
80                userInfo[UIKeyboardAnimationDurationUserInfoKey]!.doubleValue
81
82            // scroll self.tableView so selected UITextField above keyboard
83            UIView.animateWithDuration(animationTime) {
84                var insets = self.tableView.contentInset
85                insets.bottom = size.height
86                self.tableView.contentInset = insets
```

**Fig. 8.28** | Methods keyboardWillShow and keyboardWillHide. (Part 1 of 2.)

```
87                self.tableView.scrollIndicatorInsets = insets
88          }
89      }
90
91      // called when app receives UIKeyboardWillHideNotification
92      func keyboardWillHide(notification: NSNotification) {
93          var insets = self.tableView.contentInset
94          insets.bottom = 0
95          self.tableView.contentInset = insets
96          self.tableView.scrollIndicatorInsets = insets
97      }
98
```

**Fig. 8.28** | Methods keyboardWillShow and keyboardWillHide. (Part 2 of 2.)

When the keyboard is about to disappear from the screen, NSNotificationCenter sends the UIKeyboardWillHideNotification to the AddEditTableViewController and calls its keyboardWillHide method (lines 92–97), which we registered in Section 8.8.3. This method changes the UITableView's contentInset back to its original value.

## 8.8.6 UITextFieldDelegate Method textFieldShouldReturn

Figure 8.29 defines the UITextFieldDelegate protocol method textFieldShould-Return. This protocol's seven methods are optional, so here we implement only the one method we need. Method **textFieldShouldReturn** is called when the user touches the keyboard's Return key when a UITextField is being edited—i.e., the one the user touched to enter text. Such a UITextField is the first responder—the first UIResponder object that receives notification when an event occurs (introduced in Section 3.2.7). UIView is a subclass of UIResponder, so all UIViews can receive event notifications. If a given UIResponder cannot handle an event, it's delivered to the next UIResponder in the responder chain—typically that UIResponder's parent UIVew. For the complete responder chain details, visit:

http://bit.ly/iOSResponderChain

The textFieldShouldReturn method's argument is the UITextField that is currently the first responder. Line 101 calls the UITextField's resignFirstResponder method, which dismisses the keyboard.

```
99       // hide keyboard if user touches Return key
100      func textFieldShouldReturn(textField: UITextField) -> Bool {
101          textField.resignFirstResponder()
102          return true
103      }
104
```

**Fig. 8.29** | UITextFieldDelegate method textFieldShouldReturn.

### 8.8.7 @IBAction saveButtonPressed

When the user touches **Save** in the navigation bar, the @IBAction saveButtonPressed (Fig. 8.30) executes. To save a contact, the user must enter at least the contact's first and last names. Line 108 checks whether either of the UITextFields for the first and last name is empty and, if so, displays an error message in a UIAlertViewController (lines 110–117). Otherwise, lines 120–124 use NSManagedObject's setValue method to set the contact object's value for each key in the fieldNames Array. Then, line 126 notifies the delegate— the MasterViewController when adding a contact or the DetailViewController when editing a contact—that the user touched **Save**. If the delegate is the MasterViewController, it saves the new contact. If the delegate is the DetailViewController, it updates the data displayed in the DetailViewController.

```
105     // called to notify delegate to store changes in the model
106     @IBAction func saveButtonPressed(sender: AnyObject) {
107         // ensure that first name and last name UITextFields are not empty
108         if inputFields[0].text.isEmpty || inputFields[1].text.isEmpty {
109             // create UIAlertController to display error message
110             let alertController = UIAlertController(title: "Error",
111                 message: "First name and last name are required",
112                 preferredStyle: UIAlertControllerStyle.Alert)
113             let okAction = UIAlertAction(title: "OK",
114                 style: UIAlertActionStyle.Cancel, handler: nil)
115             alertController.addAction(okAction)
116             presentViewController(alertController, animated: true,
117                 completion: nil)
118         } else {
119             // update the Contact using NSManagedObject method setValue
120             for i in 0..<fieldNames.count {
121                 let value = (!inputFields[i].text.isEmpty ?
122                     inputFields[i].text : nil)
123                 self.contact?.setValue(value, forKey: fieldNames[i])
124             }
125
126             self.delegate?.didSaveContact(self)
127         }
128     }
129 }
```

**Fig. 8.30** | @IBAction saveButtonPressed.

#### A Note Regarding NSManagedObjectMethods valueForKey and setValue

We used NSManagedObjectMethods valueForKey (Fig. 8.27) and setValue (Fig. 8.30) in class AddEditTableViewController simply to demonstrate them. They're both used in Xcode's autogenerated Core Data code for classes MasterViewController and DetailViewController. This code is fragile, because the names of the Contact entity's fields could change in the data model, or you could mistype the names of the fields in the fieldNames array. In either case, Core Data runtime errors will occur. In general, it's safer to use the generated Contact class to interact with the Contact entities.

# 8.9 AppDelegate Class

Recall from Chapter 4 that every app has an AppDelegate class that conforms to the protocol UIApplicationDelegate protocol, which contains the methods iOS calls in response to events such as:

- the user launching the app,
- the app being placed into the background because another app is now in the foreground and
- the app returning from the background.

For a Core Data-enabled app, Xcode generates additional code in class AppDelegate. In this section, we discuss two changes we made to UIApplicationDelegate protocol methods and overview the Core Data additions.

## 8.9.1 UIApplicationDelegate Protocol Method application: didFinishLaunchingWithOptions:

This method is called by iOS when the app has launched and is about to begin executing. In a **Master-Detail Application**, Xcode generates code in this method to configure aspects of the UISplitViewController and its child view controllers. We added the statement

```
splitViewController.preferredDisplayMode =
    UISplitViewControllerDisplayMode.AllVisible
```

which indicates that the UISplitViewController should display both its MasterViewController and its DetailViewController if there is enough room on the screen. For an iPad in portrait orientation, this displays the MasterViewController to the left of the DetailViewController, rather than in a popover.

Xcode also sets the MasterViewController's managedObjectContext property with the statement

```
controller.managedObjectContext = self.managedObjectContext
```

As we'll discuss shortly, the AppDelegate class contains autogenerated code that creates the NSManagedObjectContext used by the MasterViewController to manage Contact entities.

## 8.9.2 UISplitViewControllerDelegate Protocol Method

In the autogenerated code for a **Master-Detail Application**, the AppDelegate class conforms to the UISplitViewControllerDelegate protocol and defines its splitViewController: collapseSecondaryViewController:ontoPrimaryViewController method. This method should return true if you want to perform any custom processing to determine which view controller to display to the right of the MasterViewController for certain scenarios. When this app runs on an iPhone 6 Plus in landscape orientation or on an iPad, we choose which view controller to display to the right of the MasterViewController, based on whether or not there are currently any stored Contacts. If there are, we display the DetailViewController; otherwise, we display the InstructionsViewController. To enable the latter, we modified this UISplitViewControllerDelegate method with the highlighted else if clause shown in Fig. 8.31.

```
77          // ADDED the check for InstructionsViewController
78          func splitViewController(splitViewController: UISplitViewController,
79              collapseSecondaryViewController
80                  secondaryViewController:UIViewController!,
81              ontoPrimaryViewController primaryViewController:UIViewController!)
82                  -> Bool {
83          if let secondaryAsNavController =
84              secondaryViewController as? UINavigationController {
85              if let topAsDetailController =
86                  secondaryAsNavController.topViewController as?
87                  DetailViewController {
88                  if topAsDetailController.detailItem == nil {
89                      // Return true to indicate that we have handled the
90                      // collapse by doing nothing; the secondary controller
91                      // will be discarded.
92                      return true
93                  }
94              } else if let topAsDetailController =
95                  secondaryAsNavController.topViewController as?
96                  InstructionsViewController {
97                  return true
98              }
99          }
100         return false
101     }
```

**Fig. 8.31** | Updated `UISplitViewControllerDelegate` method indicating that the app should handle how the `InstructionsViewController` is displayed.

### 8.9.3 Properties and Methods That Support the App's Core Data Capabilities

At the end of class `AppDelegate` are four properties and a method that Xcode generated as part of the app's Core Data support:

- The `applicationDocumentsDirectory` property is an `NSURL` containing Core Data data store's location.

- The `managedObjectModel` property is an `NSManagedObjectModel` that represents the app's data model and maps `NSManagedObjects` to the underlying data store.

- The `persistentStoreCoordinator` property is an `NSPersistentStoreCoordinator` that associates the `NSManagedObjectModel` with an actual database file. Core Data uses a SQLite database to store the app's entities.

- The `managedObjectContext` property is the `NSManagedObjectContext` that manages the app's entities. This object interacts with the `persistentStoreCoordinator` to access the data store.

- The `saveContext` method saves changes to the `NSManagedObjectContext`. This method is called by the `AppDelegate`'s `applicationWillTerminate` method, which iOS calls when an app is about to terminate. Calling `saveContext` here ensures that any remaining changes to the `NSManagedObjectContext` are stored before the application terminates.

# 8.10 Wrap-Up

In this chapter, you created the **Address Book** app, which provided convenient access to contact information stored in a database. The app enabled you to add, edit and delete contacts, and to select a contact to view its details.

You used the **Master-Detail Application** template with Core Data support, which generated all the code necessary for using Core Data to manage interactions with the app's persistent data store. Core Data hid from you the details of interacting with the underlying SQLite database.

You learned that Core Data entities are generated from your app's data model (stored in a file with your app's project name and the .xcdatamodeld extension), which describes the entities, their attributes and—for data models with multiple entities—the relationships among them. You used Xcode's Data Model editor to replace the default Event entity with a Contact entity and defined a Contact's attributes. You then autogenerated a Contact class containing a property for each attribute. You used Contact objects that Core Data mapped to the underlying relational database. You worked with various Core Data framework classes and protocols, including NSEntityDescription, NSManagedObject, NSManagedObject-Model, NSPersistentStoreCoordinator, NSManagedObjectContext, NSFetchedResults-Controller, NSFetchedResultsControllerDelegate and NSFetchRequest.

We showed that when designing a UITableViewController's cells, you can choose from several styles. You used the **Subtitle** style in which each UITableViewCell contains two UILabels—one with larger text for the cell's primary content and one with smaller text that's displayed below the primary content. You programmatically set the UILabels' contents. You also designed a UITableViewController that used the **Custom** style provided your own design for each cell.

You learned that when you know exactly how many cells a UITableViewController needs to display, you can specify predefined static cells. We used this technique to define the UITableViewController for adding and editing contacts.

We used NSNotificationCenter to register for iOS keyboard notifications that occur when a keyboard is about to appear on the screen or disappear from the screen. This app responded to these notifications to ensure that a UITextField being edited was not displayed behind the keyboard. You also used a method of the UITableViewDelegate protocol to dismiss the keyboard if the user touched the keyboard's **Return** key.

Chapter 9, App Store and App Business Issues, discusses how to prepare your apps for submission to the App Store, including testing them on the simulator and on iOS devices and creating icons and launch images. We present some of the requirements for your apps to be approved by Apple. We provide tips for pricing your apps, and resources for monetizing them with in-app advertising and in-app sale of virtual goods. We include resources for marketing your apps once they're available through the App Store. You'll learn how to use iTunes Connect to manage your apps and track sales.

# 9

# App Store and App Business Issues

Introducing the iOS Developer Program and iTunes® Connect

## Objectives

In this chapter you'll:

- Set up an iOS Developer Program profile so you can test your apps on iOS devices and submit apps to the App Store.
- Be introduced to the iOS Human Interface Guidelines for designing your apps.
- Learn how to prepare your apps for the App Store and Ad Hoc distribution.
- Learn about pricing and the benefits of free vs. paid apps.
- Learn about the *iTunes Connect Developer Guide*, which presents the steps for getting your apps approved and published.
- Learn how to market and monetize your apps.
- Learn how to use iTunes Connect to track sales and trends.
- Be introduced to other popular platforms to which you can port your apps to enlarge your market.

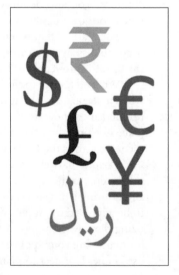

# 9.1  Introduction

In this book, we developed a variety of complete working iOS apps. Once you've developed and tested your own app—both in the iOS simulator and on iOS devices—the next step is to submit it to Apple's App Store for approval and eventual distribution. The approval process generally takes 7 to 14 days. Over the years, Apple has frequently changed the information you need to submit with your app and the submission steps. For this reason, we'll overview the key issues, then refer you to the detailed step-by-step instructions that Apple keeps up-to-date in their online iOS developer documentation.

In this chapter, we'll discuss setting up your iOS Developer Program profile so you can test your app on iOS devices and submit it to the App Store. We'll discuss Apple's *iOS Human Interface Guidelines*, which you should follow when designing your app's user interface. We'll consider characteristics of great apps. We'll overview the *iTunes Connect Developer Guide*, which shows precisely how to use **iTunes Connect** to submit your app to the App Store, track your app sales and payments, and more. We'll discuss whether to offer your app free or for a fee, and how much to charge. We'll also discuss monetizing apps via advertising and by using In-App Purchase to sell virtual goods. We'll provide resources for marketing your apps, and mention other app platforms to which you can port your iOS apps to broaden your marketplace. And, we'll point you to many online resources, mostly free, for additional information.

# 9.2  iOS Developer Program: Setting Up Your Profile for Testing and Submitting Apps

As you've seen, you can test many apps in the iOS Simulator. Some features, however, can be tested only on actual iOS devices (Fig. 9.1). Even features supported in the iOS Simulator may have slight differences from those on real devices, so Apple requires you to test your apps thoroughly on a variety of iOS devices before submitting them for approval.

| Unsupported functionality on the iOS Simulator | | |
| --- | --- | --- |
| Compass | Camera | Maps |
| Bluetooth data transfer | 3D graphics (works differently) | iPod music library access |
| Accelerometer (allows only orientation changes and simulated shaking of the device) | | |

**Fig. 9.1** | iOS device functionality *not* available on the iOS Simulator.

To test your apps on iOS devices and to submit your apps to the App Store for approval, you must join the fee-based **iOS Developer Program** at

```
https://developer.apple.com/programs/
```

You can register as an individual or as a company. Registering as a company allows you to add other members to your development team. At the time of this writing, the fee was $99 per year. Paid iOS Developer Program members can:

- Access the App Store Resource Center.

- Test apps on actual devices and have as many as 1000 beta testers for each app.

- Submit apps to the App Store for approval and distribution.

- Receive two prepaid Technical Support Incidents (TSIs) per year for code-level help from Apple engineers (for information about purchasing additional TSIs, see `https://developer.apple.com/support/technical/submit/`).

## 9.2.1 Setting Up Your Development Team

To test apps on iOS devices, you must set up your **development team**, which consists of you and perhaps other people in your organization who'll be able to log into the paid developer program website, test apps on iOS devices, add devices to the account for testing, and more. Figure 9.2 describes the roles of the various team members.

| iOS Developer Program roles |
| --- |
| *Team Agent* <br> • Has primary responsibility for the account—assigned to the person who enrolls in the iOS Developer program. <br> • Reads and accepts legal program agreements through iTunes Connect. <br> • Assigns admins and team members (see below). <br> • Makes and approves **Development Certificate** signing requests (Section 9.2.2). A Development Certificate serves as your digital identification. You'll use it to sign your app so that it can be installed and tested on your device(s). <br> • Downloads and creates **Provisioning Profiles**, which include your development certificates, devices and app IDs (alphanumeric identifiers of your choice). |

**Fig. 9.2** | iOS Developer Program roles (`https://developer.apple.com/programs/roles/index.php`). (Part 1 of 2.)

---

**iOS Developer Program roles**

*Team Agent (continued)*

- Obtains the **iOS Distribution Certificate**, used to digitally sign apps for App Store and Ad Hoc distribution (i.e., giving your app to as many as 100 devices for testing).
- Also designated as an admin if the team consists of two or more people.
- Tests apps on designated devices.
- Submits new apps and app updates to iTunes Connect.

*Admins*

- Assign admins and team members who'll be eligible to test your apps on iOS devices.
- Make and approve Development Certificate signing requests.
- Assign iOS devices to your account for testing, and register app IDs.
- Obtain iOS Distribution Certificates for App Store and Ad Hoc distribution.
- Download and create Provisioning Profiles.
- Test apps on designated devices.

*Team Members*

- Make (but do not approve) Development Certificate signing requests.
- Download and create Provisioning Profiles.
- Test apps on designated devices.

---

**Fig. 9.2** |  iOS Developer Program roles (`https://developer.apple.com/programs/roles/index.php`). (Part 2 of 2.)

When you register for the paid iOS Developer Program as a company, you're automatically designated as your company development team's **Agent**. *The Agent has the primary responsibility for the account.* If you registered as a company, you can add members to your team via the **Member Center**. Go to `https://developer.apple.com` and click **Member Center** in the toolbar at the top of the page. If you're not already logged in, do so, then follow Apple's steps at:

```
http://bit.ly/nAddiOSTeamMembers
```

For more information, read the Managing Your Team section of the *App Distribution Guide* in the iOS Developer Library.

## 9.2.2 Provisioning a Device for App Testing

Before you can test an app on a device, it must be **provisioned** for development—a process that, in most cases, is now handled for you by Xcode. Provisioning profiles and app IDs are used for provisioning. A **Provisioning Profile** specifies who can install a given app for testing. The **app ID** specifies which app can be installed. Xcode provides a default **iOS Team Provisioning Profile** and an **iOS wildcard app ID** that's used to build and install the majority of apps. Apps that use iCloud, In-App Purchase, push notifications or Game Center require an explicit app ID (Section 9.2.4).

### Development and Distribution Certificates

Apple uses **digital certificates** to verify that an app was created by you. The process used to complete this identification is called **code signing**. You'll use two types of certificates— development certificates and distribution certificates. A **development certificate** allows you to *sign your app* so that it can be installed and tested on your device(s). A **distribution certificate** allows you to sign your app so that it can be distributed for testing and, eventually to the App Store (Section 9.9).

To test an app on a device, select the device in the Xcode **Scheme** selector (Fig. 1.23), then run the app. Xcode uses your developer account—specified in Xcode's preferences (see the Before You Begin section)—to request the development certificate, then uses it to sign the app for testing purposes and installs the app onto your device.

## 9.2.3 TestFlight Beta Testing

**TestFlight** (new with iOS 8) allows you to invite (via email) up to 1,000 users to **beta test** your app before you publish it on the App Store. Before you can distribute an app with TestFlight, the app must go through *Beta App Review* and must adhere to the same app store review guidelines as apps being submitted for final approval:

> `https://developer.apple.com/app-store/review/guidelines/`

Testers simply install the TestFlight app, which then notifies beta testers when a new version of your app is available for testing. It installs the app updates, gives testers any notes you provide and allows them to send feedback. In-app purchases made during beta testing are free, but they expire at the end of the testing period. Testers have 30 days to complete testing. Figure 9.3 lists some of the benefits of beta testing your apps.

| Benefits of beta testing your app | |
|---|---|
| • Find and fix bugs. | • Discover performance issues. |
| • Receive app improvement suggestions (e.g., add, change or remove features). | • Get user interface and usability feedback. |
|  | • Prepare for future customer support questions. |
| • Testing by multiple users and on a variety of devices and iOS versions. | • Give key users or reviewers early access so they feel involved in the development process. |
| • Better understand your users and how they interact with the app. | • Collect testimonials for marketing when the app is published in the App Store. |

**Fig. 9.3**  |  Some of the benefits of beta testing your app before publication.

TestFlight also allows up to 25 development team members or admins to test your app. For more information, read the *TestFlight FAQ*:

> `https://itunesconnect.apple.com/docs/TestFlightFAQ.pdf`

For step-by-step instructions for setting up a beta test, see the TestFlight Beta Testing section of the *iTunes Connect Developer Guide*:

> `http://bit.ly/TestFlightBetaTesting`

*Creating an Ad Hoc Provisioning Profile for Beta Testing*

Before TestFlight, beta testing was performed by using **Ad Hoc provisioning profiles**, which limited testing to 100 devices that were registered in your developer account. You can still use this mechanism. The detailed steps for creating an Ad Hoc provisioning profile are discussed in the Distributing Your Beta App Using Ad Hoc Provisioning section of the *App Distribution Guide*:

```
http://bit.ly/AdHocBetaTesting
```

You'll need to register each device in your paid iOS Developer Program account before the device can be used for beta testing. You can register up to 100 devices *per year*.

### 9.2.4 Creating Explicit App IDs

The app ID part of a provisioning profile identifies an app or a suite of related apps. For apps that you'll submit to the App Store and apps that use iCloud, In-App Purchase, push notifications or Game Center, you'll need to create **explicit app IDs**.

An app ID contains a 10-character app ID prefix called a **bundle seed ID**, followed by a period (.) and an app ID suffix called a **bundle ID search string**. The bundle seed ID—generated by Apple—associates your developer team with the app ID. The bundle ID search string is an identifier that you create. Apple recommends using the reverse-domain-name style (e.g., com.*DomainName*.*AppName*) for the bundle ID search string. Once an app ID is created, it *cannot* be deleted. The steps for creating new App IDs are listed in the Maintaining Identifiers, Devices and Profiles section of the *App Distribution Guide* at:

```
http://bit.ly/CreatingAppIDs
```

# 9.3 *iOS Human Interface Guidelines*

It's important when creating iOS apps to follow Apple's *iOS Human Interface Guidelines (HIG)*:

```
https://developer.apple.com/library/ios/documentation/
    UserExperience/Conceptual/MobileHIG/index.html
```

This document discusses:

- Platform characteristics.
- Human interface principles.
- App design strategies.
- Case studies on transitioning apps to iOS from other platforms.
- User experience guidelines.
- iOS technology usage guidelines.
- iOS UI element usage guidelines.
- Custom icon and image creating guidelines.

Remember that you must submit your app to Apple for approval before it may be added to the App Store. Figure 9.4 includes some of app features and functionality required for getting approval. We discussed aspects of the HIG throughout the book. Failure to follow these guidelines could lead Apple to reject your app. The *App Store Review Guidelines* in the **App Store Resource Center** provide an extensive list of the reasons apps are rejected.

| Features and functionality | |
| --- | --- |
| • Compatible with the latest version of iOS.<br>• Valid signature in Xcode.<br>• Complies with Apple's *iOS Human Interface Guidelines*.<br>• Does not copy existing iOS functionality.<br>• Works as indicated.<br>• Does not crash.<br>• Uses only public APIs.<br>• Large and small icons are similar, so that users recognize the icon in different contexts. | • Does not use excessive bandwidth to download data.<br>• Web apps use iOS WebKit framework and WebKit JavaScript.<br>• App description for the App Store does not mention other mobile platforms.<br>• Shows an error message when the network is unavailable.<br>• Does not infringe on copyrights or trademarks of others. |

**Fig. 9.4** | Features and functionality required for App Store approval. (`https://developer.apple.com/app-store/review/guidelines/`).

Apple has published some common reasons why apps might be rejected during the review process (`https://developer.apple.com/app-store/review/rejections/`). Several of these are listed in Figure 9.5.

| Reasons for App Rejection | |
| --- | --- |
| • Software bugs—You should test on a variety of iOS devices before submitting an app for approval to ensure that it runs properly.<br>• Poor user interface design—You must follow Apple's *iOS Human Interface Guidelines* when creating your app's user interface.<br>• Missing final content—Apps that use placeholders for missing text and images will be rejected, so ensure that all of your app's final content is included. | • Missing support and contact information— Your app must include links to customer support and your contact information. Apps for children and that offer subscriptions also must include a link to your privacy policy.<br>• Broken hyperlinks—You should check every hyperlink.<br>• Lacks value—Apple may reject your app if it lacks functionality or value. |

**Fig. 9.5** | Common reasons Apple rejects apps submitted to iTunes (`https://developer.apple.com/app-store/review/rejections/`).

## 9.4 Preparing Your App for Submission through iTunes Connect

When submitting your app for approval through iTunes Connect, you'll be asked to provide an app name and description, keywords, icons, screenshots and previews (optional).

You'll also need to provide translated app data if you intend to offer localized versions of your app for international App Stores. In this section, we'll tell you what to prepare—many of the requirements are specified in the App Properties appendix of the *ITunes Connection Developer Guide* at

```
http://bit.ly/iTunesConnectAppProperties
```

Later sections in this chapter overview uploading everything for approval and refer you to Apple's step-by-step online guides.

### Keywords

When submitting your app, you'll provide a comma-separated list of descriptive keywords that will help users find your app on the App Store. This is similar to the tagging schemes used by websites such as YouTube and Pinterest, except that only you (not the general public) can provide keywords for your apps. Your keyword list is limited to 100 characters. Apple doesn't provide guidelines or suggested keywords, but it does state the following restrictions:

- You cannot use the names of other people's apps.
- You cannot use other people's trademarks.

### Icons

Design an icon for your app (your company logo, an image from the app or a custom image) that will appear on the App Store and the user's iOS device. Icons and graphics do not always scale well. For this reason, you'll typically create the required icons in various sizes so that they appear exactly as you'd like. You might want to hire an experienced graphic designer to help you create a compelling, professional icon—though this can be expensive (Fig. 9.6). For app icon requirements, see the App Icon section of the *iOS Human Interface Guidelines* at:

```
http://bit.ly/HIGAppIcons
```

| Company | URL | Services |
|---------|-----|----------|
| Fast Icon | `http://www.fasticon.com/icon-design/` | Custom, stock and free icons for use in your iOS apps. |
| Glyphish | `http://glyphish.com/` | Free and for-sale stock icons for use in toolbars and tab bars. |
| iPhone-icon | `http://iphone-icon.com/` | Custom icons for iPhone and iPad. |
| icondesign | `http://www.icondesign.dk/` | In addition to paid custom services, they offer some fee-based and free icon packages, available for download at `http://www.tabsicons.com/`. |
| AimUp Apps | `http://www.app-icon-designer.com/icon-designer-service` | Custom app icons and launch images. |

**Fig. 9.6** | Some custom app icon design firms. (Part 1 of 2.)

| Company | URL | Services |
|---------|-----|----------|
| The Iconfactory | `iconfactory.com/home` | Custom and stock icons. Also offers IconBuilder software (for use with Adobe® Creative Suite®) for creating icons in multiple sizes and formats. |
| The Noun Project | `http://thenounproject.com` | Thousands of icons from many artists. |

**Fig. 9.6** | Some custom app icon design firms. (Part 2 of 2.)

### Launch Images

Your app must have a launch screen or launch image that's displayed when the app is loading so that the user sees an immediate response while waiting for the app to load. For example, tap any of the default icons on the iOS device (e.g., **Stocks**, **Camera**, **Contacts**) and you'll notice that they immediately display a launch image that resembles the app's user interface—often just an image of the background elements of the GUI. iOS 8 app projects now include a dynamically resizable launch screen user interface that you can customize for your app, or you can continue to use launch images.

### Screenshot(s)

Take one to five screenshots of your app that will be included with your app description in the App Store. These provide a preview of your app, since users can't test the app before downloading it. To take a high-resolution screenshot, use a Retina-display iOS device. Press and hold the *Power* button and press the *Home* button—this saves an image into your device's Photos app. You can also capture screenshots from Xcode by selecting **Window > Devices**, selecting your connected iOS device and clicking the **Take Screenshot** button in the **Devices** window.

### App Previews

**App Previews**—another new App Store sales tool—are 15-to-30-second videos displayed in the App Store that allow potential buyers to see your app in action. Since they cannot try an app before purchasing it, a high-quality video preview demonstrating your app's great features could help you procure more sales. The videos are displayed before your app's screenshots on your app's product page.

To capture App Preview videos you'll need an iOS 8 device connected to a Mac running OS X Yosemite. Use the QuickTime Player to capture the video. When the video is ready, upload it to iTunes Connect for review. Though the App Previews appear in the App Stores for all countries where your app is sold, for now you may submit them only in one language of your choice.

### Contract Information

To sell your app through the App Store, the team agent must agree to the terms of the iOS **Paid Applications contract**—this may take some time while Apple verifies your financial information. If you intend to offer your app for free, the Team Agent must agree to the **iOS Free Applications contract**. To find and manage the contracts, click on **Contracts, Tax, and Banking** in iTunes Connect.

### *Additional Languages (Optional)*

You may offer your app through the various international iTunes App Stores. You can translate your app's descriptive text that's displayed in the App Store to the appropriate languages for each store (Fig. 9.7). Otherwise, the information will appear in English. You'll be asked to enter your translated text into iTunes Connect as part of the submission process (Section 9.8). You can localize the app itself to many more languages, but you can localize the text that will appear in the App Store only to the languages in Fig. 9.7.

| Languages | | | |
|---|---|---|---|
| Australian English | Finnish | Korean | Spanish |
| Brazilian Portuguese | French | Latin American Spanish | Swedish |
| Canadian English | German | Malay | Thai |
| Canadian French | Greek | Norwegian | Traditional Chinese |
| Danish | Indonesian | Portuguese | Turkish |
| Dutch | Italian | Russian | UK English |
| English | Japanese | Simplified Chinese | Vietnamese |

**Fig. 9.7** | Languages for localizing your app metadata in International App Stores (`https://itunesconnect.apple.com`).

## 9.5 Pricing Your App: Fee or Free

You set the prices for your apps that are distributed through the App Store. Many developers offer their apps for free as marketing, publicity or branding tools, earning revenue through increased sales of products and services, sales of more feature-rich versions of the same apps and sales of additional content through the apps using *In-App Purchase* or *in-app advertising*. Figure 9.8 lists ways to monetize your apps.

| Ways to monetize an app |
|---|
| • Sell the app in the App Store. |
| • In-App Purchases (see Section 9.6.1). |
| • Sell an app to a company that brands it as their own. |
| • Use iAd for in-app ads (see Section 9.6.2). |
| • Sell in-app advertising space. |
| • Use it to drive sales of a more feature-rich version of the app. |

**Fig. 9.8** | Ways to monetize an app.

### 9.5.1 Paid Apps

According to a study by Flurry, the average price of all iPhone apps (free and paid) is $0.19 and of iPad apps is $0.50.[1] At the time of this writing, we looked at the top 100 paid apps for iPhone and the top 100 paid apps for iPad; here's what we found:

- Average price for paid apps is $2.33 for iPhone apps and $3.29 for iPad apps. The bigger the screen, the more the apps cost.

- Of the top 100 paid iPhone apps, 40 were $0.99, 29 were $1.99, 12 were $2.99, eight were $3.99, seven were $4.99, two were $6.99, one was $8.99 and one was $9.99.

- Of the top 100 paid iPad apps, the most common prices were $0.99 (29 apps), $2.99 (18 apps), $1.99 (16 apps) and $4.99 (16 apps). The highest price was $9.99 (four apps). Most of the apps were in the $0.99 to $4.99 range.

These prices may seem low, but successful apps could sell thousands or even millions of copies! It's estimated that Angry Birds by Rovio sold over 648 million copies since its release in 2009[2]—ranging in price from $0.99 (iPhone version) to $2.99 (iPad version). When setting a price, first research your competition. What do their apps cost? Is yours more feature-rich? Will offering your app at a lower price than the competition attract users? Is your goal to recoup development costs and generate additional revenue?

All of the financial transactions for paid apps are handled by the App Store. Apple retains 30% of the purchase price and distributes 70% to you. Earnings are paid to you on a monthly basis within 45 days of the end of the month, though Apple will withhold payment until you exceed the payment threshold of $10. For some countries, the payment threshold is $150. For more information, see the iTunes Connect FAQ at:

```
https://itunesconnect.apple.com
```

### 9.5.2 Free Apps

According to Distimo, mobile users are more likely to make purchases from within a free app than to purchase a paid app.[3] At the time of this publication, only four of the 100 top-grossing iPhone and iPad apps were paid. You should consider offering a free "lite" version of your app with limited features or functionality to encourage users to try it. For example, if your app is a game, you might offer a free version with just the first few levels. Once users complete these, the app would provide a message encouraging them to buy your more robust app with additional game levels through the App Store. Upgrading from the "lite" version is one of the leading reasons why users purchase a paid app. Many companies use free apps to *build brand awareness* and *drive sales of their products and services*. Figure 9.9 shows a few of the companies that are employing this strategy.

Of course, you could create a popular free app and monetize by selling your business. In 2012, Facebook bought the photo-sharing app Instagram for $1 billion. Then in 2014, Facebook bought WhatsApp, a messaging app that's free for the first year ($0.99 per year after) for $19 billion!

---

1.  http://www.techspot.com/news/53294-ios-apps-are-getting-cheaper-averaging-out-at-just-19.html.
2.  http://www.therichest.com/business/companies-business/the-most-popular-paid-iphone-apps-of-all-time/9/.
3.  http://www.emarketer.com/Article/In-App-Purchases-Take-Over-App-Revenues/1010491/1.

| Free app | Functionality |
|---|---|
| Amazon® Mobile | Browse and purchase items on Amazon. |
| Bank of America | Locate ATMs and bank branches in your area, check balances and pay bills. |
| Best Buy® | Browse and purchase items on Best Buy. |
| Epicurious Recipe | Thousands of recipes from several Conde Nast magazines including *Gourmet* and *Bon Appetit*. |
| ESPN® ScoreCenter | Set up personalized scoreboards to track your favorite college and professional sports teams. |
| Nike Training Club | Numerous customized workouts from Nike's fitness experts. |
| NFL Mobile | Get the latest NFL news and updates, live programming, NFL Replay and more. |
| Taco Bell® | Find a nearby Taco Bell and check in at the restaurant, view the menu and nutritional information, play games and more. |
| Red Bull Augmented Racing Reloaded | Augmented reality racing game created by Red Bull—a popular energy drink. |
| UPS® Mobile | Track shipments, find drop-off locations, get estimated shipping costs and more. |
| NYTimes | Read the top news articles from the *New York Times*. |
| ING Direct ATM Finder | Find no-fee ATMs by GPS or address. |
| Pocket Agent™ | State Farm Insurance's app enables you contact an agent, file claims, find local repair centers, check your State Farm bank and mutual fund accounts and more. |
| Progressive® Insurance | Report a claim and submit photos from the scene of a car accident, find a local agent, get car safety information when you're shopping for a new car and more. |
| USA Today® | Read articles from *USA Today* and get the latest sports scores. |
| Wells Fargo® Mobile | Locate ATMs and bank branches in your area, check balances, make transfers and pay bills. |

**Fig. 9.9** | Companies using free iOS apps to build brand awareness.

### Freemium

You might also consider the increasingly popular *freemium* business model in which you offer your app for free, then charge a fee to add functionality. Freemium is the most successful pricing strategy for several app categories, most notably games, news and newsstand apps, books and social networking apps.[4] The top-grossing iPhone and iPad app in 2013 was Candy Crush Saga[5]—a free app that uses in-app purchase and in-app advertising to monetize—earning over $994,000 per day in the U.S. market alone![6]

---

4. http://mashable.com/2013/12/19/paid-vs-free-apps/.
5. http://mashable.com/2013/12/17/top-iphone-apps-2013/.
6. http://www.psmag.com/navigation/business-economics/flappy-bird-candy-crush-still-making-much-money-75048/.

## 9.6 Monetizing Apps

In this section we discuss how to monetize your apps by selling virtual goods, using in-app advertising and developing custom apps for businesses.

### 9.6.1 Using In-App Purchase to Sell Virtual Goods

An effective way to monetize your apps is by selling **virtual goods** (e.g., digital content) for use with the app. In-App Purchase—part of iOS's Store Kit framework—allows you to sell virtual goods through your free or paid app (Fig. 9.10). Each In-App Purchase item must be approved by Apple. For example, if you offer books for sale through a bookstore app, each book has to be approved by Apple before it's added to the catalog. According to a study by Distimo, *free* apps with in-app purchases generated the most revenue, *accounting for 92% of revenue in the App Store in November 2013.*[7]

| Virtual goods | | |
|---|---|---|
| Magazine e-subscriptions | Localized guides | Avatars |
| Virtual apparel | Additional game levels | Game scenery |
| Add-on features | Ringtones | Icons |
| E-cards | E-gifts | Virtual currency |
| Wallpapers | Images | Virtual pets |
| Audios | Videos | E-books and more |

**Fig. 9.10** | Virtual goods.

Selling virtual goods can generate higher revenue per user than in-app advertising.[8] A few apps that have been particularly successful selling virtual goods include Angry Birds, Candy Crush Saga, DragonVale, Zynga Poker, Bejeweled Blitz and NYTimes. Virtual goods are particularly popular in mobile games.

*iOS In-App Purchase*
There are two ways to use In-App Purchase:

- You can *build the additional functionality into your app*. When the user opts to make a purchase, the app notifies the App Store, which handles the financial transaction and returns to the app a message verifying payment. The app then *unlocks the additional functionality*.

- Your app can *download additional content on demand*. This content can be hosted on your own servers or on Apple's servers. When the user makes a purchase, the app notifies the App Store, which handles the financial transaction. The app then notifies the appropriate server to send the new content. The server (yours or Apple's) can verify that the app has a valid receipt from the App Store before sending

7.  http://www.distimo.com/blog/2013_12_publication-2013-year-in-review/.
8.  http://www.businessinsider.com/its-morning-in-venture-capital-2012-5?utm_source=readme&%20utm_medium=rightrail&utm_term=&utm_content=6&utm_campaign=recirc.

the content. For more information see the *Receipt Validation Programming Guide* in the developer documentation.

Your app provides the purchasing interface, allowing you to control the user experience. The Store Kit framework processes the payment request through the iTunes store, then sends your app confirmation of the purchase. To learn more about the In-App Purchase using the Store Kit framework, read the *Store Kit Programming Guide* and the *Store Kit Framework Reference*.

If your app uses In-App Purchase functionality, it's important that you select the correct category for the item you're selling (Fig. 9.11) as *you cannot modify the settings later*. For step-by-step instructions on setting up in-app purchases, read the *In-App Purchase Configuration Guide for iTunes Connect* at:

```
http://bit.ly/InAppPurchaseConfiguration
```

| Category | Description |
|---|---|
| Consumables | Users pay for the item each time it's downloaded and it *cannot* be downloaded on multiple devices. |
| Nonconsumables | Users pay for the content once. Subsequent downloads are free and *can* be used across multiple iOS devices. |
| Auto-Renewable Subscription | Users pay for access to the content for a fixed time interval. The subscription auto-renews until the user explicitly opts out. |
| Free subscription | Similar to auto-renewable subscription, but the user is not charged. |
| Nonrenewing Subscription | Users pay for content that's delivered for a set period of time (e.g., a six-month subscription). |

**Fig. 9.11** | Categorizing your products for sale using In-App Purchase (see *Creating In-App Purchase Products* at `http://bit.ly/InAppPurchaseConfiguration`).

## 9.6.2 iAd In-App Advertising

Many developers offer free apps monetized with **in-app advertising** such as banner ads and video ads. Mobile advertising networks such as Apple's **iAd Network** allow you to earn advertising revenue by including ads (banners and videos) within your apps. When a user taps an iAd banner, a screen for the advertised product launches in a web view where the user can interact with the ad without leaving your app. The user can then resume the interacting with your app. You earn advertising revenue based on a combination of the number of views and the click-through rate (CTR) on the ads. The top 100 free apps earn anywhere from a few hundred dollars to several thousand dollars per day from in-app advertising. For example, it's estimated that the wildly popular Flappy Bird app—which had over 16 million ad impressions per day—was earning $50,000 per day from in-app advertising![9] But, in-app advertising does not generate significant revenue for most apps. If your goal is to recoup development costs and generate profits, you should consider charging a fee for your app or selling virtual goods (see Section 9.6). *Unless your app is widely down-*

---

9.  `http://www.psmag.com/navigation/business-economics/flappy-bird-candy-crush-still-making-much-money-75048/`.

*loaded and used—most are not—it will generate minimal advertising revenue.* You can also use iAd to promote your own apps. For more information, see the *iAd Programming Guide.*

### 9.6.3 App Bundles

App Bundles—introduced at Apple's WWDC 2014—are groups of up to 10 paid apps that are packaged and sold at a discounted price. Users who have already purchased one or more of the apps and decide to purchase the App Bundle are credited the difference in the total price. Though you sell the bundle at a discounted price, you may sell more total apps, resulting in higher revenues.

You can offer up to 10 App Bundles at a time. An individual app may be included in no more than three App Bundles. To create an App Bundle in iTunes Connect you'll need to:

- *Name the App Bundle.* Apple suggests limiting the name to 23 characters and avoiding the words "Editor's Choice," "Essentials" and "Collection."[10]

- *Select up to 10 of your apps to include.* List your top four apps first as their icons will be visible in the App Store. All apps in the bundle must also be sold separately in each of the App Stores worldwide in which the bundle will be sold.

- *Write a description.* Say what's included and why the user should purchase the bundle (e.g., state the discount you're offering, how the apps complement each other, etc.).

- *Set the price.* The bundle price must be less than the total of the individual app purchase prices and must be more than the highest priced app in the bundle.

To learn more about App Bundles, see the *iTunes Connect Developer Guide.*

### 9.6.4 Developing Custom Apps for Organizations

You can monetize your app-development skills by providing custom business-to-business (B2B) apps to companies. The App Store **Volume Purchase Program (VPP)**[11] allows companies to purchase your B2B apps in bulk and distribute them easily to users. When uploading a custom app to iTunes Connect for approval, simply indicate the company or companies eligible to purchase the app and its release date. It will be available to only your authorized purchasers through the VPP website. Figure 9.12 lists the key VPP resources.

| URL | Description |
|---|---|
| `https://developer.apple.com/programs/volume/b2b/` | General information about the Volume Purchase Program for Business. |
| `http://www.apple.com/business/vpp/` | Enroll in the program, login to your account and learn more about how it works. |

**Fig. 9.12** | Volume Purchase Program for Business resources. (Part 1 of 2.)

---

10. `https://developer.apple.com/app-store/app-bundles/`.
11. The Volume Purchase Program is currently available in the United States, Canada, France, Spain, Germany, Italy, United Kingdom, Japan, Australia and New Zealand.

| URL | Description |
|---|---|
| `http://images.apple.com/business/docs/`<br>`VPP_Business_Guide_USA_EN_Feb14.pdf` | The Volume Purchase Program Guide discusses how to purchase, distribute and manage content, custom B2B app ideas and more. |
| `http://www.apple.com/legal/internet-`<br>`services/itunes/vppbusiness/ww/` | Volume Purchase Program terms and conditions. |
| `https://ssl.apple.com/support/itunes/`<br>`vpp/` | VPP support. |

**Fig. 9.12** | Volume Purchase Program for Business resources. (Part 2 of 2.)

## 9.7 Managing Your Apps with iTunes Connect

iTunes Connect (`https://itunesconnect.apple.com/`), which is part of the paid iOS Developer Program, allows you to manage your account and your apps, track sales, request promotional codes for your products and more (Fig. 9.13). *Promotional codes* allow you to distribute up to 100 complimentary copies of your for-sale app per update of your app.

| iTunes Connect module | Description |
|---|---|
| My Apps | Add new apps to be approved for the App Store. Enter app information including the app description, keywords, support URL, marketing URL, privacy policy URL, contact information, pricing, create in-app purchases for the app, enable Game Center (for game apps), see customer reviews, request promotional codes that allow selected users to download your paid app for free (see Section 9.10, Marketing Your App) and more. |
| Sales and Trends | View daily, weekly, monthly, yearly and lifetime sales reports. you can also view sales by territory, platform, category, content type and transaction type. |
| Payments and Financial Reports | Access your payment information and monthly financial reports. |
| iAd | Link to the **iAd Workbench** where you can create an advertising campaign to promote your app and drive traffic to your website. Your ad will appear in approved iOS apps in the App Store. You can designate the target audience and set an advertising budget. |
| Users and Roles | Add or remove authorized users for your iTunes Connect account and designate the modules each is able to access. |
| Agreements, Tax and Banking | Sign paid applications agreements to sell your apps through the App Store. Set up banking information and tax withholding. Manage your iTunes contracts. |
| Resources and Help | Contact the App Store with questions, see the list of frequently asked questions and interact with developers worldwide to ask and answer iTunes Connect questions. You'll also find links to iTunes Connect documentation. |

**Fig. 9.13** | iTunes Connect modules (`https://itunesconnect.apple.com/`).

*Crash Reporting*

iTunes reports back to iTunes Connect any app crashes from the devices on which your app is installed—assuming that the user, when setting up a device, indicated that it was OK to send Apple data. When managing an app in iTunes Connect, you can view crash information in the app's **App Details** page by clicking the **View Crash Reports** button. This information can help you fix bugs in your app, which you should do *promptly*. You might also want to consider using a third-party real-time crash reporting service (Fig. 9.14).

| Company | URL |
|---|---|
| Crashlytics | `http://try.crashlytics.com/` |
| BugSense | `https://www.bugsense.com` |
| Crittercism | `https://www.crittercism.com` |
| HockeyApp | `http://hockeyapp.net/features` |

**Fig. 9.14** | Third-party real-time crash reporting services.

# 9.8 Information You'll Need for iTunes Connect

Once you're ready to submit your app to the App Store for approval, you'll need to create a record for your app in iTunes Connect. To do so, you need the following information:

- An *availability date* for your app—You'll select the date that you wish to make your app available through the App Store. The App Store will display the app release date as either the date you enter here or the date your app is approved, whichever is later.
- An *app description*—iTunes displays this to App Store users.
- An *app icon*—iTunes displays this with the app's description.
- One or more *app screenshots* showing your app in action.
- A *version number*—This is your own number for internal version management.
- A *bundle ID* that matches your app ID.
- Various other information that we discuss below.

*App Ratings*

To publish your app in the App Store you must provide a rating—which will be displayed below the app's price in the App Store—for parental controls. Parents can restrict their children's access to the app based on the rating. On the ratings page, you'll be asked if your app contains violence, sexual content, profanity, mature themes, gambling or horror themes. Next to each, select the radio button corresponding to the frequency of such content in your app—**None**, **Infrequent/Mild** or **Frequent/Intense**. Apple will then assign one of the ratings in Fig. 9.15. As you respond to each category, your app rating will be displayed on the screen. Click the **Continue** button to proceed to the **Upload** page.

| Age rating | Description |
|---|---|
| 4+ | No objectionable material. |
| 9+ | Suitable for children 9 years and older. |
| 12+ | Suitable for children 12 years and older. |
| 17+ | Frequent or intense objectionable material, suitable only for people 17 years and older. |

**Fig. 9.15** | App ratings.

## *Pricing*

You'll also have to select the **price tier** for your app:

- Click **View Pricing Matrix** to view a list of the numbered price tiers and the corresponding app price for each. Select a tier to view a table displaying the customer price for your app in the local currency for each App Store worldwide, and the proceeds you'll receive in each currency based on that price.

- Finally, select the App Stores in which you'll sell your app by clicking the checkbox next to each country name. Click **Continue** to proceed to the **Localization** page.

## *Screenshots of Your App in Action*

To obtain screenshots:

1. Run the app on a device.

2. With the app running and your device connected to your Mac, open the Xcode **Devices** window.

3. Select your device.

4. Click the **Take Screenshot** button to save a screenshot of the app in its current state.

You can take screenshots directly on an iOS device by pressing the **Home** and **Power** buttons simultaneously. You can also take a screenshot in the simulator by selecting **File > Save Screen Shot**.

## *App Bundle ID*

The bundle ID that you use in your app's iTunes Connect record must match the bundle ID specified in your project. To specify the bundle ID:

1. In Xcode, select the project's name in the left column.

2. Select the app's name under **TARGETS**.

3. Select the **Info** tab.

4. On the **Bundle identifier** line specify the exact bundle ID you'll use when creating your app record in iTunes Connect. The bundle ID should begin with your company domain name in reverse (e.g., com.deitel) and be followed by the app name. For **Tip Calculator**, we use the bundle ID `com.deitel.TipCalculator`.

## 9.9 *iTunes Connect Developer Guide*: Steps for Submitting Your App to Apple

The *iTunes Connect Developer Guide*

```
http://bit.ly/iTunesConnectDeveloperGuide
```

provides step-by-step instructions for submitting your app to Apple for approval, then shipping your app once Apple approves it. The steps should be performed only when your app is ready for submission, because Apple places a time limit between creating the app's record and submitting the app. An exception to this is for any app that uses Game Center or In-App Purchase—both require your app to have an app record in iTunes Connect so you can test these features during development.

### Logging into iTunes Connect

By default, only the iOS development team's Agent can log into iTunes Connect, but the Agent can use iTunes Connect to set up accounts for other team members. To log into iTunes Connect, sign into the iOS Dev Center (`http://developer.apple.com/ios`) then click **iTunes Connect** under **iOS Developer Program** and log into the site.

### iTunes Connect Developer Guide *Overview*

The *iTunes Connect Developer Guide* is broken into three categories of steps:

- Steps to perform before you submit your app for approval
- Steps to perform during the submission process
- Follow-up steps to perform once your app is posted for sale in the App Store

The guide's key sections for identifying your app in iTunes Connect and submitting your app for approval are summarized in Fig. 9.16.

| Chapter | Description |
|---------|-------------|
| Overview of iTunes Connect | Presents the iTunes Connect sections and the purpose of each and provides links to various support options, including FAQs, forums and video tutorials. |
| First Steps: Identifying Your App in iTunes Connect | Discusses how to make your app stand out in the App Store, covering issues including choosing your app's name, how to write your app's marketing text, how to choose the appropriate app categories and keywords, app images, app ratings and more. |
| Creating an iTunes Connect Record for an App | Describes the key step that must be completed before an app can be submitted for approval. An app record contains all of the information for your app that appears in the App Store. |
| Configuring Store Technologies | Describes the optional step of specifying App Store technologies used in your app, if any—these include Game Center, In-App Purchase, iCloud, iAd and Newsstand. |

**Fig. 9.16** | *iTunes Connect Developer Guide* summary. (Part 1 of 2.)

| Chapter | Description |
|---------|-------------|
| Displaying on the Store in More Than One Language | Describes the optional step of uploading localized information for your app if you intend to publish the app in multiple App Store territories and multiple spoken languages. |
| Submitting the App | Discusses how to validate the information you provided in the app record, how to upload the app's binary (i.e., its executable) using Xcode or the Application Loader and the U.S. export restrictions for cryptography. |
| Setting Up User Accounts | Discusses how to set up user accounts in iTunes Connect, including test users who can help you beta test apps that use In-App Purchase and Game Center. |

**Fig. 9.16** | *iTunes Connect Developer Guide* summary. (Part 2 of 2.)

## 9.10  Marketing Your App

Once your app has been approved by Apple, you'll need to market it. Start by logging into the iOS Dev Center website at `https://developer.apple.com/devcenter/ios/index.action`, going to the **App Store Resource Center** and then clicking on the **Marketing Resources** link. Here you'll find a link to the *App Store Marketing Guidelines* (Fig. 9.17) plus several other resources. You must comply with these guidelines when marketing your apps.

| Resource | Description |
|----------|-------------|
| Download on the App Store Badge | Promote awareness by including the "Download on the App Store" badge (icon) in marketing materials. You must adhere to Apple's requirements regarding usage, placement, etc. |
| Apple Product Images | Download images of iPad, iPhone and iPod Touch devices for use, as directed, in your marketing materials on the App Store. You may use these images to display your app on an iOS device screen so it appears exactly as it appears when running. |
| Custom Photography and Video | You may use photography and video of Apple products only with written approval from Apple. You can use this to show your app at work. |
| Messaging and Writing Style | Discusses how to refer to Apple products, trademarks and URLs in your marketing copy. |
| Apps with Accessories and Product Packaging | Includes guidelines for using Apple products when marketing and demonstrating hardware accessories for use with your apps. Topics include accessory names, packaging, App Store badge placement and more. |

**Fig. 9.17** | Guidelines for marketing your iOS apps (`https://developer.apple.com/appstore/resources/marketing/index.html`). (Part 1 of 2.)

| Resource | Description |
|---|---|
| App Store Icon | Learn when it's acceptable to use the App Store icon and when you must use the **Download on the App Store** badge. |
| Legal Requirements | Discusses the legal requirements for using Apple trademarks, credit lines in publications and marketing materials, translating trademarks in other languages and more |

**Fig. 9.17** | Guidelines for marketing your iOS apps (`https://developer.apple.com/appstore/resources/marketing/index.html`). (Part 2 of 2.)

*Viral marketing* through social media sites such as Facebook, Twitter, Google+ and YouTube can help you get your message out. These sites have tremendous visibility. According to a Pew Research Center study, 72% of adults on the Internet use social networks—and 67% of those are on Facebook.[12] Figure 9.18 lists some of the most popular social media sites. Also, e-mail and electronic newsletters are still effective and often inexpensive marketing tools.

| Name | URL | Description |
|---|---|---|
| Facebook | `http://www.facebook.com` | Social networking |
| Twitter | `http://www.twitter.com` | Microblogging, social networking |
| Google+ | `http://plus.google.com` | Social networking |
| Groupon | `http://www.groupon.com` | Daily deals |
| Foursquare | `http://www.foursquare.com` | Check-in |
| Pinterest | `http://www.pinterest.com` | Online pinboard |
| YouTube | `http://www.youtube.com` | Video sharing |
| LinkedIn | `http://www.linkedin.com` | Social networking for business |
| Tumblr | `https://www.tumblr.com/` | Microblogging and social networking |
| Instagram | `http://www.instagram.com` | Photo sharing |

**Fig. 9.18** | Popular social media sites.

*Facebook*

Facebook, the premier social networking site, has more than 1.3 billion active users who, on average, have 130 friend connections.[13] It's an excellent resource for *viral marketing*. Start by setting up an official Facebook page for your app or business. Use the page to post app information, news, updates, reviews, tips, videos, screenshots, high scores for games, user feedback and links to the App Store where users can download your app. For example, we post news and updates about Deitel publications on our Facebook page at `http://www.facebook.com/DeitelFan`.

---

12. `http://pewinternet.org/Commentary/2012/March/Pew-Internet-Social-Networking-full-detail.aspx`.
13. `http://www.statisticbrain.com/facebook-statistics/`.

Next, you need to spread the word. Encourage your co-workers and friends to "like" your Facebook page and ask their friends to do so as well. As people interact with your page, stories will appear in their friends' news feeds, building a growing audience.

### Twitter

Twitter is a microblogging, social networking site with over 645 million active registered users.[14] You post tweets—messages of 140 characters or less that are distributed to all of your followers (at the time of this writing, one famous pop star had over 50 million followers). Many people use Twitter to track news and trends. Tweet about your app—include announcements about new releases, tips, facts, comments from users, etc. Also, encourage your colleagues and friends to tweet about your app. Use a *hashtag* (#) to reference your app. For example, when tweeting about *iOS 8 for Programmers, Volume 1* on our @deitel Twitter feed, we'll use the hashtag #iOS8FP1. Others may use this hashtag as well to write comments about the book. This enables you to easily search tweets for messages related to the book.

### Viral Video

Viral video—shared on video sites (e.g., YouTube, Bing Videos, Yahoo! Video, Popscreen, BuzzFeed), on social networking sites (e.g., Facebook, Twitter and Google+), through e-mail, etc.—is another great way to spread the word about your app. If you create a compelling video, perhaps one that's humorous or even outrageous, it may quickly rise in popularity and be tagged by users across multiple social networks.

### E-Mail Newsletters

If you have an e-mail newsletter, use it to promote your app. Include links to the App Store, where users can download the app. Also include links to your social networking pages, where users can stay up to date with the latest news about your app.

### App Reviews

Contact influential bloggers and app review sites (Fig. 9.19) and tell them about your app. Provide them with a promotional code to download your app for free (Section 9.7). They can receive an enormous number of requests, so keep yours concise and informative without too much marketing hype. Many app reviewers post video app reviews on YouTube.

| Name | URL |
|------|-----|
| Macworld AppGuide | www.macworld.com/category/ios-apps |
| TouchArcade | toucharcade.com/ |
| Cult of Mac | www.cultofmac.com/ |
| AppAdvice | appadvice.com/appnn |
| 148Apps | www.148apps.com/ |
| Gamezebo | www.gamezebo.com/iphone |

**Fig. 9.19** | iOS app review and recommendation blogs and websites (in order of popularity). (Part 1 of 2.)

14. http://www.statisticbrain.com/twitter-statistics/.

| Name | URL |
|------|-----|
| Appolicious™ | www.appolicious.com/ |
| The Daily App Show | dailyappshow.com/ |
| The iPhone App Review | www.theiphoneappreview.com/ |
| AppCraver | www.appcraver.com/ |
| What's on iPhone | www.whatsoniphone.com/ |
| Apple iPhone School | www.appleiphoneschool.com/ |
| Fresh Apps | www.freshapps.com/ |
| Appvee | www.appvee.com/ |
| iPhone App Reviews | www.iphoneappreviews.net/ |

**Fig. 9.19** | iOS app review and recommendation blogs and websites (in order of popularity). (Part 2 of 2.)

### Internet Public Relations

The public relations industry uses media outlets to help companies get their message out to consumers. Public relations practitioners incorporate blogs, tweets, podcasts, RSS feeds and social media into their PR campaigns. Figure 9.20 lists some free and fee-based Internet public relations resources, including press-release distribution sites, press-release writing services and more.

| Internet public relations resource | URL | Description |
|---|---|---|
| *Free Services* | | |
| PRWeb® | http://www.prweb.com | Online press-release distribution service with *free* and *fee-based* services. |
| ClickPress™ | http://www.clickpress.com | Submit news stories for approval (*free* of charge). If approved, they'll be available on the ClickPress site and to news search engines. For a *fee*, ClickPress will distribute your press releases globally to top financial newswires. |
| PRLog | http://www.prlog.org/pub/ | *Free* press-release submission and distribution. |
| i-Newswire | http://www.i-newswire.com | *Free* and *fee-based* press-release submission and distribution. |
| openPR® | http://www.openpr.com | *Free* press-release publication. |
| *Fee-Based Services* | | |
| PR Leap | http://www.prleap.com | Online press-release distribution service. |
| Marketwire | http://www.marketwire.com | Target your press release audience by geography, industry, etc. |

**Fig. 9.20** | Internet public relations resources. (Part 1 of 2.)

| Internet public relations resource | URL | Description |
|---|---|---|
| Mobility PR | `http://www.mobilitypr.com` | Public relations services for companies in the mobile industry. |
| Press Release Writing | `http://www.press-release-writing.com` | Press-release distribution and services including press-release writing, proofreading and editing. Check out the tips for writing effective press releases. |

**Fig. 9.20** | Internet public relations resources. (Part 2 of 2.)

*Mobile Advertising Networks*
Purchasing advertising spots (e.g., in other apps, online, in newspapers and magazines or on radio and television) is another way to market your app. Mobile advertising networks (Fig. 9.21) specialize in advertising iOS (and other) mobile apps on mobile platforms. Many of these networks can target audiences by location, wireless carrier, platform (e.g., iOS, Android, Windows, BlackBerry) and more. Most apps don't make much money, so be careful how much you spend on advertising.

| Mobile ad networks | URL |
|---|---|
| AdMob (by Google) | `http://www.google.com/ads/admob/` |
| iAd | `http://advertising.apple.com` |
| Leadbolt | `http://www.leadbolt.com/` |
| Tapjoy® | `http://home.tapjoy.com` |
| Nexage™ | `http://www.nexage.com` |
| Millennial Media® | `http://www.millennialmedia.com/` |
| Smaato® | `http://www.smaato.com` |
| mMedia™ | `http://mmedia.com` |
| Conversant | `http://www.conversantmedia.com/` |
| Inneractive | `http://inner-active.com/` |
| Mobclix™ | `http://http://axonix.com/` |
| InMobi™ | `http://www.inmobi.com` |
| Flurry™ | `http://www.flurry.com` |

**Fig. 9.21** | Mobile advertising networks.

You can also use mobile advertising networks to monetize your free apps by including ads (e.g., banners, videos) in your apps. Apple has not published the average eCPM (effective cost per 1,000 impressions) for ads in iOS apps; however, one source we found claims that in 2013, the eCPM for ads in iPhone apps was $0.97 and in iPad apps was $1.38 (compared to $0.88 and $1.05 for Android smartphones and tablets, respectively).[15] Most ads on iOS pay based on *click-through rate (CTR)* of the ads rather than the number of impressions generated. According to a report by Jumptap, CTRs average 0.65% on mobile in-app ads,[16] though this varies based on the app, the device, targeting of the ads by the ad network and more. If your app has a lot of users and the CTRs of the ads in your apps are high, you may earn substantial advertising revenue, and your ad network may serve you higher-paying ads, further increasing your earnings.

## 9.11 Other Popular Mobile App Platforms

According to Portio Research, by 2017 over 200 billion mobile apps will be downloaded per year (though estimates vary widely).[17] By porting your iOS apps to other mobile app platforms, especially to Android, you could reach an even bigger audience (Fig. 9.22).

| Platform | URL | Worldwide app downloads market share |
|---|---|---|
| iOS (Apple) | http://developer.apple.com/ios | 33% smartphone apps<br>75% tablet apps |
| Android | http://developer.android.com | 58% smartphone apps<br>17% tablet apps |
| Windows Phone 8 | http://dev.windows.com | 4% smartphone apps<br>2% tablet apps |
| BlackBerry (RIM) | http://developer.blackberry.com | 3% smartphone apps |
| Amazon Kindle | http://developer.amazon.com | 4% tablet apps |

**Fig. 9.22** | Popular mobile app platforms. (http://www.abiresearch.com/press/android-will-account-for-58-of-smartphone-app-down).

## 9.12 Tools for Multiple-Platform App Development

A number of products can help you develop efficiently for *multiple* platforms simultaneously. Among them is PhoneGap (http://phonegap.com), which allows you to develop your app with standard web technologies (HTML5, CSS3 and JavaScript). You submit your app to their build service, which returns app-store ready versions for various mobile platforms. Visit http://phonegap.com for their fee structure. Figure 9.23 lists several cross-platform, mobile-development tools. One disadvantage of cross-platform development tools is that not all platforms support the same features, and newer platform features may not be available.

---

15. http://smallbusiness.chron.com/average-cpm-rates-mobile-advertising-72201.html.
16. http://gigaom.com/2012/01/05/419-jumptap-android-the-most-popular-but-ios-still-more-interactive-for-ads/.
17. http://www.portioresearch.com/en/major-reports/current-portfolio/mobile-applications-futures-2013-2017.aspx.

| Tool | URL |
|------|-----|
| PhoneGap | `http://phonegap.com` |
| QT | `http://qt.digia.com` |
| Adobe Air | `https://get.adobe.com/air` |
| Sencha Touch | `http://www.sencha.com/products/touch` |
| RhoMobile | `http://docs.rhomobile.com/en/5.0.0` |
| Appcelerator | `http://www.appcelerator.com/` |

**Fig. 9.23** | Cross-platform mobile-development tools.

# 9.13 Wrap-Up

In Chapter 9, we discussed how to prepare your apps for submission to the App Store, including testing them, creating icons and launch images, and following the *iOS Human Interface Guidelines*. We discussed the steps for getting your apps approved and published. We provided tips for pricing your apps, and resources for monetizing them with in-app advertising and in-app sales of virtual goods. And we included resources for marketing your apps, once they're available through the App Store. We provided an overview of the *iTunes Connect Developer Guide*, which shows you how to use iTunes Connect to manage your apps and track sales. We provided a list of some of the other mobile and web platforms to which you might port your iOS apps to broaden your market. We also introduced cross-platform mobile app-development tools.

## Staying in Contact with Deitel & Associates, Inc.

We hope you enjoyed reading *iOS 8 for Programmers: An App-Driven Approach with Swift, Volume 1* as much as we enjoyed writing it. We'd appreciate your feedback. Please send your questions, comments, suggestions and corrections to `deitel@deitel.com`. To stay up to date with the latest news about Deitel publications and corporate training sign up for the free *Deitel® Buzz Online* e-mail newsletter at

`http://www.deitel.com/newsletter/subscribe.html`

and follow us on

- Facebook—`http://www.facebook.com/DeitelFan`
- Twitter—`@deitel`
- Google+—`http://google.com/+DeitelFan`
- YouTube—`http://youtube.com/DeitelTV`
- LinkedIn—`http://linkedin.com/company/deitel-&-associates`

To learn more about Deitel & Associates' worldwide on-site programming training for your company or organization, visit:

`http://www.deitel.com/training`

or e-mail `deitel@deitel.com`.

# Index

## Symbols

! for explicitly unwrapping an optional 149
!= (not equals) operator 84
!== (not identical to) operator **84**
? for unwrapping a non-nil optional 149
?? (nil coalescing operator) **296**
... (closed range) operator **168**
..< (half-open range) operator **168**, **169**
{, left brace 101
}, right brace 101
* (multiplication) operator 81
/ (division) operator 81
% (remainder) operator 81
- (subtraction) operator 81
+ (addition) operator 81
< (less than) operator 84
<= (less than or equal) operator 84
== (is equal to) operator 84
=== (identical to) operator **84**
> (greater than) operator 84
>= (greater than or equal to) operator 84

## Numerics

100 Destinations 29

## A

A8 64-bit chip 7
Accelerate framework 29
accelerometer **5**, 9
accelerometer sensor 243, **250**
access modifier **132**
    internal **132**
    private **132**
    public **132**
Accessibility **6**, 12, 40, 46, 67
    *Accessibility Programming Guide for iOS* 40

Accessibility (cont.)
    accessibility strings 44
    **Accessibilty Inspector** 68
    **Large Text** 7
    UIAccessibility protocol **68**
    VoiceOver **6**
    White on Black 7
    Zoom 7
accessories 29
Accounts framework 28
action **80**
    create 99
action (event handler) 99
activity 17
Ad 315
Ad Hoc distribution 315
Ad Hoc provisioning profile **317**
adaptive design **31**
**Add Missing Constraints** 93
addition 81
addLineToPoint method of class UIBezierPath **265**
addObserver method of class NSNotificationCenter **135**
AddressBook framework 28
AddressBookUI framework 26
addTextFieldWithConfigurationHandler method of class UIAlertController **148**
admin 314, 315, 316
adopt a protocol **124**
AdSupport framework 28
advertising networks
    AdMob 335
    Conversant 335
    Flurry 335
    InMobi 335
    Inneractive 335
    Leadbolt 335
    Millennial Media 335

advertising networks (cont.)
    mMedia 335
    Mobclix 335
    Nexage 335
advertising networks (cont.)
    Smaato 335
    Tapjoy 335
advertising revenue 325
Agent (for a development team) **315**
AirDrop 15, 117
AirPrint 243, 248
**AirPrint** 11
**Alignment** attribute of a **Label** 91
allObjects property of class NSSet **233**
allowsRotation property of class SKPhysicsBody **216**
alpha property of a UIView 167
altimeter sensor 250
Amazon Mobile app 323
Ambient light sensor **6**
*Android for Programmers* website xix
animated transition 205
animateWithDuration method of class UIView **189**, 190
animation xxiii, 163, 201, 281
animation frame 204
anonymous function 20, 127
AnyObject generic object type **104**
AnyObject type (Swift) **122**
API 25
app approval process 313
App Bundle **326**
app extension 16
app icons 54
app ID 314, **315**, 317
app name **49**
app platforms
    Amazon Kindle 336

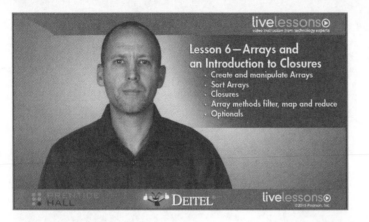